INDIA

THE MOST DANGEROUS

DECADES

India

THE MOST DANGEROUS

DECADES

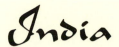

SELIG S. HARRISON

PRINCETON, NEW JERSEY

PRINCETON UNIVERSITY PRESS

1960

✧

SELIG S. HARRISON has worked for the Associated
Press in the Detroit Bureau, at the New York Foreign Desk, and for three years as a foreign correspondent covering India, Pakistan, Nepal, Ceylon
and Afghanistan. On his return from South Asia
he began this study during a Nieman Fellowship
in Journalism at Harvard University and later as
a consultant to the Modern India Project, University of California (Berkeley), and as a research
associate of the Language and Communication Research Center at Columbia University. He is the
author of scholarly studies and monographs on
caste, language, and political problems within India as well as numerous articles on issues of Indo–
U.S. relations, including several for *The New Republic*, where he has been Associate Editor since 1956.

✧

Printed in the United States of America
by Princeton University Press
at Princeton, New Jersey

TO MY PARENTS

ACKNOWLEDGMENTS

THIS work could not have been completed without the tireless cooperation and counsel of my wife, Barbara Johnston Harrison, who is no doubt correct in her judgment that "there must be an easier way" to write a book. In particular, Chapter II, "Past and Future," could not have been written without her research and early drafts over a three-year period.

For financial assistance I am in debt both to the Modern India Project, University of California (Berkeley), and to the Rockefeller Foundation, which supported my work as a research associate of the Language and Communication Research Center, Columbia University; for moral support and encouragement I am grateful especially to Chadbourne Gilpatric, Associate Director of the Humanities Division of the Rockefeller Foundation, and to Richard L. Park, guiding spirit of the Modern India Project and now Associate Professor of Political Science at the University of Michigan.

So many individuals both in India and the United States have been of help that I can only address a general word of thanks to them. However, I should like to express special appreciation to some whose ideas have helped materially in stimulating my own thought and in corroborating or downgrading my own judgments—Matthew J. Kust, Asoka Mehta, Karl W. Deutsch, Chadbourne Gilpatric, Horace I. Poleman, Richard L. Park, John Gumperz, Gene D. Overstreet and Marshall Windmiller.

It was my assignment to India as a correspondent of the Associated Press which led to this book, and I wish to record personal thanks for many kindnesses during three years' residence in New Delhi to my A.P. colleague, Harold K. Milks. My gratitude also to the Nieman Foundation at Harvard University and to Louis M. Lyons, Curator of the Nieman Fellowships, for the year of study and reflection out of which this work was to develop.

Editor and Publisher Gilbert A. Harrison of *The New Re-*

public has been most indulgent of this extracurricular activity.

Portions of certain chapters have appeared previously in *Foreign Affairs* and *The American Political Science Review*. Chapter Three, "The New Regional Elites," draws in part on an earlier paper, "Leadership and Language Policy in India," published by Princeton University Press in 1959 as part of the symposium volume, *Leadership and Political Institutions in India*.

S. S. H.

Washington, D.C.
January 12, 1960

CONTENTS

———:⁙ϑ✳Ɓ⁙:———

INDIA
THE MOST DANGEROUS
DECADES

I would now like to say that if I really thought this dismal future . . . were inevitable I would not be with you discussing the matter. If a friend of mine were suffering from an incurable disease, I would not be inclined to give him a vivid description of the nature of his disease nor a detailed outline of his future agonies. On the other hand if I believed my friend's disease curable, and if an understanding of his difficulties were a prerequisite for the cure, I would be inclined to describe his disease to him and to project its course into the future as best I could.

—HARRISON BROWN, "Problems of Survival,"
The Gideon Seymour Memorial Lecture,
Minneapolis, March 9, 1958.

I · THE POLITICS
OF NATIONAL SURVIVAL

"INDIA," warns one of her leaders, "stands the risk of being split up into a number of totalitarian small nationalities."[1]

"The future is in the hands of the gods," writes another, "but as far as I can judge, the centrifugal forces will ultimately prevail, and . . . the nation may be compelled to go through a period of political anarchy and face the risk of fascism, which is Nature's way out of disorder and misrule."[2]

When, in 1957, anxieties so often expressed in private could be committed to print, India had passed almost unnoticed from a remarkable Decade of Confidence into the first years of a struggle for simple national survival. Hope and strength were at bay. Frustration and defeat had taken the initiative. Her prophets of defeat were former Governor-General Rajagopalachari, a nationalist who is also a southerner, and Suniti Kumar Chatterji, a nationalist patriarch of Bengal. Their anxieties were the anxieties of the majority of India living in nine language territories arrayed around the north-central Ganges heartland.

India's struggle for national survival is a struggle against herself. As a civilization and as an integrated cultural whole, India has shown a power of survival rivalled only by China. But multilingual India's separate territories have failed as consistently as Europe's to hold together as a political unity. Not only is India, as Toynbee has expressed it, "a society of the same magnitude as our Western civilization . . . a whole world in herself;"[3] India is a whole world placed at close quar-

[1] Suniti Kumar Chatterji, "Minority Report," *Report of the Official Language Commission*, Manager, Government of India Press, Delhi, 1957, p. 313. Professor Chatterji is Chairman of the West Bengal Legislative Council and Chairman of the Sanskrit Commission appointed by the Government of India in 1957.

[2] C. Rajagopalachari, *Our Democracy*, B. G. Paul and Co., Madras, 1957, p. 17. Rajagopalachari adds that anarchy can be avoided "if we hasten beforehand to assure good government" in the form of a "professional authority" of senior civil servants empowered to oversee all civic life.

ters. Nowhere do so many linguistically differentiated peoples, all of them so self-aware, all numbered in millions and tens of millions, confront each other within a single national body politic. The prospect that "anarchy," "fascism," and "totalitarian small nationalities" will each torture this body politic, at one time or another in the decades ahead, is a measure not of some endemic Indian incapacity but of the challenge built into Indian nationalism.

The studies in this book probe the nature of India's peculiar challenge and seek to define accordingly certain sensitive issues that will be crucial to India's political future. To predict this or that outcome in the short-range future is on the face of it impossible. But the general lines of the long-term Indian political drama can perhaps be seen, and, to the extent that we make the effort, we may be able to cushion our minds against the shock of grotesque events. Minds conditioned by India's hopeful achievements in her Decade of Confidence will not adjust easily to an India that might at times have to postpone achievement for the more urgent business of secession here or rampant tyranny there. The adjustment will be discomfiting if only as a reminder of the British colonial argument that "there is not and never was an India, no Indian nation, no 'people of India' ";[4] that India is "a mere geographical expression like Europe or Africa."[5] When the British denied India's capacity for national unity, Indian nationalists rose to the insult and denied, in turn, that any importance at all could be attached to India's internal diversity. Yet the colonial insult holds within it the bedrock issue in India: can a unified Indian state in fact survive, and if so, what will be the political price for survival?

The upshot of these studies is that Indian nationalism will most probably survive at the price of a series of authoritarian political forms, a conclusion which suggests that we are riding for a fall when we seem to condition friendship—or foreign

[3] Arnold J. Toynbee, *The World and the West*, Oxford University Press, 1953, p. 34.

[4] Sir John Strachey, *India: Its Administration and Progress*, Macmillan, London, 1888, p. 4.

[5] Sir John R. Seeley, *The Expansion of England*, Macmillan, London, 1883, p. 92.

policy—on a particular set of institutions or the values of a particular generation of leaders. Deep-seated centrifugal forces on the one hand, and the quite contradictory urge for unified national power in the face of the unity of others, will act and interact too convulsively to leave India's present Constitution undisturbed. This interaction between extremes is characteristic of "the most dangerous decades"[6]—those decades after an underdeveloped country has discovered progress, or the hope of progress, but before progress comes rapidly enough to satisfy rising aspirations. When Indian leaders announce that agricultural extension—"community development"—workers now reach more than half of India's villages, they are declaring, in effect, that fifty percent of India has caught a glimpse of a new future and will not rest until this future has arrived. In the decades between glimpse and fulfilment "development" releases a new social awareness that soon becomes, in the uniquely compartmentalized Indian social setting, a militant group awareness. The promise of progress is the signal for a political and economic competition that intensifies as new claims to equality arise and as population growth presses the claimants into closer and closer quarters.

It is this competition for the spoils of a new time of progress that will impart a tenseness to the decades ahead, a tenseness that will be common to the politics of all underdeveloped countries but which will be aggravated, in India's case, by the strength of her ancient and rigid social rivalries. Independence was an invitation to each language territory to come into its own, invoking the memory of the golden age that each can summon forth from the millennia of Indian history. Each caste group, too, saw in a free India dedicated to equality a chance in Orwell's sense to be more equal than the rest. Caste, a social order, has provided a basis for the new economic and political competition, and the new caste competitors form ranks, as we will see, according to native linguistic regional ties. As economic competition grows, and as the political victors set the ground rules for the economic competition, so the unity and militance of regional lobbies and regional caste lobbies will grow. And

[6] Eugene Staley, *The Future of the Underdeveloped Countries*, Harper and Bros., New York, 1954, p. 174.

as the languages of each region become the languages of education and politics, new regional elites, each with a vested interest in one of ten separate regional languages, will assert new claims to dominance of administrative and political leadership.

To control centrifugal stress and strain that must get worse, in short, before it can get better, New Delhi will not be able to rely indefinitely on the "steel frame" of a cosmopolitan national civil service. For a civil service infused with the parochialism of the new regional elites will be weakened by the same internal divisions that rend the larger Indian body politic. Nor will the unitary controls available in the Indian Constitution necessarily prevent state regimes from exploiting federalist concessions which are also part and parcel of the same Constitution. So long as a single party such as the Congress maintains control in most states, the authority allocated to the states, in an unusually precise Constitutional division of powers, may not be abused. But in the event of a divergence of parties in power at the center and in a number of states—already foreshadowed by phases of Communist power in Kerala and feudal power in Orissa—a Constitutional scheme that assumes a national competition between nationally responsible parties can only serve to aggravate the competition between the states and New Delhi. A ruling state party not bound by the restraints of a ruling national party's discipline is invited by the very nature of the scheme to manipulate regional grievances at the expense of the central authority.

In the decades immediately ahead the political force most deliberately manipulating India's centrifugal stresses will be the Communist Party. Communist success in India has been largely confined, in fact, to those areas where the Communists rather than others have appropriated regional patriotism. The Communist Party is not now, as chapters five and six seek to demonstrate, a cohesive national movement with strength spread evenly over enough of India to give it any incontestable claim to national power. To take national power in a moment of anarchy or political demoralization a party commanding decisive political leverage only in certain regions, notably Andhra, Kerala and Bengal, would have to subordinate in a united front rivals who are situated in the seats of power in most other

6

regions of India. Tibet and then Chinese incursions along the Himalayan border have placed the Indian Communists on the defensive and postponed the day when such a united front might be a practical possibility. But to say that the Communist Party as now constituted is not likely to come to power is not to rule out other totalitarian experiments, which may be the linear successors of Indian Communism or which may be, on the other hand, neither "left" nor "right" but a distinctively Indian amalgam.

There are, indeed, seemingly irresistible compulsions to totalitarian experiments of one sort or another in the nature of the Indian Union. In the power relationship among the regional components of the Union there exists, as we will see, an imbalance not found in any other modern federal state. The Hindi-speaking Ganges heartland is big enough to believe in its supremacy but not big enough to practice dominion over nine sizeable rivals. This at once heightens centrifugal forces and locks the Union in a stalemate of frustration. The nationalist in a hurry seeks to escape from this frustration through surrender to a total state, which may, precisely because of India's diversity, merely be asking for trouble at some future date. In any event, the technical apparatus available to modern governments promises that India will, for better or for worse, know the total state in the decades ahead. The urge to confront other world powers on equal terms is an elemental urge common to all Indians, and the militance of regional elites, regional caste lobbies, indeed of regional chauvinism itself, can all be dissolved by the alchemy of a charismatic national leader who finds the right slogans and the right allies at the right time.

To a great extent the appeal of the Soviet and Chinese models for the Indian nationalist is the appeal of successful unitary systems, near at hand, which seem to have found the alchemy for dissolving disunity. The economic example of the Soviet Union telescoping development into forty years gains special significance as an example, at the same time, of multilingual diversity overcome. The Soviet Union was the one foreign country visited by the secretary of the Indian Government commission appointed in 1955 to consider language policy because, he explained, while there is "no precedent" for India's linguistic complexities, the Soviet Union provides "the most important instance . . . of a successful tackling of the problems of multi-lingualism."[7] Prime Minister Nehru has repeatedly emphasized that "China's strength is its unity." "While sectional interests eat at the roots of our national unity," he said on his return from China in 1954, "China has no such problem." Nehru pointed out that

in India, we have a Parliament in the Centre with legislatures in the states which guarantee regional autonomy. But in China any decision taken by the central government is the nation's decision and accepted all over the country.[8]

While "both India and China have had to contend against provincialism," Nehru said on an earlier occasion, "generally speaking, the Chinese have tried to get over it by getting rid of the provinces themselves."[9]

For Nehru the Chinese model was not an example to be imitated but one more foil for reminding Indians that national unity is their single overriding challenge. Wherever he has gone across his vast constituency since Independence, whatever his immediate pronouncement on the affairs of India or the world, Nehru has appealed above all for national solidarity. "My profession," he said on one occasion, "is to foster the unity of India."[10] Nehru tried every technique of diversion and stall available to a politician to avert the redrawing of most of India's state boundaries according to language lines, warning that "a boiling cauldron" was being stirred up, a "Pandora's Box" opened, and reiterating, when the inevitable came to pass, that he would have "preferred to wait."[11] Nehru's forebodings of national disintegration explain, if they do not necessarily justify, some of his infidelities in practice to professions preached. The Indian occupation of Kashmir is a case in point. Not to insist on Kashmir's place in the Union would be

[7] Report of the Official Language Commission, p. 481.
[8] Hindu Weekly Review, November 8, 1954, p. 4.
[9] Prime Minister's Speech on Linguistic States, Press Information Bureau, Government of India, New Delhi, July 7, 1952, p. 12.
[10] National Herald, February 10, 1956, p. 1.
[11] Prime Minister's Speech on Linguistic States, p. 10; Hindustan Times, January 19, 1953, p. 1; The Hindu, October 3, 1953.

to concede the possibility that other parts of the Union could secede and indeed, in the Indian nationalist view, would invite them to do so. When Kashmir gained autonomous rights in certain spheres in 1953, some of them later withdrawn, other regional leaders were quick to point out that what Kashmir could have, they could not be denied. Nehru's nightmare is a separatist chain reaction in which one region's defiance of the central authority touches off another's until the whole structure comes down. For Nehru the nightmare always ends in stalemate. The regions are exhorted but not disciplined. But the nightmare can also be a totalitarian rationale for coming down hard on all regions in the name of nationalism.

It must be conceded, of course, that the prospect for India held forth in these studies would differ materially were certain assumptions to prove unjustified. One of these assumptions will certainly not go unchallenged: that in little more than ten or fifteen years, as events are now moving, there will be no very widely shared unifying language common to all parts of India. This assumption rests first on the fact that English is declining precipitously, and conversely, that the regional languages are gaining rapidly; and secondly, on the belief that the Constitutional designation of Hindi to serve as the official language of the Union, according to a timetable fixed in advance, was in the first place a piece of political self-delusion on the part of India's leaders. No one who reads the debates of the Constituent Assembly on the language provisions of the Constitution and then places them alongside the embittered present-day recollections of nationalists in the non-Hindi regions can fail to share this belief to some extent. The debates amply confirm the allegation made ten years later by the respected southern nationalist newpaper, *The Hindu*, that the one-vote margin which decided the designation of Hindi was made possible only because Congress members of the Constituent Assembly "had to obey the Party's directive."[12] "It was very largely at the importunacy of the north Indian Hindi-speaking members of the Congress Party," recalls a distinguished non-Hindi Congress

[12] *The Hindu*, January 27, 1958, p. 6.

9

leader, "that the people in non-Hindi areas agreed to accept Hindi, a majority of them with reservations."[13]

If one assumes that only a miniscule few outside Hindi territory will learn Hindi well enough to use it in significant degree, and that English, as a difficult-to-learn, non-Indic language, will be the property of a relatively small scientific and bureaucratic elite, then one can only suppose that the separate regional languages will each grow in importance and that there will be, accordingly, not one central focal point for intellectual and political life but ten separate focal points in each of India's ten linguistic territories. There will be a generation of provincial politicians and bureaucrats, in short, literally unable to talk meaningfully to one another on a national stage. The fact that this generation will itself be ambivalent, eminently susceptible to some new nationalist charisma, does not obviate, for the interim, the shift of intellectual and political life to the regional capitals. From this supposition of ten separate linguistic centers of attraction flows the conclusion advanced in chapter three that the national civil service will be subjected to unprecedented stress and strain.

The prospect suggested in these studies could also be critically altered should tension with neighboring powers impart a sense of common cause in the face of common danger. One cannot take it for granted, however, that external danger would in fact evoke a rally-round-the-flag response. Thus in the case of China the distinct possibility exists that sustained pressures over the years would aggravate internal divisions. Those not on the direct line of exposure might ask themselves why they should bear the risks of common cause and seize instead on a moment of national crisis to further sectional aspirations.

The struggle in India shapes up as one of prolonged indecision. The regions may irreversibly win, inflicting a slow, malignant fever on the Indian body politic. But the chances are at least equally strong that India will find her way to present a consolidated front to the outside world. The real question is: What will be the cost of this integration? Will authoritarian experiments in integration, carried forward with disregard for

[13] P. Subbarayan, "Minute of Dissent," *Report of the Official Language Commission*, p. 319.

10

local integrity, amount to no more than experiments in violence?

The cost of integration will almost surely be periodic political crises as each invasion of state prerogatives sets off reaction and counter-reaction. In this intermittent tug of war, already in progress, the most tragic figure is the politician or bureaucrat whose base is in his home region but who has had at the same time cosmopolitan experience. As a product of the nationalist era he knows well what he does when he takes the regional side. He does not exploit crises to undermine the Union but to make the most of his best bargaining position. While he reassures himself that India will survive, in fact he saps the vitality of Indian nationalism when it most needs nourishment. Divided in his loyalties, he leans now to one side, now to the other.

In the final analysis the struggle for national survival in India is a struggle within every Indian. If a high symbol of hope can be held forth by the central authority, hope for economic progress rapid and equally shared, then the latent parochial instinct in every Indian need not rise up "like the hood of a cobra"[14] to engulf a whole people in desperation. But if hope falters, if enough come to believe that the nation is not to rise together, then the visceral response of every man is to fall back on his parochial self for protection against others who are, in turn, falling back on their own parochial selves.

Who will risk letting his rival score the first point? Who will risk the sacrifices of nationalism when another may meantime act in narrower self-interest? India's dilemma was summed up by a member of Parliament representing the state of Orissa, a poor relation next to the more prosperous states of Bengal to the northeast and Bihar to the northwest. "My first ambition," he said, "is the glory of Mother India. I know it in my heart of hearts that I am an Indian first and an Indian last. But when you say you are a Bihari, I say I am an Oriya. When you say you are a Bengali, I say I am an Oriya. Otherwise, I am an Indian."[15]

[14] *Bhoodan*, August 15, 1956, p. 4.
[15] Lokenath Misra, M.P., *Debates on the Report of the States Reorganization Commission*, Lok Sabha Secretariat, New Delhi, December 1955, Vol. I, col. 647.

Two social psychologists, one Indian and one American, studied two separate groups of Indians in 1953 and arrived at the same measure of the challenge to Indian nationalism. The Indian study showed that in Marathi-speaking Poona university students and slum housewives volunteered the very same adjectives, as often as not derogatory, when asked to characterize other regional groups. Tamils were, among other things, "dark"; Gujaratis, "fat" and "spineless."[1] In the Hindi center of Lucknow the American researcher encountered similar regional stereotypes: he discovered, moreover, that the stereotypes applied by university students to other regions of India were more consistent than those attached to foreign countries. "Whereas fifty percent of the Lucknow residents chose the main stereotype 'domineering' for the most stereotyped nation, the British," reports Robert T. Bower, "we find two-thirds to three-quarters of the total sample agreeing on the qualities of groups like the Punjabis and Bengalis."[2]

Certainly images so defined, held in common by so many, cannot have their origins in the personal or even group experience of the recent past. Their strength is the strength of age, of roots deep in the triumphs and humiliations of a venerable history. In a dispersed and isolated peasant society men knew only their immediate environs and war provided the most memorable occasions of inter-regional contact. Now the new mobility between regions has promoted a new national consciousness, but this increased contact has, at the same time, revived latent memories of a history in which Indian periodically fought Indian. "Fratricide," warns V. K. Krishna Menon, "is part of our national heritage. I fear that we do not yet realize the danger

[1] V. K. Kothurkar, "Some Provincial Stereotypes: An Essay in Social Perception and Thinking," *Journal of the University of Poona (Humanities)*, April 1954, pp. 103-110.
[2] *The Indian Student*, Bureau of Social Science Research, American University, 1954, pp. 25-28, 47-56, esp. p. 56.

that lies hidden in this aspect of our modern being."[3] Most simply put this danger is that Indians will not be able to forgive and forget the past. The valued legacies of their past greatness now belong nominally to all Indians; but because this greatness was not achieved in any instance within a unified Indian body politic, few Indians today are in agreement on who achieved what.

For all the temples and traditions the fact remains that there exists no one historical golden age cherished in common by all or even most citizens of the Union. Each region can claim its own golden age somewhere in the millennia of Indian history, but one region's golden age was often another's dark age. The pride of the Ganges plain is in memories of Maurya and Gupta emperors who ruled all of the north from Gujarat on the west to Bengal and Orissa on the east, and who ventured south, in the case of the Mauryas, into Karnataka and Andhra. Orissa, however, prefers the memory of its own imperialisms, and Bengal reminds us not of the Mauryas and Guptas but of the Palas, who in their heyday dominated much of the old Maurya and Gupta territory. Andhra's golden ages were the ages of Andhra hegemony over neighboring Karnataka, Maharashtra, or Tamilnad. But the Karnataka-based Chalukya and Rashtrakuta dynasties had their day at the expense of Andhra- and Maharashtra-based powers. Karnataka's imperium came while Maharashtrian power was still nascent; and when Maharashtra did take form, the Marathas, in turn, ranged over most of middle India and beyond. Similarly, those historical moments when high-riding Tamil power overflowed into Andhra and Karnataka are golden ages primarily in the Tamil history books.

Nehru, speaking in Parliament in 1952, referred in understandable despair to "these ancient historical memories." In modern times, he exclaimed, India cannot afford to think in the old terms of "warring empires or imperial entities conquering other places. If the Andhras think of the ancient Andhra empire, if history is invoked to say that 'in the year 1000 A.D., Gujarat spread right up to there,' if the Maharashtrians think

3 "Public Administration—Federalism and National Unity," *National Herald*, February 15, 1957, p. 8.

of the old Maharashtrian empire, and so on, this leads inevitably to thoughts now of spreading out . . . vis-à-vis your neighbor."[4] The shapers of most nationalisms have had the stuff of history as their primary raw material. Their exhortations to sacrifice for a better tomorrow have carried the promise of a revival of vanished glories. But Nehru and the molders of Indian nationalism are denied any powerful appeal to a shared political past and must in effect disown much of Indian history. Their appeal becomes diluted and loses all definition when, in invoking a proud cultural past, they must at the same time inveigh against the shame of historic political strife. The nationalist can make of the fratricides of the past only a solemn catechism, a dire portent to be recalled as the leader is followed on faith into the future. The regionalist on the other hand need disown nothing. He is free to excite the losers in past strife to new vengeance—and the victors to new aggrandizement. For all practical political purposes the past with all its powerful memories is abandoned to the regional rivals of Indian nationalism.

Any attempt to relate India's past to an analysis of her present and future is limited by the fact that India, unlike ancient Greece, Rome, and China, did not write her political history as she went along. Indian thought and social patterns can be traced in a remarkable and continuous body of literature. But there is in political history no unanswerable final authority, and the political manipulator, regionalist or nationalist, can act as his own historian. In the Independence movement the nationalist argument for unity was, as it still is, that Hindu civilization has always aspired to political unity, did in fact attain unity in the Maurya and Gupta periods, and would have found its own contemporary expression but for Moghul and then British appropriation of the modern opportunity for unity. Regional historians, on the other hand, emphasize their separate regional histories, conjuring up, in effect, an India divided neatly throughout time into much the same regional units that are the present basis of the Union. The most mean-

[4] *Prime Minister's Speech on Linguistic States,* Press Information Bureau, Government of India, July 7, 1952, p. 18.

ingful view of Indian history for the present analysis seems to lie somewhere in between.

The political history of India can be viewed as the history of three large geographical arenas—north, Deccan and south—set off from one another by profound physiographic differences. The west to east flow of so many major rivers in a country lying north to south has accentuated the natural separation between northern and southern plains and a vast tableland in between. The Ganges plain and its appendages were the most that any north Indian dynasty controlled for any length of time, the southern plains and their outworks all that most southern rulers saw as their proper horizon, and the Deccan tableland the province of middle Indian emperors who marched their armies back and forth from ocean to ocean. Three relatively separate Indian political histories can be written. Within each of the three basic arenas, regional linguistic and political identities took form, as history progressed, around agricultural core areas within confines imposed by geography.[5] From the beginning people gravitated to the same fertile core areas that are, even now, India's centers of population density; and these agricultural heartlands became the nuclei for emergent regional identities that grew in strength despite the intermittent rise and fall of empire.

These regional identities are old and persistent: literary tradition in most regional languages or their precursors can be traced without difficulty to the first centuries after Christ, and there are, in all of the regional languages, more or less unbroken literary traditions at least eight centuries old. It is the persistence of these identities throughout Indian history that

[5] For discussions of the coincidence between language and geography in India, see David K. Hartley, "Language Regions and Linguistic Provinces in India" (M.A. dissertation, University of Chicago, December 1955), esp. pp. 34-35; M. B. Pithawalla, "Correlations Between Linguistic (Cultural) Regions and the Physiographic Divisions of India, Burma and Ceylon," Science and Culture, Vol. 9, May 1944, esp. pp. 467-468; C. D. Deshpande, "The S.R.C. Report, A Geographical Commentary," The Indian Geographer, August 1956, entirety; Lanka Sundaram, "Linguistic States," Times of India, April 30, 1952, p. 6; Pandit Jaychandra Narang Vidyalankar, "The Regional and Linguistic Structure of India," The Cultural Heritage of India, Sri Ramakrishna Centenary Memorial, Calcutta, Vol. III, pp. 123-152.

gives political dynamism to regional historical memories today. But it is important to distinguish between the strength of historical memories as a force to be manipulated in present-day politics and the actual situation at any moment in Indian history. India was never a political unity, but neither did India experience at any time in her long past fixed and crystallized political division into the ten distinct regions now demarcating the Union. Her disunity was a loose affair of shifting dynastic boundaries. The overarching fact was a common Hindu civilization sharing a dominant Sanskritic cultural legacy. Hindu India more than most peasant societies gave scope to this subcontinental cultural unity, despite political disunity, because mass cultural participation was inherently proscribed by the caste system. Indeed, the system assured that the low-caste majority in all regions could not become, as that perceptive student of nationalism, Karl W. Deutsch, would put it, "socially mobilized";[6] thus a cosmopolitan Brahman elite at the apex of Indian life had a free field to carry forward the common Hindu civilization. At the base the inert low-caste millions did not generate significant independent cultural expression, and the regional languages served essentially, therefore, as vehicles for the secondary transmission of the dominant pan-Indian culture embodied in a common fund of Sanskrit literature.

India's dilemma today lies in the fact that the same industrial age that provides the technological basis for a unified subcontinental state also emancipates low-caste millions whose cultural energies are now self-generating, and must now find expression in newly-vitalized regional languages. The dilemma is profound because there is no modern parallel for the old Sanskritic standard, because the renascent regional languages are so immovably entrenched in their historic territories, and because now, for the first time, political boundaries are crystallizing in accordance with time-honored linguistic boundaries. The dimensions of India's dilemma are nothing less than the deep dimensions of her history: a history in a political sense of three Indias, each having in its compass interacting regional

[6] *Nationalism and Social Communication*, Technology Press and John Wiley and Sons, New York, 1955, entirety.

16

identities that have held their ground, persistently, against the day of their modern coming of age.

The Ganges and Its Dependencies

First of these Indias, first in nearly every sense, is the north Indian complex of regions centering in the basin of the holy Ganges. The Aryan[7] nomads who crossed into India from Persia in the second millennium before Christ and advanced across the Gangetic plain brought with them a language (a branch of the Indo-European linguistic family) which, evolving into Classical Sanskrit, was to become the unifying medium of the new composite Hindu civilization. The Aryans were the prime movers who gave "form and unity . . . discipline and order"[8] to the civilization arising from Aryan interchange with the earlier Dravidian and Austric settlers; and the new Hindu scriptures, written in the language of the Aryans, had as their setting north Indian Aryan territory.

The sacred importance conferred on "Aryavarta" in the Sanskrit texts guaranteed at the outset a pre-eminent position to the Ganges heartland in Indian life. But this pre-eminence, a basic source of instability in the present-day Union, as we will see, does not primarily or even largely derive from the place of the Ganges in Hindu mythology and its consequent power of attraction for Hindu pilgrims from all parts of India. The facts of geography are even more fundamental. From beginning to end the Ganges basin is a wide, immensely fertile alluvial plain, "one of the world's greatest expanses of rich, tillable soil . . . one of the world's greatest agricultural regions."[9] This expanse, hemmed in as it is by the Himalayan ranges to the north and the forested slopes and ragged desolation of central India, constitutes a great natural enclosure inherently destined for political consolidation. The eastward flow of the

[7] "Aryan" is, strictly speaking, a linguistic and not an ethnic term and thus one might properly refer only to "Aryan-speakers." However, both Indian and non-Indian scholarship commonly uses "Aryan" to denote the early settlers who brought the Indo-Aryan language to India.

[8] S. K. De, "Beginnings of Indian Civilization," *The Indo-Asian Culture*, January 1956, p. 279.

[9] Kingsley Davis, *The Population of India and Pakistan*, Princeton University Press, Princeton, New Jersey, 1951, p. 10.

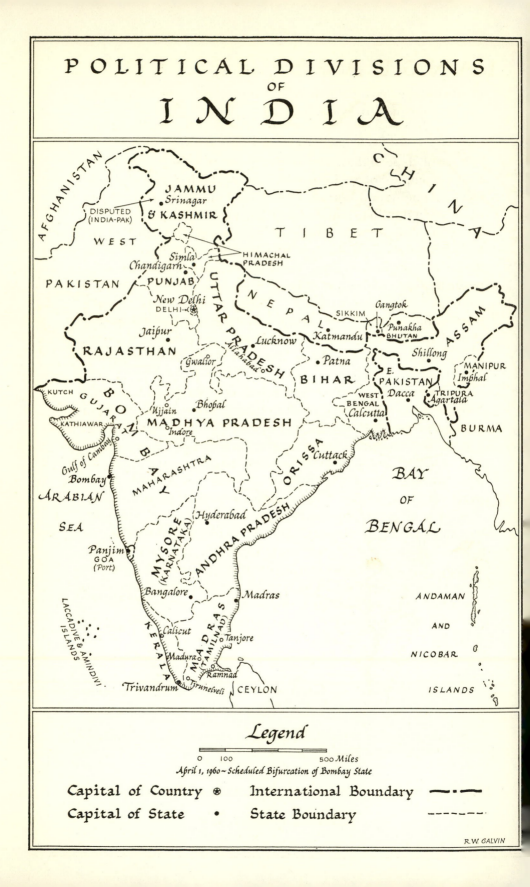

POLITICAL DIVISIONS
OF
INDIA

AFGHANISTAN

JAMMU
• Srinagar
& KASHMIR

DISPUTED
(INDIA-PAK)

TIBET

CHINA

WEST

PAKISTAN

Simla
Chandigarh
PUNJAB

HIMACHAL
PRADESH

New Delhi
DELHI ⊛

UTTAR PRADESH

NEPAL

SIKKIM • Gangtok
Katmandu • Punakha
BHUTAN

ASSAM

Jaipur

RAJASTHAN

Gwalior

Allahabad

Lucknow

• Patna

BIHAR

Shillong

MANIPUR
• Imphal

E.
PAKISTAN
Dacca

WEST
BENGAL
Calcutta

TRIPURA
• Agartala

KUTCH

GUJARAT

KATHIAWAR

Ujjain

Bhopal

MADHYA PRADESH

Indore

BURMA

Gulf of Cambay

Bombay

ARABIAN

SEA

MAHARASHTRA

ORISSA

Cuttack

BAY

OF

BENGAL

Panjim
GOA
(Port)

MYSORE
(KARNATAKA)

Hyderabad

ANDHRA PRADESH

Bangalore

• Madras

ANDAMAN

AND

NICOBAR

LACCADIVE & AMINDIVI
ISLANDS

KERALA

Calicut

Madura

Trivandrum

MADRAS
(TAMILNAD)

Tanjore

Ramnad

Tirunelveli CEYLON

ISLANDS

Legend

0   100   500 Miles

April 1, 1960 ~ Scheduled Bifurcation of Bombay State

Capital of Country ⊛   International Boundary — · —

Capital of State   •   State Boundary   - - - - -

R.W. GALVIN

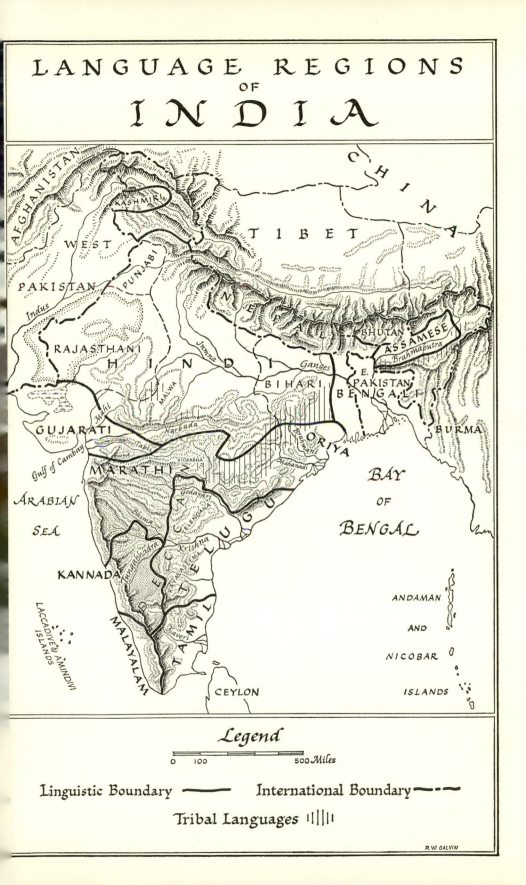

LANGUAGE REGIONS
OF
INDIA

Legend

0   100   500 Miles

Linguistic Boundary ———   International Boundary ———

Tribal Languages ⵏⵏⵏ

R.W. GALVIN

Ganges, Panikkar emphasizes, "leads to the integration of population in a closed area, bound together by the river and its tributaries."[10] Once on the plain, the way for any conqueror was easy. The Aryan story is the story of all subsequent foreign land invaders and indigenous imperial powers in north India. A power-base anywhere on the plain offered the opportunity for conquest up and down the unimpeded Gangetic expanse.

Whenever an imperial dynasty managed to unite the Ganges plain, the dynamism generated by this concentration of power inevitably spilled over into all of north India and just as inevitably failed to extend more than briefly beyond the Vindhyan barrier into the Deccan. The Maurya and Gupta empires of early north Indian history provide cases in point. The scattered Gangetic kingdoms of Aryan times began about 600 B.C. to coalesce into larger units—Kosala, Avanti, Vatsa near modern Allahabad, Magadha in southern Bihar.[11] Before the end of the fourth century Magadha had expanded into the Maurya empire. Chandragupta Maurya stretched his power from Bengal on the east to the Hindu Kush on the west, only to be outdone in imperial authority by his famed grandson, Asoka Maurya (c. 273-232 B.C.), who ruled in addition Gujarat, Orissa, and the northwest Deccan to the borders of Karnataka and Andhra and incorporated his conquered territories into what was for that day a unified imperial structure. But soon after Asoka, the empire disintegrated. The Guptas who established the next great north Indian empire six centuries later and presided over north India's classical golden age did not attain even Asoka's limited territorial jurisdiction. Beyond their northern boundaries the Guptas had to be content with parts of central India and Orissa and spasmodic military expeditions such as Samudragupta's celebrated foray to the Krishna River in Andhra. In less than two hundred years, at the end of the fifth century A.D., the main Gupta dynastic line had retreated before rebellious feudal chiefs to its local base in Bihar. The

10 K. M. Panikkar, *Geographical Factors in Indian History*, Bharatiya Vidya Bhavan, Bombay, 1955, p. 30.
11 R. C. Majumdar et al., *An Advanced History of India*, Macmillan & Co., London, 1956, pp. 55-57.

Delhi Sultans and the Moghuls, who founded the only other extensive and comparatively long-lived north Indian empires prior to the British, eyed the Deccan, too, but in attempting to defy geography and extend their power beyond their natural northern arena they were, like all the others before them, overextending themselves.[12]

Even within their north Indian limits, northern imperial rulers never established, up to Moghul times, more than the loosest sort of political control over the regions beyond their home bases. Aggrandizement was a Hindu monarchic ideal; annexation was not. Although, to secure his home base, a king might annex his immediate neighboring kingdoms, when he embarked on his *digvijaya* or clockwise conquest of the "Four Quarters,"[13] he did so normally for pelf and prestige and not for the extension of any permanent machinery of bureaucratic power. He might take his troops to outlying regions periodically to show off his strength—to remind them, in the parlance of modern strategic doctrine, of his deterrent power. But conquered feudatory units ordinarily remained intact within an empire, often under their own kings, retaining their autonomous identity for all their payment of homage and tribute. When the empire dissolved they reverted back to their old independent status as a matter of course.[14] Thus, in the case of north India, the growth of separate regional identities in Gujarat, Bengal, and Assam persisted despite the recurrent subordination of these regions to the dominant Ganges heartland. Their geographical proximity exposed them to the ambitions of each Gangetic empire as it arose. Yet because they were, in a sense, so near and yet so far—geographically self-contained and each separately strong—they were able to reassert independence when imperial authority disintegrated.

[12] For an extension of this thesis, see K. M. Panikkar, *Geographical Factors in Indian History*, pp. 75-82.

[13] H. G. Rawlinson, *India: A Short Cultural History*, Frederick A. Praeger, New York, 1952, p. 106.

[14] For brief discussions of the place of conquered constituent units within the ancient Hindu empire, see R. C. Majumdar, ed., *The History and Culture of the Indian People*, Bharatiya Vidya Bhavan, Bombay, Vol. III, 1954, pp. xxiii, 13, 345, and Vol. V, 1957, pp. xiii-xiv; W. H. Moreland and A. C. Chatterjee, *A Short History of India*, Second Edition, Longmans, Green and Co., London, 1944, pp. 24 and 146.

Bengal, for example, while tied by the river to the main Gangetic plain and thus intrinsically exposed to its power, enjoys at the same time a definite measure of geographical separation that has throughout history assured a separate regional identity. Just before the Ganges makes its great southern turn toward the Bay of Bengal the highlands of Chota Nagpur break the otherwise unimpeded eastward sweep of the plain to the sea. The steep Rajmahal hills reach to the very banks of the Ganges to cut off all but a northern corridor of Bengal from the rest of the basin. Accompanying this physical separation is the climatic separation that distinguishes wet, rice-growing Bengal, seasonally subjected to cyclonic rainfall, from the comparatively drier plain. With its deltaic terrain of "new mud, old mud and marsh,"[15] its constantly shifting river beds, Bengal is not easily traversed east to west. Even today no through road connects Dacca in East Bengal and Calcutta in West Bengal, all of 150 miles, and the rail-boat route linking them rambles for 380 miles.[16] The east-west division within Bengal, which made regional unity no mean achievement for Bengali dynasties, made Bengal's incorporation as a region into any Ganges-based power system still more difficult. Bengal has been on the far fringes of most north-south trade and cultural exchange, separated, as Nirmal Kumar Bose points out,[17] even from its immediate southern neighbor by the west to east flow of the Mahanadi, which gives Orissa its "horizontal"[18] direction. Although most empires in command of the rest of the Ganges sooner or later made it a dependency, Bengal was enough of an integrated region, for all of its subdivisions, to carry on independently for centuries at a time, and, in the case of the Pala period (c. 750 to c. 1050), to provide the base

[15] O. H. K. Spate, *India and Pakistan: A General and Regional Geography*, Methuen and Co., London, 1954, p. 522.

[16] *Ibid.*, p. 533. Richard L. Park, "The Rise of Militant Nationalism in Bengal: A Regional Study of Indian Nationalism" (Ph.D. dissertation, Harvard University, 1950, p. 38), discusses the "subtle differences in cultural traditions" in the two Bengals.

[17] Nirmal Kumar Bose, *Modern Bengal*, Reprint No. 10, Center for South Asian Studies, Institute for International Studies, University of California, Berkeley, 1959, pp. 1-3.

[18] K. M. Panikkar, *Geographical Factors in Indian History*, p. 30.

for a dominant north Indian empire when the main Gangetic power had ebbed.

The middle of the eighth century saw the emergence of two large northern kingdoms contesting for imperial control of north India: the Pratihara Rajputs in the west, based at Kanauj near modern Allahabad, and the Palas of Bengal in the east. Dharmapala, after uniting Bengal and subduing Orissa, marched to Kanauj and made the Palas the paramount power in north India for a century. "Never before or since, until the advent of the British," pronounces Bengal's distinguished historian, R. C. Majumdar, "did Bengal play such an important role in Indian politics." The reigns of Dharmapala and his successor, Devapala, he writes, "constitute the most brilliant chapter in the history of Bengal."[19] Bengali regional consciousness today gains its immediate inspiration from Bengali initiative in the Independence movement, and, to an even greater extent, from the vitality of a Bengali literary achievement distinctive in its humanist emphasis and notable both in quantity and quality among Indian regional literatures. But historical memories of the Palas and their eleventh century Sena successors are alive at the back of Bengali minds. Bengalis were influenced by a sense of their history when they rose in righteous passion against threats to their regional integrity in 1905, at the time of the British partition of Bengal, and again, albeit diffused by Hindu-Muslim differences, at the time of the partition of the subcontinent in 1947. They are influenced by a sense of their history when they look suspiciously upon the Hindi plain in contemporary politics.

Assam, in turn, off in India's northeast corner, looks with suspicion of its own on neighboring Bengal. The narrow Brahmaputra valley, which is the major settled area of Assam, is even more isolated from the rest of India than Bengal. But while Assam was separated from the Ganges heartland and was left relatively unmolested by Gangetic emperors, the Assamese did know and fear—and feel different from—adjacent Bengal. The Ahoms, Bodos, and Kacharis who settled Assam between the eleventh and fourteenth centuries were Mongoloid tribes

[19] *The History and Culture of the Indian People*, Vol. IV, 1955, pp. 48 and 52.

and the Assamese have as a consequence a stronger Mongoloid strain than the Bengalis. Today tensions between Assam and Bengal that may be in the first instance economic—competition over jobs, for example—are aggravated by Assam's historic awareness that it is a hinterland next to politically and culturally assertive Bengal. When Bengal calls on Assam to relinquish the districts of Goalpara, Garo Hills, and Cachar for the sake of the allegedly repressed Bengali language, Assam counters with a demand for Cooch Behar, citing historic periods of dominion over territory since usurped by the Bengalis.[20]

Unlike Bengal and Assam, Gujarat, despite its geographical seclusion in another corner of India, has enjoyed few periods of unrelieved isolation. When not part of an empire based in the Ganges heartland, Gujarat was subject to the ambitions of Deccan regimes or outside invaders from the northwest. The attraction was the maritime riches pouring into Broach and other Gulf of Cambay ports, even in ancient times, from the western shores of the Arabian Sea, and later from Greece, Rome, and Europe. Gujarat's maritime riches made a passable empire resplendently wealthy; Gujarat offered, also, an agricultural heartland in the alluvial plain between the Sabarmati and Mahi rivers. The region was cut off from easy access to Gangetic India by the Aravalli range, the Rajasthan desert, and dissected jungle land on its eastern flank. However, a natural link between Gujarat and the plain lay in the pivotal region of Malwa—roughly present-day Gwalior, Bhopal, and Indore—a link, too, between the north and the Deccan. Ancient and medieval trade routes from the Ganges to the Arabian Sea followed this natural passage and then the valleys of the Narbada and Tapti rivers to the Gulf. Control of Malwa—"the invariable appanage to the domains of every monarch, native or barbarian, who became the master of the Gangetic plain"[21]—provided the key to control of Gujarat, and con-

---

[20] *Memorandum of the Assam Pradesh Congress Committee*, Submitted to the States Reorganization Commission, Congress House, Gauhati, May 26, 1954, pp. 7-8 and 8-10.

[21] O. H. K. Spate, *India and Pakistan: A General and Regional Geography*, p. 577, quoting the 1931 *Census*, Vol. xx, Part i, p. 3.

versely, served as the symbol of Gujarat's own resurgence when Gangetic or Deccan empires declined. Thus the three-century golden age of the Solanki dynasty (961-1297 A.D.)—the age of Siddharaja, the popular conquering hero, and Hemachandra, the great Jaina classical scholar—was also the age of Gujarati hegemony over Kutch and Kathiawar, over parts of western Rajasthan, over the north Konkan coast of Maharashtra, and, at the apogee of empire, over Malwa. When Gujarat regional champions argue their differences today with neighboring Maharashtra, they cite the greatness of the Solankis, of ancient Aparanta[22] and medieval Gurjaradesa,[23] deploring the "dismemberment" by the Marathas and the British of "this Gujarat, which had been the richest part of India both in natural and social wealth, Gujarat that was reckoned to be the second political power of India after that of Delhi during the medieval period."[24]

The persistence of separate regional identities in north India in the face of recurrent Ganges-based empires has been accompanied and indeed reinforced from the very beginning of Indian history by the formation of separate regional languages. The periods of imperial unification were too brief and too widely spaced in time, the periods of isolated regional independence too frequent and prolonged, and above all, the facts of geography too powerful, for linguistic development to have followed any other course. The original Aryan language mingled with Dravidian, Austric, and Sino-Tibetan linguistic forms and slowly but ineluctably developed along regional lines.

Linguistic evidence[25] shows that some centuries before Buddha

[22] K. M. Munshi, *Linguistic Provinces and the Future of Bombay*, National Information and Publications Ltd., Bombay, 1948, p. 26; and *Formation of Maha Gujarat*, Memorandum submitted to States Reorganization Commission by Amrit Pandya, General Secretary, Maha Gujarat Parishad, Vallabh Vidyanagar, Kaira District, Bombay, 1954, pp. 4, 10-11.

[23] *Formation of Maha Gujarat*, pp. 1, 11-12; and K. M. Munshi, *Gujarata and its Literature*, Longmans Green and Co., Bombay, 1935, pp. 74-79.

[24] *Formation of Maha Gujarat*, p. 57.

[25] Scientific linguistic research into the origins of the Indo-Aryan languages of India has been carried on rapidly and fruitfully ever since Dr. G. A. Grierson began it all late in the nineteenth century. His monumental findings, presented in *Linguistic Survey of India* (Vol. I, Part 1, Introductory, Government of India Central Publication Branch, Calcutta, 1927) still provide the basis, as well as

(c. 563-483 B.C.), this evolving Aryan language was spoken in at least three distinct regional forms—northwestern (Udichya), middle (Madhyadesiya), and eastern (Prachya). The northwestern form was the mother tongue of Panini (sixth century B.C.), who relied on this dialect and its midland neighbor when preparing the first complete grammar of Classical Sanskrit. This standardized Sanskrit, as it was perfected by Panini's successors Katyayana (fourth century B.C.) and Patanjali (second century B.C.), and as it came into literary use, was to remain immutable for the next two thousand years as the vehicle of Brahmanical culture. But the spoken languages, or *prakrits*, continued to change imperceptibly. Initially the process of change was most rapid in the case of the eastern *prakrit*, no doubt because the dominant political power center of the day was the eastern-based Magadha empire: the Magadha metropolis of Pataliputra, present-day Patna, was not only the political capital of the north but also the cultural and consequently linguistic focal point. Moreover, the Buddhist and Jaina protestant religious movements, which made such deliberate use of the spoken languages, were centered in the east. The *prakrits* first took literary form under the auspices of these officially-patronized sects as the media for both canonical and non-canonical Buddhist and Jaina literature. The *prakrit* rock inscriptions of Asoka also attest to a threefold linguistic evolution of north India. From 100 A.D. the line of development of the *prakrits* becomes clear, and one recognizes with ease the three distinct languages, in each case literary, as well as spoken, which were the precursors of the modern north Indian languages.

The great western Sauraseni *prakrit* was used over a wide area but was centered in the Ganges-Jumna region near Mathura (Surasena of the Sanskrit texts). Reflecting the disorganized life

---

the point of departure, for all the succeeding study. An excellent modified work following Grierson is T. C. Hodson, *India: Census Ethnography, 1901-1931*, Government of India Press, New Delhi, 1937. Through the decades linguistic evidence has been piling up which dates, refines, and in some cases, of course, alters Grierson's suppositions. For a short up-to-date discussion of the early development of the Indo-Aryan languages from the time of the ancient Vedic Sanskrit, see R. C. Majumdar, ed., *The History and Culture of the Indian People*, Vol. II, 1951, pp. 278-284.

of the Ganges plain in the Maurya-Gupta interval, Sauraseni had been succeeded by 500 A.D. by separate but closely related forms corresponding to the geography of western India. These successor languages are called *apabhramsas* by linguistic historians. Thus the form spoken then in Gujarat and western Rajasthan (Marwar) was the precursor of modern Gujarati. Prior to Gupta times the Saurashtri dialect of Maharashtri, a *prakrit* of the Deccan, had been the language of Gujarat.[26] Then when the Guptas ruled Gujarat from Ujjain, a seat of intense Sanskritic culture, Gujarat drew culturally closer to the Gangetic plain.[27] By the last stage of the *prakrits* (c. 500 A.D.), most traces of Saurashtri were disappearing from the Gujarat-western Rajasthan form in favor of Sauraseni influences from the midland; and in later periods of political autonomy, especially the fifteenth and sixteenth century period of Muslim rule, Gujarati gradually took on an identity separate even from the western Rajasthani dialects.[28] The form of Sauraseni spoken in the Ganges-Jumna doab was the direct ancestor of the related dialects—Khari Boli native to Meerut, Braj Bhasha around Mathura, Kanauji, and Bundeli—that developed in later centuries and are known jointly today as Western Hindi. The form of Punjabi spoken today in the Indian sector of Punjab can also be traced to this *apabhramsa*. Modern Rajasthani derives from the old Malwa form, but now its various dialects cover a broadened area extending over the whole of present-day Rajasthan.[29]

In the east the Magadhi *prakrit* localized, too, into clearly defined *apabhramsas*. A Magadhi form was spoken in Bihar

[26] T. C. Hodson, *India: Census Ethnography, 1901-1931*, p. 22, and *Formation of Maha Gujarat*, pp. 7 and 28.

[27] See K. M. Munshi, *Gujarata and its Literature*, pp. 9-19, for a brief history of Gujarat from the earliest times through the Gupta period.

[28] S. K. Chatterji, *Languages and the Linguistic Problem*, Oxford Pamphlets on Indian Affairs, No. 11, Oxford University Press, London, 1945, p. 14.

[29] The languages derived from the Sauraseni prakrit remained closely related through the early stages of modern language development, and it is unsettled whether the language of the Rajput bardic poetry of the late twelfth and thirteenth centuries should be classified as a form of early Hindi or of Old Western Rajasthani-Gujarati.

and, by 1000 A.D., had become the modern Bihari dialects.[30] Bengal in the period of the Palas had two related *apabhramsas*, Gauda in Gangetic Bengal and Dhakki in eastern Bengal, corresponding to the geographical division that persists even today in the political division between Indian West Bengal and Pakistani East Bengal. Both modern Bengali and Assamese are lineal descendants of these dialects of the Magadhi *prakrit*, though eastern Bengali, the modern form of Bengali spoken in Dacca, more closely approximates the old Dhakki dialect.

A third north Indian *prakrit*, Ardhamagadhi (Half-Magadhi), was indefinitely located between Sauraseni and Magadhi and influenced by both. This, the sacred language of the Jains, ultimately became the so-called Eastern Hindi grouping of dialects—Avadhi, Bagheli, and Chhattisgarhi.

Here it must be emphasized that the Ganges heartland, which is often treated in this work as a monolithic unit, is monolithic, strictly speaking, only in its relation to other regions of north and south India. Although physiographically a single whole, the Gangetic plain cannot, by its very size, receive an equal distribution of rainfall; the Bengal monsoon progressively loses force on its northwesterly course. Thus the plain divides broadly into eastern, middle, and western parts.[31] The relatively dry western extremity—roughly, the Ganges-Jumna doab, Rohilkhand to the north and Bundelkhand to the south—corresponds more or less to the linguistic territory of the Western Hindi dialects. Allahabad marks the eastern limit of this grouping and the beginning of the Eastern Hindi group reaching south into Madhya Pradesh and east to Bihari territory. The confusion and controversy over the future character of the "Hindi" that is India's Constitutionally-designated Union language reflects in part this linguistic diversity within Hindi territory. To most of its proponents "Hindi" describes a highly Sanskritized version

[30] Bihari divides into the three dialects of Bhojpuri in western Bihar, Magadhi in south Bihar, and Maithili in north Bihar.

[31] O. H. K. Spate (*India and Pakistan: A General and Regional Geography*, p. 494) agrees with Stamp (L. Dudley Stamp, *Asia: A Regional and Economic Geography*) that the Ganges basin, apart from Bengal, must be delineated geographically into upper and middle zones, and he draws an imprecise dividing line "running roughly from the Ganges-Jumna confluence at Allahabad across to the NNW-SSE section of the Gogra."

of the existing literary Hindi, a purist version that is being developed in the face of a twofold opposition: those who want the new standardized Union language to correspond to the Hindustani already spoken in a standard form common to most towns of the Ganges plain,[32] and those, on the other hand, who want to preserve highly-developed dialects such as Braj Bhasha in the Western Hindi area and Avadhi within Eastern Hindi territory.[33]

Punjab, Rajasthan, and Bihar are treated throughout this work as part of a single Gangetic regional system encompassing in linguistic terms varying degrees of "mutual intelligibility." Such separate character as each may have is a sub-regional manifestation within the Gangetic system. Punjabi, although a highly developed language, is not the undisputed majority language of an homogeneous linguistic territory, and in this sense it must be distinguished from other regional languages emphasized in this work. The political struggles against Hindu power waged by the Sikhs under the Punjabi banner are not the struggles of a separate "Punjabi" region against other regions. They are waged within a larger Gangetic regional complex in which Eastern and Western Hindi, Hindustani (notably its Muslim variant of Urdu), and Punjabi have an interlocking relationship and thus a joint relationship to the rest of India.

The Deccan—Fact and Memory

The interplay of unity and diversity that is the grand pattern of Indian history has been exemplified separately within each of the three arenas of Indian history. In the case of middle India, the immemorial pattern of regional subdivision was as definite as in Gangetic north India. Geography assured four separate linguistic and political identities within the seemingly integrated Deccan tableland.

[32] For a useful case study, see S. K. Chatterji, "Calcutta Hindustani—A Study of a Jargon Dialect," *Indian Linguistics*, Vol. i, 1931, Parts ii-iv.

[33] For an interesting discussion of dialect differences within Hindi territory, see John Gumperz, "Language Problems in the Rural Development of North India," *Journal of Asian Studies*, January 1957, esp. p. 257; and "Some Remarks on Regional and Social Language Differences in India," *Introducing India in Liberal Education*, University of Chicago Press, 1957, pp. 69-88.

Bordered by long lines of mountains, high on the west, broken and lower on the east, the rocky Deccan plateau is India's oldest land-mass—the remnant, some geologists believe, of a now-submerged land block once connecting with Africa. The plateau slopes to the east and its great river systems, the Mahanadi in Orissa, the Godavari spanning Maharashtra and Andhra, and the Krishna with its Bhima and Tungabhadra tributaries in Maharashtra and Karnataka, all follow the eastern slope in that west-to-east river flow so characteristic of India. On the map, the Krishna and Godavari, rising near the Arabian Sea and emptying some 900 miles away on the other side of the peninsula, give a coast-to-coast unity to the Deccan.[34] But the broad, shallow Deccan rivers, dependent on the monsoon rains and almost dry in the hot season,[35] cannot be navigated from region to region; and the ancient gneisses and granites of the Deccan do not, in any case, offer a suitable repository for an agricultural expanse comparable to the Ganges plain. The Krishna and Godavari pass from one largely self-contained geographic territory to another.

Ancient and deep lava flows enrich the soil of the west-central portion of the plateau: this is Maharashtra with its rich black cotton land in the north and in the river beds, with its flat-topped, often steep-sided buttes. Where the lavas end to the south and east, Maharashtra ends and Karnataka and Andhra begin. The high southern portion of the plateau rises, at places, as much as twice the 2,000 foot Deccan average, setting off Karnataka. Andhra divides into two distinct parts: the bleak eastern extension of the plateau, called Telengana in its northern sector and Rayalaseema to the south, shades off into the unusually fertile Krishna-Godavari deltas. Coastal Orissa, stretching north of the deltas, has, like Andhra, a hinterland of its own on the plateau proper. In this case the Gondwana hinterland is a sparsely-populated jungle waste that presses almost to the coast, insulating Orissa throughout history from all but the most determined conquerors.

[34] "Deccan" is used interchangeably to describe both the plateau and the plateau together with its coastal extensions.
[35] O. H. K. Spate, *India and Pakistan: A General and Regional Geography*, p. 35.

Despite this natural separation between each of its regions, the Deccan possessed enough general unity as an entity apart from north and south to make the political unification of the whole plateau and its coastal extensions the goal of most powerful empires arising in middle India. No one region had the central dominating position occupied by the Ganges plain in the north, and this being so, strong dynasties based in any of the Deccan regional heartlands were equally emboldened to attempt an imperial role. The pivotal historic agricultural heartlands were the rich Vidarbha cotton tract of northern Maharashtra, Karnataka's Dharwar black soil belt, near the Krishna-Tungabhadra doab, and the Krishna-Godavari deltas. What made the unification of these seats of empire possible, in the absence of a unifying Ganges, was a series of natural march-lands. The rocky belts of Telengana connected Maharashtra with the deltas and the Krishna-Tungabhadra doab led onto a passable expanse of flat country between Karnataka and Andhra. Maharashtra's low-lying ridges offered no insuperable obstacle to the relatively open line of march from Karnataka to Vidarbha. Thus the early Satavahanas (c. 230 B.C.–200 A.D.) and the Chalukyas and Rashtrakutas in later centuries (c. 550-1200 A.D.) were able in spite of rough terrain and great distances to maintain direct or indirect rule over most of the Deccan. The armies of great Deccan empire builders, like the Chalukyas' Pulikesin II and the Rashtrakutas' Govinda III, made their way back and forth between geographic territories which, albeit slowly developing their separate regional character, did not conform to a more or less established pattern of linguistic and political identities until the thirteenth century.

In emphasizing this thirteenth century watershed our intent is not to suggest that Deccan regional evolution differed in its pace from the parallel processes taking place to the north and south. When a pan-Deccan dynasty declined, the emergent regional identities encompassed within the dynasty showed the same staying power evident in the north: in the Satavahana-Chalukya interregnum, for example, the perennial regional core areas each threw up independently strong ruling houses, the Vakatakas in Vidarbha, the Vishnukundins in Andhra, and the Kadambas in Karnataka. The contrast does seem striking, however, between what was an essentially pan-Deccan political and cultural pattern prior to the thirteenth century and the more identifiable regional pattern afterward. This contrast serves to illustrate the relative unimportance of regional identities in the early history of most parts of India and their unprecedented importance in the very different Indian environment today.

While the languages of the Deccan were taking separate shape prior to the thirteenth century, they were not confined, in this formative period, within clearly demarcated regions. Fifth-century inscriptions testify to the separate existence at that point of nascent Kannada and Telugu.[36] Nevertheless, the two languages remained closely related for at least another five centuries and shared the same script until the thirteenth century. The earliest extant work in Kannada is the *Kavirajamarga* (c. 850 A.D.) and in Telugu Nannaya's version of the *Mahabharata* (1020 A.D.). In the tenth century the two were so close that the great poets Ponna and Pampa, though born in Andhra, wrote in Kannada.[37] The roots of Marathi can be traced to the old Maharashtri prakrit, which became, under the Satavahanas in the second and third centuries, a highly-developed literary vehicle. Later the Vakatakas also used Maharashtri. Yet this linguistic precursor of modern Marathi was for centuries re-

[36] Little is known of the beginnings of the Dravidian languages. It is clear that Tamil is the oldest of them. They all derive from some parent Dravidian tongue. Inscriptional evidence provides the only information so far of early Telugu and Kannada. Telugu linguist B. R. Krishnamurty of Andhra University in an interview with the author stated that prakrit inscriptions of the second century B.C. show village names in Telugu. K. A. Nilakanta Sastri (*Dravidian Literatures*, S. Viswanathan, Madras, 1949, p. 33) traces the beginnings of Telugu from fifth and sixth century A.D. inscriptions. Seventh century inscriptions are recognized as the earliest evidence of Telugu by K. Lakshmi Ranjanam ("Early Telugu Poetry—Nannaya to Tikkana," *Triveni*, Vol. IX, No. 10, April 1937, pp. 47-48) and Rayaprolu Subba Rao ("Leaders and Landmarks of Telugu Literature," *Triveni*, Vol. XI, No. 10, April 1939, pp. 9-10). A. P. Karmarkar (*A Cultural History of Karnataka*, Karnataka Vidyanardhaka Sangha, Dharwar, 1947, p. 119) points to fifth century A.D. inscriptions as the earliest pure Kannada so far found. See also R. C. Majumdar, ed., *The History and Culture of the Indian People*, Vol. IV, pp. 221-223.

[37] P. T. Raju, *Telugu Literature*, The International Book House, Ltd., Bombay, 1944, pp. 3-8. Rayaprolu Subba Rao, "Leaders and Landmarks of Telugu Literature," pp. 10-13.

stricted as a spoken language to northern Maharashtra. Kannada, meanwhile, was spoken much farther north than its present limits and possibly reached as far as the upper Godavari —now the northern part of the *Desh* sector of Maharashtra. "The region which extends from the Kaveri as far as the Godavari," states the *Kavirajamarga*, "is the country in which Kannada is spoken. . . ."[38] Although the Sravana Belgola inscription (c. 983 A.D.) indicates that Marathi existed in the tenth century, Marathi territorial limits did not move southward, and the present Deccan regional pattern take form, until the time of the Chalukyan collapse.

It was when the aging Chalukyan empire was supplanted in the late twelfth century by three of its feudatories—the Yadavas in the Maharashtra lava country, the Hoysalas in Karnataka, and the Kakatiyas in Telengana—that the unified life of the Deccan had finally come to an end. Kannada and Telugu, having drifted more and more apart in the late Chalukyan period, now began a process of final separation. Marathi came into its own as the medium of the early saint poetry. In 1291 Dnyaneshwar completed his great Marathi exposition of the *Bhagavad Gita* and soon after Marathi had displaced Kannada everywhere on the lavas.

The fact that the Deccan had until the thirteenth century a measure of political unity linking geographic regions enhanced its meeting-ground role in the evolution of a unified Hindu civilization. When a single empire maintained contact on one border with the north, through Malwa, and on another with the southern dynasties, the horizons of this empire were in the most literal sense cosmopolitan. The Deccan empires acted as agents for cultural transfer back and forth between north and south, mediating, as it were, between cultural extremes. Linguistically, Sanskrit-related Marathi and Oriya ab-

---

[38] The *Kavirajamarga* has been quoted at this point by many writers. Among them are K. A. Nilakanta Sastri, *A History of South India from Prehistoric Times to the Fall of Vijayanagar*, Oxford University Press, Madras, 1955, pp. 375-376; and *Census of India, 1951*, Vol. xiv, "Mysore," Part i, Government Press, Bangalore, 1954, p. 183. See also P. B. Desai, "Research Work in the Nizam Karnatak," *Karnatak Historical Review*, Vol. i, No. ii, September 1931, pp. 28-31, for a discussion of the territorial limits of early Karnataka.

sorbed Dravidian elements, while Dravidian Kannada and Telugu became heavily impregnated with Sanskritic influences; Deccan sculptural styles and temple architecture[39] similarly evolved as a blend of north and south, and "the inseverable Godhood of the Aryan Vishnu and the non-Aryan Siva"[40] found expression in the non-sectarian tenor of Andhra and Maharashtra Hinduism.

By the same token, however, the persistence of so much supra-regional life in the Deccan is a most awkward fact for modern regional patriots. As one example, the Satavahanas, also known in history as the Andhras, are claimed today as a Telugu dynasty and were indeed based in their closing years in the Krishna-Godavari delta land. But scholars are now placing their beginnings and much of their history in the upper Godavari country that is within modern Maharashtra.[41] The Satavahanas patronized the Maharashtri prakrit popular in a day when the Telugu language was still taking form. At the same time they cannot be assigned to a Maharashtra which, as we have seen, had not yet attained a separate identity. Most modern Marathi patriots do not even make the claim. The Marathi historian Bhandarkar does, on the other hand, lay claim to the Rashtrakutas, arguing that they originated in what is now Maharashtra and indeed gave the region its name.[42] Yet the evidence pointing to Kannada origins for the Rashtrakutas appears equally, if not more, persuasive.[43] On the face of it, Karnataka has a convincing claim to the Chalukyas, who clearly favored the then-coalescent Kannada language over any other

[39] See R. C. Majumdar, ed., *The History and Culture of the Indian People*, Vol. v, p. 530, Vol. iii, pp. 516-535; and A. P. Karmarkar, *A Cultural History of Karnataka*, pp. 142-145.

[40] R. C. Majumdar, ed., *The History and Culture of the Indian People*, Vol. iii, p. viii.

[41] K. A. Nilakanta Sastri (*A History of South India*, pp. 88-89) gives the Satavahanas this upper Godavari origin. For statements that they were Andhras, see P. Chenchiah and Raja M. Bhujanga Rao Bahadur, *A History of Telugu Literature* (The Heritage of India Series), The Association Press, Calcutta; W. H. Moreland, *A Short History of India*, p. 63; *Census of India, 1951*, Vol. xiv, "Mysore," p. 183.

[42] R. G. Bhandarkar, *Early History of the Dekkan*, Third Edition, Chuckervertty, Chatterjee and Co., Calcutta, 1928, pp. 78-81, 106.

[43] R. C. Majumdar, ed., *The History and Culture of the Indian People*, Vol. iv, p. 17, fn. 2, cites Kannada as the mother tongue of the Rashtrakutas; Vol. iii, p. 198, states them to be of Kannada stock.

and had their seats of empire within what is now Kannada territory. The claim loses some conviction, though, when one considers the scholarly speculation that the Chalukyas were originally Central Asian invaders.[44] Moreover, Karnataka's regional center of gravity has now shifted south. The sites of the Chalukyan capitals, Badami (near the Krishna-Tungabhadra doab) and Kalyani (in present-day Bidar), lay relatively near Kannada border territory still contested by Maharashtra.[45] All that can be said with strict accuracy in the case of the Chalukyas is that if they are to be called something, if they "belong" to any one region, they are Kannada property. For the regional patriot this is enough. But the historical reality at any moment in time prior to the thirteenth century was that the regions of the Deccan, like most regions of India, were still inchoate and ill-defined. The dynastic identity had more relevance than the emergent regional identity.

Today the very confusion and uncertainty in historical studies that are so incomplete encourages the regional patriot in his efforts to appropriate pre-thirteenth century history. In the Kannada version of Deccan history the statement that the Satavahanas are "wrongly designated as Andhras" is accompanied by the flat contention that none of the early Deccan dynasties was in any sense Maharashtrian.[46] All the dynasties become Kannada by a process of elimination. "After a glorious epoch of the Satavahana rulers, Karnataka enjoyed a unique and solemn glory for a period of 1,000 years under the rulership of the vigorous dynasties of the Kadambas, the Chalukyas, the Rashtrakutas, and others."[47] Similarly, the Andhras go from their plausible claim to the Kakatiyas (c. 1200-1326 A.D.) to

[44] Historians have been inclined to trace the Deccan Chalukyas to the Gurjar invaders of northwest India who gave their name to Gujarat. More recent research, however, gives them a Kanarese origin. R. C. Majumdar, ed., *The History and Culture of the Indian People*, p. 227, states that the Gurjar identification seems to be untenable. The Chalukyas themselves, as was the habit of many of the Deccan and southern dynasties, trace their origins to Ayodhya. For this, see R. G. Bhandarkar, *Early History of the Dekkan*, p. 83.

[45] For useful correlations of ancient historical locations throughout India with modern boundaries see the maps in C. Collin Davies, *An Historical Atlas of the Indian Peninsula*, Oxford University Press, Indian Branch, 1949.

[46] A. P. Karmarkar, *A Cultural History of Karnataka*, p. 25.

[47] *Ibid.*, p. 1. See also pp. 22, 26; and S. R. Sharmal, "Jainism in Karnataka," *Karnatak Historical Review*, Vol. I, No. 1, March 1931, p. 31.

the blithe embrace of the Vijayanagar Empire (c. 1327-1565 A.D.). Krishnadeva Raya (c. 1509-1530 A.D.) and most of the Vijayanagar emperors did, in fact, give their greatest patronage to Telugu. Vijayanagar is remembered today in Andhra as the golden age of Telugu poets, from Srinatha, who set the literary fashion in the fourteenth century, to Peddana, poet laureate of Krishnadeva Raya's court. In separating historical memory from historical fact, however, one must keep in mind that Vijayanagar was a multi-lingual empire in which Kannada and Telugu still co-existed in a single political unit. Although Telugu enjoyed the greatest favor, official patronage was also accorded to Kannada. The Lingayat movement, which had spread over both Karnataka and Andhra in the centuries immediately preceding Vijayanagar, had created a bi-lingual literary climate: Andhra-born Somanatha wrote Lingayat texts in both languages,[48] and the Vijayanagar poets Srinatha,[49] Bhima Kavi,[50] and Peddana[51] continued in varying measure in the bilingual tradition. Clearly, then, Andhra can make no exclusive claims on the strength of linguistic homogeneity. Nor can Vijayanagar be labelled wholly "Andhra" in its lineage. Historians speculating on the empire's origins find it likely that feudatories and lieutenants drawn from both Karnataka's Hoysalas and Andhra's Kakatiyas allied to found Vijayanagar.[52] The imperial capital actually lay in what is clearly Kannada territory. All the same, in the clash of regional patriotisms today, the manipulator in Andhra does not hesitate to disregard all Kannada complications and call Vijayanagar Telugu.

Because Vijayanagar lies in the relatively recent past its cul-

---

[48] K. A. Nilakanta Sastri, *A History of South India*, pp. 383 and 389.

[49] *Ibid.*, p. 388. P. T. Raju, *Telugu Literature*, pp. 3-8, 24-26.

[50] K. A. Nilakanta Sastri, *A History of South India*, p. 383.

[51] *Ibid.*, p. 395.

[52] For example, see K. Ramakotiswara Rau, "The Triple Stream," *Triveni*, Vol. IX, No. 6, December 1936, p. 5; P. Ramamoorty, "The Empire of Vijayanagara," *Triveni*, Vol. IX, No. 6, December 1936, pp. 20-21; S. K. Aiyangar, *Some Contributions of South India to Indian Culture*, University of Calcutta, 1923, pp. 292-298. Both W. H. Moreland (*A Short History of India*, pp. 149 and 174) and *Census of India, 1951* (Vol. XIV, "Mysore," p. 9) make Hoysala nobles and vassals the founders of Vijayanagar. The Empire is popularly known both as the Karnataka Empire (R. C. Majumdar, ed., *The History and Culture of the Indian People*, Vol. IV, p. 220) and as the Andhra Empire.

tural and political glories provide unusually rich and malleable
material for the manipulator. The even more recent memory
of Sivaji (c. 1627-1680 A.D.) and the Peshwas gives to Maharashtra a history uniquely capable of elaboration through reference to a still extant and accessible historical record. Sivaji
and his successors are rousing symbols in the political struggles
of Maharashtra today, primarily because their story has come
down to the present as word-of-mouth folklore. Moreover, Sivaji's
exploits against the Moghul Aurangzeb are remembered as something more than retaliation against Islamic insults: they symbolize rightful Maharashtrian leadership of a Hindu cause
that other regions were unable and indeed not meant to exercise. All the rest of *sahishnu* or "passively suffering" India is
distinguished from *jayishnu* or "conquering" Maharashtra; it
is the *Maharashtra Dharma*, the duty of Maharashtra, to exercise benevolent leadership for all the sacred regions of the
Hindu motherland.[53] Sivaji would have led all India to a
realization of its glories as a great Hindu power, in the Maharashtrian *mystique*, but for his untimely death at fifty-three;
and so would the Marathas after him "if they had not been un-
expectedly called upon to face an organized Western power."[54]
With all the odds against them, we are reminded, the Marathas
still spread their benevolent hegemony over an arc extending
southeast as far as Tanjore in Tamilnad, northwest as far as
Surat in Gujarat, and even to Delhi.[55] For their part the
Gujaratis fail to recall a benevolent Maratha presence. Sivaji's
agents, according to K. M. Munshi, looked on Gujarat "more
as a treasure to be robbed than a country to be governed."[56]
The Bengalis commemorate the Maratha free-booters—those
"slayers of pregnant women and infants . . . expert in robbing
the property of everyone and in committing every sinful act"[57]

[53] See G. S. Sardesai, *The Main Currents of Maratha History* (rev. ed.), Phoenix
Publications, Bombay, 1949, pp. 11, 14-16.
[54] *Ibid.*, p. 68.
[55] *Ibid.*, p. 29.
[56] K. M. Munshi, *Gujarata and its Literature*, pp. 207-208.
[57] W. H. Moreland, *A Short History of India*, p. 269, citing Sir Jadunath
Sarkar, *Bihar and Orissa During the Fall of the Moghul Empire*, Patna, 1932,
pp. 36-39.

—with nursery songs equating Marathas and depredation.[58] But Maharashtrian historians write of "liberators and defenders of the faith" and go on to conclude that, were it not for the British, Maharashtra would have presided over India's entry into the industrial age.[59] The Maharashtrian *mystique* is in any case a major fact of the contemporary Indian scene. Toynbee notes that the dissolution of the British Raj, like the previous liquidation of the Moghul Raj, has been followed by a scramble for power. This time "neither the Maratha's valor nor the Bengali's penmanship" triumphs. The twentieth century victor

is the Gujarati with his business sense. The Gujarati industrialist is, in fact, the British sahib's principal heir; and Bengal, with her wings broken by partition, may resign herself to being eclipsed. But what about the Maharashtrian, with his masterful character and his unforgotten past political greatness? Shades of Sivaji, Gokhale and Tilak! Are their kinsmen to resign themselves to becoming Gujarat's helots? Today the Maharashtrian is carrying a chip on his shoulder. I augur that more will be heard of him again before long.[60]

Although Orissa can claim a regional history as old as the rest of the Deccan, Orissa has no Sivaji or Krishnadeva Raya whose relatively recent exploits can form the stuff of word-of-mouth folklore. The Oriya regional patriot must reach back two thousand years to Kharavela (c. 180-150 B.C.)[61] to rival the heroes who performed in later centuries in the center of the Deccan stage. Orissa remained, so far as the main Deccan drama was concerned, virtually off-stage, its ties equally close to Bengal. The Orissa coastal lowlands are difficult to negotiate from both north and south; the Mahanadi-Brahmani delta fan, perennially subject to flood, can be traversed only along a narrow strip at the head of the delta, the site of Cuttack;[62] and the Gondwana hinterland, wild and forested, blocks off the region on

---

[58] Sukumar Dutt, *The Problem of Indian Nationality*, University of Calcutta, 1926, p. 35.

[59] G. S. Sardesai, *The Main Currents of Maratha History*, p. 28.

[60] Arnold J. Toynbee, *East and West*, Oxford University Press, 1958, p. 100.

[61] See *Orissa Review*, Orissa Monuments Special, Public Relations Department, Government of Orissa, Vol. vi, 1949, p. 49; *Orissa in Pictures* (pamphlet), Public Relations Department, Government of Orissa, p. 5; *Orissa—A New State with a Past and a Future* (pamphlet), Public Relations Department, Government of Orissa, p. 13.

[62] The historic importance of Cuttack is discussed in *Orissa Review*, p. 1.

the west. This physical isolation made "Kalinga" a distinct identity even in the *Mahabharata* and *Ramayana*. The boundaries of Orissa expanded and contracted, north and south, depending not only on the fortunes of its own rulers but also on those of northern and southern neighbors. All of it or parts of it were variously conquered by the northern Mauryas and Guptas, the Satavahanas and Chalukyas of the Deccan, the Palas of Bengal, the Rayas of Vijayanagar. There were powerful dynasties after Kharavela that gave Orissa intermittent regional golden ages: the Gangas (c. 500-900 and 1070-1430 A.D.) and the Gajapatis (c. 1450-1540 A.D.). In the age of the later Gangas Orissa was the headquarters of a kingdom extending, at one point, from the Ganges to the Godavari. In this period the Orissan prakrit dialect, a sub-form of the old Magadha prakrit, developed into modern Oriya, which rapidly became the medium for a considerable prose literature. But the glories of Orissa left little impact in histories written outside Orissa. In this case, the fact that a region did not build the biggest empires and has always been, relatively speaking, on the fringes of Indian history, may be as important in modern inter-regional relationships as the real or imagined greatness of other regional pasts.

Eden in South India

"Tamilaham or the home of the Tamils," declares a solemn tract, "was in the hoary past the southern region of the large island known as Navalam . . . one of the first land formations on either side of the equator. . . . It included Lemuria or the Lost Continent . . . [and] was the cradle of human civilization." The first of three great deluges tore Australia, China and Africa from Navalam, the second severed Ceylon, and in the third, Tamils fled by land and by sea as far as Ireland and China. "Traces of this wide dispersion are found in Palestine, Egypt, Italy, Scandinavia, and far-off Erin in the names of places with the suffix *ur*, in the modes of life pursued, in the resemblances of the Tamilian myths to those of Greece and to the northern sagas."[63]

[63] M. S. P. Pillai, *Tamil India*, The South India Saiva Siddhanta Works Publishing Society, Tinnevelly, Ltd., Madras, 1945, pp. 1-4.

None but the most lyrical Tamil patriots insist on this version of ancient Tamil importance: others consent to the arrival of the first Tamils after the great deluge, as survivors, perhaps, of Noah's adventure, or acquiesce in Sir John Marshall's suggestion that the Sumerian precursors of Babylon and Assyria may have been the offshoot of a prior south Indian civilization.[64] The Tamil loyalty oath is addressed not to the origins of all human civilization but specifically to Tamil priority within the Indian historical scheme of things. Here regional pride allows no debate. Tamil patriots took it as settled that their antecedents had indeed been first on the Indian scene when disinterested scholars three decades ago perceived Dravidian traces in the artifacts of the Indus Valley civilization, India's oldest known, predating even the Aryan arrival by some 1,500 years. The discoveries at Mohenjodaro and Harappa together with recent studies in anthropology and linguistics still leave many riddles of early Indian history unresolved.[65] But the fact that a remnant of the Dravidian language family can even today be found in Baluchistan indicates that northwest India must have been, as Horace Poleman has put it, the home of "either the advance guard or the rear guard of Dravidian culture."[66] No doubt can remain that nineteenth-century European and Indian historians and Sanskritists left us a grossly inaccurate picture of ancient India. Their preoccupation with the Aryan north virtually shut out the Dravidian south.

In Aryan Sanskritic lore the southerners of Vedic times are *asuras* or demons and non-Aryans generally *dasyus* or slaves. The archetypal Aryan Brahman sage, Agastya, ventures south in the *Mahabharata* much as a missionary goes to the Hottentots.

[64] See T. R. Sesha Iyengar, *Dravidian India*, Vol. I, published by author, Madras, 1925; V. Kanakasabhai, *The Tamils Eighteen Hundred Years Ago*, South India Saiva Siddhanta Works Publishing Society, Tirunelveli, Madras (rev. ed.), 1956; P. T. Srinivas Iyengar, *History of the Tamils From the Earliest Times to 600 A.D.*, C. Coomerasawmy Naidu and Sons, Madras, 1929.

[65] For a concise discussion of the scientific evidence so far available on the ethnic and linguistic origins of Dravidian India, see K. A. Nilakanta Sastri, *A History of South India*, pp. 49-63. Another version of Indian ethnology is in H. G. Rawlinson, *India: A Short Cultural History*, pp. 9-13.

[66] Horace I. Poleman, "Historical Aspects of the Language Problem in India," Seminar Paper No. 3, Seminar on Leadership and Political Institutions in India, Berkeley, California, 1956, p. 3.

To be sure, Agastya also appears in Tamil accounts, and scholars conclude from his presence in historical memory on both sides of the Vindhyas that he personifies allegorically early Aryan contact with the south. But the Tamil memory of the north-south encounter happens to be precisely the opposite of the Vedic memory. Instead of wise and heroic Aryans subjecting savage southerners, the Tamil patriot tells us, on the contrary, how "from a barbarian he [the Aryan] developed into a civilized being on his coming into contact with the highly civilized Dravidian."[67]

The Bengali philologist S. K. Chatterji typifies the new consensus that non-Aryan India had a major part in the creation and elaboration of Hindu civilization. Hindu culture, he asserts, "was not an Aryan culture imposed by a superior, civilized, white Aryan or Indo-European-speaking people upon backward or savage, dark-skinned, non-Aryan aboriginals. . . . It was in fact the joint creation of the Aryan and non-Aryan."[68] This conclusion is as unacceptable to many Tamil Brahmans as it is welcome to Tamil non-Brahman scholars and propagandists whose political vendetta against the Brahmans and the north rests, as we will see in chapter four, on the allegation that the Tamil Brahmans are Aryan interlopers defiling a once-pure Tamil culture. In Tamilnad the very fundamentals of history are the grist of political debate. Thus the publication in 1955 of a book on south Indian history[69] by the eminent K. A. Nilakanta Sastri was as much a political as a scholarly event. As a Brahman, and worse, a "Brahman believed to be of Telugu ancestry," Nilakanta Sastri emphasized, according to a non-Brahman reviewer, "the 'Aryanization' of south India—it would be more appropriate to speak of 'the Indo-Aryan infiltration into south India.'" Nilakanta Sastri, said the reviewer, presented

[67] P. Chidambaram Pillai, *Dravidian and Aryan* (pamphlet), published by author, Nagercoil, 1936, p. 2.

[68] S. K. Chatterji, "The Basic Unity Underlying the Diversity of Culture: The Origins and Meaning of Indian Culture," *Interrelations of Cultures*, UNESCO, Paris, 1953, pp. 161-162. See also S. K. Aiyangar, *Some Contributions of South India to Indian Culture*; and Gilbert Slater, *The Dravidian Element in Indian Culture*, Ernest Benn Ltd., London, 1924.

[69] *A History of South India.*

39

selected facts that would "fit in with his theory that Tamil could not have been fully developed before the spread of Sanskrit."[70]

The non-Brahman case for the antiquity of Tamil civilization hinges in good part on the antiquity of a developed Tamil language. Scholars agree that Tamil antedates its three related sister southern languages, Malayalam, Kannada, and Telugu, which together with Tamil and certain minor languages form the Dravidian language family. But the comparative age of Tamil and Sanskrit remains a subject of controversy. Nilakanta Sastri dates the origins of Tamil to inscriptions in the third century B.C.[71] In non-Brahman eyes this deliberately minimizes the advanced state of ancient Tamil to support the hypothesis of a superior—and more ancient—Sanskrit. Whether Tamil is in fact "a language as ancient as and coeval with, if not older than, any ancient language alive or dead"[72] has not yet been confirmed by linguists and historians. The Tamil mythology which places the roots of the language 9,000-odd years before Christ[73] cannot be converted by any available evidence into historical fact. Having dismissed mythology, however, scholars are unable to fix with certainty an agreed estimate of the antiquity of Tamilnad and its language. Some believe that the earliest extant Tamil grammar, *Tolkappiyam*, must date back centuries before Christ—at least five centuries, says a non-Brahman scholar, even "by the most rigid canons."[74] The fact that early Tamil verse forms show little similarity to Sanskritic metres is also advanced in behalf of the Tamil case.[75] But the case is far from proved. The most that can be said with certainty is that the three ancient Tamil states, Chola, Pandya, and Chera, were in existence as of the fourth century B.C. and figured conspicuously enough in the literature of the Asokan period a century later for Nilakanta Sastri to conclude cau-

[70] S. J. G., *The Tamil*, Colombo, Ceylon, June 1955, p. 4.
[71] K. A. Nilakanta Sastri, *A History of South India*, pp. 86-87.
[72] *Tamil: The Language and Literature*, Delhi Tamil Sangam, June 1950, p. iv.
[73] K. A. Nilakanta Sastri, *A History of South India*, p. 111; and see the use of this legend by M. S. P. Pillai in *Tamil India*, p. 47.
[74] Xavier S. Thani Nayagam, *Nature in Ancient Tamil Poetry*, Tamil Literature Society, Tuticorin, 1953, p. xii.
[75] T. R. Sesha Iyengar, *Dravidian India*, p. 79.

40

tiously: "The Tamils . . . must have had a settled polity and lived in well-ordered states for some time before Asoka could think of starting his friendly intercourse with them."[76]

Whatever the precise age of the Tamil regional identity, there can be no doubt—placing the facts of geography next to the speculations of history—that the Tamil country was the seat of a very old, self-contained civilization. The Tamilnad plain, stretching south and west as the peninsular platform recedes inland from the Andhra coast, offers a decided contrast to the Deccan tableland lying above and beyond. Next to the Ganges basin, the Kaveri delta, Tamilnad's most fertile granary, provides India's greatest natural setting for political consolidation. The Ganges and Kaveri at opposite ends of the subcontinent are, as Panikkar puts it, "the two focii of Indian civilization."[77] Now corresponding roughly to the site of Tanjore District, the Kaveri delta was the seat of dominant Chola dynasties in Tamilnad off and on for more than twelve centuries. To the south the Pandya dynasties, equally long-lived, were the perennial rulers of the Tirunelveli black soil tract and the dry farm belt from Madura, their capital, to Ramnad; and to the west, along the Kerala coastal strip between the Western Ghats and the sea, the Cheras completed the "Trirajya" or "Three Kingdom" triumvirate of ancient Tamilnad. The boundaries of the Tamil plain were for the most part the outer limits for the ambitions of Tamil kings. However, where the boundaries are relatively undefined, as in the Rayalaseema area now forming the southwestern extremity of Andhra, a self-confident Tamil regime often challenged the Deccan imperial power of the day for possession of all the peninsula up to the Tungabhadra. The coastal belt immediately north of the Kaveri was another beckoning passageway and a standing invitation to northern excursions— most frequently to the Andhra deltas and on occasion beyond. The invitation proved irresistible at the eleventh-century zenith of Tamil power when the emperor Rajendra sent his army through Orissa as far as Bengal and "the war elephants of the

[76] *A History of South India*, p. 82.
[77] *Geographical Factors in Indian History*, p. 24.

Chola drank the water of the Ganges. . . ."[78] But such grandiose expeditions were exceptions to the rule of Tamil history.

Tamil emperors were content to forego the wealth of the Deccan because their geographical position gave them access to the rich and ancient East-West ocean trade route and thus to the wealth of a great maritime power. The key to the self-generating prosperity of the early Tamils and an impressive part of the case for a pre-Aryan Tamil civilization can be found in this maritime orientation. Egyptian records attest to the presence of south Indian products in Egypt as far back as the second millennium before Christ. Chinese and Babylonian sources similarly date trade with south India at least to the seventh century B.C. The sandalwood, rice, and peacocks shipped to Babylon, moreover, bore Dravidian rather than Sanskrit names.[79] Later south India carried on an immense trade with Greece and Rome during their imperial centuries. A dynasty uniting in one sovereignty the Tamil plain, the Kerala coastal strip to the west, and, if possible, the Andhra deltas, looked next to the sea, to the lucrative trade passing from the Mediterranean and Africa to China. For more than ten centuries after the beginning of the Christian era Tamilnad was intimately involved culturally with Indonesia, Malaya, Viet Nam, and Cambodia,[80] as a result of its trade ties, and evidence of this involvement is still pronounced today. Great military armadas of the Cholas and of the Sri Vijaya Empire of Sumatra and Malaya were contending for control of the Indian Ocean at a time—the eleventh century—when only the Vikings, among the European powers, were equipped for comparable adventures. As maritime powers, as controllers of the Kaveri rice bowl, Tamil empires stood on an impregnable economic base. Thus they were able to forestall Deccan incursions and to develop a political and cultural identity as strong and vital as any in India.

If Tamil chauvinists exaggerate, in short, they do so unnecessarily, for Tamilnad can in fact look back on a prolonged and

[78] H. G. Rawlinson (*India: A Short Cultural History*, p. 182) extracts this line from a Tamil poem.
[79] K. A. Nilakanta Sastri, *A History of South India*, p. 76.
[80] Xavier S. Thani Nayagam, "Tamil Cultural Influences is South East Asia," *Tamil Culture*, Vol. IV, No. 3, July 1955, pp. 1-18.

virtually continuous historical golden age corresponding roughly to the first thirteen centuries of the Christian era. The classical Sangam Age at the beginning of this thirteen-century span gains its name from three Sangams, or colleges of learned men, which in the traditional account were officially-sponsored literary high commands empowered to sanction or reject Tamil literary works for inclusion in a body of accepted Tamil literature. This "accepted" literary output, now preserved as a collection of some 2,279 Tamil poems written by some 473 poets, plus 100-odd anonymous pieces, constitutes a high order of literary achievement. Precisely what period of time this output covers remains uncertain. While all agree that the Sangam Age opens known Tamil literary history, the Sangams themselves are dated variously over a period of 9,990 years, if Tamil mythology is to be believed, or over a mere 150 years, sometime in the first three or four centuries of the Christian era, if Nilakanta Sastri is correct.[81] In any case the existence of the poetry provides the tangible stuff for dreams of vanished Tamil glories.

The simple but elegant poetry of the Sangam Age, free from "over-refined speculation," drawing on "a world essentially of the here and now,"[82] is idealized in modern Tamilnad as unstained by Brahmanism,[83] emphasizing good conduct, love, and above all, the glories of nature. "In a corner of peninsular India," writes a Tamil Jesuit intellectual, "a people developed an interpretation of Nature the like of which was never conceived on the plains watered by the Ganges, or on the banks of the Nile, or the Tiber, or on the shores of the Aegean Sea."[84] The Tamil heartland along the Kaveri is the *marudam*[85] region of the ancient Nature poetry, a garden of Eden named for the myrtle tree so plentiful in this "sea of green fields."[86] The Tamils of this halcyon day live with the "unsophisticated spontaneity" of Virgil's shepherds,

[81] K. A. Nilakanta Sastri, *A History of South India*, p. 111.

[82] A. Srinivasa Raghavan, "A Note on Tamil Literature," *Orient Review*, September 1956, p. 50.

[83] A. Senthamilan (pseudonym—"A Lover of Tamil"—for a prominent non-Brahman), "Cultural Conflicts in Tamilnad," *Quest*, April 1955.

[84] Xavier S. Thani Nayagam, *Nature in Ancient Tamil Poetry*, p. xvi.

[85] *Ibid.*, p. 92.   [86] *Ibid.*, p. 27.

in houses built . . . in the center of a garden . . . dancing under the bowers, holding their meetings under umbrageous trees, feasting in the open, indulging in the pleasure that only those in warm climates know in bathing in tanks and rivers and the sea, decorating themselves even in daily life with garlands and leaves.[87]

A royal hero of this Tamil Augustan Age was the Chola king Karikala, patron of the arts[88] and doer of brave deeds, who singlehandedly overpowered a battalion of prison guards, it is said, when jealous relations conspired to deny him his rightful throne,[89] and who succeeded later in subduing all the kings of the Tamil country. Centuries after his death legends about Karikala multiplied to the point where some credit him with the conquest of all of India up to the Himalayas.

In a political sense the centuries following the Sangam Age are inconveniently disarrayed for purposes of any modern evocation of the Tamil past. The Tamil kings were subdued by unknown rivals: the Pandyas do not reappear until the sixth century and the Cholas until the ninth. But a continuous Tamil literary tradition can be traced through the dark interval and, indeed, some of the greatest Tamil literary achievements accompanied Buddhist and Jaina religious hegemony in this period of south Indian history. The noted *Kural*[90] was written by the weaver known to history as Tiruvalluvar and usually identified as a Jain. "There hardly exists in the literature of the world," says Albert Schweitzer, "a collection of maxims in which we find so much lofty wisdom."[91] The *Kural's* couplets provide an all-embracing code of ethics addressed to three of the four Hindu objectives of life—righteousness (*dharma*), worldly prosperity (*artha*), and love (*kama*). Complete as it is and, more important, credited as it is to a non-Brahman, the *Kural* enables Tamil non-Brahmans today to claim their own Veda. The Bud-

---

[87] *Ibid.*, p. 10.

[88] V. Kanakasabhai, *The Tamils Eighteen Hundreds Years Ago*, p. 69. See also K. N. S. Pillai, *The Chronology of the Early Tamils*, University of Madras, 1932, pp. 128-131.

[89] "Karikala Chola," *Hindu Weekly Review*, July 7, 1958, p. 11.

[90] V. V. S. Aiyar, trans., *The Kural* or *The Maxims of Tiruvalluvar*, The Bharadvaja Ashrama, Sheramadevi, South India, 1916.

[91] *Indian Thought and its Development*, Adam and Charles Black, London, 1951, p. 203.

dhist and Jaina period also produced the classic *Silappadikaram* epic of Kovalan and his wronged wife Kannagi and the lesser epic *Manimekalai.*

Buddhist and Jaina predominance in the Kaveri plain and the Pandya country ended soon after the sixth-century rise of the Pallava dynasty to dominance in Tamilnad. Just who the Pallavas were is not clear; their political history is almost blank between their arrival from the north in the fourth century and their center-stage prominence from about 600 to 900 A.D. That the Tamil memory of the Pallavas is not entirely cordial can be seen in the Tamil use of the word "Pallava" as a synonym for rascal or robber.[92] The Pallavas may have been Satavahana viceroys who usurped control of their southern Andhra viceroyalty on the demise of the Satavahanas and then expanded into the Chola country. Or they may have been, as some say, indigenous Tamil rivals of the Cholas. Whatever the case, the ambitious Pallavas, who alternated with the Pandyas in dominating the south for three centuries, were vigorous promoters of Brahmanism, the last of the dynastic carriers of north Indian Sanskritic culture to the south. As great military conquerors who pushed the northern Tamil frontier into the Andhra delta land, as patrons of the arts instrumental in the creation of the Dravidian style of structural temple architecture exemplified in the Kailasanatha temple at Kanchi, the Pallavas are embraced, today, as part of the Tamil tradition.

During the period of Pallava power in Tamilnad, the Kerala coastal belt on India's southwestern tip began to break away from its previous Tamil connections. The breach was an inevitable one because of the sharp geographical separation of Kerala from the rest of south India by the Western Ghats. The southern extremity of this mountain barrier stretches from north to south between Tamilnad and Kerala with only one major opening—the Palghat Gap at the western end of the Coimbatore plateau. The Gap was the key to control of Kerala for any Tamil regime and made the Coimbatore plateau, ancient Kongu

92 H. G. Rawlinson, *India: A Short Cultural History*, p. 194.

Nad, a bone of contention between rival Tamil powers. The Western Ghats dictated not only the political boundary but the climatic boundary: the Ghats block the monsoon as it sweeps in from the Arabian Sea so that an inordinate amount of rainfall drenches the Malabar Coast. The tropical fertility, which makes five acres of land enough for a family's sustenance in Kerala, differs sharply even from the deltaic prosperity of the Kaveri plain.

In the Communist view of Indian history it is the fact that, in Kerala, "field cultivation does not, in a normal year, require artificial irrigation by canals and other forms of public works,"[93] which explains why, despite its geographical separation, Kerala cannot claim a succession of strong centralized kingdoms. "While the need of a central organization for the development of irrigation led to a centralized imperial state in other parts of India," writes E. M. S. Nambudripad, formerly Chief Minister of Kerala, "the absence of this need made for a state with a far smaller area under its control in Kerala."[94] Nambudripad opts for that school of historical thought that depicts the early Chera kingdoms, paralleling the Cholas and Pandyas, as loose collections of divided principalities tied to the Kaveri rather than as distinctive and politically unified regional states. In the case of Kerala, one school of thought carries as much conviction as another. Little is certain in the obscure history of this long-isolated region. Whatever the case during the Chera period, it seems reasonably clear that when the Cheras declined, the Perumals, who are often cited as the next great imperial rulers of early Kerala, commanded only formal allegiance from subject chieftains. Kerala remained divided into petty disputatious principalities until Maharajah Martanda Varma of Travancore embarked on his unifying adventures in the eighteenth century.

Throughout the long centuries of disunity and isolation Kerala nonetheless enjoyed an economic prosperity based on a vigorous sea commerce with countries across the Arabian Sea. Her language, meanwhile, was progressively separating from

[93] E. M. S. Nambudripad, *The National Question in Kerala*, Peoples Publishing House, Bombay, 1952, p. 16.
[94] *Ibid.*, p. 52.

Tamil. Even in Chera times the Tamil of Kerala was a distinct dialect.[95] By the tenth century Malayalam was a separate language, by the twelfth century a language with the beginnings of its own literature. The tenth century origins of Malayalam are explained in various ways. In the Nambudripad version of Kerala history, which was the "official" explanation in India's first Communist-controlled state, the rise of an unprecedented "feudal landlordism" following the fall of the Perumals is said to mark a new measure of freedom from the Kaveri.[96] Former Chief Minister Nambudripad's treatise on Kerala history is the most comprehensive effort of its kind by any regional Communist leader. Yet, ironically, Kerala Communist success, while based in good part, as we will see in chapter six, on deliberate identification with regional interests, has involved only a marginal appeal to an historical memory notably weak compared with that of most other regions.

Certainly Kerala, placed next to Tamilnad with its impressive history, presents a pale shadow. The regional patriot in Kerala rarely appeals to historical memory. He exploits instead a sense of discrimination at the hands of the Tamils and the central government. Historical allusions pervade the Tamil regional appeal, on the other hand, even when it is nominally addressed to the here and now. The Tamil appeal is made with the greatest abandon in the name of the Sangam Age, which is still lost in the never-never land between legend and history and lends itself, as a consequence, to the most lyrical flights of regional fancy. But the ninth to thirteenth century age of the imperial Cholas provides a more recent and less debatable example of Tamil greatness. At the height of their power in the eleventh century the Cholas united all of south India for the first time as a single political unit. Rajaraja the Great and his son Rajendra I, Tamilnad's proudest royal heroes, pushed the limits of Tamil power north to the Tungabhadra. The sea power of the Cholas had a splendid symbol in the cosmopolitan

[95] See A. C. Sekhar, *Evolution of Malayalam*, Deccan College Dissertation Series: 10, Poona, 1953; and T. Lakshmana Pillai, "Are Malayalis Tamilians?" *Kerala Society Papers*, Vol. II, series 7, 1931, pp. 1-18.

[96] E. M. S. Nambudripad, *The National Question in Kerala*, p. 55.

port city of Puhar at the head of the Kaveri delta, a commercial crossroads for goods from China to the Mediterranean. Rajaraja's Siva temple at Tanjore is the architectural gem of south India. The Chola Nataraja bronzes remain to this day the epitome of south Indian sculptural excellence. No Chola court in the imperial golden age was without a poet laureate to celebrate a great victory, such as Kulottunga's Kalinga (Orissa) war, with a war poem like Jayangondar's *Kalingattupparani*.[97] In the twelfth century the poet Kamban produced his classic Tamil version of the *Ramayana*, still treasured today as a Tamil literary masterpiece.

Bhakti and the Regional Languages

In a study of the development of the regional languages the Chola period has a special significance. This was the age when the movement for a popular Hinduism that had taken root in Tamilnad under the Pallavas and Pandyas acquired both standardized form and deepened philosophical content. The pandits of the Chola era codified and canonized the Tamil hymns of their predecessors, the Nayanars and Alvars, who had taken the inspiration for Tamilnad's devotional (*bhakti*) movement, in turn, from the North's popular religious efflorescence in the Gupta Age. Buddhism and Jainism had gravely challenged a Hinduism, which was in reality Brahmanism, simply by speaking over the heads of the Brahmans to the lower castes. To expunge the heretical sects from Tamilnad, the mystic saint-worshippers of Siva, the Nayanars, and of Vishnu, the Alvars, preached in place of metaphysics an emotional Hinduism offering salvation through *bhakti* or uncomplicated devotion to God. The *puranas* handed down from the Gupta period provided a storehouse of easily comprehensible mythology, which the saints disembodied from its original Sanskrit[98] and carried to the countryside in Tamil: the Tamil hymns of the Nayanars and Alvars comprise the Saivite *Tirumurai* and the

[97] K. A. Nilakanta Sastri, *Dravidian Literatures*, p. 9.

[98] Some historians maintain that Sanskrit was not the original language of the *puranas*, which were originally written, according to this view, in the *prakrits*. A brief account of this position can be found in R. C. Majumdar, ed., *The History and Culture of the Indian People*, Vol. III, p. 296, n. 1.

Vaishnavite *Nalavira Prabhandam* still used in Tamil Hindu worship.[99] Providing a philosophic rationale for the popular *bhakti* preached by the mystics were the great *acharyas* of the Chola age,[100] notably Ramanuja, who adapted the earlier Vedantic speculations of Sankara to the needs of a mass religious revival.

The significance of the Chola period cannot be overemphasized because here for the first time, in the Nayanar and Alvar hymns, a regional language became the medium of a sacred liturgy central to the regional practice of Hinduism. Here, too, Tamilnad, having drawn inspiration from the north in the first place, now retransmitted a revitalized popular Hinduism to all regions of India at precisely the moment when Hinduism was to need renewed strength for the dark centuries of Islamic hegemony. Coming out of the south at this critical period was the *Bhagavata Purana*: in this beloved scriptural story of the youthful Lord Krishna Vaishnavite writers throughout the Deccan and the north would find their "gospel of *bhakti*."[101]

Like Buddhist and Jaina reformism the *bhakti* movement, typifying the broad popular Hindu revival of which it was a part, emphasized the use of the regional languages as a means of reaching the lower castes and thus had an important part in regional language development. Instead of transposing Sanskrit metres to the regional languages, the *bhakti* poets deliberately employed the native or *desi* metres characteristic of each language.[102] The peculiar importance of *bhakti* in this respect lies in the fact that it came at a time when the regional languages were already well along in their development, ready to respond to new stimuli. Kannada had been in literary use for

---

[99] J. S. M. Hooper, *Hymns of the Alvars*, The Heritage of India Series, Association Press, Calcutta, 1929, pp. 19-20. See also K. A. Nilakanta Sastri, *A History of South India*, pp. 5, 404, 407; K. G. Sesha Aiyar, "Kulasekhara Alvar," *Kerala Society Papers*, Series 1, 1928, pp. 30-39.

[100] Kenneth Morgan, ed., *The Religion of the Hindus*, Ronald Press Co., New York, 1953, pp. 232-233.

[101] R. C. Majumdar, ed., *The History and Culture of the Indian People*, Vol. IV, p. xxii.

[102] K. Ramakrishnaiya, *Desi in South Indian Languages and Literatures*, Korada Publishing House, Madras, 1954, pp. 2, 42, 128, 132. (Telugu text partially translated for the author.)

three centuries under the Jains before Karnataka's Saivite expression of *bhakti*, the Lingayat movement,[103] turned to the popular language to spread its creed through the simple, still-recited *vacana* literature. With Lingayat influence spilling over into Andhra, Telugu, until then used primarily for translations from the Sanskrit, became for a brief interval a medium of Lingayat *puranas* and propaganda. The anti-Brahman bias of Lingayatism and of the Haridasa cult,[104] its companion Vaishnavite movement, typified most of the regional variations on the *bhakti* theme. Paralleling Lingayatism in Maharashtra was the anti-caste Mahanubhav Panth, among other manifestations of the *bhakti* spirit, which set in motion reformist forces soon to merge in the Vithoba cult[105] with its succession of some fifty mystic saints over a four-hundred year period. The first of the Maharashtra *bhakti* mystics, Dnyaneshwar, although a Brahman, frankly directed his Marathi paraphrase and commentary on the *Gita* to the lower castes. In his use of Marathi and his bias against Brahmanical monopoly of the Sanskrit texts he set the pattern for Maharashtra's deeply-rooted popular culture. All the Maharashtra saints, whether an emotional Namadev or Tukaram taking devotional *abhangas* to the villages or a more literary and philosophical Ekanath, wrote in Marathi and in so doing established a progressively more vital language.

The imprint of the *bhakti* movement in the Ganges valley can be found on almost all its treasured literature, whether written in Avadhi, the language used by Ramanand's Rama-worshipping followers (Raidas, Kabir, Tulsidas) or in the Braj Bhasha adopted by the Krishna cult (Surdas, Biharilal).[106]

[103] A vivid lay account of this movement is found in Masti Venkatesa Iyengar, *Popular Culture in Karnataka*, Bangalore Press, Bangalore City, 1937, pp. 18-36.

[104] Narayana Rao B. Kalamdani and Ananta Rao P. Karmarkar, "The Haridasa Movement in Karnataka," *The Karnataka Historical Review*, Vol. IV, Nos. 1 and 2, January-July 1937, pp. 87-95. See also Masti Venkatesa Iyengar, *Popular Culture in Karnataka*, pp. 58-89.

[105] For an interesting discussion of the Vithoba cult and its contemporary significance in Maharashtrian regional life, see Maureen L. P. Patterson, "The Cult of Pandharpur," (paper), South Asia Studies Program, University of Pennsylvania, 1952.

[106] Lala Sita Ram, *Selections from Hindi Literature*, University of Calcutta,

Avadhi and Braj Bhasha developed as the literary vehicles of a popular religiosity extending over centuries and as such acquired a linguistic legitimacy denied, so far at least, to the contemporary standard Hindi, which must now be artificially fashioned out of these and other independently powerful dialects within the Gangetic region. Indeed, the very multiplicity of these competing traditions in the Ganges valley, with the added complication of the later Urdu heritage of the Muslim elite, has been a major reason for the weakness and lack of prestige of Hindi. In every other region the *bhakti* movement had left a single dominant linguistic tradition.

Although much older than the fourteenth and fifteenth centuries, Bengali also came into its own as a literary language during the Vaishnavite revival of this period. The amours of Radha and Krishna as recounted in the lyrics of Chandidas,[107] and in the fervid *kirtan* devotionals are still sung today. The sixteenth-century Bengali mystic Chaitanya made the Chandidas poetry part of the sacred literature of his sect[108] and sponsored the use of Bengali as passionately as the Brahmans sought to suppress the "vulgar" regional language.[109] Popular Hinduism took full possession of Bengali literature. As in most regions the *Ramayana* and *Mahabharata*, among other Sanskrit texts, were translated into the regional language, though in translating them the Bengali poets gave the epics a distinct Bengali flavor, and "ancient heroes and heroines became Bengalis almost to a fault."[110] In Orissa, too, Sarala Das "sang the *Mahabharata* in a rugged folk-song way, depicting the national character of Orissa in the character of the Pandavas and Kauravas."[111] To his successor, Balaram Das, who wrote the Oriya version of the *Ramayana*, Orissa was "a short-cut India with its Ganges called

---

1921-1926, Book VI, Part I, pp. x-xi, Part II, XVII-XX. Ram Awadh Dwivedi, *Hindi Literature*, Hindi Pracharak Pustakalaya, Banaras, 1953, pp. 33, 51, 63, 66.

[107] A discussion of Chandidas is found in J. C. Ghosh, *Bengali Literature*, Oxford University Press, London, 1948, pp. 38-40.

[108] Annadasankar and Lila Ray, *Bengali Literature*, The International Book House, Ltd., Bombay, 1942, pp. 11-14.

[109] *Ibid.*, pp. 32-33. Also J. C. Ghosh, *Bengali Literature*, p. 35.

[110] Annadasankar and Lila Ray, *Bengali Literature*, pp. 33-34.

[111] Kunjabehari Das, *A Study of Orissan Folklore*, Visvabharati, Santiniketan, 1953, p. 124.

Mahanadi, its Kailas called Kapilas."[112] Unlike Bengal, however, Orissa had its age of puranic translations first and then, in the sixteenth century, its *bhakti* revival. Chaitanya in Bengal provided the inspiration for the Oriya *bhakta* Deena Krishna. The sixteenth century was also the period of Assam's great *bhakta* Sankara Deva.[113]

In the case of Gujarat, a local expression of popular Hinduism called *akhyana* verse caught on a century before the northern Vaishnavite movement was swept into Gujarat by the lovelorn Rajput poetess Mirabai and by Gujarat's own Krishna *bhakta,* Narasinha Mehta. Gujarat's *gagaria bhata* troubadour has wandered from village to village since the early fifteenth century, calling the villagers together with a drumbeat on his *gagara* or copper pot to listen to recitals of the *puranas* in Gujarati verse—*puranas* hitherto heard only in Sanskrit.[114] "Men of sentiment," said Bhalana (c. 1426-1500 A.D.), the father of the *akhyana,* "men fond of the *puranas,* desire to hear them but their desire remains unfulfilled. Bhalana has, therefore, composed this poem in *bhasha.*"[115] Even the great Gujarati writer Premananda (1636-1734) was a *gagaria bhata.*

Significantly, although popular Hinduism initially represented a conscious appeal over the heads of the priesthood to the lower castes, the lower castes did not necessarily have within it a dominant role. Much of the leadership of the *bhakti* movement rested with Brahmans who were endeavoring to broaden the base of Hinduism but who were by no means seeking to alter it in its essentials. A Namadev (tailor) or Tukaram (graindealer) was balanced by a Dnyaneshwar or an Ekanath—a Raidas by a Tulsidas. The *bhakti* movement, while giving the low-caste millions a place in Hinduism, did not involve a process of cultural emancipation comparable to the release of linguistic energy now accompanying mass literacy in the regional languages. At the same time, however, the release of linguistic

---

[112] *Ibid.,* p. 125.

[113] B. K. Barua, *Assamese Literature,* The International Book House, Ltd., Bombay, 1941, pp. 16-34.

[114] An absorbing account of Gujarat's *gagaria bhata* tradition is found in K. M. Munshi, *Gujarata and its Literature,* pp. 117-119.

[115] *Ibid.,* p. 119.

energy taking place today draws much of its strength from the *bhakti* heritage. Through *bhakti* the Hindu faith of each region found some of its most honored expression in the regional language. Recorded expressions of the *bhakti* spirit during the centuries of Islamic attacks on Hinduism became a strong link for each region with its past. The regional languages became, through their use as vehicles of religious thought and lore, something far more meaningful to each region than mere *patois* or folk languages. When Western political and social ideals stirred nineteenth century India, the highly-developed regional languages provided an obvious outlet for the rising generation of Indian leaders.

Most of the new generation became an English-speaking generation because, as we shall see in the next chapter, British rule made English the passkey to intellectual and administrative employment. Still, the regional languages were links to a past that the new generation wished to recapture, and there began to be those, even among the English-speaking leadership, who consciously attempted to use the regional languages for modern cultural expression. Beneath the surface of the Western-oriented elite culture a literary renaissance was beginning in the regional languages, some of its early products crude and imitative of English models but others, as in the Bengali historical novels of Bankim Chandra Chatterjee or the Telugu classics of Guruzada Apparao, authentic expressions of a deep cultural ferment. Moreover, as the languages of everyday speech, these were the only possible vehicles for any mass independence movement. To mobilize a mass following, the English-speaking Congress Party leadership pamphleteered at the grass roots in the regional languages and helped promote the revival of regional literary effort to spread the political message of the day. This new mass-oriented regional effort released energies that have progressively increased in breadth and power. In India today the low-caste millions are in the throes of an unprecedented process of "social mobilization" and, still more important, "cultural mobilization."

It is because this process is so totally unprecedented that the nationalist rationale explaining away the absence of political

53

unity in Indian history rests on a false consolation. Past obstacles to unity are contrasted with a present which, we are assured, now offers for the first time the technical opportunity for national integration. "If the United States had a long history going back hundreds or thousands of years before modern science and industry revolutionized life," writes Nehru, "probably the country would have been split up into many small units as happened in Europe. The coming of the British in India synchronized with developments in transportation, communication and industry, and so it was that British rule succeeded at last in establishing a political unity."[116] But is this the whole of it? The coming of the British, while paralleling modern developments in transportation and communication, also coincided with and indeed was responsible for a new burst of vitality in the regional languages—a rebirth which is still in its beginnings and which may well in a matter of decades define regional divisions as they have never been defined before. In contrast to the India of one thousand years ago, disunited by default in a welter of political jurisdictions, India now faces the prospect of disunity by the deliberate design of regions face to face in a single state. One must agree with the dean of Indian sociologists, G. S. Ghurye, who observes matter-of-factly, struck by the new vitality of the regional languages, that "there are far greater potentialities of fissiparous tendencies in India today than in the . . . India of the tenth or eleventh century."[117]

[116] Jawaharlal Nehru, *The Unity of India*, Lindsay Drummond, London, 1948, p. 13.
[117] "Indian Unity—Retrospect and Prospect," *Group Prejudices in India*, Vora, Bombay, 1951, p. 120.

III · THE NEW REGIONAL ELITES

THE UPSURGE of the regional languages radically distinguishes the India now emerging from the India of the past two thousand years. In the past the diversity of emergent regions did not undermine a pan-Indian cultural unity because the regions never challenged the cultural monopoly of a cosmopolitan Brahman elite. Sanskrit spanned all regions: the Hindu classics written in Sanskrit served as a common fount for regional cultural expression, which was most often a popularized variation on pervasive Sanskritic themes. This dominance of Sanskrit and of a national Brahman elite was as complete as the corresponding cultural and political quiescence of the non-Brahman millions.

When English became the common language of a new national elite, India remained unified at the top; and though some non-Brahmans entered this English-speaking elite, most of India continued to remain quiescent at the bottom. Then the new elite discovered nationalism and the industrial age, setting in motion a process that now permits no corner of India, no caste group, to remain quiescent, and thus denies to future national elites the old monopoly on cultural vitality. The Independence movement and Independence itself have activated millions who are, in their linguistic behavior, doing what comes naturally—expressing a new mass social consciousness through their own languages.

To say that the regional languages are in some cases yet to arrive at popular literary standards bridging spoken dialects, yet to become fully developed conveyances for Western concepts new to Indian experience, is merely to say that in the decades ahead these languages will be in the throes of revolutionary creative development. Certainly as the languages of farm and factory, of time-honored literatures and a rapidly spreading pulp culture, they will be the natural vehicles of mass education and mass political awareness. As a consequence, they will carry greater dynamism than any "linking language"[1] that Indians may be able to agree upon for purposes of inter-regional communication; moreover, as this chapter seeks to demonstrate, their rise may very well destroy the cosmopolitan character of the national civil service, which is so often placed on the credit side in any balance sheet of India's prospects.

Has any other civilization experienced a linguistic revolution so vast, so precipitate, so complex as India's? Can the linguistic preconditions of cultural and political renascence at the local level be reconciled with unified political and administrative leadership at the national level? Assuming that a reconciliation does emerge, through long trial and error, can representative institutions survive? How will India relieve the political tensions implicit in the coexistence of regional institutions conducted in the regional languages and national institutions that seem certain to be carried on for an indefinite period in English?

The Legacy of English

The coexistence of English and the regional languages presents problems new in degree—as regional language literacy spreads—but not in kind. Tensions between the English-speaking elite and champions of the regional languages afflicted India throughout British rule. On the one hand, five generations of Indian leaders were compelled by British edict to receive their education through the medium of English. Yet this was also the period when the new contact with Western thought was inspiring a burst of literary effort in the regional languages. Not the English themselves, Gandhi once charged, but "our own English-knowing men have enslaved India."[2] When Gandhi came on the scene, he found for the raw material of revolutionary leadership an elite disembodied from indigenous culture, unable, in the most literal sense, to speak to the people in their

[1] Nehru's phrase in *The A.I.C.C. Economic Review*, February 15, 1958, p. 28— a pointed substitute for the use of "national" language so objectionable to non-Hindi regions.

[2] Cited in *The Speeches and Writings of Annie Besant*, G. A. Natesan Co., Madras, 1921, p. 249.

own language. Nehru himself typifies this "English" Indian. There is a couplet heard from Delhi schoolchildren:

A-B-C-D-E-F-G
Ismay nikala Panditji.

Which means, liberally translated,

A-B-C-D-E-F-G
Out of this (i.e. English education) came Panditji.

Gandhi used the disembodied "English-knowing men" for his superstructure at the same time that he found leaders rooted in local life as the base-support for his new machine; and ironically, the British had erected the superstructure for him. The colonial educational regime that produced a nationwide bureaucratic "steel frame" also brought the unified pan-Indian Congress challenge. Lord Macaulay's Education Minute of March 7, 1835, set the direction for British educational policy—in essence a language policy. English became the medium of university education; and by 1857 a university degree, which meant, in effect, facility in English, was mandatory for higher government employment. It is relatively unimportant whether this man or that did become, as Macaulay's Minute envisioned, "Indian in blood and color, but English in taste, in opinion, in morals and in intellect." The enduring fact is simply that a governing elite acquired a language that had "a wider currency simultaneously all over the country than any other language in the history of India."[3]

The linguistic revolution of 1835 was astonishingly complete not only because the British were thorough in their work but because Indian leaders such as Ram Mohan Roy saw in English the key to the West and were as willing as the British to de-emphasize the "vernaculars." As for the British, they were necessarily thorough. Their urgent everyday dependence on clerks and bureaucrats competent in English led them to build the entire educational edifice to suit their needs, emphasizing higher education and neglecting, accordingly, both primary

[3] M. Mujeeb, "Indian Education—Retrospect and Prospect," *Pacific Affairs,* September 1953, p. 213.

education and its logical vehicle, the regional languages.[4] The medium of instruction during British rule was normally the regional language during the primary period (ages six to ten) as well as during the middle period (ten to fourteen). By the middle period, however, English figured in the curriculum, and in the higher phase leading to university admission (fourteen to sixteen) English was the sole medium. University education was divided into three two-year stages, the intermediate, B.A., and M.A., with English the sole medium of instruction at all levels. Secondary education pointing to a university career tended to become more and more English-oriented; secondary education in the regional medium, merely "a truncated version of the secondary course minus English, designed mainly for those who could not afford to go in for [higher] secondary education and wanted to qualify themselves for the cadre of primary teachers or for the lower public service ranks which did not require English."[5]

As a result of British language policy, according to one estimate, the Indian student spent one-third of his time on the study of English alone.[6] From the initial admiration of Ram Mohan Roy the attitude to English turned to deep resentment. Votaries of the Indian languages, indeed of Indian education itself, seized upon the legacy of British language policy to explain what was undoubtedly a state of cultural havoc. With a large proportion of students, not fully at home in any language, unable to follow lectures delivered in English, it became increasingly incongruous, as the Punjab University Inquiry Committee reported in 1929, to find Indians by the hundreds of thousands reciting Shakespeare, Shelley's "Skylark" and Milton's "Ode on the Morning of Christ's Nativity." "They have never seen a skylark," observed the Committee. "They do not know why a highborn maiden sits in her tower."[7]

This legacy of English could be dismissed, and was dismissed,

---

[4] The impact of British language policy on Indian education is discussed in K. G. Saiyidain, J. P. Naik, and S. A. Husain, *Compulsory Education in India*, UNESCO Studies on Compulsory Education No. 11, Paris, 1952, pp. 13-15.

[5] *Ibid.*, p. 63.

[6] Sir Philip Hartog, *Some Aspects of Indian Education, Past and Present*, Oxford University Press, London, 1939, p. 10.

[7] Cited in S. N. Chib, *Language, Universities, and Nationalism in India*, Oxford University Press, London, 1936, p. 3.

more blithely during the freedom movement than the realities of nation-building now permit. It was a major article of the Gandhian faith that English should give way to the regional languages in education and administration. Gandhi pleaded that a linguistically alienated Indian leadership could not in fact lead a profound national regeneration, arguing, as Indians from President Rajendra Prasad down continue to argue,[8] that original thought demands the use of the mother tongue. Gandhi, denying the alleged "poverty" of Gujarati as an intellectual medium, declared that in reality "no language is poor. We have hardly had time to speak since we have begun to act. Gujarat like the rest of India is brooding. Language is shaping itself."[9]

Tagore, too, lamented that

We pass examinations, and shrivel up into clerks, lawyers and police inspectors, and we die young. . . . Once upon a time we were in possession of such a thing as our own mind in India. It was living. It thought, it felt, it expressed itself. But it has been thrust aside, and we are made to tread the mill of passing examinations, not for learning anything, but for notifying that we are qualified for employment under organizations conducted in English. Our educated community is not a cultured community, but a community of qualified candidates.[10]

"A language," he said, "is not like an umbrella or an overcoat, that can be borrowed by unconscious or deliberate mistake; it is like the living skin itself."

[8] Prasad expressed his belief, at the centenary celebrations of Calcutta University in 1957, that even in pre-Independence India original intellectual contributions were greater among those who received their education through the mother tongue than among those educated in English. (*Hindustan Times*, January 21, 1956, p. 6.) Even the Official Language Commission, cool as it was to the claims of the regional languages, states in its *Report* (Manager, Government of India Press, Delhi, 1957, p. 77) that "both comprehension and expression of the students have improved" where Indian languages have been introduced as the medium of instruction. See also D. P. Mukerji, "The Intellectuals in India," *Confluence*, January 1957, p. 453; and Humayun Kabir, *Education in the New India*, Harper and Bros., New York, 1957, entirety, for recent elaborations of this view.

[9] K. M. Munshi, *Gujarata and its Literature*, Longmans, Green, and Co., Bombay, 1935, p. 6.

[10] Rabindranath Tagore, *Creative Unity*, Macmillan and Co., London, 1922, pp. 176, 180. In his Bengali essay *Siksar Vahan* (The Medium of Instruction), Tagore conceded the desirability of English for those pursuing post-graduate studies.

The pressure to replace English with the mother tongue was concentrated first on secondary education officials who could not plead, like university educators, that adequate textbooks were lacking in the regional languages, and who were clearly on the defensive side of any professional pedagogical argument in insisting on an alien medium of instruction at this stage of education. With the increasing use of the mother tongue in secondary schools, however, Indian universities, too, soon came under increasing attack for their use of English in instruction, and most of all in the entrance examination. In 1937 Punjab and Calcutta universities became the first Indian universities to permit the use of the regional language in entrance examinations in all subjects except English itself. Sir Philip Hartog, chairman of the Simon Commission's education committee, warned at the time that as the entrance examination goes, so would go all language policy in Indian education.[11]

What Language for Education?

By the time Independence came, nothing less than a complete shift to the regional languages as the university medium would satisfy the advocates of the mother tongue. In the sharpened controversy defenders of English pointed to the shortages of textbooks and adequately trained teachers in many Indian languages. Hindi enthusiasts advocated Hindi as the medium of instruction. Both of these foes of the regional language medium warned that without a uniform medium throughout the country India's intellectual unity, and ultimately her political unity as well, would be gravely jeopardized.

For the English-speaking educational elite control of administrative and teaching posts was at stake. The editor of the former Gandhian weekly *Harijan* charged bluntly in 1953 that "English education gave rise to some vested interests which continue to dominate us even today. The English-educated formed a caste by themselves."[12] Finance Minister Morarji Desai was even more explicit:

[11] Sir Philip Hartog, *Some Aspects of Indian Education, Past and Present*, p. 44.

[12] M. P. Desai, *Our Language Problem*, Navajivan Publishing House, Ahmedabad, 1956, p. 7.

The position today is that professors are teaching through English. They have old notes prepared in English, and they teach referring to those notes. Now if the medium of instruction is changed, then they shall have to study and prepare fresh notes; they shall have to study the language through which instruction is given. Therefore the professors object to the change in the medium of instruction.[13]

But there were regional intellectuals with their own vested interests. Little doubt remained after January 1948, when independent India's first National Education Conference assembled in New Delhi, that the regional language advocates had gained the offensive. It was a lone voice, indeed, raised by A. Lakshmanaswami Mudaliar, then vice-chancellor at the University of Madras. Pleading for English, he told the conference that to introduce Tamil as the sole medium there would spell "absolute disaster." "I tried to look into the figures of the people who would be in a position to teach through that particular language," Mudaliar warned, "and I found to my surprise that practically all colleges would have to reshuffle their teaching staff. For very important subjects, where recruitment of the teaching staff is not on a provincial basis but on an all-India basis, it will mean that there will be an absolute halt to the progress of higher education."[14]

While some might have agreed, few, if any, voiced their agreement. The conference appointed a committee consisting of university vice-chancellors and prominent specialists, and the committee's own doubts could be read between the lines of its recommendation that English should be replaced by regional languages within five years. "It would be necessary," said the committee,

to reconcile ourselves to the idea of having the regional languages as the media of instruction and examination at the university stage when English ceases to hold the position enjoyed during years of British rule.[15]

[13] *Selected Speeches of Morarji Desai*, Chandrakant Mehta, ed., Hind Kitabs, Bombay, 1956, p. 75.

[14] *Verbatim Record of the Educational Conference of 1948*, Ministry of Education, Government of India, Pamphlet No. 61, Government of India Press, 1949, pp. 56, 59.

[15] *Report of the Committee on the Medium of Instruction at the University Stage—1948*, Ministry of Education, Government of India, Pamphlet No. 57, Government of India Press, 1948, pp. 11, 36.

Similarly, the University Education Commission spoke with unabashed inconsistency when it declared a year later that English

has become so much a part of our national habit that a plunge into an altogether different system seems attended with unusual risks. It appears to us, however, that the plunge is inevitable.[16]

It was one thing, however, to order English banished in five years and quite another to conjure up the necessary textbooks and teachers to install the regional languages. Nor were the "English-knowing" powers-that-be in Indian education possessed of the will necessary even to begin to find a way. At its meeting in August 1950, the Inter-University Board warned against a deterioration in educational standards should English be abandoned.[17] Conference after conference of professors of English urged the central and state governments and universities to stage the transition from English to the regional languages or to Hindi "in a gradual manner."[18] University vice-chancellors lobbied, most notably in the case of a special committee in 1954, for "sufficient time" to permit teachers to equip themselves for the new medium, *sufficient* meaning *indefinitely* to opponents of English.[19] Regional exasperation at this impasse found expression in two successive meetings of the Congress Working Committee in 1954. In April the committee reminded the nation that normally future university teaching should be conducted in the regional language, with an option to use Hindi or English only in special cases. Again in July, the committee reiterated this position.[20]

[16] *Report of the University Education Commission*, Government of India Press, 1949, Part I, p. 478.

[17] *Proceedings* of the special meeting of the Inter-University Board, August 1950, cited in *Report of the Committee on the Medium of Instruction*, Bombay University, 1955, p. 7.

[18] For example, see the resolution of the conference of English professors, New Delhi, January 1953, cited in *Proceedings of the 20th and 21st Meetings of the Central Advisory Board of Education* (November 1953, and February 1954), Ministry of Education, Government of India, Government of India Press, 1955, p. 13.

[19] Cited in *Proceedings of the 20th and 21st Meetings of the Central Advisory Board of Education*, p. 252.

[20] *Times of India*, April 7, 1954, p. 1; *Hindu Weekly Review*, July 5, 1954, p. 16.

To the textbook-teacher objection a Gandhian educator exclaims:

> Books are not going to fall from the heavens! What writer or publisher would care to bring out college books in Gujarati or Marathi or Bengali when there is no market for them. If a university decides that from a particular year instruction will commence in a particular language, books are sure to flow soon into the market. It is a simple question of demand and supply.[21]

For English-speaking teachers to shift their linguistic gears, he concedes, would be "at first a stupendous task." At the same time he points to the inevitable vicious circle:

> Whenever we shall try to bring over the change, this difficulty is bound to crop up. It is the difficulty of a transitional stage. The students instructed by such professors in the regional or Hindi language will, in their turn, when they become professors, naturally be more at home in the new medium. If the process is not started at all, whence are the professors thoroughly efficient in and capable of teaching in the native media going to be obtained?[22]

But if textbooks must break the vicious circle the state and central governments will have to budget accordingly. Poona University called publicly in 1955 for state assistance in the preparation of Marathi textbooks, and a Gujarat University official has estimated that it would cost at least 4,000,000 rupees ($920,000) to finance at one stroke the initial translations and textbooks necessary for any drastic changeover to Gujarati.[23] Even $920,000, of course, does not cover the broad field of reference literature that would ultimately have to be made available for higher studies in Gujarati.

It is interesting to note the experience of one of the pioneers in the use of the regional language medium, Nagpur University, which has permitted the use of Hindi and Marathi as examination media since 1950, and has made it nominally compulsory since 1954 that students select either Hindi or Marathi as their medium for undergraduate arts and science courses. Even here,

[21] A. L. Majumdar, "When Should the Change be Effected?" *Harijan*, February 7, 1953, p. 1.

[22] *Ibid.* For a discussion of problems of standards in language teaching in India, see K. G. Saiyidain, P. P. Naik, and S. A. Husain, p. 124. See also *Proceedings*, Travancore-Cochin Legislative Assembly, July 23, 1952, p. 2009.

[23] *Times of India*, March 28, 1956, p. 6.

as a result of the textbook-teacher dilemma, the university has reported that "provision is made for special permission in certain cases to offer the English medium, and such permission is granted on a liberal scale." For science education, especially, English remains unchallenged at Nagpur as at most universities. A breakdown of the undergraduate examinations in 1954 showed that fourteen percent of the 2,036 students in non-science courses chose the English medium, while eighty-eight percent of 1,032 science students used English.[24] The undisputed place of English in science education is further illustrated by the use of English as the medium of instruction for undergraduate science courses leading to the degree. Viewed over a five-year period from 1951 to 1956, the number of those electing to use the mother tongue for the intermediate science examination remained virtually constant (with failures through the regional medium on the increase); and in non-science courses, too, failures were greater for the regional-medium students.[25]

In the final analysis, political accident will, in most cases, decide when a particular region will act to provide the wherewithal for the colossal task of rapid conversion to the regional language. The decision in universities must be made consistent with educational policy in secondary schools,[26] on the one hand, while being consistent, on the other hand, with national decisions governing the nature of the role of Hindi as the Union language. For many years the Hindi controversy will linger in one form or another, complicating what would otherwise be a direct conflict between English and the regional

[24] Computed from statistics provided by the Registrar, Nagpur University.

[25] *Times of India*, January 5, 1956, p. 6.

[26] The controversy over the medium of instruction in secondary education concerns not the medium of instruction, which is conceded to be the mother tongue, but the stage at which Hindi and English should be introduced. See *Report of the Committee on Secondary Education in India*, Bureau of Education, Ministry of Education, Pamphlet No. 52, Government of India Press, New Delhi, 1948, p. 4; *Report of the Secondary Education Commission*, 1953, Ministry of Education, Government of India Press, New Delhi, 1953, p. 73; *The Hindu Weekly Review*, January 2 and 23, 1956, for accounts of a meeting of the All-India Council of Secondary Education; and *The Hindu Weekly Review*, January 2, 1957, p. 4, for an account of a session of the Central Advisory Board of Education that recommended the compulsory study of three languages in secondary education.

languages. The Hindi enthusiast sees no reason why Hindi cannot be sufficiently promoted in secondary education to serve as the university medium throughout India. The committee on the medium of instruction appointed by the Bombay University Syndicate braved popular wrath in this multilingual state to recommend in 1955 that ultimately Hindi become the medium. But the committee set a period of ten years, ending in 1970, during which English should remain in force while Hindi is gradually introduced.[27] This was understandably viewed on the one hand as a blow to the regional languages, and on the other as a veiled victory for English. It was a suspect recommendation if only because a minority of Hindi enthusiasts, for precisely the considerations of national unity that prompt their dedication to Hindi, frankly prefer the continuance of English to the division of Indian higher education into regional compartments.

Barring total centralized domination of Indian education, it is doubtful that Hindi can become the medium of secondary or higher education in any substantial number of institutions outside Hindi territory.[28] Even if non-Hindi-speaking educators did not fear for their own future in a Hindi dispensation, merely on competitive professional grounds, their contempt for Hindi as a language still in their view to be developed and standardized for modern intellectual purposes would prevent its expansion. Not only do those in the Hindi region continue to wrangle among themselves, as they did in pre-Independence years,[29] over Sanskrit versus Persian words. Still more fundamental, writes Chakravarti Rajagopalachari,

Hindi is still in its infancy. It is in an undeveloped stage. In Delhi Parliament, members from Jawaharlal Nehru down express them-

[27] *Report of the Committee on the Medium of Instruction*, Bombay University, entirety.

[28] For examples of opposition by non-Hindi educators to the introduction of Hindi as the medium of instruction, see *Report of Indian Languages Development Conference*, Poona University Press, Poona, 1953; comments by South Indians at the All-India Hindi Sammelan, 1955, quoted in *The National Herald*, December 31, 1955, p. 1; *Report of the Committee on the Medium of Instruction*, Bombay University, esp. p. 37; *The Hindu Weekly Review*, October 9, 1956.

[29] For example, see Z. A. Ahmed, *National Language for India*, Kitabistan, Allahabad, 1941.

selves briefly and clearly whenever they speak in English. They leave no room for doubt in what they say. But when they use the Hindi medium they repeat themselves quite often and still find it difficult to express their ideas precisely, correctly and fully. This difficulty arises because of the poverty of the Hindi language and of its want of growth. Hindi vocabulary lacks in precision. So our first act should be to put Hindi to school, rather than to ask the Tamil people to learn Hindi.[30]

Whereas, in Bengal, the educated will be as familiar with Tagore as with English-language literature, in the Hindi area there are no universally accepted literary traditions and there are many among the educated who have not read any of what they refer to as Hindi literature.

It is precisely in the name of Hindi's development and standardization, of course, that the advocates of a highly Sanskritized Hindi press their claims. But it is problematical whether this kind of artificial development would not in fact stop Hindi dead in its tracks as a developing language. Champions of Sanskritization not only want to drive out Urdu and Persian words now in use—to insist, for example, on *sachiva* for "minister" rather than *wazir*—but they just as insistently object to the retention of English words that have gained popular currency. Thus for "rickshaw," we confront *thrichakara manushya vahana*, meaning literally "a vehicle that has a man as its third wheel"; for "telephone," *doora sravana yantra*, "a device for hearing from afar," and for "railway," *lohapatha gamana*, "going over the iron path."[31]

Since it is necessary first of all, in standardizing a language, to agree on sources for new terminology, the stalemate of indecision in which Hindi is caught undoubtedly accounts for its slow development and for its consequent failure to radiate outward into the non-Hindi regions. Delays in the changeover to

---

[30] *Kalki* (Tamil weekly), Madras, April 19, 1955. See also S. K. Chatterji, "Note of Dissent," *Report of the Official Language Commission*, p. 297.

[31] See G. Rajanna, "Linguistic Controversy and Educational Policies," *Hitavada*, February 19, 1954, p. 4; H. C. Kaila, "Zealots and Hindi," *Times of India*, February 28, 1954, p. 12; C. Kunhan Raja, "The Future Role of Sanskrit," *Adyar Library Bulletin*, Vol. 13, Part I, February 17, 1949, p. 7; and for a Communist view, *Indian Literature*, No. 3, 1953, p. 55. The specific controversy over the nature of Hindi on All-India Radio figures in *National Herald*, February 17, 1946, pp. 8-9, and March 24, 1946, p. 6, and *Proceedings*, House of the People, June 27, 1952, col. 2666.

Hindi as the language of administration in Uttar Pradesh, the major Hindi-speaking state in India, were attributed in 1955 to the lack of an accepted English-Hindi lexicon of technical, legal, and administrative terminology.[32] Moreover, as we have noted in the previous chapter, the would-be developers of a standardized Hindi constantly confront choices among words from alternative possible sources: the Hindustani already spoken in a standard form common to most towns of the Ganges plain, and highly-developed dialects such as Braj Bhasha in the Western Hindi group and Avadhi in the Eastern Hindi group. The linguist John Gumperz has described, after field studies in the Hindi region, the villager's inordinate linguistic parochialism, his limited acquaintance even with district-wide variants of Hindi beyond his own immediate circle of villages, let alone new manufactured region-wide forms.[33] Most of the effort to spread the new standard Hindi is directed at the educated elite and thus little is done to eliminate this diversity within Hindi territory. Although some other regional languages must, like Hindi, still bridge their spoken dialect forms in literary standards, the fact that Hindi is even more inchoate than most rules it out as the nation-wide medium of university education.

If, then, Hindi is not to be the medium, what can be expected in the contest between English and the regional languages? For the present, clearly, the regional languages are on a slow but continuing ascendancy. "The trend is quite unmistakable . . . fast gathering strength," reported the Official Language Commission.[34] The trend is, indeed, so unmistakable that one of its most determined opponents, Bombay University Registrar S. R. Dongerkery, who in 1950 foresaw "possible disaster overtaking university education in India"[35] as a result of conversion to the regional languages, conceded in 1957 that the "rational" solution to the medium controversy would, after all, be to let

---

[32] *Times of India*, April 7, 1955, p. 5.

[33] "Language Problems in the Rural Development of North India," *Journal of Asian Studies*, January 1957, p. 257. See also Gumperz, "Some Remarks on Regional and Social Language Differences in India," *Introducing India in Liberal Education*, University of Chicago, 1957, pp. 69-80.

[34] *Report of the Official Language Commission*, pp. 76, 173.

[35] S. R. Dongerkery, *Universities and National Life*, Hind Kitabs, Bombay, 1950, p. 48.

the regional languages take the place of English.[36] While a final policy remains to be decided in many Indian universities, at least sixteen are, even now, teaching some non-scientific undergraduate courses in Indian languages.[37] If there is any probable pervasive pattern in what will by its very nature be a fluid situation, it is the pattern now evident in Calcutta University. There S. K. Chatterji points to the increasing use of "a bilingual jargon," mixing English with Bengali. To make up for the inadequacies of the regional language, and to make the most of English words already in use, instructors and students are evolving a working compromise between English and the regional language that will leave instructors free to lecture by improvisation, and students free to write their examinations in the regional language.[38] Ultimately, as the regional languages are used for more and more original intellectual effort, English will be displaced to a marginal position as a medium of instruction.

One barometer that will indicate the extent to which the regional languages are actually becoming the primary media of higher education is their use for theses and post-graduate dissertations. Similarly, as Sir Philip Hartog has forewarned, it will be important to watch the entrance examination. The prestige of English will depend first upon whether it remains as the examination medium, and should that go, whether it is a compulsory subject on the examination. But in any event, sooner or later, it seems probable that English will in most regions be pushed to a marginal position as a medium of instruc-

[36] *Times of India*, January 26, 1957, p. 1.

[37] These are Agra, Allahabad, Banaras, Bihar, Calcutta, Gujarat, Karnataka, Lucknow, Nagpur, Osmania, Poona, Roorkee, Saugor, Thackersey, Vallabh Vidyanagar, and Visvabharati. This collation is based on *Report of the Official Language Commission*, p. 461; on *Hindi and the Regional Languages as Optional Media of Instruction in Universities in India*, a statement prepared for the author by the Education Ministry, Government of India, November 1955; and an extensive correspondence with registrars of all universities on the Education Ministry register. It should be noted that only two of these, Vallabh Vidyanagar in Gujarat and Osmania in Andhra, are Hindi- or Hindustani-medium institutions outside Hindi territory. The remainder include Hindi-medium institutions in Hindi territory as well as institutions using non-Hindi regional languages.

[38] S. K. Chatterji, *Scientific and Technical Terms in Modern Indian Languages*, Vidyoday Library, Calcutta, 1954, p. 42.

tion and will instead occupy a new place as the pre-eminent second language. By a recent estimate there are at least 3.6 million English literates in India.[39] But the decline in the extent and standards of English instruction is already a fact of the Indian scene, and while this decline can over a period of time be slowed down, it is doubtful whether it can be reversed.

In 1955 the Bombay University committee on the medium of instruction noted that students entering the university by and large received their secondary education through the regional languages. Their defective knowledge of English, said the committee, made it impossible for them to follow lectures delivered in English, and "in order to enable students to follow lectures in English with ease, teachers have been instructed to use simple language, to dictate summaries of lectures at the end of the period, and to hold special classes of small groups."[40] Since the Secondary Education Commission had reported even in 1953 a "serious dearth of well-qualified and experienced teachers who can handle English classes in schools and college," and as a consequence, "rapid deterioration in the standards of English at the university stage,"[41] the Central Advisory Board of Education was doing little more than voicing a wish when it said in 1957 that English should be a compulsory subject in secondary schools.[42] With better methods of instruction, of course, methods adapted to India rather than merely transferred intact from Great Britain, it is entirely possible that English will gain some new vitality.[43] English will gain greatly, too, from its link with the increasingly technological orientation of Indian education. The ambitious technician-administrator who wishes to go outside his region will realize far more sharply than the political administrator the inescapable necessity of English as a window to world progress in his field. But it must

[39] *Report of the Official Language Commission*, p. 33, cites this number as "adequately literate" in English.

[40] *Report of the Committee on the Medium of Instruction*, Bombay University, p. 38.

[41] *Report of the Secondary Education Commission*, p. 69.

[42] *Times of India*, January 18, 1957, p. 1, and January 22, 1957, p. 6.

[43] This is discussed in Humayun Kabir, *Education in the New India*, pp. 131-132, and *Report of the Official Language Commission*, p. 78.

be recognized that the linguistic momentum in India is on the side of the regional languages.

No enforcement sanctions, constitutional or otherwise, are available to the central government should it wish to prevent universities from converting to the regional language. The Constitution clearly labels education a prerogative of the states. All that the central government can do, as the Official Language Commission put it, is to "hold a continuous watching, supervisory brief over the progress of the national policy for languages."[44] Beyond exercising its power of persuasion to the political limit, the central government can employ only its power to make financial grants to bring a measure of uniformity to university policies. Here the sensitivity of universities to any suggestion of outside interference is so imbedded that the mere prospect of the new University Grants Commission in 1955 was enough to sound the alarm in Parliament.[45] When a select committee reported on legislation establishing the Commission, six non-Hindi members filed dissents. One charged that a commission able to "pay the piper" would also "call the tune" and proposed instead that regional commissions should be appointed to insure regional control.[46] Although the Commission has, once established, gained steadily in power, chairman C. D. Deshmukh complained on one occasion that he had scant funds to carry out any substantial program and that "national aspects of education continue to be neglected."[47]

Surveying the general prospect in Indian education, in short, one must prophesy a period of prolonged linguistic pandemonium. Unless the central government asserts virtually total control over education, as certain leaders advocate,[48] the re-

[44] *Report of the Official Language Commission*, p. 242.

[45] For information relating to central versus state control of university education, see Sir Philip Hartog, *Some Aspects of Indian Education, Past and Present*, p. 22; *Report of the University Education Commission*, esp. pp. 450, 711; *Education in Universities in India, 1950-51*, Ministry of Education Pamphlet No. 153, Government of India Press, New Delhi, 1954, Table No. 13, pp. 78-79; Gardner Murphy, *In the Minds of Men*, Basic Books, 1953, p. 256; S. R. Dongerkery, *Universities and National Life*, p. 62.

[46] *Times of India*, July 30, 1955, p. 6.

[47] *The Hindu Weekly Review*, December 15, 1956, p. 8.

[48] For example, see *Hands Off Bombay*, Memorandum submitted to the States

gional languages can be expected to displace English in time as the media of higher education. As matters stand the Education Ministry exercises ineffective influence in regional educational councils and the regional universities are more or less free to go their separate linguistic ways. Sooner than we think the issue will no longer be what medium, but how to forge new educational tools suited to a linguistic generation equipped to pursue education solely through the regional language.

What Language for Leadership?

Once university education has, in fact, passed clearly to the regional languages, pressure to permit use of the regional languages in national as well as local civil service examinations will become irresistible, and when this happens, the "steel frame" of a national bureaucracy may very well become eroded, decosmopolitanized, subject to the same regional stresses as the larger Indian body politic. Indeed, the controversy over the university medium of instruction is, to a remarkable degree, a controversy over the medium of national civil service examinations.

The peculiar importance of the national civil service competition cannot be overemphasized in a society in which government employment enjoys such unusual prestige, and in which educated unemployment, constantly on the increase,[49] is in so many cases the unemployment of frustrated aspirants to the 37,000 new jobs each year in a national bureaucracy totalling more than 700,000.[50] The prestige which attaches to intellectual employment and the opprobrium associated with manual labor is, of course, part and parcel of a hierarchy of caste prestige which places intellectual Brahmanism at the top. This hierarchy of prestige will be toppled as the caste hierarchy topples and as educational reforms reduce the white-collar out-

Reorganization Commission by the Bombay Pradesh Congress Committee, Bombay, 1954, p. 25.

49 See *Outline Report of the Study Group on Educated Unemployment*, Government of India, New Delhi, January 1956, esp. p. 11; and Edward Shils, "The Intellectuals, Public Opinion, and Economic Development," a paper read at a conference on "Problems of Economic Growth," Tokyo, April 1957.

50 *Report of the Official Language Commission*, p. 477.

put of Indian universities. But this will be a process spread over many years. In the meantime the prestige of government employment will give decisive prestige to any language permitted as the medium of the civil service examination, most especially the examination for the so-called "higher" select national services such as the Indian Administrative Service. When a Marathi-speaking aspirant wins entry to the I.A.S., he insures, in turn, the entry of numberless other Marathi-speakers in lesser posts within his jurisdiction.

Undoubtedly the civil service examination is the end-all of higher education for a "disproportionate" share, as the Official Language Commission cautiously observed, of "the best talent from amongst the educated youth of the country."[51] When an American psychologist asked students in major Indian universities in 1954 what educational goals the ideal institution should emphasize, 22 percent specified: "Help pass examination for administrative service."[52] A Lucknow University study showed that 47 percent of liberal arts students and 51.4 percent of science students joined the university in the years 1949 to 1953 to get ready for government posts,[53] and former Vice-Chancellor P. V. Kane of Bombay University has deplored the fact that "the Government of India and the state governments are the greatest employers of the products of our universities. . . . Whatever one may say about the pursuit of higher education for its own sake, most of the students join the universities in the hope of securing government appointments."[54]

Former Congress Secretary Sriman Narayan saw the prestige of the government job and argued that the expansion of Hindi depended on at least optional status for the Union language as an examination medium. Otherwise, he feared, the lure to use English as the medium of instruction in higher education would persist.[55] But, to insist on Hindi as an optional

[51] *Report of the Official Language Commission*, p. 186.

[52] Robert T. Bower, *The Indian Student*, Bureau of Social Science Research, American University, Washington, D.C., September 1954, p. 10.

[53] Cited in Myron Weiner, *Party Politics in India*, Princeton University Press, 1957, p. 10.

[54] *Report of Indian Languages Development Conference*, p. 27.

[55] *Times of India*, October 6, 1954, p. 1.

72

medium is to insure that the regional language advocates will insist with equal vigor on the option to use the regional languages, for the native speaker of Hindi would obviously be more at home competing in his own medium than a speaker of another regional language competing through a language not his own, whether Hindi or English. At present, examinations for the 1,539 regular posts in the Indian Administrative Service and the 937 posts in the Indian Police Service must be written in English. For the long haul, however, this place of English as the *de facto* all-India administrative language is not consistent with declared national intentions.

Champions of Hindi and the regional languages alike have invariably coupled the demand for optional media in the civil service examination with the demand for abandonment of English as the medium of higher education. Even partisans of Gandhian basic education, which is designed primarily as a preparation for village life, plead that their programs cannot fully utilize the regional languages so long as English remains the language of bureaucratic recruitment; "the changeover, therefore, is essentially a matter of who will bell the cat first."[56] When the subcommittee on the medium of instruction urged delegates to the National Education Conference in 1948 to reconcile themselves to the regional languages, the subcommittee conceded in the same breath that national civil service examinations "may be conducted through the language of the region," though successful candidates should be required to pass a test in Hindi.[57] Similarly, the University Education Commission, while urging that English "continue as the medium for federal business . . . until the provincial educational institutions have spread the federal language adequately," clearly appeared impressed by the fears of the non-Hindi regions. Granted that Hindi will be the Union language, the report asks,

How will it affect the participation in the affairs of the federation of those whose mother tongue is different? Members of the federal

[56] Satya P. Agarwal, "Problems Facing Basic Education in India Today," Seminar Paper No. 22, Seminar on Leadership and Political Institutions in India, Berkeley, California, 1956.

[57] *Report of the Committee on the Medium of Instruction at the University Stage,* p. 5.

legislature will be required to speak in the federal language; federal acts, statutes, ordinances, orders, resolutions, proclamations, reports and budgets will issue in the federal language; members of the central government, officials of the secretariat, judges of the federal court will employ it. How will all this affect the personnel of the legislature, the executive and the judiciary? Will it give to those whose mother tongue is Hindi an undue advantage and a disproportionate influence in the affairs of the state? Will this arrangement deprive the central government of the valuable services of the intellectual elite of India irrespective of the regional and linguistic provenance?[58]

If fears for the non-Hindi regional elites can be expressed so forcibly even in the course of a recommendation for the spread of Hindi, then it is, understandably, a mere reflex for regional leaders to go consistently a step further, demanding that the mother tongue be permitted as an optional medium for the civil service examination. Although the nominal victory remains to be made actual, Congress and government policy already recognize this regional demand. Responding to regional clamor which was a response, in turn, to the demands of the Hindi champions, the Congress Working Committee said in April 1954, that candidates should be free to write their examinations, according to their choice, in Hindi, English, or the regional languages.[59] Nehru pointed out at the time that Yugoslavia conducts civil service examinations in all of its languages.[60] In May 1955, the Home Ministry announced that the Government of India would accept the Congress policy as its own,[61] and in September 1957, the Working Committee again registered its "definite opinion" that Hindi and the regional languages should be permitted as optional media.[62]

But precisely because it would be such a far-reaching step the actual implementation of declared policy is postponed and postponed, and behind the scenes at least, it is bitterly opposed.

[58] *Report of the University Education Commission*, p. 320.

[59] *Congress Bulletin*, No. 3, April 1954, esp. p. 123.

[60] *Congress Bulletin*, No. 4, May 1954, p. 166.

[61] *Report of the Official Language Commission*, p. 202. M. P. Desai, in his Dissent, p. 374, described this declaration as the government's "outstanding" act in language policy from 1950 to 1955.

[62] *A.I.C.C. Economic Review*, September 15, 1957, p. 11.

For the English-speaking leadership of today it seems, in many instances, inconceivable that the leadership of tomorrow should be divided into linguistic compartments. That eminent veteran of the Indian Civil Service, A. D. Gorwala, without committing himself between Hindi and English, declared that "clearly" the national administrator "should be sufficiently proficient in the central language to be able to answer his question papers in it."[63] Although the Official Language Commission envisaged the possibility that a regional language might have to be admitted as an optional medium when it had attained sufficient usage in higher education,[64] the Commission betrayed alarm at this prospect in numerous roundabout allusions.[65] At one point the Commission observed that "some of us do hope that, when the time comes for taking a decision on this issue, it may be found that the introduction of the regional language media for these examinations is not necessary."[66] So sensitive did the Commission appear to be on this score, in fact, that it went to great lengths to avoid discussing at all, on the record, why it feared opening the examinations to the regional languages.[67] Even two non-Hindi spokesmen who dissented from the alleged pro-Hindi bias of the Commission's Report emphasized that they, too, feared the consequences of any change in the examination medium. Both S. K. Chatterji of Bengal and P. Subbaroyan of Tamilnad argued for the continued requirement that the examinations be written in English as "the only way to maintain the unity of India through the services."[68] Like political bodies the world over whose response to seemingly

---

[63] A. D. Gorwala, *The Role of the Administrator, Past, Present, and Future*, Gokhale Institute of Politics and Economics, Poona, 1952, p. 29.

[64] *Report of the Official Language Commission*, p. 203.

[65] *Ibid.*, p. 198. The Commission refers to the continued use of English as "one way of obviating the necessity for admitting the medium of regional languages [other than Hindi]."

[66] *Ibid.*, p. 201.

[67] Instead, the Commission discussed at length (*ibid.*, pp. 193-197) what Commission member M. P. Desai described as the "technical matter" of equitably grading examinations given by examiners divided on language lines. "It is surprising," said Desai (p. 374), "that the Commission almost appears to show its aversion to it [the Government of India's May 1955, announcement endorsing Congress policy on the regional language option] by basing its argument on . . . a technical matter of moderation."

[68] *Ibid.*, pp. 301, 326.

insoluble dilemmas is to appoint a committee, the Committee of Parliament assigned to pass on the recommendations of the Official Language Commission said in 1959 that it had "no objection in principle" to the admission of the regional languages but wanted an expert study panel to determine whether the changeover could be accomplished short of certain technical steps which would, it said, "destroy the services' all-India character."[69]

Whatever the languages permitted as the media of competitive examinations at all levels of bureaucratic employment, these languages will, it is clear, gain by this status a prestige and power of attraction attainable in no other way in the decades ahead: the prestige and attractive power of a select few white-collar jobs sought by tens on tens of thousands of the educated unemployed. The power of economic incentive that government language policy can exercise is illustrated in the case of the Marathi minority in the former state of Madhya Bharat. The *Times of India* reported in 1955 that Marathi was only an optional subject in the high school examination in predominantly Hindi-speaking Madhya Bharat and that the tendency to pursue languages other than Marathi was gaining ground even among pupils whose mother tongue is Marathi. The secretary of the local Marathi Sahitya Sammelan attributed this to "the existing economic stresses and strains," meaning, explained the reporter, "that the better prospect of official jobs that education in Hindi would offer tomorrow was weaning away Maharashtrian boys from Marathi to Hindi. If this tendency was allowed to grow, the Sammelan was afraid there would soon be a generation of Maharashtrians unlettered in Marathi."[70]

This instance of competition between Hindi and Marathi, it must be noted, occurred in a distinctive local setting in which Marathi had never been more than an alien import of erstwhile ruling princes. It was a state government in Hindi ter-

---

[69] *Report of the Committee of Parliament on the Official Language*, Government of India Press, New Delhi, 1959, p. 22. The Committee feared in particular the so-called quota system dividing the civil service competition into specified regional language quotas.

[70] *Times of India*, February 1, 1955, p. 6.

ritory that used its political leverage to oust Marathi and to elevate Hindi. On a national scale a very different balance of power prevails, and it is unlikely that the potential leverage for the Hindi cause residing in the examination medium can ever actually be exploited. The non-Hindi regions will see to that. When Rajagopalachari railed at the suggestion in 1955 that all examinations for recruitment to high civil service posts would ultimately be conducted in Hindi, "a foreign medium, foreign in so far as Tamils are concerned,"[71] Home Minister G. B. Pant hastily reassured him that the spread of Hindi in other spheres "need not be inextricably bound up with the language or languages that may be adopted for conducting the all-India examinations."[72] Hindi, in short, can become an optional language for the examinations, as a practical political matter, only in its capacity as a regional language. And once Hindi is given optional status so must all other regional languages.

If we assume that university education will pass into the regional languages, then the eventual admission of the regional languages in civil service competitions must also be assumed. While English will no doubt remain an optional medium, as well as a compulsory subject in the examination proper, English will not enjoy its present prestige as the sole language permitted for the examinations. As languages enjoying equal prestige, the regional languages will command for their speakers the same attractive power exercised for so long by English. Indian leaders will be enabled to communicate by a common knowledge of English, learned as a second or third language,

[71] *Kalki*, April 19, 1955. For the reaction of the Madras University Syndicate when the use of Hindi as the examination medium was proposed in 1955, see *Times of India*, September 19, 1955, p. 9. Bombay University's Committee on the Medium of Instruction reported a split on the examination issue in its *Report*, p. 31, with "some members" favoring permission to use the regional languages. Poona University reflected Marathi support for the use of the regional languages in a statement cited in the Bombay *Report*, p. 36. Orissa's Biswanath Das expressed his region's fears of Hindi dominance in the services in the *Constituent Assembly Debates*, September 13, 1949, Vol. 9, No. 33, p. 1396. See also *Hands Off Bombay*, p. 25.

[72] *Indian Express*, June 4, 1955, p. 1. For similar assurances by President Rajendra Prasad, see *Times of India*, August 13, 1955, p. 1, and *The Indian Worker*, August 22, 1955, p. 4.

but this is likely to be a most difficult and labored communication process.

The rise of a new generation of Indian leaders rooted in their local linguistic settings will, it is true, provide a great fillip for local progress in all fields. India's language problem, as Maurice Zinkin has pointed out, "is in one aspect a problem of making the leadership of the educated effective. A society in which there are no officials, or works managers, or professors, who do not really understand the people under them is clearly able to change much more quickly than one in which there are severe barriers to downward communication."[73] By the same token, the continued pre-eminence of English would retard communication between leaders and led. India's dilemma, however, is precisely that the linguistic preconditions for making the leadership of the educated effective at the local level may prove incompatible with the need for cohesive political and administrative leadership at the national level. As the regional languages gain new prestige, as the regional capitals become the centers of cultural vitality in India, the number of men who are educated in cosmopolitan intellectual surroundings will rapidly dwindle. All Indian life must suffer from this decline of cosmopolitan leadership, but the most immediate and perhaps most critical effects will come in the national civil service. In place of men relatively fortified against parochial pressures the new bureaucrats may be as vulnerable as any other Indians. The face of tomorrow can already be seen in some of the new regional-minded civil service recruits. As a result of the trend to "all-out linguistic universities," V. K. Krishna Menon warned even in 1957, "we have very largely broken up the national character of our higher public services."[74]

The New Regional Elites

But does the fact that the rising generation lacks cosmopolitan polish necessarily mean that it cannot attain a cosmopolitan world view? Not at all, insist advocates of the mother tongue,

[73] Maurice Zinkin, *Development for Free Asia*, Essential Books, 1956, p. 197.
[74] V. K. Krishna Menon, "Public Administration—Federalism and National Unity," *National Herald*, February 15, 1957, p. 8.

and conversion to the regional languages will neither erode the administrative structure of Indian unity nor lead to intellectual regionalization. "Provincialism is bad," grants a Gandhian spokesman. "But is it alleged that it is born because of the regional language? Surely not. Is it not there even though we have English as the common medium today?"[75] The new regional intellectual life, according to this forecast, will turn to the outside world as well as to the rest of India for inspiration. The fact that it is carried on within the linguistic boundaries of Tamilnad or Maharashtra or Orissa will not fence it in.

Left to themselves, great intellectuals in any language most certainly look to universal horizons. But India in the decades ahead will not leave intellectuals to themselves. In each region writers and intellectuals will be caught in an atmosphere of political ferment that will, in most instances, emphasize and honor parochial rather than universal values. The decline of English has already led to a sharp decline in educational standards, which may be only an interim phenomenon but which will, for many years, intensify this parochial political atmosphere. Moreover, great writers and intellectuals with universal horizons are few and far between in any language. Intellectual activity in each region will to a considerable extent be the pulp culture of popular writers who will address themselves to the swelling millions of new literates in the regional languages. This pulp culture will, by its very nature, be predominantly parochial in its horizons. Men of stature in the new generation of Indian leadership will attain their full height in spite of, but only in spite of, this intellectual climate.

The fact that the new dynamism of the regional languages is the companion of political awakening and expanding education on a colossal mass scale explains, above all, why this dynamism will initially yield up regional pulp cultures rather than cultural achievement universal in its horizons. In sheer numbers India's linguistic revolution is without precedent. For example, when we speak of India's 16.6 percent literacy,[76] we

[75] M. P. Desai, *Our Language Problem*, p. 73.

[76] *Census of India, 1951*, Paper No. 5, "Literacy and Educational Standards," New Delhi, Government of India Press, 1954. Recent estimates are higher.

should translate this into the human terms of 60,000,000 persons and bear in mind that the number of literates for a particular regional language runs as high as six million for Bengali or Marathi or Malayalam.[77] Percentages conceal the human dimensions of a linguistic convulsion that will be adding tens of millions to literates in the regional languages at the same time that English literacy will be expanding, if it is indeed expanding, in mere hundreds of thousands. Even in a statistical projection that is based on the most favorable possible assumptions for both Hindi and English we can foresee unmistakably the scope of this convulsion. Assuming a combined population of 635 million in India and Pakistan by the year 2000, Karl W. Deutsch estimates that in both countries English literacy would not exceed forty million. Literates in other languages would total 200 million, 135 million of them literates in languages other than Hindi and its Pakistani Union language counterpart, Urdu.[78] Deutsch assumes the same rate of growth in English literacy in the next forty years that was recorded during a period—1901 to 1931—when English enjoyed the patronage and support of an imperial ruling power. For Hindi, too, he assumes a similar rate of growth, which is equally generous in view of the fact that Hindi will not begin to enjoy the prestige and support from an indigenous Indian Government, confronted with opposition from its own non-Hindi constituents, enjoyed by English during British rule. But even if we must bear in mind that his projections for Hindi and English can be cut by as much as half in favor of the regional languages, Deutsch demonstrates powerfully, still, that we can look to tens upon tens of millions of new literates in Indian languages.

When we add to the sheer size involved in the expansion of the regional languages the fact that new literates will be, for the most part, only partial literates, we can see even more clearly why the new regional pulp cultures will be limited in their horizons. In rural India most children who go to school at all

[77] *Bhoodan*, July 21, 1957, p. 7.

[78] *Nationalism and Social Communication*, Technology Press and John Wiley and Sons, 1954, pp. 108-110, 204. Bengali and Urdu are both designated as Union languages in Pakistan.

leave school before reaching the fifth grade; that is, before attaining "permanent literacy." Less than one child in five, and in many rural areas not more than one in ten,[79] gets full elementary education in a society in which facilities are limited and in which the ideal of free public education has yet to gain priority over the need for extra hands in the fields. This may change, but only over a long period of time. Studies in eighteen cities of south India conducted by the Southern Languages Book Trust showed that seventy-five percent of all literates— 1.7 million people—had left school before the fifth grade.[80] The rapid expansion of literacy that is now beginning will create a vast audience of partial literates, competent enough to search for new horizons through reading but not competent enough to absorb more than the most simplified popular journalism. Publishers and writers alike will devote their major attention to this burgeoning market. Nor will there be much incentive for writers who can be literary big fish in small ponds to venture forth under the searchlight of exacting critical appraisal. To satisfy the new literates, especially the partial literates, writers will "write down," in a literary sense, and what they write about will be the stuff of local life that the local mass audience knows best.

It is only natural, of course, to draw on the touch and smell of local life, and even such a distinguished regional literary figure as the late Tamil novelist "Kalki," R. Krishnamurthy, consciously harked back to past glories in Tamil life. The National Academy of Letters had in mind such giants of the regional literatures, no doubt, when it observed, outlining a series of projected historical studies, that "in the thought content of every literature, there are various elements, some narrow, parochial, or jingoistic, some transcending all local or artificial barriers and emphasizing the kinship of man with man." Where necessary to discuss thought content of a regional literature, advised the Academy, "the emphasis might be on the latter

[79] Ministry of Education Studies cited in W. S. Woytinsky, *India: Awakening Giant,* Harper and Bros., New York, 1957, p. 130.
[80] Martin P. Levin, *Marketing of Popular Books in South India,* Southern Languages Book Trust, Madras, 1956, p. 3.

kind rather than on the former."[81] In and of itself emphasis on local traditions and local life is not out of the ordinary in the intellectual life of any region in any country, and it is, indeed, often the rich substance of the very greatest universal literature. But it is a fine line which divides local color from local pride, and a finer one still which separates pride from jingoism. In the atmosphere that increasingly pervades most regions of India, literary and political consciousness become one and the same. Thus, reports a chronicler of the movement for a Kannada-speaking state, the playwright Kailasam was "the voice of resurgent Karnataka. What W. B. Yeats desired for Ireland, Kailasam achieved for Karnataka." There can be no quarrel with the elated observation that "all Karnataka walked on his stage,"[82] but it is fair to wonder to what extent all India—not to mention all the world—will find an equal place in the new regional literatures.

Even when he was urging regional intellectuals to "work for our one culture, which is the common background of our regional local diversities," a Gandhian proponent of the mother tongue was adding, as an afterthought, that "the trouble is, much loose talk of separate cultures appears to go on in this connection."[83] This is precisely the trouble. As a group of Indian writers concluded, confessing their ambivalence on the mother tongue issue, "the regionalization of the medium of instruction . . . may improve expression but it will limit thought."[84] The use of regional textbooks, written by authors reared in the new regionally-limited intellectual environment, can all too easily infuse a parochial content into the grist of education itself. The States Reorganization Commission warned that even now textbooks in some states include songs "exalting the regional idea." History books used in the earliest years of education "have disclosed a marked tendency to exaggerate the

---

[81] Sahitya Akadami, New Delhi, *Annual Report, 1954-55*, Appendix 6, p. 21.

[82] A. N. Krishna Rao, "Portrait of a Playwright," *Lekhaka*, July 1953, p. 30, and "Bird's-eye View of Modern Kannada Literature," *Lekhaka*, November 1953, pp. 29-32. For another revealing view of a regional literature, see K. C. Panigrahi, "Oriya Literature," *The Illustrated Weekly of India*, July 26, 1953, pp. 26-27.

[83] M. P. Desai, *Our Language Problem*, p. 86.

[84] Indian Congress on Cultural Freedom, March 29-30, 1951, *Proceedings*, p. 57.

past achievements of the dominant linguistic groups," a tendency which the Commission believed to be "inevitable . . . in language-based states."[85] The Commission's belief is confirmed to some extent in a study of history teaching in Indian schools published by the Ministry of Education. Six states now teach regional history as the history course for at least one year of elementary schooling, and one state, Orissa, teaches regional history for three of the first six years of elementary education.[86] But the study dismisses these regional history courses as inadequate and unduly subordinate to other history courses, pointing to the absence, by and large, "of any systematic treatment of the history of the regional group. . . . Indian history cannot be studied as a unit, any more than the history of Europe. There are many civilizations within an all-comprehensive Indian civilization. Linguistic and cultural groups have histories distinct from the history of India as a whole."[87] In the future there may well be more rather than less history teaching which "exalts the regional idea." How much more, and how much, in the process, students will fail to find in education a window on the world outside their region, will be decided by the course of political events. Like the medium of instruction itself, the content of education could be taken out of regional hands should a central regime disregard the existing Constitution or write a new one providing for greater national control over Indian education. But present trends, as S. K. Chatterji observed in the case of Bengali university students, are in fact resulting in "an increasing lack of interest in all-India happenings and in world events (except in some limited spheres among a small number of students). Regionalism and even parochialism are encroaching upon the domains of a broad and enlightened nationalism and a cultured internationalism, with slogans of all sorts stifling the sense of actualities."[88]

[85] *Report of the States Reorganization Commission*, Manager, Government of India Press, Delhi, 1955, p. 39.
[86] K. P. Chaudhury, *Content of History in Indian Schools*, Ministry of Education, 1952, Pamphlet No. 9, Tables, pp. 14, 43.
[87] *Ibid.*, pp. 2-3, 43.
[88] S. K. Chatterji, Minority Report, *Report of the Official Language Commission*, p. 296.

As weekly and daily journalism shift more and more to the regional languages, present trends will gain more and more momentum.

In a 1958 survey, the Indian languages claimed 9,712,000 of a total newspaper circulation of 13,089,000, and 2,620,000 out of a total for dailies of 3,606,000.[89] There are at least 6,000,000 males in India who do not know English but who are sufficiently proficient in a regional language to read a newspaper. Yet the circulation of regional language newspapers has tapped only thirty percent of this number. As female literacy increases, the regional language press will be the major beneficiary, for already, as the Press Commission points out, "in a large number of households it would appear to be the practice to take, in addition to the English newspaper, another paper in an Indian language, mainly for the use of female members of the household." All things considered, concluded the Commission, "the English newspapers do not have any considerable scope of adding largely to their circulation. But Indian language newspapers have great possibilities and in the next few years, we might expect that their circulation would increase to double the present figures."[90]

In its economic struggle with the English-language competition, the regional language press won an important tactical victory when the Indian Government accepted the so-called "price-page schedule" recommended by the Press Commission. Under this plan, which its sponsors claimed would help small and medium-sized papers against entrenched monopoly, the government is to regulate the price charged for newspapers according to the number of pages. This would presumably reduce newspaper dependence on advertisements—especially government notices—and force greater reliance on sales and subscription revenue. It would be impossible for a favored newspaper fattened by government advertising patronage to go on the market at a price equal to the skimpier competition, which

[89] *Annual Report of the Registrar of Newspapers for India, 1958*, Ministry of Information and Broadcasting, 1959, pp. 8-9. See also *Report of the Press Commission*, Part I, Manager of Publications, Delhi, 1954, p. 15.
[90] *Ibid.*, pp. 22-23.

in the Indian scene normally happens to be regional language newspapers.[91]

Each new breakthrough in script reform will promote the expansion of the regional-language press. Script reform is a prerequisite for the effective use of the regional languages in typewriters,[92] type-setting machines,[93] and teleprinters[94] because Indian scripts, as written now in all their time-honored complexity, number in some cases twice as many separate symbols as English.[95] With simplified scripts, and with new type-setting methods such as the "photo-setter" recently developed in the United States, regional language publications will be able to leap-frog from their present nineteenth century printing modes, including hand-set types, to the most up-to-date printing technology.

Even if the English-language press does continue to prosper, its influence will decline, relatively speaking, as the new literates turn to the regional language press. The English-language press will address the well-to-do in cosmopolitan centers, while the regional language papers, which often sell for one anna (one cent) or less per copy, will bid for the widening mass market in the hinterlands. More than forty percent of the weeklies published in regional languages—every language has at least ten—are published from towns of less than 100,000 population.[96] The regional language press will set the linguistic standard for the new regional pulp cultures, reaching out, as it

[91] See *Times of India*, September 15, 1955, p. 1, and August 21, 1955, p. 7; also *New York Times*, September 8, 1956, p. 36.

[92] For an example of resistance to script reform, see *Report of the Kannada Typewriter Committee*, Bangalore, Director of Publications, 1951. The Committee reported the protest of a "learned gentleman that he would rather forego the luxury of a typewriter than let a body of enthusiasts 'murder this ancient script' for satisfying the 'craze of a handful of moneyed men'" (p. 7).

[93] *Times of India*, July 10, 1955, p. 11, and November 9, 1955, p. 10. See also *Report of the Press Commission*, Part I, p. 109.

[94] The Official Language Commission recognized the implications of teleprinters in the regional scripts when it recommended that, instead, teleprinters need be developed only in the Devanagri script, which could be used for all regional languages. See *Report of the Official Language Commission*, p. 240.

[95] W. Norman Brown, "Script Reform in Modern India, Pakistan, and Ceylon," *Journal of the American Oriental Society*, Vol. 73, No. 1, January-March 1953.

[96] *Report of the Press Commission*, Part I, p. 16.

does, to all social levels and to remote villages, just as it has been the testing ground for the regional languages in the past. In the early days of *Swadesamitran,* editor G. S. Iyer wrote in a simple Tamil style that did much to take the language away from "the hide-bound Pandits and Palavars,"[97] and in Telugu, as another example, it was the rise of the Telugu press that began to standardize the language in a form close enough to the spoken medium to be intelligible to a mass audience.[98]

As regional language newspapers become more and more vital, parochial political trends will gain, too, in their vitality, fed by the inordinate parochialism of editorial standards in the regional language press. On the whole, reported the Press Commission, the regional language press downgrades not only international news, but even national news, in marked contrast to the English-language press.[99] In his case study of press reaction to the report of the States Reorganization Commission, V. K. Narasimhan found that the regional language papers gave overwhelming emphasis to recommendations concerning their own regions, while "the English papers generally had a wider perspective."[100] Inadvertently, Narasimhan explains why this is so in the course of a tribute to one publisher for permitting the editors of his two newspapers, one Tamil and one English, to decide policy in each case with a free hand. As it happened, said the editor of the Tamil paper, his opposition to the Commission's recommendation that two Tamil districts go to Kerala was "influenced by the strength of public sentiment in the areas concerned." The English-language paper, though also published in Tamilnad, reached a cosmopolitan audience and could afford to argue on cosmopolitan ground.[101]

97 *Report of the Press Commission,* Part II, p. 105. See also Murray Fowler, "The Segmental Phonemes of Sanskritized Tamil," *Language,* Journal of the Linguistic Society of America, Baltimore, July-September 1954, p. 360.

98 *Report of the Press Commission,* Part II, p. 202. For an interesting discussion of problems of language standardization in north India, see John Gumperz, "Language Problems in the Rural Development of North India," *Journal of Asian Studies,* pp. 251-259.

99 *Report of the Press Commission,* Part I, pp. 259-260.

100 V. K. Narasimhan, *The Making of Editorial Policy: A Case Study of Press Treatment of the S.R.C. Report,* P. Varadachari and Co., Madras, 1956, p. 29.

101 *Ibid.,* p. 36.

Next to newspapers, motion pictures will provide the strongest fillip for the regional languages in the decades ahead, for India's film output, exceeded only by that of the United States and Japan in footage, is concentrated overwhelmingly in the regional languages. Out of 3,479 films (35 millimeter) certified by the Central Board of Film Censors from 1951 through 1956, only 644 were English-language films, including Western imports.[102] In addition to Hindustani films, Bengali, Marathi, Gujarati, Tamil, Telugu, and Malayalam films can all claim sufficient audiences to support thriving "Little Hollywoods" in Calcutta, Bombay, Madras, and the Punjab. Political control through the Central Board of Film Censors can conceivably be exercised to check the use of films for purposes objectionable to the central authority. Similarly, the central monopoly of the air through the All-India Radio can conceivably assure that the primacy of the regional languages in radio, and eventually television, need not feed parochial currents to the extent that will be inevitable in printed media. But the mere fact that the regional languages will gain virtually total ascendancy in all media will, generally speaking, contribute to a climate in each region that enshrines parochial rather than universal values.

In this climate the impulse for scholars and professional men to migrate from one region to another will most probably subside in all but exceptional individual cases. Even if he has studied other Indian languages, the young scholar[103] will think twice before assailing alien university bastions where he will

---

[102] *Report of the Official Language Commission*, p. 47.

[103] When Education Minister Maulana Azad asked state education authorities in August 1949, to reserve a "substantial percentage of admissions and appointments for persons belonging to other provinces," all states pleaded limited facilities and some, such as Madras and Orissa, frankly pointed to "the language difficulty." For a detailed account, see *Proceedings*, Central Advisory Board of Education, January 1951, Bureau of Education Pamphlet No. 110, New Delhi, 1952, pp. 158ff. The Pharmacy College of Gujarat University warned that its "national" character would suffer from the introduction of the regional language medium, according to the *Times of India*, March 28, 1956, p. 6. For an American educator's view, see the unpublished lectures of Olive I. Reddick, director of the U.S. Educational Foundation in India, "Problems Facing the Indian Democracy," in which Doctor Reddick predicts flatly (p. 4) that "obviously," as a consequence of the regional language medium, "the former interregional association of students and teachers will languish behind linguistic barriers."

be, linguistically at least, an outsider, nor will the lawyer who can make his fortune within one convenient linguistic world go out of his way to build a cosmopolitan practice. If ambition can be counted on to arouse the impulse for careers national and international in their scope, this will be the ambition of the most determined few, while the majority in all walks of life will find worlds enough to conquer in the churning new life of home regions, which number, after all, tens upon tens of millions.[104] The determined few who build cosmopolitan careers will constitute one elite at the very pinnacle of Indian leadership. Beneath this national elite, however, successor to the present generation of Indian national leadership, new regional elites will arise, and it is these regional elites which will command decisive social and political power. The rise of these regional elites, each divisible along regional caste lines as we will see in the following chapter, will exercise profound influence on the future of Indian political life.

This new generation of "political nouveau riche," as one member of Parliament contemptuously put it,[105] will be stamped by its partial or complete inability to cope with English and its relatively humble place on the Indian social scale. What appears in the Indian Constitution as a language problem, Sir Ivor Jennings observes, is in reality "a class division which is also a language division," in short, "the use of English by the wealthier classes."[106] With the rise of the new regional elites, which is to say, in part, the rise of a lower middle class,[107] the linguistic co-existence now found within Indian political life will to some extent be replaced by a state of tension. Already, Asoka Mehta notes,

[104] The "regional immobility among the educated classes" is stressed in *Outline Report of the Study Group on Educated Unemployment*, p. 12.

[105] Frank Anthony, Anglo-Indian Member of Parliament, speaking in the Debate on the Andhra State Bill, *Proceedings*, House of the People, August 27, 1953, col. 1691.

[106] Sir Ivor Jennings, *Some Characteristics of the Indian Constitution*, Oxford University Press, 1953, pp. 21-22.

[107] For a discussion of the relation between the rise of the regional languages and the rise of a lower middle class, see Nirad Chaudhuri, "The Language Question for the Millions," *The Statesman*, January 2, 1953, p. 10.

a new group prejudice is emerging in political parties. It is the group strength of persons inadequately educated. The prevalence of a foreign language, English in the case of India, as the official language of the country, has created a special type of monopoly. Only a handful of men who know English are able to operate effectively in political and administrative matters. As a strong opposition grew up against Latin in Europe in the Middle Ages, so in India against the English-knowing 'neo-Brahmans' an opposition is growing up.[108]

It is the depth of this tension between the educational "haves" and "have-nots" that is ignored in the more optimistic projections of tomorrow's linguistic pattern. Whether the language of national political life continues to be English or, contrary to all signs, should ultimately be Hindi, the notion of a body politic controlled by the "haves" who know the common language disregards, in both cases, the rise of the new regional elites. Here, for example, is one rosy look into the linguistic future of Maharashtra:

This is the year 1975. In order that the administration be conducted in Marathi a Marathi-speaking state has been formed. . . . The language in all grades of education and of all business and life in the state is Marathi.

The central government and all central offices and the supreme court conduct their business in Hindi. The local government and the local high court receive communications from the center in that language and publish a Marathi version of such of them as are of general interest immediately so that the people know from an authoritative source what the center is saying and desiring.

All communications from the state to the center will be in Hindi.

Important orders and reports and decisions of local government and the state high court are put into Hindi and communicated to the center for information and record.

The highest offices in the state employ only those who can read Hindi, write Hindi and speak it fairly well.

The center will have in its employment only persons who along with a first class knowledge of Hindi know two or three of our languages tolerably well.

This would be true of our ministers and supreme court judges. . . .[109]

[108] Asoka Mehta, *Group Prejudices in India*, M. B. Nanavati, ed., C. N. Vakil, Bombay and Vora, 1953, p. 43.

[109] Venkatesa Iyengar, in *Report of the Indian Languages Development Conference*, pp. 49-50.

But will the higher offices in any state in fact be free to limit employment to "those who can read Hindi, write Hindi, and speak it fairly well"? Will state and central ministers, as a matter of actual practice, necessarily know Hindi? On the contrary, the successful claimants to high bureaucratic and political posts at state and central levels alike will be those who can back up their claims with real local power. Those who can read, write, and speak Hindi with reasonable competence may be, outside the Hindi region, among the lowest rather than the highest in the hierarchy of power. Similarly, although English will more than likely command greater prestige than Hindi and will be learned as a second language by some holders of local political power, many of those who can read, write, and speak English with reasonable competence will not be at home in regional life and will most often be found on relatively low niches in the hierarchy. Theirs will be the perquisites of the hired technician. The man of independent political resources will, on the other hand, most often know only his regional language. His archetype can be seen today in the Tamil Congress manager Kamraj Nadar, who trusts his English so little that he has a translator at his side in all conferences with Nehru, or the Kerala leader Mannath Padmanabhan, who took his successful 1959 campaign against the Communist Ministry to the people in powerful platform-Malayalam, the only language he knows. For India to produce a local leadership bilingual to any substantial degree would be without precedent in history. Both history and the reality of local life in India point to a structure of political power in which the new regional elites will corner commanding positions.

There was a great deal of truth to the charge that the agitation for linguistic provinces was inspired in part by local claimants to government jobs. "Let us be frank and accept the Dal-Roti (Beans and Bread) basis of this enthusiasm," exclaimed an Indian political scientist. "It is the middle class job hunter and place hunter and the mostly middle class politician who are benefited by the establishment of a linguistic state, which creates for them an exclusive preserve of jobs, offices and places by shutting out, in the name of the promotion of culture, all outside competitors."[110] The pressures for patronage are unusually powerful, as A. D. Gorwala has observed, in a social order which makes it "a man's clear duty to provide for his relatives, near and distant, as well as for his *biradri* or brotherhood."[111] Moreover, while competing pressures tend to be diffused in New Delhi, the concerted pressures of dominant groups at the state level are more difficult to withstand. Chakravarti Rajagopalachari's plea in 1957 for a new national body of overseers to assure integrity in government was at bottom a plea that "the administrative services should be saved from the pressures of state politics."[112] As the States Reorganization Commission found, however, the pressures of state politics cannot be wished away. The Commission's objections to language and residence requirements which restricted state civil service recruitment to "sons of the soil"[113] did lead to reform legislation designed to assure equity for linguistic minorities.[114] But when the Commission made the more crucial proposal that fifty percent of centrally-recruited civil servants employed by state governments should be non-residents, recruited outside the states in which they would serve,[115] state leaders were so vocal in their protests that the scheme had to be dropped.[116]

As the "sons of the soil" who control political life in all re-

[110] Krishna Mukerji, *Reorganization of Indian States*, Bombay, Popular Book Depot, 1955, p. 31.

[111] A. D. Gorwala, *The Role of the Administrator*, p. 22. For other discussions of nepotism in Indian political life, see Gorwala, *Report on Public Administration*, Planning Commission, New Delhi, April 1951, pp. 64-65; Nirad Chaudhuri, "The Language Question for the Millions"; *Hindustan Times*, February 10, 1953, p. 4; *Hindu Weekly Review*, July 15, 1957, p. 7; and Barbara Ward, *The Interplay of East and West*, New York, Harper and Bros., 1957, pp. 64, 70.

[112] C. Rajagopalachari, *Our Democracy*, Madras, B. G. Paul and Co., 1957, p. 14.

[113] *Report of the States Reorganization Commission*, New Delhi, Government of India Press, 1955, p. 230.

[114] *Hindustan Times*, April 28, 1957, p. 6.

[115] *Report of the States Reorganization Commission*, p. 231.

[116] *Times of India*, November 4, 1955, p. 3. Supporting the Commission proposal in Parliament, H. C. Heda charged that "higher-ups in the state services many times associate themselves with this group or that group." This is reported in *Proceedings*, House of the People, December 15, 1955, col. 96. For details of the national controversy over the Commission's proposals for protecting the civil services against state pressures, see *Times of India*, September 28, 1955, p. 1; October 12, 1955, p. 1; November 10, 1955, p. 1, and May 2, 1956, p. 6; and *National Herald*, December 15, 1955, p. 1.

gions become more and more clearly a generation apart, a generation with its own vested interest in the regional languages, even those individuals who do learn to be bilingual will be drawn for all practical political purposes into the new regional elites. There will be few places indeed where English will be the key to substantial local power and influence. Courts of law, for example, closely wedded as they are to English by the very nature of a British juridical legacy, are likely to be conducted in the regional languages up to and perhaps including state High Courts. Former Home Minister K. N. Katju pointed helplessly in 1954 to the writing on the wall,[117] and the Official Language Commission, reporting a "clear trend," prophesied that the "subordinate judiciary in the different states will come to function almost wholly in the respective regional languages in course of time."[118] Article 348 of the Constitution lays down the specific injunction that, irrespective of other language policy, the language of the Supreme Court and the state High Courts will remain English until Parliament designates otherwise. But as if anticipating eventual conversion to the regional languages even in state High Courts, the Constitution decrees, at the same time, that in such an eventuality the High Courts must continue to prepare their authoritative, binding versions in English. Thus the ambitious lawyer, who is often, as in other countries, a lawyer-politician, will feel less and less compulsion to master English. In the state legislatures, where "the large bulk of speeches"[119] are already delivered in regional languages, and where even ministers know only their mother tongue,[120] English will be heard less and less in the decades ahead.

In states constituted on a linguistic basis, of course, it will be all to the good for government to be conducted in the popular medium. Indeed, the multilingual confusion in the legislatures of Bombay, Madras, Hyderabad and Madhya Pradesh was a powerful argument on the side of linguistic provinces. In the

[117] *Times of India*, October 9, 1954, p. 7. See also *Times of India*, January 5, 1955, p. 3.
[118] *Report of the Official Language Commission*, p. 164.
[119] *Ibid.*, p. 173.
[120] *Report of the States Reorganization Commission*, p. 36.

legislature of now-defunct Hyderabad, deputies could use any one of six official languages.[121] In Bombay, which survived as a multilingual unit in the reorganization of states, six languages could be heard in bewildering succession. To a scholar who studied official reports of the Assembly debates—complete with interruptions, switches from one language to another, and wrangling over nothing more than which language a member should use—it seemed obvious that "few, if any, of the M.L.A.'s are able to follow all the Assembly proceedings."[122] The fact that English, which provided the one link across linguistic barriers inside the Assembly, is a language alien to most of the people outside, constituted the crux of the case for the division of Bombay into its regional parts.

But conversion to the regional languages will be one thing in the political life of homogeneous linguistic regions and quite another in the national affairs of a multilingual subcontinent. Unless central educational controls can assure sufficient training in English, or unless Hindi is taught on a scale which now seems unimaginable, it is entirely possible that India will be led in not too many years by a generation of bureaucrats and politicians literally unable to talk meaningfully to one another on a national stage. On the other hand, and here is India's dilemma, even if a new generation of leadership does receive the linguistic equipment to govern a unified nation, it is possible that this generation will constitute a subcaste of linguistic technicians with little actual power.

Representative national leadership may in fact become less and less representative in direct proportion to the rise of the new regional elites. For the politician competent solely in his regional language may be compelled to remain in his local sphere, while one competent in English or Hindi who does go to Parliament may typify a cosmopolitan minority disembodied

121 *Proceedings*, Hyderabad Legislative Assembly, Government Press, Hyderabad, March 28, 1952, p. 183.

122 Maureen L. P. Patterson, "The Bombay Legislative Assembly: 1952-56," Seminar Paper No. 20, Seminar on Leadership and Political Institutions in India, Berkeley, California, 1956, p. 23. For other examples of the problems of multilingual states, see *Hindustan Standard*, October 20, 1952, p. 5; and *Proceedings*, Travancore-Cochin Legislative Assembly, November 8, 1952, p. 1145.

from cultural and political life in the constituencies. In many cases the cosmopolitan political and administrative leader has a camaraderie with the English-speaking Army officer[123] and businessman as natural as his contempt for the provincial politician and intellectual. The rule of a Westernized elite would only be a latter-day example of India's age-old pattern in which government has been a political overlay conducted in a court language unknown to most of the people. But neither the Sanskrit-speaking autocrats of fifteen hundred years ago nor the English-speaking autocrats of the recent past had to contend with enfranchised new literates by the millions in the regional languages.

Will trial and error produce a characteristically Indian compromise? Is it possible that bi- or tri-lingualism will develop as the rule rather than the exception and that Indian leaders will become linguistically cosmopolitan on a scale unprecedented in history? Can speakers of the regional languages, Hindi, and English coexist in a stable body politic? Perhaps the incentives to learn English and Hindi will produce substantial national leadership competent in one of these languages, while still others competent primarily in the regional languages are propelled willy-nilly to New Delhi by their unrivalled strength in their regions. Speaking with a measure of authority, itself eloquent enough to compensate for their linguistic rough edges, such regional leaders might manage somehow to function at the national level.[124] Yet precisely how, no one, least of all Indian leaders themselves, can now foresee.

[123] English is the medium for all five of the armed forces officer training entrance examinations, according to the *Report of the Official Language Commission*, p. 184. The long-standing policy initiated during British rule that made English not only the medium of secondary preparatory schools for the armed forces but also the medium of the entrance examination for these schools has been subjected to increasing pressure. Elementary education, at least, should be in the regional languages, even for Army officers-to-be, argued the Bihar state government in a memorandum cited as Appendix M, *Proceedings of the 18th Meeting of the Central Advisory Board of Education* (October 1951), Ministry of Education, Government of India, Government of India Press, 1953, p. 171.

[124] Article 120 of the Constitution, which stipulates that the Speaker of each chamber of Parliament "may permit" members to speak in their mother tongue in place of English or Hindi, is discussed in *Report of the Official Language*

In the heat of the Andhra State debate in 1953, former Home Minister K. N. Katju, a Hindi champion, impatiently shouted at a South Indian Communist orator:

Personally, I cannot understand the notion of democratic institutions and Parliament, elected on adult franchise, functioning in a sort of multi-lingual atmosphere. Supposing in this House, very many honorable friends speak in the national language, I believe there must be about one hundred members here who say we are unable to follow. But supposing you were to say that the national language is not known—and English, I entirely agree, has got no future here—supposing every one of us were to speak in our regional language, what will happen? We speak here in order to make ourselves under-stood, not for love of our own voice. We speak to bring other people round to our views, and to appreciate the other person's views. Sup-posing we were to speak in our own regional languages, the thing would become a Babel. . . . I say you cannot have democratic insti-tutions functioning properly on a multi-lingual basis.

Mr. Deputy Speaker (Ananthasayanam Ayyangar): Even otherwise also it happens. Even if there are no linguistic provinces, if English goes out and they do not know Hindi, what will happen?[125]

Commission, p. 150. The Commission also foresees (p. 152) that it would "not be beyond the limits of feasibility" to install simultaneous translation procedures similar to those used in the United Nations.

[125] *Proceedings*, House of the People, Debate on the Andhra State Bill, August 27, 1953, cols. 1724-1725.

THE EQUATION between Hindu unity and Indian unity is the facile first answer to all doubts about the future of the Union. Hindu unity, it is said, pervades all regional differences; Hindu society is a national society. But if the common identity of all Hindus in a non-Hindu world gives validity to Indian nationalism in its world setting, this vaunted unity is vulnerable, at the same time, to powerful regional stresses on its home ground. The most powerful centrifugal stresses threatening Indian unity are unmistakably resident within the Hindu social order. With its complex interaction of centrifugal and centripetal forces, Hindu society may not, after all, provide the foundation for a unified modern state.

Hindu tradition has its unifying strength in a symbolism that even in the earliest Hindu scriptures encompasses all India. The *Rig Veda's* River Hymn pointedly projects the unity of the motherland on a national scale. It was an adaptation of the River Hymn that became the Puranic prayer now recited when a Hindu performs his *sandhya,* or water purification ritual, before his daily bath: "Oh ye Ganga, Godavari, Narmada, Kaveri, and Indus, come ye and enter the water of my offering." Here the Hindu imagines waters from the north, east, west, and south of the subcontinent mingling in the waters of his small pot. The major pilgrim centers that the orthodox should visit as an imperative religious duty draw Hindus to such geographically dispersed points as Mathura and Banaras in the north, Ujjain in central India, and Kanchipuram in the far south. In the eighty-first chapter of the *Garuda Purana,* which reviews the holy places, all of India passes in review from the Himalayas to Cape Comorin. "The underlying principle in the determination of these sacred places," writes Radha Kumud Mookerjee, "was to treat the entire country as a single sacred unit, and to spread the conception of such sacredness among the unlettered millions."[1]

[1] R. K. Mookerjee, *The Fundamental Unity of India,* Longmans, Green & Co., London, 1914, p. 46.

What Mookerjee set forth with scholarly rigor in *The Fundamental Unity of India* nationalist tracts repeated and repeated throughout the freedom movement. To counter the British claim that India was not a nation at all, Indian historians sought to establish a record of Hindu political unity and Hindu cultural nationalism equal to the challenge. Even President Rajendra Prasad, chief of state in a secular republic, pointed to the Hindu epics—*The Ramayana* and *The Mahabharata*—as embodying "the common links in the realm of thought, literature and social customs of the various regions."[2] The latest ideologian of India's cultural unity, Ramdhari Sinha Dinkar, whose book carried a foreword by Nehru, declares exultantly that "because of this story (*The Ramayana*) the whole country has one idea, one inspiration—one personification of manly virtue."[3] Through the integrating power of *The Ramayana*, maintains Dinkar, Rama in the north and Shiva in the south became "more or less assimilated" in a common mythological heritage that gradually eroded the differences separating north Indian Vaishnavite Hinduism and south Indian Shaivism. Nor can it be disputed that thanks to *The Ramayana* and *The Mahabharata* all regional literatures throughout India draw on a common fund of Hindu culture. Folklore is often only a local variation of themes from the two epics, and Valmiki's original saga of Rama has itself been translated into all Indian languages: *Kamban Ramayana* (Tamil) in the 10th century; *Dwipad Ramayana* (Telugu) in the 12th century; *Ram Charitam Ramayana* (Malayalam) in the 14th century; *Balaram Das Ramayana* (Oriya) and *Kritti Bas Ramayana* (Bengali) in the 15th century; *Ram Charitamanas Ramayana* (Hindi), *Torave Ramayana* (Kannada), and *Bhavartha Ramayana* (Marathi) in the 16th century.

Despite this common fund of tradition, however, Hinduism is in a social and political sense as much a force for disintegration as for integration. Neither King nor Pope embody for Hindu-

---

[2] Rajendra Prasad, *India Divided*, Hind Kitabs, Bombay, 1946, p. 67. See also *Times of India*, December 10, 1954, p. 1. For a discussion of *The Ramayana* as a source of national unity, see the report of the All-India Writers Conference, *The Hindu*, April 20, 1954, p. 1.

[3] Ramdhari Sinha Dinkar, "Rama as a Figure in Synthesis," *Samskriti Ke Char Adhyaya (Four Phases of Culture)*, Hindi, Rajpal and Sons, Delhi, 1956, p. 70.

ism the controlling discipline common to other major religions. Unlike Confucianism in China, as a notable example, Hinduism has never brought forth on an enduring basis its own centralized political institutions. In this inchoate character lies the unifying capacity to accommodate great diversity. But at the same time the complete absence of institutional forms has made it impossible for Hinduism to control the centrifugal strains built into its unique social order—a social order which is the most pervasive accompaniment to being Hindu.

Caste and Region

This social order, caste, is usually seen in terms which would denote an integrating rather than disintegrating role. The fourfold division of Hindus into *varnas*, Brahman, Kshatriya, Vaisya, and Sudra, exists in all parts of India and would seem, therefore, to signify a pan-Indian caste edifice giving all Hindus a close social relationship to one another. In fact, however, the structure of caste in India divides into a series of self-contained regional caste structures that are threaded together only loosely within the all-embracing hierarchy of Hindu society. By and large, the linguistic boundary is the caste boundary. Caste limits inter-dining and inter-marriage to an endogamous unit (*jati*), which may be native to a single village or may spread across an entire region but which is, in almost all cases, confined within linguistic limits. It is because caste ties do not cross linguistic borders that Hinduism, for all its unifying power, is vulnerable to centrifugal forces within.

In place of a vertical view of Hindu caste groups ranked on an ascending scale of *varnas*, irrespective of regional location, it is more meaningful to view the Hindu social order horizontally as a succession of regional subcastes that coincide at right angles with linguistic regions. Caste not only divides Indians into high-born and low-born, but into regional sub-caste compartments whose members behave as members of their compartments. To K. M. Panikkar each of these 3,000-odd regional subcastes can be described as an extended joint family. "Beyond this," he writes, "the Hindu in practice recognizes no society or community. This is the widest social group

98

that the Hindus evolved . . . the bedrock on which Hindu social organization is built."[4]

Hindu kinship organization, writes the anthropologist Irawati Karve, follows roughly the linguistic boundary, which circumscribes "the widest area within which marital connections are established and outside of which kinship hardly ever extends."[5] From this each region gets what Karve calls its distinctive "cultural *gestalt*." The dominant caste grouping in each region draws to itself other groups, embracing them over time in a network of common social practices across the heartland of the region. Karve cites the fact that in Maharashtra, nearly forty percent of the total population consists of various inter-connected peasant-proprietor caste groups embraced by the terms Maratha and Kunbi. The Maratha-Kunbi group "has a certain clan organization, certain marriage customs and a particular type of kinship organization which in its turn is based on one type of cross-cousin marriage and on clans organized on an hierarchical principle." Around this Maratha-Kunbi group of castes can be placed other castes who imitate Maratha peculiarities, such as the Mali or gardener, the Navi or barber, the Parit or washerman, and the Mahar and Chamar untouchables. Even some Brahman castes, such as the Deshastha Rigvedi Brahmans, have become closely associated with the Marathas as a result of their proximity in everyday life.

Recently the caste council of the immigrant Gujar caste in northwest Maharashtra, which does not practice the cross-cousin marriage practiced by most agricultural castes in the region, allowed one such marriage after a heated two-day debate and the imposition of a token fine on the families involved. When Mrs. Karve, who was in the village when this incident occurred, asked on what basis the caste council consented to such a marriage, she was told by an elder: "One cannot resist the customs of the

[4] *Hindu Society at Cross Roads*, Asia Publishing House, Bombay, 1955, pp. 12, 17. See also D. R. Gadgil, *Notes on the Rise of the Business Communities in India*, Institute of Pacific Relations, New York, 1951, p. 1.

[5] *Kinship Organization in India*, Deccan College Monograph Series, Number 11, Deccan College Post-Graduate and Research Institute, Poona, 1953, p. 1. See also David G. Mandelbaum, *Materials for a Bibliography on the Ethnology of India*, Department of Anthropology, University of California, Berkeley, 1949, p. 2.

land in which one lives. After all, a fish cannot wage a feud against water."

The rules of *gotra* permit Hindus to marry where the mothers' *gotras* and the respective fathers' *gotras* are different. In thus avoiding marriages of kin removed by less than two degrees, *gotra* gives "a wider and wider circle for seeking marital alliances," but it is a circle which, while likely to extend over several administrative districts, does not exceed the boundaries of the linguistic region.[6]

Anthropologists, sociologists, and historians agree that modern communications and transportation have pushed the boundaries of caste from the traditional village extension of the joint family to what are now regional alliances of kindred local units. "In the beginning of the 19th century," states G. S. Ghurye, "linguistic boundaries fixed the caste limits."[7] The British anthropologist Eric J. Miller has demonstrated in a detailed case study of the Malayalam-speaking region that caste was traditionally "a system of territorial segmentation" in which the bedrock unit was either the village (*desam*) or at most the chiefdom (*nad*). Then, with modern social change,

the change from a closed to an open society, the old boundaries, dependent on political cleavages, now became porous, ceasing to mark the limits of social relations within individual castes. This has enabled castes to establish internal bonds of solidarity over wide areas. The last fifty years have seen the growth of a formal regional organization for practically every caste, with the avowed aim of . . . raising the status and prestige of the caste as a whole and freeing its members from exploitation and victimization by other castes.[8]

"British rule freed the jinn from the bottle," summarizes M. N.

[6] Karve discusses kinship organization throughout this work. See esp. pp. 9-17. The *Memorandum* submitted by the Indian Association to the States Reorganization Commission (Calcutta, 1954, p. 27) discusses the kinship between castes in Manbhum and Dhalbhum districts of Bihar and Bengal castes. "The castes of both have intimate kinship with similar communities in West Bengal" and the Dayabhaga school of law prevails, it is argued, rather than Bihar's Mitakshara.

[7] G. S. Ghurye, *Caste and Class in India*, Popular Book Depot, Bombay, 1950, p. 23. See also pp. 19 and 32; and J. H. Hutton, *Caste in India*, Oxford University Press, London, 1951, p. 10.

[8] Eric J. Miller, "Caste and Territory in Malabar," *American Anthropologist*, Vol. 56, No. 3, June 1954, pp. 418-419.

Srinivas.[9] Roads, railways, postal and telegraph facilities, cheap paper, printing (especially in the regional languages), and finally the coincidence of political units and party organizations with linguistic areas, have all enabled and even impelled castes to organize as they had never done before. When caste riots broke out in Madras in 1957, they were not the local riots of a century ago, which would hardly have attracted national and even world attention, but the conflict of Maravar and untouchable factions united throughout an entire administrative district.

"The increasing solidarity of castes over large geographical distances," Kingsley Davis has observed, "has led in some ways to a strengthening of the caste spirit, a spirit which has a new element in it: it is competitive."[10] This is indeed a spirit new to caste, for the traditional role of caste has been the very reverse, to minimize competition and to promote the spirit of live-and-let-live. In this traditional atmosphere the fact that the ethical prescriptions of Hinduism teach an in-group exclusiveness, a loyalty to one's *biradri* or brotherhood, spelled strength for each caste without vitiating the strength of the system as a whole. But for caste to become the basis of economic and political competition, which was the inevitable accompaniment of its geographical expansion, is to magnify all of its worst features.[11] Where it once exercised social control at the level of functionally integrated villages,[12] caste now reinforces economic and political conflict, which occurs for the most part within the same linguistic regional boundaries demarcating the newly extended caste alignment.

Even more menacing than regional pressures as such, warns

9 M. N. Srinivas, "Caste in Modern India," *Journal of Asian Studies*, August 1957, p. 530.

10 *The Population of India and Pakistan*, Princeton University Press, 1951, p. 175.

11 See Kingsley Davis, "Social and Demographic Aspects of Economic Development in India," in *Economic Growth: Brazil, India, Japan*, Simon Kuznets, ed., Duke University Press, 1955, pp. 304-305.

12 Oscar Lewis, discussing this functional integration as it has operated in the so-called *jajmani* system of village economic organization (*Village Life in North India*, University of Illinois Press, 1958, pp. 83-84), declares that "the decline of the *jajmani* system will not necessarily be followed by an automatic or speedy disintegration of the caste system. Instead, caste may continue to take on new functions and manifestations."

D. R. Gadgil, is the fact that caste can no longer perform its integrative function. In the past, he points out, "social and economic gradations roughly corresponded to the gradations of caste. But now that we want equality and have decided to get rid of the caste system, we face the problem of preserving the live-and-let-live philosophy."[13]

To enshrine equality is in effect to tell all castes that it is every man—which is to say every group—for himself. If the promise of economic progress is the main promise of freedom for the dispossessed, then it is only natural for a scramble to ensue when the rate of economic development fails to bring a new world overnight. Caught in a never-never world of frustration, somewhere between newly aroused desires for equality and the scant spoils of progress that are actually available, it is inevitable for a man to turn to a loyalty he knows and understands to fortify his quest for equality with those above him and to assure that he is "more equal" than those below. While in time some dissolution of Hindu values and social ties will follow industrialization and urbanization, while in time successful members of rising castes will forsake their group allegiances for a broad new middle class consciousness,[14] in the decades immediately ahead most Hindus will pursue equality as members of caste lobbies.

Far from dissolving under the impact of economic change, therefore, caste is, if anything, stronger than ever before. "Men discover sooner or later," writes Karl Deutsch, "that they can advance their interests in the competitive game of politics and economics by forming coalitions . . . coalitions which will depend to a significant degree on social communication and on the culture patterns and personality structure of the participants."[15] With power now a living reality in the new democratic dispensation, every caste and region wants to claim its share.

[13] "Caste, Regionalism, and Nationalism," Report of a Seminar on Interdisciplinary Indian Studies, Poona, 1955, Deccan College Post-Graduate Research Institute, pp. 26-27.

[14] For an interesting discussion of the Indian middle classes, see Humayun Kabir, *The Indian Heritage*, Harper and Bros., 1956, pp. 140-142.

[15] "Growth of Nations," *World Politics*, January 1953, p. 183. See also Sasadhar Sinha, "Some Dangers of Disunity," *The Statesman*, January 26, 1957, p. 10.

Thus the low caste striving for equality strives for it within the caste system. When a low caste becomes newly-rich as a result of new economic opportunity, it does not repudiate its group identity but rather uses its new resources to win a higher and therefore more secure place, as a group, within the caste hierarchy, imitating the Sanskritic rituals of educated higher castes, which are themselves more and more exposed to Westernization.[16] It is the prestige of the Sanskritic ritual and the interlocking religious and social ties of Hindu society which above all prevent class from replacing caste. In seeking to explain why newly-rich individuals do not take on a class rather than caste identity, F. G. Bailey, reporting on his study of an Orissa village, observes that

to improve his position in the ritual system of rank . . . the rich man cannot throw off his poorer caste-fellows. . . . The most that the wealthy within a caste group can do to lighten their upward passage by jettisoning poorer caste-fellows is to form a subcaste.[17]

But, he adds, subcastes are not easily formed: at least two unrelated families are required in the first instance, and "members of a caste group often derive from one ancestor." Moreover, the rich find the ranks of united higher castes closed to them, while the poor, sensing that "mobility adheres to groups and not individuals . . . support their own 'middle classes' in the struggle against higher castes."

The constitutional provisions guaranteeing specified numbers of government jobs, legislative seats and school admissions to designated untouchable and low castes have sharpened caste consciousness on an enormous scale. For, numerically, it is the very castes that are submerged in Hindu society that are also the strongest. The Backward Classes Commission listed 2,399 "backward" communities in 1953, excluding untouchables, 913 of the major ones accounting alone for 116 million people. Yet for all the blessings that "backwardness" confers, thus con-

[16] The phenomenon by which Brahmans are becoming more Westernized at the same time that other castes are becoming Sanskritized is discussed in M. N. Srinivas, "A Note on Sanskritization and Westernization," *Far Eastern Quarterly,* August 1956, pp. 490, 493.

[17] *Caste and the Economic Frontier,* Manchester University Press, 1957, p. 270.

solidating caste consciousness, these constitutional guarantees only institutionalize a group awareness that would in any case exist to a great extent. Since the upper castes often refuse to recognize the achievement of an individual member of a low caste who may, for example, acquire education, the individual invariably concludes that mobility on any significant scale must be a group phenomenon.[18]

In an economy of plenty social lines are eroded by the change to urban life, but in an economy of scarcity the lines harden. "Envy and acquisitiveness become the dominant emotions," comments Asoka Mehta, "and each class, each group, each individual is engaged in grabbing."[19] Where there is economic development, the issue becomes who shall get rich from it. Where there are limited educational facilities, jobs, and promotions, it is not plans for expanding the facilities that excites men but rather how the younger sons of one caste group can elbow out another for the lion's share in the region. A sociologist who studied a sample of 3,467 persons in Bangalore, a modern metropolis by Indian standards, found inter-caste marriages "extremely rare."[20] This is not surprising when it is realized that even those upper castes at the very pinnacle of Hindu society guard their group identity with especially rigid strictures against outside pollution—and competition—when the caste shifts from a rural to an urban environment. Thus the Chitrapur Saraswat Brahmans, a wealthy and influential caste

[18] For an interesting account that illustrates this contention, see Bernard S. Cohn, "Changing Status of a Depressed Caste," *Village India*, University of Chicago Press, 1956, esp. pp. 74-76. Other discussions that the author has found helpful in considering the impact of economic change on caste solidarity are: Gardner Murphy, *In the Minds of Men*, Basic Books, 1954, esp. pp. 62-69 and 93-116; Asoka Mehta and Achyut Patwardhan, *The Communal Triangle in India*, Kitabistan, Allahabad, 1942, p. 99; Srinivas, "Caste in Modern India"; P. C. Joshi, "Casteism—The Problem and its Solution," *National Herald*, February 24, 1957; K. V. Sundaresa Iyer, *Democracy and Caste*, Minerva Printers, Madura, 1956, entirety; B. R. Chauhan, "Recent social trends among depressed classes in Rajasthan," *Agra University Journal of Research* (Letters), Vol. III, December 1955, pp. 158-161, and D. P. Mukerji, "Presidential Address," *Agra University Journal of Research*, p. 4.

[19] Presidential address, Asoka Mehta, Socialist Party Convention, Madras, July 1950.

[20] Noel P. Gist, "Caste Differentials in south India," *American Sociological Review*, April 1954, p. 128.

of 18,900 concentrated in the Bombay area, has continually extended its communal organization to keep the caste together in Bombay and to corner for it the benefits of urban life. The Chitrapur Saraswats are only one of forty-two castes in India that operate regular caste publications.[21] "While it is disquieting that we have lost our agricultural moorings with the movement of our population from villages and towns to bigger cities," a caste leader wrote in the 336-page *Chitrapur Saraswat 1956 Census Report and Directory*, "it is heartening that we have recorded substantial progress"—22 caste-operated educational institutions, 13 fraternal and social agencies, and 12 housing cooperatives. It is unfortunate, he lamented, that the 1945 Directory did not contain comparable institutional statistics; "for such comparison would have shown the community's will to function as a separate entity represented by the word 'community' reflecting its fortunes and even its failures vis-à-vis those of the rest of the country."[22]

So long as the institution of caste persists, of course, the fact that all Hindus belong in common to a social system with so many interlocking pan-Indian features will in one sense connect the local caste tie to the larger Hindu loyalty. But at the same time the regional limits of the operative caste unit render it inevitable that caste—setting as it does the social boundaries of the competition for economic and political power—will be as divisive as it is unifying.

Behind the Banner of Language

For this reason the linguistic demarcation of state boundaries in India intensifies conflict between castes. Their power relationship changes. The balance of power between castes in a multilingual political unit with its many caste groups differs radically from that in the smaller linguistic unit. This has already been apparent in Andhra, where two rival Telugu peasant-proprietor castes, the Kammas and Reddis, have kept the state in political upheaval since its formation in 1953. Before the

[21] G. S. Ghurye, *Caste and Class in India* (third revised edition, 1957), p. 231.
[22] *The Chitrapur Saraswat 1956 Census Report and Directory*, Kanara Saraswat Association, Bombay, 1956, esp. Introduction.

separation of Andhra from multilingual Madras State, the Kammas and Reddis were lost in the welter of castes. In Andhra they face each other as titans.[23] Similarly, the formation of Maharashtra will heighten the political struggle among the major regional caste groups—the Marathi Brahmans, the Maratha peasant-proprietors and the Mahar untouchables.

It was a distinguished Mahar son, the late Law Minister B. R. Ambedkar, who perceived from the special vantage of one beyond the pale of caste what linguistic reorganization held in store. Ambedkar warned on many occasions against Maratha subjugation of the Mahars in a linguistically-defined Maharashtra. Switzerland, Ambedkar told Parliament, has no difficulties as a multilingual state

because there linguism is not loaded with (caste) communalism. But in our country linguism is only another name for communalism. . . . Take Andhra. There are two major communities spread over the linguistic area. They are either the Reddis or the Kammas. They hold all the land, all the offices, all the business. The untouchables live in subordinate dependence on them. Take Maharashtra. The Marathas are a huge majority in every village in Maharashtra. In a linguistic state what would remain for the smaller communities to look to?[24]

In Gujarat, he warned the Dar Commission in 1948, the "Anavil Brahmans form a dominant class in some parts. In other parts it is the Patidars. It is quite likely the Anavils and the Patidars will reduce the condition of the other communities through subjection." Foreseeing that in a linguistically-defined Maharashtra, the Marathas, "as the dominant community, will become sole heir to all political power which the area gets,"[25] Ambedkar demanded guarantees that the Mahars would enjoy full civil rights. Six years later protagonists of Maharashtra went

[23] See a case study of Andhra caste rivalries in chapter six and in an earlier study by the author, "Caste and the Andhra Communists," *American Political Science Review*, July 1956.

[24] *Hindustan Times*, September 3, 1953, p. 3. See also B. R. Ambedkar, *Thoughts on Linguistic States*, Bombay, Ramkrishna Press, 1955, pp. 34-35; B. R. Ambedkar, "Linguistic States-need for checks and balances," *Times of India*, April 23, 1953, p. 4; and Srinivas, "Caste in Modern India," p. 542.

[25] "Maharashtra as a Linguistic Province," statement submitted to the Linguistic Provinces Commission, Thacker & Co., Bombay, 1948, pp. 34-35.

to great lengths to assure him that "no government, whatever its communal complexion, could afford to tolerate or ignore any harassment of the minority within its jurisdiction."[26]

The South Indian untouchable member of Parliament, R. Velayudhan, has often expressed a similar outcaste's-eye view of the conjunction between caste and language region. Velayudhan declared in 1953 that the linguistic idea "is a dangerous idea, from the very cardinal point of view of the future social structure of India." Unlike Europe, "here the one fundamental basis was the caste social structure. And if the states are now redistributed on the basis of language alone, it is really the caste idea which is behind it."[27] On another occasion, Velayudhan branded the formation of linguistic states "a great danger . . . a reactionary move which will result in bringing the caste system back into the country in a ferocious form."[28]

In a sprawling linguistic region such as Maharashtra, the lines of the operative subcaste unit may form on the basis of intra-regional territorial divisions rather than of the region taken as a whole. Three distinct sections of Maharashtra—Desh surrounding Poona, Vidarbha to the northeast, formerly a part of Madhya Pradesh, and Marathwada to the southeast—each to some extent circumscribe separate subcaste power groupings. Thus, while Ambedkar feared the dominant Marathas, from the perspective of Vidarbha (where Marathas comprise 24 percent of the population, compared to nearly 40 percent in Desh) it is the fear of domination by Poona's Chitpavan Brahmans that looms large. A Congress untouchable leader in Vidarbha joined Ambedkar in opposing a single Marathi state, but his argument was that it would re-establish the "one-caste rule" of Maharashtra's Peshwa era.[29] The Brahman view from

[26] Memorandum submitted by Maharashtra leaders, V. P. Pawar, B. M. Gupte, M. D. Joshi, and T. R. Deogirikar, published by B. M. Gupte, Swatantraya, Poona, 1954, and cited in Krishna P. Mookerji and Suhasini Ramaswamy, *Reorganization of Indian States*, Popular Book Depot, Bombay, 1955, p. 61.

[27] House of the People, *Proceedings*, August 19, 1953, Debate on the Andhra State Bill, cols. 1090-1091.

[28] *Proceedings*, House of the People, February 17, 1953, Debate on motion on address by the President, col. 438.

[29] *Sakal*, Poona, October 14, 1954, p. 1.

Vidarbha, on the other hand, was that a single state would be inadvisable because it would infect the docile Vidarbha Marathas with the arrogance of their Desh brethren. The best efforts of Brahmans in the Desh, warned M. S. Aney of Nagpur, former governor of Bihar, have not

penetrated deep enough to break the barriers of communalism and the spirit of jealousy and antagonism in a large section of the population which has now the right to vote and to rule the country. If this be correct, I consider it wrong to bring any other blocs of large population which are comparatively free from these pernicious traits under their political authority and dominant influence.[30]

In view of the prospect of Maratha dominance in a single Maharashtra, why have the Chitpavan Brahmans joined the Marathas to support the Maharashtra movement? The answer lies partially in the head start of the Brahmans, who are confident that they can become the main beneficiaries of liberation from Gujarati influence in composite Bombay. Ambedkar once added his cynical belief, in a conversation with the writer, that "the Brahmans hope they will get something by licking the boots of the Marathas, and they are looking to the future to preserve their position with the new majority." But even more decisive is the distribution of subcaste lines within the Marathi-speaking region. The Marathas themselves are divided into five major clans. First in the hierarchy are those claiming descent from Marathas close to Shivaji, such as K. S. Jedhe. Beneath this elite stands a lesser aristocracy known as the "96 families," and beneath these three other major clans embracing the rank and file of the Maratha peasant-proprietors. Conceivably, as particularism divides into particularism in any future Marathi-speaking state, clan divisions might dissipate Maratha strength and preserve Brahman hegemony by default. When the late B. G. Kher relinquished the Bombay Chief Ministership in 1953 to serve as High Commissioner in London, a Maratha might have succeeded him had Maratha leaders been able to reach agreement between B. S. Hirey and another caste

---

[30] *Memorandum* submitted to the States Reorganization Commission, Dr. Madhao Shridhao Aney, Poona, 1954, p. 45.

luminary, Y. B. Chavan, who ultimately did become Chief Minister.[31]

Political competition in a representative system was bound to give casteism "a new lease on life,"[32] as Vinoba Bhave put it, if only because the single-member constituency inherently favors—barring gerrymandering—any social group in any country which happens to live together in close proximity in a particular locality.[33] The political role of caste is widely conceded in the Indian press,[34] and invariably, the most perplexing election surprises become crystal-clear when the caste factors in a constituency come to light.[35] But the strength of caste in Indian political life is not the diffused strength of scattered local caste factions, each organized to elect its own single member of a state assembly or Parliament. It is because caste lobbies function coherently on the basis of entire linguistic regions— for all their potential division, even the Marathas are a relatively unified lobby—that caste assumes such irrepressible importance. United blocs in a state party machine demand their share of the spoils when the party comes to power, and often, as Ambedkar argues, it is indeed a caste bloc which agitates in the first place for the very creation of a state as a means to strengthening its own position.

Nor is it new for the linguistic demand to "cloak the political ambitions of a community or an individual."[36] As long ago as

[31] The Maratha clans are described in Irawati Karve, *op.cit.*, p. 156. See also Maureen L. P. Patterson, "Caste and Political Leadership in Maharashtra," *Economic Weekly*, September 25, 1954, p. 1065; and Ambedkar (*Thoughts on Linguistic States*, p. 27), who asks: "What affiliation has a Maratha of Satara got with a Maratha of Aurangabad?"

[32] *Hindustan Times*, April 29, 1957, p. 2. Congress secretary Sriman Narayan declared that "the present system of elections has undoubtedly given strength and encouragement to casteism" in an editorial in *A.I.C.C. Economic Review*, April 15, 1956, p. 4.

[33] This is cited as a major justification for sweeping reform of the Indian electoral system in an interesting discussion by S. S. More, *A.I.C.C. Economic Review*, July 15, 1957, p. 9.

[34] For example, see *Times of India*, January 21, 1957, p. 6; *Hindustan Times*, April 29, 1957; *National Herald*, March 24 (p. 6), April 21 (p. 6), and April 29 (p. 4), 1957.

[35] Thus, the defeat of U. P. Congress boss C. B. Gupta in 1957 involved caste defections engineered by the opposition, according to the *Hindustan Times*, March 3 (p. 5) and March 4 (p. 8), 1957.

[36] *Times of India*, April 5, 1955, p. 6.

the turn of the century a popular Bengali couplet razzed the leader of the Bihar movement for separation from Bengal:

> Sachchidananda Sinha
> By the nine Gods he swore,
> That ere the year was o'er
> He should be a judge at Bankipore.

Sinha hailed from the Bihar capital of Patna, and the couplet was recalled by a north Bihar separatist, Lakshman Jha, as a defensive counterthrust when he was stung by ridicule from Patna. Jha's movement for a separate Mithila Republic in Maithili-speaking north Bihar is commonly attributed to the desire of Mithila's Darbhanga Brahman subcaste to gain a separate enclave of power far from the political monopoly of the Rajputs and Bhumihars in Bihar politics.[37]

The Andhra movement for provincial autonomy became in its final stages a mass expression of the regional patriotism of all Telugus, but in its beginnings the Andhra demand drew motive force from regional caste factors. Initially the leadership in the Andhra movement came from the Telugu Brahman, who took a reluctant second place to the dominant Tamil Brahman in the cultural and political life of multilingual Madras State. The Telugu Brahman lawyer saw in a separate Andhra state a chance to break the government-supported monopoly that the Tamil Brahman lawyer enjoyed in Andhra legal business. The Telugu Brahman bureaucrat wanted the government patronage in Andhra that went more often to his Tamil Brahman rival. The Telugu Brahman poet or novelist understandably wanted a political setting in which excellence in his own mother tongue would be an asset and not a curiosity. But by the late 1930's, the leadership of the Andhra movement and of all Andhra political life had broadened as more and more of the sons of non-Brahman peasant-proprietors broke through the Brahman monopoly on education. The two largest of these non-Brahman

---

[37] Lakshman Jha, *Mithila—A Union Republic*, Mithila Mandal, Darbhanga, 1952, p. 59. See also *Times of India*, February 8 (p. 6) and February 22 (p. 8), 1956; and Purshottam Tricumdas, Address of Chairman, *Proceedings*, Socialist Party convention, Nasik, 1948, p. 1.

caste groups, the Kammas and Reddis, emerged as rivals for the limited political and economic spoils that were available to them in the multilingual confusion of Madras caste groups. The Kammas and Reddis, their strength diffused in the welter of Madras castes, became vigorous advocates of an Andhra State in which their place in the power structure was sure to enlarge.[38]

In Kannada-speaking Karnataka, caste conflict over whether a linguistic state should be formed even more clearly exposed the possible effects of linguistic reorganization on the caste power balance. The lines of rivalry in Karnataka are much the same as in Andhra, with the conflict between the Brahmans and non-Brahmans even less important than the conflict between two powerful, predominantly peasant-proprietor subcastes within non-Brahman ranks, the Lingayats and Vakkaligas. Strictly speaking, the Lingayats should be classified as a religious sect in which assorted subcaste groups are allied in a common anti-Brahman reform movement, Virashaivism, dating back to the 12th century. But in practice the Lingayats now function as a broad regional subcaste, all the more powerful for "an ecclesiastical organization comparable in thoroughness to that of Catholic Rome."[39] Their rivals for power are the Vakkaligas, nearly half of whom belong to a single subgroup—the Gangadikar Vakkaligas, centered in the area comprising the southwest corner of the former state of Mysore, and often called the most distinctively "Kannada" of all caste groups, with no historic or other ties outside the region.[40]

The transition of the Lingayats from a loose sectarian alliance of subcaste groups into a unified regional force seeking to enhance its position through linguistic reorganization may typify the solidification of regional caste consciousness in other parts

[38] A Tamil deputy opposed to the formation of Andhra charged in Parliament (House of People, *Proceedings*, Debate on the Andhra State Bill, August 27, 1953, col. 1689) that the new state would only serve to satisfy "those unabashedly communal elements who think in terms of loaves and fishes of office." See also *Self-Critical Report of the Andhra Communist Committee, January 1948-February 1952*, Part Two, March 1949-March 1950 (a party document not intended for publication), and *Eastern Economist*, July 16, 1954, p. 3.

[39] *Mysore Gazetteer*, Vol. 1, Government Press, Bangalore, 1927, p. 143.

[40] H. V. Nanjundayya, *Mysore Tribes and Castes*, Mysore University, 1931, Vol. 1, pp. 125-126; Vol. 3, p. 175; Vol. 4, p. 81.

of India. Soon after the turn of the century, a Dharwar District Lingayat leader founded the Virashaiva Mahasabha on the strength of the argument that only a united caste consciousness could rescue the Lingayats from their depressed plight in Karnataka society. The Mahasabha perceived that while Lingayats were in a minority in the existing princely state of Mysore, they might well dominate a united Karnataka, embracing Kannada-speaking districts of Bombay and Hyderabad. In time the movement for a linguistic state—until then a fancy of the Kannada Brahman literati—became a lever to displace the Vakkaligas as the dominant non-Brahman community in Mysore and to give the Lingayats outside Mysore a better entree to power than they could expect as outsiders in multilingual Bombay. From the Bangalore session of the Mahasabha in 1927, which demanded formation of Karnataka state, the full power of the Lingayat religious organization stood behind the Karnataka movement.[41] The Virashaivite clergy could look to greatly increased importance in a Lingayat-dominated Karnataka, and the priestly leader of one of the major Lingayat *maths* or pilgrimage centers personally presided at many rallies for a Karnataka state.[42]

Assessing the Vakkaliga claim that Lingayats would dominate the proposed linguistic Karnataka, the States Reorganization Commission accepted the estimate

that Lingayats or Veerasaivites constitute about 35 to 40 percent of the population in the Kannada areas outside Mysore at present. The . . . Vokkaligas constitute a little less than 29 percent of the population of Mysore. In united Karnataka it has been estimated that a little more than 20 percent of the population may be Lingayat and between 13 and 14 percent Vokkaligas. It is clear that no one community will, therefore, be dominant, and any one

---

[41] *Report of the First Virashaivite Mahasabha* (Kannada); M. S. Kesair, *History of the Virashaivite Mahasabha*, 1933, p. 1; and Minchina Balli, *Karnataka Darshan* (Kannada), Dharwar, 1937, p. 31. Cited in a note prepared for the author by Neglur Ranganath, MA, BT, LLB, Dharwar, pp. 14-16. For a good description of Brahman-Lingayat relations see Basaraj Kattimani, *Janivara Shivadara* (Brahman Thread-Lingayat Thread), 1947.

[42] "A note on the Kannada portions of Anantapur District," Karnatak Ekeekaran Mahasamiti, in *Replies and Memorandum to the Linguistic Provinces Commission by the Representatives and Associations of Madras-Karnataka, 1948*, All-Karnataka Unification Sangh, Mangalore, p. 110.

section can be reduced to the status of a minority if other groups combine against it. . . . It is not unnatural in these circumstances for those who expect to be reduced in their relative position to view the proposed change with disfavor.[43]

While granting, however, that it was "not entirely un-understandable" for the Vakkaligas to see a specter of rampant Virashaivism, the Commission recommended that all things considered Karnataka should be formed.

Immediate personal clashes for control of a unified Karnataka Congress organization were unavoidable. One claimant to power, Mysore's Vakkaliga Chief Minister K. Hanumanthaiah, was challenged and eventually displaced by Lingayat S. Nijilingappa, veteran leader of Congress forces in the Kannada areas outside of Mysore. Moreover, a factional division within Mysore's Vakkaligas themselves raged between Hanumanthaiah and a rival whose victory over Hanumanthaiah in a 1954 intraparty fight created a schism between the ministerial and party Congress organizations in the state. So virulent did the Lingayat-Vakkaliga controversy become that little effort was made to keep it behind the scenes. At a 1953 conference advocating united Karnataka, the presiding officer referred openly to "these fears of communities and sections."[44] The Vakkaliga stake in the status quo was only too obvious, wrote *Times of India* Editor D. R. Mankekar, and "thus we find once again, on lifting the linguistic cloak, casteism and love of office grinning at us."[45]

But at stake in the Lingayat-Vakkaliga rivalry is not only the power of Virashaivism and political patronage in all its many forms. At bottom it is the economic gain expected to follow the establishment of a beachhead in government that motivates caste political rivalries, especially at a time when widening economic opportunity in India coincides with an increasingly active government economic role. For example,

[43] *Report of the States Reorganization Commission*, Manager, Government of India Press, Delhi, 1955, p. 91.
[44] Presidential Address, K. R. Karanth, *Report*, Second session, Akhand Karnataka Rajya Nirman Parishad, Hampi, Vijayanagar, December 3, 1953, S. P. Works Limited, Mangalore, p. 6.
[45] *Times of India*, June 29, 1955, p. 6. See also October 26, 1955, p. 6; and *New Age*, October 23, 1955, p. 4.

although the Lingayats are in numbers predominantly peasant-proprietors, the most influential group in Lingayat councils, next perhaps to the priesthood, is the sect's distinct trading caste, the Banajiga Lingayats. The Karnataka Pradesh Congress Committee complained in 1948 that there were "few capitalists" in Mysore and only three textile mills.[46] Even the negligible industry that did exist in Mysore had been promoted by the Maharaja of Mysore, and private initiative—to some extent Banajiga initiative—was far more evident in Lingayat-majority Kannada regions outside Mysore.[47] The Banajigas hope to keep their head start over a number of Gangadikar Vakkaligas who have entered urban trading and, indeed, to go beyond their traditional wholesale trade in a Lingayat-dominated Karnataka. In the former distribution of Lingayat strength between the multilingual states of Mysore, Bombay, and Hyderabad, the Banajigas faced competition on all sides from better-situated rivals—especially India's entrenched Marwari merchant castes of Rajasthan.

The Ubiquitous Marwari

It is Marwari power that looms before the potential local investor throughout India, not only in Karnataka but in virtually every linguistic region. In addition to the large-scale industrial power of well-known Marwari entrepreneurs such as G. D. Birla, Marwari moneylenders wield widely diffused power in far-flung villages and provincial towns. This peculiarly cosmopolitan economic position and the supra-regional social position that it reflects—so marked a contrast to the notion of a regional caste *gestalt*—is an unusually sensitive political factor in the Indian setting.

Until the early 19th century the Marwaris were merely petty local lenders. But British rule gave money a new importance in a crumbling village economy and enforced the debtor's obli-

[46] *Linguistic Provinces and the Karnataka Problem,* Karnataka Congress Committee, Hubli, 1948, p. 33.

[47] R. R. Diwakar, *Union Karnataka and Mysore,* 1948, cited in *Statistical Information on the Karnataka State in India,* Karnataka Pradesh Congress Committee, 1952. William McCormack, in *Social Styles in Dharwar Kannada* (a paper read at a panel on "Language and Culture Dynamics in South Asia," Chicago, 1957), discusses the economic power of the Banajigas.

gations by law. With rapidly inflated power and wealth the Marwaris branched out into trading. Buying up grain, butter, cloth, gold, and even opium in areas of plenty, they shipped their inexpensively gotten gain to areas of scarcity for resale at huge profits. By World War I, the Marwaris possessed both the economic leverage and the business sophistication to get a good share of war contracts and then to go on to speculate in shares and commodities. Since then Marwari power has climbed steadily. The British-erected "managing agency" structure of industrial organization, bringing a wide range of enterprises under a single managerial roof, was made to order for highly centralized family empires. In World War II, the Marwaris advanced into Indian banking, and by 1947 there were at least 16 jute mills, 54 cotton mills, 35 rice mills, 24 oil mills, 15 sugar mills, and 11 *dal* mills under Marwari ownership. So entrenched is this mercantile and industrial elite today that eight Marwari families, some of them related by marriage, hold 565 directorships in Indian industry, banking, and insurance.[48]

Although the term Marwari is often applied loosely, and can be used to signify all 4,276,514 speakers of the Marwari dialect of Rajasthani, it most accurately describes members of certain Vaisya castes native to the Marwar area of Rajasthan. Ninety percent of the Marwaris belong to three specific caste groups, Oswals, Agarwals and Maheshwaris, and most trace family lines to two particular Marwar towns, Nawalgarh and Pilani. Some subsects of the Oswals and Agarwals were converted to Jainism in the 16th century. But all these caste groups claim common descent from certain Rajput kings, which gives them, according to one authority, a stronger bond of unity than is usually found among other castes of the same *varna*. This common mystique of Rajput descent has produced a chosen-people complex, "a strong sense of astrological destiny."[49] Cutting across all the

[48] Bhimsen Kodia, *The Marwari Community in India* (Hindi), cited in D. R. Gadgil, *Notes on the Rise of the Business Communities in India*, p. 18. See also D. R. Gadgil, "Indian Economic Organization," in *Economic Growth: Brazil, India, Japan*; M. M. Mehta, *Combination Movement in Indian Industry*, Friends Book Depot, Allahabad, 1952, p. 29, and *Structure of Indian Industries*, Popular Book Depot, Bombay, 1955.

[49] Harry A. Millman, "The Marwari, a Study of a Group of the Trading Castes of India" (MA thesis, University of California, 1955, p. 4).

castes is the horizontal dividing line between so-called *bisas* or descendants of princes and princesses, and *dasas* or descendants of princely unions with handmaidens of princesses. Thus when one of the Maheshwari Birlas married in 1922 into one of the caste's *dasa* families, the Kolwars, it was only the proud self-confidence of the powerful Birla family that forbade his out-casting.

Wherever the Marwaris go in India, the ties that bind remain indissoluble under the impact of the strongest regional solvents. Acharya Vinoba Bhave scolded Marwari traders whom he encountered dwelling in a world of their own within the Tamil town of Erode:

> You carry on trade and business in Tamilnad. There must also be many Tamil people doing business who are similar to you in ways of thinking and living. When you live in Tamilnad and are going to live here, what is the propriety in looking for a husband or a wife for your children in Marwar, nearly a thousand miles away?[50]

This tightly knit solidarity, tight even by the standards of the Hindu social order, is especially important for a community that operates on a much more thoroughly cosmopolitan scale than other prominent business communities, such as the Gujarati *banias* or the Parsis. "Though they are found especially concentrated in certain regions," comments D. R. Gadgil, "Marwaris are more generally spread over the whole country than any other group of business communities"—even as village money-lenders.[51]

---

[50] *Bhoodan*, November 14, 1956, p. 3. See also B. R. Agarwala, "Caste and Joint Family in a Mobile Mercantile Community," *Bombay University Sociology Bulletin*, September 1955, pp. 138-145.

[51] D. R. Gadgil, *Notes on the Rise of the Business Communities in India*, p. 6. In *Federating India* (Gokhale Institute of Politics and Economics, Poona, 1945, p. 96), Gadgil charges that British rule, "with its indifference to the disintegration of regional societies, has been favorable to the spread everywhere of aggressive non-indigenous moneylenders." See also Helen B. Lamb, "The role of business communities in the evolution of an Indian industrialist class," *Pacific Affairs*, June 1955 (reprinted by Economic Development Program, India Project, Center for International Studies, Massachusetts Institute of Technology, March 14, 1955). On p. 11, Mrs. Lamb notes that Marwari strength "is derived in part from the fact that the group is ubiquitous; it does business throughout all India and in this respect, the Marwari are quite unlike the Parsis and Gujaratis who have operated largely from their home base in Western India."

On the Indian prestige scales, business communities as a group rank near the bottom. The moneylender is the traditional symbol of avarice and greed, exacting interest seldom less than 25 percent, and often twice that high, from peasants who must borrow when grain is scarce—and prices high—only to repay at harvest time when prices are low.[52] For the dominant business community in most regions to maintain external pan-Indian connections that must loom overwhelming indeed in provincial eyes is, therefore, to add insult to injury. As an outsider, the Marwari is absolved from the restraints of customary regional business behavior. Nor does he make any pretense of sympathy for regional aspirations. The All-India Marwari Federation opposed linguistic reorganization,[53] and the Marwaris as a rule show only casual respect for the regional languages, stressing Hindi instead in school from the ages of five to fourteen and learning only enough of the regional languages to get along.[54] At the same time Marwaris buy up newspapers in the regional languages, controlling 23 percent of the readership in Maharashtra, 37 percent in Tamilnad, and 55 percent in Andhra.[55] Beyond Rajasthan, the Marwari is an outsider everywhere, a ready target for regional propagandists who link him with the central government. He is the *bete noire* not only of the rising local caste with its would-be entrepreneurs, but of all who are or have ever been in the toils of his usury. While he is more of an evil demon in some regions than in others, the Marwari (or the Gujarati *bania*) is, in almost all regions, the central villain in regionalist propaganda and a focal point of factionalism when he pursues local political power.[56]

[52] Frank J. Moore, "Peasants and Moneylenders: A Study of Short-Term Agricultural Credit in India" (Ph.D. dissertation, University of California, 1955, p. 67).

[53] *Times of India*, February 11, 1956, p. 3.

[54] Millman, *op.cit.*, describes Hindi instruction, p. 53, and the *Economic Weekly*, August 28, 1954, points out the utility of Hindi for all-India business intercourse.

[55] *Report of the Press Commission*, Part I, Manager of Publications, Delhi, 1954, p. 21.

[56] For references to the epithets leveled at the Marwaris Seth Govind Das and Brijlal Biyani in Congress factional in-fighting in Madhya Pradesh, see *Times of India*, December 28, 1954, p. 6, and *Hindustan Standard*, July 28, 1953, p. 3. The case of C. B. Gupta, U. P. Congress leader and member of a

With its proximity to the capital of Marwari and Gujarati power, Bombay City, and to both Gujarat and Rajasthan, Maharashtra even more than most regions looks on Marwaris and Gujaratis as a present danger and as prime scapegoat for its little developed economy. Bombay City, divided as it is between a Marathi-majority working class and Gujarati entrepreneurs, provides inflammable political tinder when regional politicians are in search of riots as they were in early 1956. In Maharashtra proper, what little industry does exist is controlled not within the region but from Bombay. For example, six out of seven of the mills in the Marathi industrial center of Sholapur are operated by Bombay managing agencies.[57]

Even in this center of anti-Brahman strife, the Marwari or Gujarati *sahukar* who lends money in rural Maharashtra is quite as much a villain to the impoverished villager as the Brahman himself. In the 19th century anti-Brahmanism did not divert Marathi hostility from the outside moneylenders then spreading over Maharashtra. The official post-mortem on the so-called Deccan riots of 1875 in Poona and Ahmednagar districts reported that "the Marwari *sahukars* were almost exclusively the victims of the riots, and in villages where *sahukars* of other castes shared the moneylending business with Marwaris, it was usual to find that the latter only were molested."[58] It was the Marwaris to whom the Maharashtra political leader S. S. More pointed immediately when the writer asked what could arouse the illiterate villager's passion for a Maharashtra linguistic state. More, one of the organizers of the region's Peasants and Workers

non-Marwari Vaisya caste, is described in *Hindustan Times*, October 25, 1953, p. 1, 2nd section, and *Delhi Express*, October 29, 1953, p. 1. Alleged Marwari influence in Bengal Congress affairs as a major election charge by P. C. Ghosh, state P.S.P. leader, is reported in *The Statesman*, February 1, 1957, p. 1. Even in their native Rajasthan, reports Phillips Talbot in his American Universities Field Staff letter dated March 12, 1957, p. 8, Marwaris active in the election campaigns were the "cause of some uncharitable comment."

[57] In the *Poona Daily News*, October 3, 1954, K. P. Joshi, President of the local Banks Association, also points to the small number of local banks in Maharashtra. See also E. R. Dhongde and L. B. Manikatti, "An inquiry into the economic conditions of Sydenham College students," *Sydenham College Magazine*, August 1954-March 1955, pp. 11-20, Table 15.

[58] Government of Bombay, *Report of the Committee on the Riots, 1875*, Government Central Press, Bombay, 1876, p. 23.

Party, political front for the Maratha caste, said that a separate Maharashtra

> would be in the interests of the peasants and workers, and they know it because the Marwaris are all over our countryside. They come from Rajasthan and they are moneylender, trader, and landlord all rolled into one. These people are the monetary sinews of the Congress in Maharashtra as well as elsewhere and they are regarded as some kind of foreign oppressors by the peasantry in my region. That is why they want them to go, and they feel they would have to go if we had Samyukta Maharashtra rather than the composite Bombay State where they can control the setup.[59]

Supporters of a united Maharashtra professed to see the fine Marwari hand behind the demand for separate statehood by Marathi-speaking Vidarbha, formerly the southwest corner of Madhya Pradesh. The powerful Maratha caste—39.1 percent of the population in the Desh or Maharashtra proper—comprises only 24 percent of Vidarbha, where it plays a poor second in Congress politics to a dominant faction led by a Marwari publisher. Pro-Maharashtra forces, said a *Times of India* report, maintain "that most of the so-called protagonists of Vidarbha are persons of non-Marathi origin and have been supporting bifurcation of the Marathi areas with ulterior motives of serving vested interests."[60] The ulterior motive—it did not need to be elaborated—was that Marwari power could go a long way in a small unit but would be swallowed up in Maharashtra by overall Maratha caste strength. Most Maratha leaders in Vidarbha supported a united Maharashtra, and when the States Reorganization Commission recommended a separate state, Maharashtra Congress leader N. V. Gadgil charged that "from the very minute of the report, land has been passing into the hands of capitalists who are rejoicing on the formation of Vidarbha."[61]

Gadgil's resentment of the Marwaris is so extreme that in a

[59] Interview with S. S. More, July 1, 1953. See also S. S. More, *Democracy Stabbed*, Nirmal Press, Poona, 1949, p. 10.

[60] November 3, 1955, p. 6. See also Maureen L. P. Patterson, Brahman Versus Non-Brahman Controversy in Maharashtra," term paper, University of Pennsylvania, November 12, 1951, p. 13, and Patterson, "Caste and political leadership in Maharashtra," pp. 1065-1067.

[61] *Times of India*, October 28, 1955, p. 5.

1952 Parliament debate he declared India could never progress economically without "abolishing the exploitation of the parasitic elements." At that point the Bengali Jan Sangh leader S. P. Mookerjee interjected: "Is that Maharashtra versus Gujarat?" Gadgil shot back: "It is versus Bengalis also. You are not free from that capitalistic insect. In due course, banking, insurance, trade and particularly wholesale trade must be taken over by the government."[62]

To say that Bengal does not enjoy freedom from the Marwaris was a masterpiece of understatement, for there is no single greater numerical concentration of Marwaris anywhere in India than in Calcutta. As Asia's biggest base for supplies to the Allied armies, Calcutta was the scene of a wartime bonanza. Chittaranjan Avenue in the heart of the city is a Marwari stronghold, and while Bengalis control the city's small business, Marwaris dominate the commodity exchanges, the stock market, real estate, industry, and even banking. It was only a moderate outburst of Bengali spleen for a former editor of Calcutta's *Hindustan Standard* to threaten in 1954 that "if monopoly capital and Hindi chauvinism are allowed to dominate the scene, we shall have to suffer further territorial disintegration of India that is Bharat."[63]

From a vantage point close to Bengal, the principal pamphleteer for a separate Mithila state in North Bihar complains that local trade "is mostly in the hands of people of the west, especially from Marwar. The inter-provincial or inter-district trade is generally handled by Marwaris, while retail redistribution is carried on by our poor *banias* who are dependent on their mercy." Not the local Maithili language, but Hindi, is used "in the shops run by Agarwals and Marwaris. Cotton textile has been our specialty from time immemorial. But the British asked us to stop our own manufacture and purchase our cloth from their Lancashire. Now under Delhi we are asked to pur-

[62] *Proceedings*, House of the People, December 17, 1952, col. 2612. For a similar outburst by Gadgil, see *Proceedings*, House of the People, December 14, 1955, col. 300.

[63] Dhirendranath Sen, *A Case for Linguistic States*, Uttarayan Limited, Calcutta, 1954, p. 9.

chase it from Ahmedabad and Bombay."[64] Similarly, in Orissa to the south of Calcutta, the princes and landlords organized in the Ganatantra Parishad attack Marwari power.[65]

But from the south, that most distant outpost of Marwari expansion, come the shrillest protests against alleged economic imperialism. When businessmen in the Telugu-speaking region celebrated the Silver Jubilee of the Andhra Chamber of Commerce, an analysis of local banking facilities in the Silver Jubilee volume bewailed the fact that most credit in Andhra "has been in the hands of Marwaris, who lend their own money."[66] Nehru, campaigning at Alleppey in Travancore-Cochin in 1951, saw a wall poster demanding: MARWARIS! GUJARATIS! GO HOME! "There would be a sensation," he exclaimed, "if somebody said in Delhi, 'Travancoreans quit!' The Central Secretariat is overflowing with them."[67] The Marwaris and Gujaratis have figured in the propaganda of all parties in Kerala, and one group identified with Syrian Christian merchants, the Kerala Socialist Party (a local group not connected with the national Socialist parties), made its major battle cry the expulsion of north Indian finance. "The central government just dances to the tune of millionaires like Dalmia, Birla, Singhania and Goenka," protested the KSP. "Each has got his own industrial pocket from where he wants to grow and spread."[68]

The industrially "underdeveloped" south as a whole suffers from an understandable economic persecution complex. South Indian business communities have reason to envy the ubiquitous Marwari—reason which even the record does not show, for the

[64] Lakshman Jha, *Mithila—A Union Republic*, p. 54. See also *Mithila Will Rise*, Mithila Mandal, Darbhanga, 1955, p. 20; and Mithila Socialist Party, *Constitution and Program*, Lakshman Jha, Chairman, p. 7, published by Mithila Socialist Party, Darbhanga, printed by Sudhakar Press, Darbhanga.

[65] *Policy Statement*, part 2, and *Economic Program* adopted by the executive committee, Ganatantra Parishad, Bhawani, Patna, March 29, 1951.

[66] *Andhra Chamber of Commerce Information Bulletin—Silver Jubilee Souvenir*, January 27, 1954, pp. 8, 12, 297.

[67] *The Pilgrimage and After*, A.I.C.C. Publication, 1952, p. 9.

[68] *Socialist Review*, January 1949, p. 2, published by Pouran Press, Ernakulam. The writer also discussed KSP policies with party leader Matthai Manjuran on September 10, 1952. The Communist weekly, *People's Age*, October 24, 1948, p. 5, attacked the KSP belief that "local capitalists want to industrialize Travancore, while the others want to prevent it."

record may show south Indian ownership of firms or banks that in fact depend on north Indian banking sources. For all their wealth next to most south Indians, the Chettiar money-lender or the Naidu landowner cannot begin to compete with the big Marwari operator. The Naidus and Chettiars moved into cotton trading, then ginning, and finally textile milling to put the Tamil center of Coimbatore on the Indian industrial map.[69] But there are few Coimbatores. As moneylenders, traders, and financiers,[70] the Chettiars especially are in direct competition with the Marwaris, and the Marwari head start is so great as to be almost overpowering. It is not surprising that jealous Tamil entrepreneurs risk substantial funds in a political cause that can ennoble their pursuit of private interest with ringing universal slogans.

The Brahman and the Bania

The cause that serves this purpose for the Tamil industrialists is the so-called "Blackshirt" movement, composed of two kindred groups, the Dravida Kazagham or Dravidian Federation, and the Dravida Munnetra Kazagham or Dravidian Progressive Federation. Founder E. V. Ramaswami Naicker, known as Periyar or Great Sage, left his post as Tamilnad Congress secretary in 1922 to join the anti-Brahman Justice Party when he lost out in a bid for party leadership. After he narrowly defeated the Brahman candidate for the presidency, a Brahman leader allegedly moved a no-confidence motion before Periyar could take office—"only because he is not a Brahman," as one of his defenders charged.[71] For more than twenty years Periyar then led the Justice Party's parliamentary efforts in behalf of non-Brahman representation in government and schools. By the

[69] James J. Berna, S.J. ("Entrepreneurship in Madras State," Ph.D. thesis, Columbia University, 1958, p. 39) describes the emergence of Coimbatore first as a textile center and, more recently, as a center for engineering and other industries.

[70] Allene Masters, "The Chettiars," *Population Review*, Journal of the Indian Institute for Population Studies, January 1957, p. 22, citing twenty subcastes within the Chettiars, refers to the Nattukottais as the major moneylending subcaste and the "most influential" of the Chettiars.

[71] "The Congress is a Brahman Dominated Organization—Views of an Experienced Person," *Objectives of the Dravida Kazagham*, Dravida Kazagham, Madras, 1949, p. 36.

1945 conference of the party at Salem he had decided to found a more militant mass organization, the Dravida Kazagham. Periyar maintained that the non-Brahmans in Tamilnad, constituting as they do 97 percent of the population, should not be called "non-Brahmans" at all but should have a positive identity as members of a Dravidian nation entitled to sovereign independence from the Indian Union. On the eve of Indian Independence he warned that "we must guard against a transference of power from the British to the Aryans."[72] Members were enjoined to sign a pledge to support separation from the Indian Union. With the birth of the Kazagham, the Dravidian movement adopted the black shirt as its trademark. "Members of the Kazagham should wear black shirts whenever possible," the Constitution said, "as a symbol of the present day downtrodden condition of the Dravidians."[73]

But Periyar's popularity suffered a disastrous blow in 1949 when, at the age of 72, he married a 28-year-old girl, providing a pretext for his ambitious lieutenant, C. N. Annadurai, to secede with his followers to found the Dravida Munnetra Kazagham. Today Annadurai is the dynamic force in the Dravidian movement. Although a member of the Mudaliar caste, he deliberately gives his movement a proletarian flavor, orienting his appeal not to such prosperous non-Brahman communities as his own or the Vellala[74] landowners (commonly known by their title of Pillai), communities that had been Periyar's mainstay, but even more to the non-Brahman masses—the rank and file Nadars, Maravars, and Adi-Dravida untouchables. Annadurai's admirers exaggerate when they call him "the Dravidian Mao," but there is no doubt that this powerful orator is the single most popular mass figure in the region.[75]

72 *The Hindu*, February 11, 1946, p. 4.
73 "Aims and Constitution of the Dravida Kazagham," *Our Aim*, Dravida Kazagham, Madras, 1950.
74 The Vellalas go to great lengths to demarcate their own antecedence from lesser non-Brahmans, and historian M. Arokiaswami (in "Origin of the Vellalas," *Journal of Indian History*, April 1955, p. 25) stresses that the caste originated as the Velir chieftains of Sangam times.
75 See A. S. Venu, *Life of Annadurai*, Kalai Manram, Madras, 1953, entirety; *Hindustan Times*, September 6, 1953, p. 8; and T. C. Ganesan, "C. N. Annadurai," *Swatantra*, September 10, 1953, p. 20.

The fact that the Dravidian movement is essentially a social protest of the Tamil masses against Brahmans and even elite non-Brahmans at the top of the caste hierarchy makes it no less serviceable as a channel for protest against alleged north Indian economic imperialism. Indeed, as an alliance of aggrieved Tamil castes, the Dravidian movement typifies the political potential of regional caste groups united behind a catch-all slogan against a "foreign" scapegoat. In the case of the Tamil non-Brahmans, the intruders who impinge on the domain of the true indigenous inhabitants of the region are the Brahman—an Aryan fifth columnist—and the northern trader. Both symbolize the cosmopolitan elements of a Hindu social order in which regional subcastes hold a strong sense of their own local interests and identity. The Dravidians, charges A. S. Venu, confront a new Indian imperialism with two faces: "a peculiar combination of the Brahman and the Bania, of orthodoxy and avarice, of Manu and the Mammon."[76]

The Brahman as a symbol of Dravidian protest is actually the entire Hindu social order in which the Tamil non-Brahman sees himself placed at the very bottom of the scale. To comprehend the depth of this racial complex it is necessary first to consider the integral importance of color throughout India in the very concept of caste. The caste hierarchy stands on color, as it has since the earliest Sanskrit dicta in which even the word *varna*, for the fourfold division of Brahman, Kshatriya, Vaisya, and Sudra, literally means color. There are in India's ethnic kaleidoscope Brahmans who are darker than non-Brahmans, but the caste hierarchy descends in a general sense from a fair Brahman downward. Though the color line that marks off Hindu from Hindu is a silent, elusive fact of life in India, it is a fact nonetheless, and one that is less elusive than usual when marriages are arranged. With fair skin so highly prized, it is a comedown indeed to marry beneath one's color.

---

[76] A. S. Venu, *Dravidasthan*, Kalai Manram, Madras, 1954, p. 20. For almost identical language in the context of Maharashtra (language employed by a political scientist, not a propagandist), see S. V. Kogekar, "Bombay," *The Indian General Elections: 1951-52*, S. V. Kogekar and R. L. Park, eds., Popular Book Depot, Bombay, 1956, p. 34: "The opposition to the Brahman and the Baniya— the scapegoats for all evils in the land—had a ready appeal in the rural areas against the background of the anti-Brahman movement in Maharashtra."

Inspired by a plea from Chakravarti Rajagopalachari for marriages free from color dictates, the *Hindustan Times* once asked with the delicate understatement of the rhetorical question:

Do our young men, in pursuit of beauty (often judged by the color of one's skin), refuse to marry dark girls and thereby wreck many a home? There is no disguising the fact that tendency is there among young men. . . . This stupid 'color prejudice' which is working havoc in society is, in Mr. Rajagopalachari's view, 'a vital matter and not a joke.' . . . The stupid craze for mere color is capable of ruining not only individual lives but national destinies.[77]

The color line not only divides Indian from Indian and North from South, but cuts off Indians from other colored peoples. The fact that a pyramid of color snobbery stands in the midst of the Hindu social structure inevitably complicates Hindu relations with Negroid races. Certainly neither the American nor African Negro finds his contact with the high-caste Hindu to be a joyous festival of racial solidarity. The upper-caste Hindu who traces his history back to the same racial roots as Western white peoples lays down a psychological barrier before the Negro as solid as it is without malice. The Reverend James Robinson, a New York Negro minister who visited India in 1951, "vehemently criticized Indian students in America," according to one account, "for not mixing with Negroes and failing to study their problems of racial segregation."[78] An American Negro residing in India as a CARE official wrote in a local newspaper that in United States universities, "Indian students rarely socialize with Negro students. . . . At one of the largest and most famous midwestern universities . . . the Indian students' social aloofness was a topic of constant conversation among Negro students who found great friendliness among the Chinese, Japanese, and Korean students." Within India, he added, "one finds color prejudice operative in the most blatant manner among the Indians themselves."[79] In his study of American images of China and India, Harold R. Isaacs found that

[77] *Hindustan Times* (*Evening News*), June 14, 1953, p. 2; see also *Hindustan Times,* February 11, 1954, for an account of a play, *Hum Hindustani,* based on the theme of a Punjabi-Tamil marriage.
[78] *Indian Express,* October 20, 1951, p. 1.
[79] Letter from C. Sumner Stone, Jr., in *Mail,* Madras, January 24, 1957, p. 6.

American Negro images of India were often resentful recollections of Hindu color prejudice. One Negro who had visited India recalled "arrogant" light-skinned Punjabis in Delhi who "would always refer to South Indians in a sarcastic manner . . . contemptuous of them because they were so black."[80] African students in India have publicly objected to discriminatory treatment. In February 1955, five Indian Government scholarship students from Rhodesia, Uganda, Nyasaland, and Kenya told the Delhi Rotary Club that the group had suffered "immense psychological torture" through constant discourtesies. "If India is against colonialism," said one, "it should not discriminate against colonials of darker hue."[81] A leading editor hastily reassured the Africans that the color complex in India was merely a hangover of the soon-to-die caste system.[82]

The Hindu posture toward Negroes has often been explained by a strict caste-outcaste analogy in which the Negro is a dark-skinned equal of the untouchable and therefore instinctively shunned. But the problem is not that simple. The caste Hindu intellectual is a bundle of contradictions. On the one hand, he believes that in the present period of world history all colored peoples are in the same joint relationship to the white West— which must therefore be confronted jointly. With white overlordship in India still a painful memory, he transfers a portion of his hunger for national self-respect into an emotional united front with the entire colored world. A lynching in Georgia or a stoning in Little Rock does indeed seem to be a direct attack on him.

At the same time, however, he sets himself in a distinct class apart. He takes pride in the fact that the early Aryan migrants who established Hindu society fanned out of a racial core that was neither Negroid nor Mongoloid. He looks back to Hindu golden ages without parallel in the heritage of most other colored peoples. In the clash of these opposite psychological currents, he wonders whether he really deserves to suffer a fate in common with other colored peoples who have no racial

[80] *Scratches on Our Minds*, John Day and Company, New York, 1958, p. 287.
[81] *Times of India*, February 5, 1955, p. 1.
[82] *Times of India*, February 11, 1955, p. 3.

common ground with the dominant nations and who never were on top of the international heap. A vague exasperation tinges his world view, and inevitably, his view of dark-skinned "inferiors" in his own society.

The late Unni Nayar reflected southern sensitivity on this score when he attributed this irreverent verse to an unusually dark nobleman of Malabar:

> Brahman the creator, absent minded
> or in his cups
> while making me,
> tilted the entire bottle of ink
> into the clay,
> the wretch![83]

For the Tamil non-Brahmans, perhaps the darkest of the dark in the subcontinent, the color line built into Hindu society sets up a barrier before not only the Brahman but all fairer-skinned India. The Dravidian movement exploits this color line, pointing to the Brahman as the archetype of a still greater enemy, Hinduism itself, which by its very nature underwrites color bias. "A Hindu in the present concept may be a Dravidian," declares A. S. Venu, "but a Dravidian in the real sense of the term cannot and shall not be a Hindu."[84] The Dravidian argument is based on the very substance of Hindu mythology, and *The Ramayana*, so proudly hailed as a force for synthesis, becomes the basic text cited to establish Aryan iniquity. In Dravidian propaganda the southward march of Rama to the lair of the evil King Ravana, abductor of Sita, is nothing less than the allegorical story of the triumphal Aryan progress over the original Dravidian inhabitants of India. To many a non-Brahman Tamil, the legions of monkeys Rama encounters in the southern jungles appear to be none other than the Dravidians. Thus the epic is a racial insult before half told. The Dravidian movement rewrites *The Ramayana* to cast Ravana as a Dravidian hero repelling Rama, the invading Aryan generalissimo. Touring dramatic troupes parody the epic, improvising with

[83] *My Malabar*, p. 3.
[84] *Dravidasthan*, p. 13.

day-to-day allusions to local personalities and events. When Rajagopalachari, a Brahman, was Chief Minister of Madras in 1954, he ordered police to search out the troupes, which were forced to perform in clandestine gatherings, and even took to the All-India Radio to mobilize a "Ramayana Protection Committee."[85]

Like the dramatic troupes, Dravidian pamphlets "exposing" Kamban's Tamil Brahman version of *The Ramayana* dwell on alleged obscenities in the original Valmiki version. The Brahmans, it is said, fancified Valmiki for Tamil consumption. Dravidian propaganda denies that the movement opposes religion as such, maintaining that it is Hinduism, not the new Dravidian faith, which desecrated God. For literally hundreds of pages, Dravidian pamphlets catalog hoarded wealth in the temples and alleged lusts of the Brahmans and their gods and goddesses. Thus, we are told, Valmiki's fine print betrays the Brahmans of Rama's day as liquor addicts and meat eaters while the non-Brahmans exalted virtuous conduct.[86] Rama, Sita, and Dasaratha, far from being heroic, were cunning, immoral, and deceitful. The very basis of *The Ramayana's* plot, Rama's dismay at Sita's abduction, is questioned in one reminder that Sita actually accused Rama of past infidelity in pleading that he take her with him in his forest exile.[87] Valmiki allegedly chronicles the cruelty of a Brahman who deliberately plotted the death of a Sudra for having dared to do penance in the sacred forest.[88] Worst insult of all, Valmiki traces the origin of castes to the cow, with the Brahmans deriving from the bovine face and the Sudras from the backside.[89]

In addition to lampooning the Hindu pantheon, the Dravidian movement challenges even the right of the Brahmans to preside at weddings and other Hindu ceremonial functions.

[85] *Times of India*, September 29, 1954, p. 6, and December 3, 1954, p. 1, and *The Hindu*, March 8, 1954, p. 6.

[86] Chandrasekhar Pavalar, *Ramayana Araichi—Ayodhya Kandam (Researches into Ramayana)*, Kudiarasu Pathipakam, Madras, 1950, pp. 35, 218.

[87] Chandrasekhar Pavalar, *Ramayana Araichi—Bala Kandam*, Kudiarasu Pathipakam, Madras, 1949, p. 75.

[88] Chandrasekhar Pavalar, *Guana Suriyan*, Kudiarasu Pathipakam, Madras, 1951, p. 130.

[89] *Ramayana Araichi—Bala Kandam*, p. 40.

Periyar himself barnstorms the Tamil countryside, performing so-called "self-respect" marriage ceremonies for non-Brahmans— ceremonies with neither the pomp of the usual Hindu cere- mony (boy and girl need only to be introduced in the presence of relatives to be pronounced duly wed) nor the high fee exacted by the Brahman priests. He wages intermittent idol-smashing campaigns, inciting wholesale destruction of images of Hindu gods such as Lord Krishna.[90] In some Tamil centers non-Brah- man *maths* have been established with their own *adipathis* or priests. The anthropologist Kathleen Gough found in an in- tensive study of one Tamil village that the local Mother God- dess was a non-Brahman deity, worshipped even by Brahmans second to their own deities and regarded as an aspect of Shakti, but "clearly not one of the Sanskrit pantheon." Her temple straddles two non-Brahman streets in the center of the village, and she is worshipped daily by a non-Brahman priest.[91]

Sanskrit stands as a rigid linguistic dividing line between the standard Hinduism common to the cosmopolitan Brahmans, irrespective of region, and regional Hindu forms that arise from the life of regional subcaste groups. In the eyes of the Tamil Brahmans, charges one prominent non-Brahman intellectual,

all the non-Brahman communities of Tamilnad constitute the Sudra caste of the Aryan system. Tamil is therefore, in effect, the language of the Sudras, which the Brahmans had perforce to adopt for their mundane intercourse with the Sudras amongst whom they lived. It is not that the Brahmans are so crude as to broadcast such views openly, but this is the subtle but unmistakable assumption which underlies their attitude to the Tamils and their language.[92]

Most Brahmans deliberately attempt to suppress Tamil, runs this accusation, and it was past Brahman chicanery that dis- placed Tamil as the language of Hindu liturgy in Tamilnad. Tamil devotional songs of the Alwar and Nayanar saints could not be sung until recently in Tamilnad temples until the Brah- mans had finished their worship. Now some non-Brahmans,

90 For example, see *Delhi Express*, September 28, 1952, p. 1.
91 E. Kathleen Gough, "The Social Structure of a Tanjore Village," *Village India*, University of Chicago Press, 1955, p. 48.
92 A. Senthamilan (pseudonym for A. Subbiah, prominent Madras banker), "Cultural Conflicts in Tamilnad," *Quest*, October 1955.

including some who do not support the Dravidian movement, want to restore Tamil to the temples. It was news throughout India when the Sire of the Kunrakudi *math*, more popularly known as Kunrakudi Adigalar, came out on the side of a Tamil liturgy in 1955. The Kunrakudi Adigalar and his allies, reported the *Times of India*, "have come forward to deliver the Gods from the unintelligible Sanskrit rigmarole showered on them during Puja."[93] If the *Archanas* are recited in a language understandable to the average devotee, argued the Adigalar, there would be no anti-God demonstrations in the state and even leaders of the Dravidian movement could be won over to Hinduism. "Surely," he said, "the Gods will understand Tamil as much as they understand Sanskrit." A Dravidian tract similarly complained that "there is no meaning in worshipping Tamil gods, in Tamilnad, in a north Indian language."[94] But another Tamil religious leader, the Sire of the Ahobila *math*, passionately defended "God's own language," and a conference of orthodox priests protested against any change in the liturgy. If Tamilnad's temples and pilgrimage centers should to any substantial extent cut off their Sanskrit bonds with north India, their cosmopolitan place in pan-Indian Hindu culture would clearly decline in importance, and in time it is indeed possible, as the orthodox insist, that pilgrim traffic from north to south would dwindle.

But to the non-Brahman masses it is both plausible and eminently comprehensible to make of "Sanskrit rigmarole" and the priests who chant it a simple grim explanation for a host of grievances. When a political movement finds powerful evocative symbols it summons them for all their worth, and the Dravidian movement has discovered a double-barrelled power in those twin villains, "the Brahman and the *bania*." The discovery is doubly useful for its simultaneous appeal to the masses and to such leaders of regional subcaste interests as the Chettiars in Coimbatore. First the movement bewails the south's scant industry, charging that the Marwari powers behind the throne in New Delhi want to keep the south as their own private

[93] May 20, 1955, p. 6.
[94] Kunrathol, *Jeevavukku Bathil (Answer to Jeeva)*, Madras, 1954, p. 18.

preserve. The benighted south has simply passed from British hands to still worse Marwari tyranny. Next, the threat of Hindi is laid to "the Brahman-Bania government."[95] When it comes right down to it, in fact, the Marwaris are to blame for everything:

The cloth market is monopolized by the North. Nothing need be said about the moneylending business. It is a matter of common knowledge that north Indians who were a few settled at Sowcarpet are today spread all over the Presidency. . . . The helpless peasant who loses his only hut and the small bit of land to the Marwari moneylender . . . remembers to the end of his life that a north Indian deprived him by unfair means of his food and shelter. To him all north Indians are the same, be they moneylenders or cloth shop owners. The petty retail trader, who winds up his provisions store—owing to uneconomic competition in the shape of price reduction from formidable north Indian cartels—finds later that they have raised commodity prices to a very high level. . . . Moneylending has resulted in many south Indians becoming insolvent. Sometimes the accrued high rate and unfair interest has rendered south Indian families close to ruination. In fact north Indian migration is the root cause for the present downtrodden state of south Indian society.[96]

The Dravidian movement champions the cause of the Chettiar or the Naidu who claims discrimination at the hands of central government economic czars. Tamil Brahman bureaucrats in league with the Marwaris, charge Dravidian leaders, demand bribes before granting the legitimate rights of non-Brahman businessmen. On one occasion permission is refused in New Delhi to "the great industrialist, Mr. G. D. Naidu of Coimbatore, to start a radio factory and a blade factory of his own."[97] Another Coimbatore industrialist wants to import equipment from Japan to begin a lamp factory but allegedly cannot get import clearance from a government board friendly to the existing Marwari-controlled lamp industry.

95 A. S. Venu, *Dravidasthan*, p. 34.
96 S. Vedaratnam, *A Plea for Understanding: A Reply to the Critics of the Dravidian Progressive Federation*, Vanguard Publishing House, Conjeevaram, 1951, p. 33.
97 A. S. Venu, *op.cit.*, p. 51.

New Claims to Power

Inevitably any government with the economic ambitions of the Indian Government will be caught in such political cross-fire. For the increasingly important economic role of government at both national and state levels inevitably shifts the competition of regional interest groups from the stock exchanges to the bureaucratic and political arena. Government not only controls the imports needed by would-be private investors but government influence pervades all industrial expansion in India through the central and state finance corporations that loan capital for new enterprises. Who is to sit on the directorates of these corporations? Who is to get the loans? Who is to assure day-to-day economic justice on the part of the twenty industrial enterprises controlled by the central government but organized and managed as private limited companies?[98] With contracts big and small to be allocated, contracts which can make millionaires overnight, it is no small matter who sits on government boards. For the modest operator, it is no small matter who controls the local irrigation and electric-generating systems linked to hydroelectric development; who decides the distribution of power and water, and who sets the rates. Clearly, in the pursuit of economic gain, the rising local caste group has a heavy stake in cornering political power.

This rising local caste group may be the *avant garde* of a region's own Vaisya caste—aware that the moneylender must either gamble some capital in industrial investment or clear the field for others. Or it may even be a Brahman group, as in Maharashtra, where the Chitpavan Brahmans of Poona have turned more and more to industry. But it is most likely of all to be non-Brahman peasant-proprietor castes such as the Kammas in Andhra or the Vakkaligas in Karnataka. In the wealthy upper crust of the 45.7 million agricultural owner-cultivators recorded in the Census lies great dormant economic power, grown fat through the high prices of foodstuffs, sometimes black market,

[98] George B. Baldwin ("Public Enterprise in Indian Industry," *Pacific Affairs*, June 1957, p. 11) observes that it "is hard to understand" why the private limited company—"this private form of public enterprise"—should have been selected in India.

132

and through compensation payments for acreage appropriated under land reform. In some localities this economic power has been multiplied many times through moneylending to poorer peasants, tenants, and agricultural laborers, combined with wholesale marketing of the borrower's produce on a commission basis.[99] "Dominant" peasant-proprietor castes, as the Backward Classes Commission observed, "may not belong to the upper castes in the religious or orthodox hierarchy, but by their wealth and prestige they dominate the whole village scene. Brahmans and Banias have to bend before their will."[100] To the Brahmans the Kammas or Vakkaligas are Sudras, but the "dominant" castes themselves often claim past tribal military glories and demand respect as Kshatriyas[101] corresponding to their antecedence and their economic power. High prices for food and cash crops during World War II made many peasant-proprietor castes prosperous indeed, and for such fortunates as the Kammas, presiding over productive delta land, these were bonanza years not only in cash but in new political capital.

Maurice Zinkin points out that in most Asian countries the businessman is not an integral part of the social structure but rather

a member of a close-knit small community within the country itself, a Marwari or a *bania* in India, a Khoja or a Bohra in Pakistan. As the great peasant communities rise to power—and their rise to power is the inevitable long-run result of adult suffrage, as one can already see in India—they are liable more and more to want a share of the profits and jobs of business, either through special privileges in licenses and permits or through more nationalization or through state-assisted cooperation.[102]

[99] W. C. McCormack ("Factionalism in a Mysore Village," *Leadership and Political Institutions in India*, Richard L. Park and Irene Tinker, eds., p. 42) cites the example of Morsralli village in Bangalore District, Mysore State. See also Frank S. Moore, *op.cit.*, p. 64, and *Report of the Backward Classes Commission*, Vol. I, Government of India Press, 1956, p. xxiii.

[100] *Report of the Backward Classes Commission*, p. xxiii.

[101] See K. M. Panikkar, *Caste and Democracy*, Leonard and Virginia Woolf, Hogarth Press, London, 1933, p. 11, and *Hindu Society at Cross Roads*, Asia Publishing House, Bombay, 1955, p. 9.

[102] Maurice Zinkin, *Development for Free Asia*, Essential Books, 1956, p. 223. "The arrival of large numbers in state assemblies belonging to the middle peasantry" is noted in W. H. Morris-Jones, *Parliament in India*, University of Pennsylvania Press, 1957, p. 127.

It is the younger sons of these peasant communities who comprise the most significant segment of the rising regional language intelligentsia, the ever more insistent claimants to intellectual and political leadership in the state capitals and in New Delhi. They know well that their entire future is at stake in such seemingly minor matters as what language is used for a civil service examination or a university lecture. Embodying as they do a pivotal section of the regional population, that locally-entrenched and in many cases numerically-strong section which is the magnet of the region's *gestalt,* these peasant-proprietor castes see themselves as the front-runners of the rise of the region as a whole. In so doing they exemplify the peasant-proprietors of any country and any time, whose insularity and low mobility make them, as Carl J. Friedrich put it twenty years ago, "the compact mass which stands behind uncompromising, emotional nationalism . . . in the sense of love for their own country or region."[103]

Today the peasant-proprietors wield the economic power which makes them the most insistent immediate claimants to political and economic power. But with every passing year new claims are made as other communities begin to sense their potential.[104] As progress seeps deeper and deeper, more and more non-Brahman communities that do not own land, laboring communities submerged until now, will assert their new economic and political strength. Just as the growth of town life gave the medieval serf a route of escape from his bondage to the landed gentry, so the Indian industrial revolution emancipates tenant farmers and migrant labor from their feudal attachment. In her case study of the Tamil village, Kumbapettai, Gough found that Brahman landowners had sold out one-third of the village land

[103] "The Agricultural Basis of Emotional Nationalism," *Public Opinion Quarterly,* April 1937, p. 60.

[104] Although he lumps proprietor and non-proprietor together, the Kamma leader N. G. Ranga lists six specific communities in *Outlines of National Revolutionary Path,* Hind Kitabs, Bombay, 1945, p. 54: "During the last fifty years, several castes like the Jats of the UP, Punjab and Rajasthan, the Bhumias of the UP and Bihar, the Gonds of the C.P., the Reddis, Kammas, and Telagas of Andhra, the Marathas of Maharashtra, the Nadars, Kallars, Maravas, and Vellalas of Tamilnad, the Thiyas of Malabar . . . and various other peasant, Harijan and working class communities have revolted against social degradation."

in the past twenty years; as a result 37 percent of all non-Brahman caste Hindus in the village no longer depend for their subsistence on Brahman landowners, and 78 percent of the Adi-Dravida untouchables no longer work as tied laborers for payment in kind.[105] Once off the land, the enterprising leadership in such submerged communities quickly makes itself felt in economic and political life.

The rise of regional caste lobbies is most noticeable in the south, where populous Kammas or Vakkaligas loom large within homogeneous linguistic regions. But even in Uttar Pradesh smaller castes that do not loom large separately in this sprawling unit can through coalitions find political strength. In Uttar Pradesh the motley alliance of lower castes known as "AJGAR" (A for Ahir cattle breeders, J for Jat peasants, G for Gadariya sheep breeders), which happens to be the Hindi word for python, twines its coils in and out of state political life.[106] In north Indian regions with greater homogeneity castes such as Bihar's Yadava cattle-breeders,[107] Gujarat's Patidars, and Saurashtra's Kada Kunbis and Lada Kunbis[108] function as compact regional lobbies.

In the clamorous competition that will accompany India's economic progress, the linguistic boundary to caste will reinforce the lines of economic rivalry, first within linguistic limits between contesting caste groups and, at the same time, across linguistic lines between regional caste lobbies whose interests overlap. On one side in this competition stands the rising local caste with its would-be entrepreneurs. Ranged in opposition may be the ubiquitous Marwari, who confronts competitors in all regions, or rivals from neighboring regions who happened to get a head start. If there will be no holds barred in this contest, it is not only because the rupture in the Brahman

[105] E. Kathleen Gough, "The Social Structure of a Tanjore Village," *op.cit.*, p. 36.

[106] AJGAR is mentioned in S. V. Kogekar and R. L. Park, "Uttar Pradesh," *The Indian General Elections: 1951-52*, p. 164. See also the description of AJGAR in *Report of the Backward Classes Commission*, Vol. I, p. xxii; and the *National Herald*, April 29, 1957, p. 8, which notes that 22 Ahirs were elected from predominantly Ahir constituencies in the 1957 elections.

[107] Kogekar and Park, *op.cit.*, p. 2.

[108] *Ibid.*, p. 16.

monopoly on education has opened the field to all comers. The struggle will be grim because both the newcomers and the past masters are all so rigidly set apart into contesting groups, groups which get their peculiar *esprit de corps* and will to win from religious sanctions. Perhaps, as the nationalist argues, the Hindu pantheon to which all castes must answer will exercise a saving cohesive force no outsider can grasp. Yet to the outsider one inescapable question remains: Will cohesion come in time? Sooner or later, a contest between social groups dissolves into a more diffuse contest as the clash of ambitious individuals and new economic lobbies overlaps social alignments. In time some of the new competitive economic lobbies may become national caste lobbies insofar as they represent the fusion and coalition of regional caste blocs. But the contest in India, if it dissolves at all, will dissolve later rather than sooner. In the decades immediately ahead the unity of India must withstand the centrifugal strain of a contest conducted more and more relentlessly according to the rival regional alignments built into Hinduism itself.

———— ∷Ә∗Ꮥ∷ ————

HISTORY will answer whether India's uniquely fragmented social order—divided first into linguistic regions and then at right angles into regional castes—was made to order for Communist exploitation or made to confound hopelessly the Marxist-Leninist scriptures. For their part the Indian Communists have proceeded on the assumption that social divisions are made to be exploited. Like all parties the Communists in any given region have either claimed the chauvinism of region and caste as their own or have lost out to others who have harnessed this elemental force stronger than party or ideology. But unlike other parties, the Indian Communists have not stumbled by mere accident of circumstance into their strategy. They have deliberately made it their business to become the political custodians of regional patriotism. It is a special concern of Communist Parties in all countries—beginning with the Soviet motherland—that the volatile "national question" shall serve rather than frustrate the cause.

On the day that Stalin died, Prime Minister Nehru, speaking in the Indian Parliament, recalled Indian Ambassador Sarvapalli Radhakrishnan's last call at the Kremlin only three weeks earlier. Stalin expressed himself, Nehru reported, in favor of peace. "He sent his good wishes to our country and to some of us. And it was interesting how he discussed with our Ambassador some of our cultural problems, showing a certain knowledge which was a little surprising. He discussed—and it may interest the House—the languages of India, their relationships, their parentage, their extent, and our Ambassador gave him such replies as he could on the subject."[1] To Indians Nehru's overtones were unmistakable, for to show too much interest in India's sensitive linguistic fragmentation is less "surprising"

[1] The text of Nehru's speech was issued by the Press Information Bureau, Government of India, March 6, 1953.

than suggestive of hostile divisive intentions. But hostile or not, Soviet consciousness of India's multilingual dilemma arises naturally out of the Soviet Union's own experience.

The Soviet Example

The Soviet state itself is a multilingual union of peoples,[2] and long before the Soviets the Czarist Empire traditionally asserted a vast dominion over non-Russian regions to the east and south. The Czars, in fact, behaved as unabashed Great Russian imperialists, banning printing in such highly developed non-Russian languages as Ukranian. Thus nationalist grievances spread among non-Russian minorities at the same time that socialist thinkers in Europe were wondering how to adjust to the sharpening national tensions in the Austro-Hungarian and Ottoman Empires. Marx and Engels could disregard the "national question," but as the twentieth century opened it was clear that socialism could continue this neglect only at its peril.

For most European social democrats it seemed enough to concede the right of all nations to self-determination but to suffice with a declaration, one step short of programmatic action. By the time the Bolsheviks faced up to the problem, however, non-Russian grievances were so acute that Lenin with his sense for tactics was quick to perceive that declarations were not enough. Though Lenin was a rigid doctrinaire in his fundamental assumptions, Richard Pipes has observed, he was also notably flexible in his choice of means. Once he recognized the utility of nationality as a weapon against the established order, he used it for all it was worth.

Lenin's emphasis on the national question was to culminate in a vital alliance between the Bolsheviks and the nationalists in critical stages of the Revolution. Pipes records that the Communists on the whole succeeded in winning nationalist support

[2] The latest official population figures, on the basis of the 16 "Union Republics," show a total 200,200,000, divided into 112.6 in Great Russians, 40.6 in Ukrainians, and these remaining components: Byelorussian 8; Uzbek 7.3; Kazakh 8.5; Georgian 4; Azerbaidzhan 3.4; Lithuanian 2.7; Moldavian 2.7; Latvian 2; Kirghiz 1.9; Tadzhik 1.8; Armenian 1.6; Turkmen 1.4; Estonian 1.1; and Karelo-Finnish .6. From *Naroduve khozyaistvo SSSR* (*The National Economy of the USSR*), Central Statistical Administration of the USSR, 1956, p. 18 (translated for the author).

when they most needed it, and in the Urals and the Northern Caucausus, it was the alliance between Communists and nationalists that "helped tip the scales in favor of the Soviet regime." It was only their inroads in the Rada or local nationalist assembly that enabled the Bolsheviks to seize the capital, Kiev, in the showdown struggle for the Ukraine.

Lenin looked on national tensions "as something to exploit, not something to solve," comments Pipes.[3] But he perceived that the very future of the new Soviet state depended on the successful integration of the non-Russian regions into the Union. It was Lenin who insisted on the most scrupulous treatment of national adjustments when the Revolution was being consolidated. Moreover, as early as 1922 Lenin perceived the importance that Soviet nationality policy would hold as a future propaganda symbol in Asia. "This is a world-wide question," he declared, "without exaggeration, a world-wide question. Here one must be archstrict. This applies to India, to the East; here it is necessary to be careful a thousand times over."[4] In a letter attacking "great Russian chauvinism," Lenin declared that it would be "unforgivable opportunism if on the eve of the emergence of the East, and at the beginning of its awakening, we should undermine our prestige there with even the slightest rudeness or injustice to our own minorities."[5] He thus took Stalin's side on the form of the new Soviet constitution at the Twelfth Party Congress in April 1923. Western-oriented Bolsheviks such as Rakhovsky and Bukharin wanted a constitution that would impress European onlookers, especially the Germans. But Stalin countered that it mattered much more to impress the East by giving proper constitutional status to Eastern peoples within the Soviet State who are "organically linked to India and China." Even the very name of the Soviet State was decided as "Union of Soviet Socialist Republics," rather than "Russian Union

[3] Richard L. Pipes, *The Formation of the Soviet Union*, Harvard University Press, 1954, p. 35.
[4] Z. Levina, "Great Role of V. I. Lenin in Organizing the Union of Soviet Republics," *Pravda*, July 11, 1955, cited in *Current Digest of the Soviet Press*, August 22, 1956.
[5] Cited in Pipes, *op.cit.*, p. 42.

of Socialist Republics," only on Stalin's initiative.[6] "The fact of the matter is," said Stalin, that

the whole East regards our union of republics as an experiment station. Either we shall, within the union, find a correct solution for the national problem in its practical application and establish truly fraternal relations and true collaboration between the peoples —in which case the entire East will see that our federation is the banner of its liberation, an advance guard, in whose steps it must follow—and that will be the beginning of the collapse of world imperialism; or we, the federation as a whole, shall commit errors, undermine the confidence of the formerly oppressed peoples in the proletariat of Russia, and deprive the union of republics of that power of attraction which it possesses in the eyes of the East—in which case imperialism will win and we shall lose.[7]

In a 1925 speech to Communist trainees for Asian organizing, a speech cited often by the Indian Communists ever since, Stalin looked ahead to an India in which many nations would emerge:

Now, India is talked about as one entity. But there can be hardly any doubt that in the case of a revolutionary upheaval in India, many hitherto unknown nationalities, each with its own language and its own distinctive culture, will emerge on the scene.[8]

From the very outset the Soviets have attempted to persuade Asians not only that "we solved the national question," but that indeed only the Marxist-Leninist-Stalinist scriptures are addressed to the special challenge of organizing for rapid economic development in a multilingual state. To a great extent the attractive power of the Soviet Union in Asia can be explained precisely in these terms. It is commonly said that the example of the undeveloped Soviet Union mobilizing its resources in the short space of forty years is compelling to Asians. But it is little recognized that the record of economic achievement is seen in

[6] Frederick C. Barghoorn, *Soviet Russian Nationalism*, Oxford University Press, 1956, pp. 33-34. See also Barghoorn, "Nationality Doctrine as a Weapon of Soviet Totalitarianism," a paper read at the convention of the American Political Science Association, Washington, September 1953.

[7] J. V. Stalin, *Sochineniia*, v, 236-238, 264-266, cited in Robert C. North and X. J. Eudin, *Soviet Russia and the East, 1920-27*, Stanford University Press, 1957, p. 62.

[8] S. Dimanshteiu, "Otnoshenie Marksizma-Leninizma K Voprosu Ob Assimiliapsii Natsional 'nostei," *Revoliutsiia I Natsional 'nosti*, No. 7, 1935, pp. 57-63 (translated for the author).

close conjunction with the fact that the Soviet Union, too, confronted the challenge of national consolidation that now faces the new multilingual states. Nor could the Soviets fail to know that their attractive power is derived in part from the multilingual nature of the Soviet state. It was natural for the Soviets with their own voluminous literature on nationality problems to perceive the uniquely sensitive importance of the multilingual composition of other states.

When multilingual states such as India and Indonesia were still under colonial rule the Soviets found special response to their claims. For as Morris Watnick writes, the Soviets could contrast their own national policy with the national subjugation intrinsic to colonialism. The multinational composition of the USSR enabled indigenous Communists "to confront their audience with the glaring disparity between the possibilities of ethnic equality and the actualities of Western arrogance and discrimination."[9] First Czechoslovakia, finally Hungary have raised profound doubts about Soviet respect for national rights. But the myth of Soviet nationality policy has outlived most others in the Soviet mythology in the West and seems destined to die hard as well in the East.

Soviet propagandists couple their claims on the treatment of national minorities with pretensions to benign international intentions, solemnly declaring that the USSR "regards as a sacred principle of its foreign and home policy the equality of the peoples, respect of their independence and national sovereignty."[10] Counter-propaganda within India to debunk the Soviet claims has come only from a few anti-Communist pamphleteers and such ideologically certain political leaders as Jayaprakash Narayan.[11] Only recently have anti-Communist

[9] Morris Watnick, "The Appeal of Communism to the Underdeveloped Peoples," *The Progress of Underdeveloped Areas*, Bert F. Hoselitz, ed., University of Chicago Press, 1952, p. 156.

[10] N. Matyushkin, "The October Revolution Ended National Oppression," *New Age*, New Delhi, November 20, 1955, p. 17.

[11] C. L. Gheevala provides a rare example of such anti-Communist pamphleteering in *Linguistic States and the Communist Approach*, Bombay Citizens Committee, 1954. Jayaprakash wrote in 1947 (*In The Lahore Fort*, Sahityalaya, Patna, 1947, p. 5) that centralized one-party rule made the rights of Soviet Republics mere "paper freedoms."

émigré groups directed propaganda to India. The Committee for the Liberation of Turkestan was a lonesome voice when it warned Indians in 1952 to look for ulterior motives when "the Soviet tiger in the skin of the Indian sheep demands even that the campaign to spread Hindi cease."[12] When a delegation of Kalmuks told of its plight in India, the Indian weekly *Janata* commented that in the "country of the big lie, perhaps the biggest lie was that of the independence of its component peoples in the sovereignty of the autonomous republics."[13] But the lie continues to attract many believers in India, so deep has it penetrated the national intellect.

In analyzing the impact of the West in Asia, K. M. Panikkar maintains that from the very beginning the Soviet Union has approached Asians in the name of its dedication to national justice. The "well-defined national policy" of the Revolution, says Panikkar,

had an irresistible appeal to struggling dependencies, colonies and semi-colonial countries in Asia . . . Lenin and Stalin proclaimed the equality and sovereignty of the peoples of Russia and the right to freedom of development of national minorities. This was indeed an explosive statement, and all the nations of Asia struggling for freedom heard it with a new hope. This emphasis on national self-determination and ethnic separateness of minorities had an immense effect in shaping opinion in Asia during the next quarter of a century.[14]

In 1932, a Soviet writer said that the Soviets had already resolved national tensions, and "all the colonies, in particular India, can see from the results of the fourteen years of existence of the Soviet Union what can be achieved."[15] Nehru returned from his 1936 Soviet visit to report that "the problem of minorities has been largely solved there,"[16] and twenty years later Nehru still

12 A. Uluktuk, "On the Soviet Tiger in the Skin of the Indian Sheep," *Turkeli*, Review of the Committee for the Liberation of Turkestan, May-June, 1952, nos. 5-6 (translated for the author).

13 May 29, 1955, p. 15. See also International Peasant Union, *Communist Conspiracy in India*, Washington, 1951, p. 11.

14 *Asia and Western Dominance*, George Allen and Unwin Limited, London, 1953, p. 250.

15 *Anti-Imperialist Review*, March-June, 1932, Vol. 1, Nos. 4-5, p. 253.

16 Jawaharlal Nehru, *Soviet Russia*, Chetana, Bombay, 1949, p. 83.

ranked "the handling of the language issue"[17] as one of the major items of interest on his return visit in 1955.

Soviet propaganda systematically reiterates the characteristic contention of *Soviet Land,* organ of the New Delhi Soviet Embassy, that "the Soviet state differs radically from capitalist multinational states in each of which one nation dominates, while others are subjugated."[18] The Embassy's weekly mimeographed publication, *News and Views of the Soviet Union,* devotes a special section in each issue to achievements of the Central Asian Republics.[19] Soviet cultural missions to India invariably spotlight Central Asian delegates, in part, of course, because they are Asian, but even more so to accent their national respectability in Soviet life.[20] Indian cultural delegations visiting the Soviet Union find their itinerary heavily oriented to Central Asia.[21] When the Soviets "liberated" Azerbaijan in 1946, Moscow Radio's prompt announcement that the Azerbaijan language had "regained its lost rights" in schools and administration won more attention in some of the Indian press than the fact of aggression itself.[22] Similarly, in 1955, Moscow Radio could proclaim that all sixteen Soviet republics would henceforth have their own foreign ministries, even though this never actually happened, a piece of propaganda duplicity which the most sophisticated Indian newspapers did not question.[23] The Indian press reprints learned dissertations by Soviet scholars on na-

[17] *The Indian Worker,* July 2, 1955, p. 1.

[18] M. Raginsky and S. Rosenblit, "The Soviet Union—a voluntary union of equal nations," *Soviet Land,* August 25, 1950, p. 1. Another article in *Soviet Land,* in which the same theme is stressed, is V. Ivnonv, "Federation and Autonomy in the USSR," November 3, 1952, Vol. 11, No. 247.

[19] For example, see "What are Autonomous Soviet Republics, Autonomous Regions and National Areas?" December 29, 1952, Vol. 11, p. 10; and "Union of Free Peoples," December 22, 1952, Vol. 11, No. 285.

[20] See *Kommunist Tadzikhistan,* "To the Peoples of the East," poem by the Stalin Prize winner Tursun-Zade, October 9, 1951; "Month in India," a report by the delegation led by Tursun-Zade; and "Forty-seven Days with Soviet Delegations," June 27, 1953.

[21] "Indian Cultural Delegation in the USSR," *Soviet Land,* August 10, 1951, p. 18.

[22] *National Herald,* December 27, 1946, p. 1.

[23] "New Soviet Enigma," *The Christian Science Monitor,* May 5, 1955, p. 1 (second section). See also "More Powers for Republics," *Times of India,* February 12, 1955, p. 1.

tionality theory,[24] provided by the Soviet Embassy, and pro-Soviet Indians fill the literary supplements with eulogies of state-directed translation efforts designed "to evolve a multinational Soviet literature."[25]

When the Soviet leaders Bulganin and Khrushchev toured India in 1955, they combined relentless emphasis on Soviet national policy with acute sensitivity to the regional sequence of their itinerary. In New Delhi they assured the Parliamentary Association for the Development of Hindi that the USSR will devote greater study to "the Indian languages, in particular the Hindi language."[26] Arriving in Calcutta, however, Bulganin extended greetings of "the multinational people of the Soviet Union." For his tributes to Tagore and Bengali culture, and for his bald assertion that Bengal suffered "greater sacrifices in the struggle for India's independence than any other state," Khrushchev won rave notices from Calcutta's leading newspapers, which called his speech "the highest of all felicitations accorded to Calcutta in her civic history,"[27] and "solace to those whose minds have been frustrated by Bengal's endless miseries."[28] In Poona he praised the "courageous and valiant Marathas, who bravely defended the national independence of their native land."[29] It was in Kashmir, however, that the Soviet leaders could best exploit nationality slogans, for Kashmir with its measure of autonomy is acutely conscious of its special status in the Indian Union.[30] "Friendly collaboration of peoples is specially dear to us," said Khrushchev, "and we understand it." At the same time that he thus addressed himself to the Kashmiris,

[24] Professor Eugene Steinberg, "Lenin and the Soviet State," *The Hindu*, January 20, 1946, p. 6.

[25] S. V. Kondapi, "Soviet Example Best for Encouragement," *Praja Patrica*, Madras, December 1952, p. 4.

[26] *New Age*, November 20, 1955, p. 3; November 27, 1955, p. 8. See also December 11, p. 11; December 15, p. 4.

[27] *Ananda Bazar Patrika* (Bengali affiliate of *The Hindustan Standard*), Calcutta, December 1, 1955, p. 1.

[28] *Jugantar* (Bengali affiliate of *Amrita Bazar Patrika*), Calcutta, December 1-2, 1955, p. 1.

[29] *Pravda*, November 26, 1955, cited in *Current Digest of the Soviet Press*, January 11, 1956.

[30] *Times of India*, December 11, 1955, p. 4. See also *Speeches During Sojourn in India, Burma, and Afghanistan*, Tass Representative in India.

he made a gesture to the Big India Dream (Dag Hammarskjold's expression) which still lingers in Hindu nationalist hearts. Deploring Partition, Khrushchev declared that "we are absolutely convinced that when passions have calmed down and people realize the significance of such an artificial division of India, they will regret it."[31]

Although Communist China enjoys greater internal homogeneity than either the Soviet Union or India, Peking's propaganda, too, contrasts its own national program with "old China, in which the ruling class consistently carried out a policy of national oppression." Peking claims that even before 1949, the Chinese Communist Party "helped the national minorities in their struggle. Since the liberation, it has striven to bring about complete national equality." By October 1953, reported a minorities commissar, fifty of China's sixty minority nationalities had been granted regional autonomy, including administration of local finances.[32] That the Chinese Communist leaders are well aware of India's linguistic landscape was clear to a visiting Indian editor, Chalapathi Rao of the *National Herald*. Chou very pointedly asked him, said Rao on his return, "how the regional language press was developing. He was glad that the Indian languages press was making headway."[33] But Tibet, so close to home, was a much more damaging blow to Chinese prestige than Hungary had been in the Soviet case. A Yugoslav organ observed that "settlement of the national question in multi-national states has a large significance" and thus "the problem of Tibet . . . has a great interest . . . for multi-national India."[34]

[31] The Soviet cultural delegation to India in 1954 featured the Azerbaijan singer Rashid Beibutov, whose two major songs in New Delhi—Iqbal's *Sare Jahan Se Accha Hindustan Hamara (Our Hindustan Is The Best In The World)* and H. N. Chattopadhyaya's *Surya Asta Hogaya (The Sun Has Set)*—were rendered in such well-coached Hindi that the *Hindustan Standard* rhapsodized: "One would be very near the truth in saying that never before have these songs been sung so well." See *Hindustan Standard*, February 4, 1954, p. 1; *The Statesman*, February 4, 1954, p. 1; and *The People*, January 10, 1954, p. 2.

[32] Liu Chun, Vice Chairman of the Commission on Nationalities Affairs, "National Minorities Enjoy Regional Autonomy," *Peoples China*, January 1, 1954.

[33] M. Chalapathi Rao, *National Herald*, June 20, 1952, p. 4.

[34] *Review of International Affairs*, Belgrade, April 16, 1959, p. 11.

How Many Indias?

But for all their propaganda value Soviet and Chinese claims of national equality at home are significant primarily as a backdrop for the separatist political programs of local Communist parties. The so-called first tactical principle of Leninism enjoins the "obligatory consideration of the particularly and specifically national elements in each individual country."[35] The Soviet Union has manipulated internal differences as a direct weapon of its foreign policy, deliberately seeking to strain the structure of national unity and democratic institutions in states outside its orbit. Conversely, when Soviet foreign policy interests could best be served by calling off the wolves, the Soviets have sought to restrain Communist parties. Communist manipulation of "national" differences is an unusually flexible weapon even by Communist standards. It can be used or repudiated, depending upon expediency, with equal support from the Leninist-Stalinist scriptures. While affirming the right of national self-determination to the point of secession, which supports local Communists in separatist programs, the Soviet literature on nationality specifies at the same time that it is only the proletariat, whose will is embodied in the Communist Party, that can decide whether it is in the interests of the nation on a given occasion to exercise this right.

Communist strategy in Asia has explicitly advised the use of this weapon from the very beginning. In the early twenties, Soviet emissaries made a brief effort to build a regional Asian "Inter-Colonial Union," but ever since this abortive attempt "it is on national soil alone that Communist movements have thrived."[36] Pan-Islamism and pan-Asianism have been roundly denounced as reactionary ideologies;[37] in the Middle East, needless to say, as Walter Z. Laqueur wrote as early as 1955, national-

[35] Cited in Resolution on the Reports of the National Trade Union Centers of Asian and Australasian Countries, *World Trade Union Movement*, organ of the World Federation of Trade Unions, December 1949, p. 40.

[36] Milton Sacks, "Communism and Regional Integration," *South Asia in the World Today*, University of Chicago Press, 1953, p. 204.

[37] E. Zhukov, "Obostreniye Krizisa Koloniyalnoi Sistemy," *Bolshevik*, December 15, 1947, pp. 51-64 (translated for the author).

ism "has paved the way for and occasionally collaborated with Communism."[38] As early as 1933, the *Pan-Pacific Worker* advised the Indo-Chinese Communists to build party organizations on the basis of national lines rather than French administrative boundaries and to exploit the fact that merchants and usurers were in most cases Annamites.[39]

Soviet advice could not have been more explicit than the dictum of V. V. Vassilieva in the Indian Communist monthly that "Comrade Stalin's teachings on nations bear world historic significance. The majority of the countries of the east comprise multi-national states, and . . . the experience of the solution of the national question in the Soviet Union is really invaluable."[40] The Indian Communists have elevated to a high doctrinal pedestal Stalin's last speech on October 14, 1952, which provides a double-barreled pretext for anti-Western nationalism and "national" disruption within multilingual states:

Formerly, the Bourgeoisie was regarded as the head of the nation; it upheld the rights and independence of the nation and placed them above all else. Now not a trace remains of the national principle. Now the . . . banner of national independence and national sovereignty has been thrown overboard. There is no doubt that it is you, the representatives of the Communist and democratic parties, who will have to raise this banner and carry it forward, if you want to be patriots of your country, if you want to become the leading force of the nation. There is nobody else to raise it. That is how matters stand today.[41]

After Stalin's death Indian Communist writers hailed his writings as the fountainhead of all knowledge on nationality. Stalin was credited with having perceived the unique evocative

---

[38] "The Appeal of Communism," *Middle East Journal*, Winter, 1955, p. 21, and *Communism and Nationalism in the Middle East,* Praeger, 1956, entirety.

[39] Orgwald, "Tactical and Organizational Questions of the Communist Parties of India and Indochina," *Pan-Pacific Worker*, 1933, p. 73.

[40] *The Communist*, July-August 1950, p. 101. The same issue of the Communist monthly contains an article by I. Verkhovtsev on the 25th anniversary of Stalin's 1925 speech to the University of the Peoples of the East in which he predicted the emergence of national differences in India. Another example of Soviet emphasis on the national question in Indian Communist periodicals is the article by Professor I. Levin, "Soviet Federalism," *Marxist Miscellany*, Vol. 7, April 1946.

[41] Stalin, Speech at the 19th Congress of the Communist Party of the Soviet Union, October 14, 1952, cited in *New Age*.

power of "national" slogans to puncture the fatalist apathy that afflicts the low man on the Asian economic scale. Without doubt "national" slogans do, in fact, provide an emotional receptacle wide enough to channel myriad accumulated grievances. While specific economic grievances may at one time touch one group or another in a region, the "national" grievance can be presented as the common concern of all. Moreover, in Asia, predominantly agricultural as it still is, Communists and indeed all would-be political manipulators confront a special difficulty in mobilizing the peasantry. The peasant-proprietor, large or small, is normally associated with conservative values by any doctrine in any country. But in Communist doctrine, conceived in terms of urban proletarian dominance, the archetypal peasant is not only conservative but downright dull. Incapable of enough class-consciousness to come to his own economic self-defense, he is politically penetrable only through emotional loyalties. Stalin thus seemed to be addressing himself directly to the Indian Communists when he termed "the national question, virtually the peasant question." The peasant question, deduced Kerala's Communist Chief Minister E. M. S. Nambudripad,

is a question of how the peasantry forms itself into the main army of the national movement. It is a question not merely of a few changes in agrarian relations, but a question of the peasantry being transformed from an incoherent mass of scattered individuals to an organized class which in its turn is allied to all those classes struggling for freedom and democracy.[42]

To the Bengali Communist theoretician on nationality, S. N. Mazumdar, Stalin's works are "very important politically. . . . Stalin's teachings in Marxism and linguistics are of immense

[42] E. M. S. Nambudripad, *New Age*, June 1953, pp. 20-22. See also *New Age*, July 1956, p. 13; J. Stalin, *The National Question Once Again*, 1925, cited in G. Adhikari, ed., *Marxism and the Question of Nationalities*, People's Publishing House, Bombay, 1943, p. 2; Adhikari, *Indian National and Hindu-Muslim Unity*, Current Book Distributors, Sydney, 1945, p. 14; Adhikari, *Pakistan and Indian National Unity*, People's Publishing House, Bombay, 1944, pp. 4, 25, 26; and S. Parameswaran, *The Peasant Question in Kerala*, People's Publishing House, Bombay, 1951, p. 1. In *New Age* (May 13, 1956, p. 3) the Bengal Communists report that their 1956 campaign against merger with Bihar proved to be "a really *national* movement . . . one of those rare instances where the *kisans* on a considerable scale joined the middle class and working class."

significance for a multi-national country like India."[43] Stalin's teachings in linguistics, of course, amount primarily to his 1950 articles, "On Marxism in Linguistics," which came as the Kremlin's final intervention in the Soviet Union's so-called linguistic controversy.[44] When the eminent linguist N. Y. Marr carried his doctrinaire class analysis of language too far, he impeded Soviet instruction programs in Russian as well as linguistic research in the relation between Russian and other Slavic languages. This research was politically important first of all in the European setting,[45] but it was no accident that Mazumdar attached great importance to the linguistic controversy outside Europe. The Soviets themselves were well aware of its implications abroad,[46] sensitive as always to the relevance of their nationality theory in Asia. Stalin himself implied that Marr's antipathy to the concept of national, as distinct from class, languages hampered Asian Communist exploitation of national sentiment.[47] It was typical of the cynical Soviet use of nationality theory that at home Marr's repudiation was needed to facilitate the repression of languages and the domination of one, Russian, while abroad Stalin's demolition of Marr cleared the theoretical decks for linguistic separatism. India is perhaps the extreme example of this resilient Communist doctrine on nationality, for Soviet and Indian Communist policy have followed a classic cycle from unreserved separatism between 1946 and 1953 to sweetly reasonable dedication to national unity when Stalin's death signalled a softened Soviet approach to South Asia.

[43] S. N. Mazumdar, "Stalin's Work on Linguistics," *New Age*, March 1954, p. 55. See also J. V. Stalin, *The National Question and Leninism*, Moscow, Foreign Languages Publishing House, 1950, p. 8.

[44] "On Marxism in Linguistics," *Pravda*, June 20, 1950, in *The Soviet Linguistic Controversy*, Kings Crown Press, New York, 1951, p. 85.

[45] Henry Kucera, "Soviet Nationality Policy; The Linguistic Controversy," *Problems of Communism*, March-April 1954. See also G. Akhvlediani, "For a Leninist-Stalinist Path of Development in Soviet Linguistics," *Pravda*, June 27, 1950, p. 4.

[46] For example, in one of the initial documents in the linguistic controversy, G. P. Serdyuchenko, Report to the 85th anniversary of N. Y. Marr's Birth, *Current Digest of the Soviet Press*, June 17, 1950, stresses that Soviet nationalism is "of the greatest world-wide historic importance."

[47] J. Stalin, "Replies to Comrades," *Pravda*, August 2, 1950, p. 2, reprinted from *Bolshevik*, No. 14, 1950, in *The Soviet Linguistic Controversy*.

Even before Independence, the Indian Communists were well aware of the relevance of Soviet nationality doctrine for the Indian scene. The draft program of the nascent Indian Communist Party in 1930 declared that only an "Indian Federal Soviet Republic would be capable of insuring to national minorities their right to self-determination, including that of complete separation."[48] Later, when Hindu-Muslim conflict overshadowed all Indian political life, Indian Communist theoreticians turned to nationality doctrine to find a rationale for supporting the Muslim League in its Pakistan demand. As late as 1938, confesses the Marathi Communist theoretician on nationality, G. Adhikari, "we were yet wrapped up in the theory, like the rest of the nationalists, that India was one nation and that the Muslims were just a religious cultural minority." Many Indian Communists had been "shocked by the formulation that India was not one nation," but the party leadership had it out with dissenters in May 1941.[49] Then, at the historic "Quit India" session of the Congress Working Committee on August 8, 1942, Communist committee members came out against the demand for an immediate British withdrawal and called instead for prior agreement with the Muslim League.[50] The Communist line thenceforth urged Congress to concede "what is just and right" in the Pakistan demand.[51] "The rational kernel of the Pakistan demand," wrote Adhikari, is that "wherever people of the Muslim faith living together in a territorial unit form a nationality . . . they certainly have the right to autonomous state existence just like other nationalities in India such as Andhras, Karnatakis, Marathis, and Bengalis."[52]

[48] "Draft program of action of the Communist Party of India," *International Press Correspondence*, December 18, 1930, cited in *The Communist Party of India*, United States Office of Strategic Services, Research and Analysis Branch, No. 2681, August 1945. See also "Lessons of the Lahore Congress," a manifesto signed by Brajesh Singh, *Revolutionary Age*, February 1, 1930, Berlin (mimeographed), which calls for provincial autonomy and linguistic demarcation of state boundaries.

[49] G. Adhikari, *Pakistan and National Unity*, p. 29.

[50] *Bombay Chronicle*, August 9, 1942, p. 1. See also *People's Age*, August 3, 1942, and *People's War*, September 20, 1942.

[51] Adhikari, *Pakistan and National Unity*, p. 8.

[52] *People's War*, October 15, 1944. See also Adhikari, *Pakistan and National Unity*, p. 7, and *Party Letter*, October 16, 1943.

It was the Communist line on Pakistan that contributed as much as any other single factor to the ultimate wartime break between the Congress and the Communists. To be sure, the line on Pakistan was only part of the broader "People's War" line: the Communists were able to use it as a means of camouflaging their opposition to the Congress anti-war stand. But on top of the Communist line-up with the British, the alliance with the Muslim League was, in nationalist eyes, unforgivable. At the "Quit India" session Nehru approved a Communist-inspired pledge that the future Indian constitution "should be a federal one . . . with the residuary powers vesting in the units,"[53] which G. Adhikari boasted "came very near to recognizing the right of self-determination."[54] But this 1942 "victory" began a controversy with the official Congress leadership that ultimately resulted in Communist expulsion from the Congress. In December 1945, the Congress Working Committee voted to remove all Communist Party members from Congress office.[55] Nehru drafted a subcommittee report which charged that "without doubt Communist support of the Muslim League's claim for Pakistan had added to the prevailing estrangement."[56] "After all," agreed P. C. Joshi, "the real issue which sharply divides us today is not people's war, but our advocacy of self-determination."[57]

By the eve of India's Independence in 1946, Communist leaders were sufficiently aware of sharpening regional consciousness to apply their new line with sweeping abandon to all regions and indeed to the entire future of the Indian Union. The Pakistan movement had inspired their "advocacy of self-determination" in the first place, but the prospect of Congress rule in a free India now gave to the separatist line a peculiar new importance, "a source of strength against the day when major

[53] Cited in P. C. Joshi, *Communist Reply to the Working Committee Charges*, People's Publishing House, Bombay, March 1946. See also P. C. Joshi, *Congress and the Communists*, People's Publishing House, Bombay, 1944, p. 25.

[54] G. Adhikari, *Pakistan and National Unity*, p. 7.

[55] *National Herald*, December 14, 1945, p. 1. See also D. K. Rangnekar, *The Congress-Communist Tangle*, National Youth Publications, Bombay, 1945, pp. 23-24.

[56] *National Herald*, December 15, 1945, p. 2.

[57] P. C. Joshi, *Communist Reply to the Working Committee Charges*, Bombay, March 1946.

national parties would take power at the center."[58] In the 1946 election campaign the Communists demanded that power go not to the provisional central government headed by Nehru but to fourteen sovereign regional constituent assemblies, each empowered to decide whether or not to join the new Indian Union. "The delegates to the all-India constituent assemblies should have no more authority than that of plenipotentiaries," wrote P. C. Joshi. "Full and real sovereignty shall reside in the national constituent assemblies which will enjoy the unfettered right to negotiate, formulate and finally to decide their mutual relations within an independent India on the basis of complete equality."[59]

Nehru struck back angrily in the election campaign, shouting to mill workers in Kanpur that he was

greatly surprised at the treacherous attitude of the Indian Communists, who want to create a dozen or perhaps more divisions of India. The part that the Communist Party has played during recent years has no relation with communism, and if there is any party which has done the maximum harm to the cause of communism, it is the Communist Party of India which has by its treacherous policy isolated itself from the masses.[60]

Nehru's *National Herald*,[61] reviewing a book by P. C. Joshi at the time of the elections, declared that "the Communists know that Britain will never get out of India unless she is kicked out. But before that, let India be divided into bits so that the Indian National Congress may end . . . leaving the Communists free to make a revolutionary conquest of India part by part. Thus would Comrade P. C. Joshi become the Stalin of the Indian Soviet Republic."[62] Still another attack, speculating on the postwar Soviet role in Asia, looked Moscow squarely in the eye:

It would not at all suit the USSR to have one or two big powerful

---

[58] Gene D. Overstreet and Marshall Windmiller, *Communism in India*, University of California Press, Berkeley, 1958, p. 308.

[59] P. C. Joshi, *For the Final Bid to Power—Freedom Program of the Indian Communists*, People's Publishing House, Bombay, 1946.

[60] *National Herald*, March 9, 1946, p. 1.

[61] Nehru and members of his family held controlling interest in the *National Herald* prior to his assumption of office as Prime Minister.

[62] D. P. J., *National Herald*, January 6, 1946, reviewing P. C. Joshi, *A Free, Happy India*, People's Publishing House, Bombay.

neighbors to the South. A big country like India or China cannot be 'persuaded' against her will to become a sphere of influence. On the contrary, it would insist on becoming an equal and a big world power. Together China and India can successfully resist any onslaught from the North or from the Anglo-Saxons. The emergence of a strong India or China is therefore not at all conducive to present Soviet plans of expansion. Pakistan would provide the best means for penetrating India's body politic . . . a small and weak state.

In fact Soviet and Communist policy . . . has opted in favor of splitting the country into many autonomous units. They deny that there is any such thing as an Indian nation. The Communist plan appears to be for a Balkanization of India.[63]

When, in the midst of the election campaign, Communist delegates at the Udaipur session of the All-India States Peoples Conference, Congress arm in the princely states, pressed a resolution for the convocation of sovereign constituent assemblies in each region of India, Kashmir leader Sheikh Abdullah scornfully responded that "the creation of small independent states is the pastime of imperialist powers. This amendment is born of an inferiority complex. The Communists, while propagating the secession idea, have completely ignored the opposite point of view. This conference should not encourage disintegration." Nehru told the conference that a government of free India "could never function if the federating units refused to owe allegiance to the center and wanted to form separate states of their own. The Congress does not want to compel any unit to join the federation against its will. At the same time, with freedom for a unit to secede, it would be impossible for a federal or unitary government to carry on. The constant threat of separation would demoralize the atmosphere, and planning for economic betterment . . . would be impossible."[64]

Yet despite attacks the Communist Party in its memorandum

---

[63] Kautilya, "Pakistan, Russia and the Communists," *National Herald*, February 10, 1946, p. 6. See also *National Herald*, April 7, 1946, p. 4, and April 11, 1946, editorial, "Russia and Pakistan."

[64] *National Herald*, January 3, 1946, p. 1. Nehru attempted to favor *self-determination* without endorsing specifically the right to *secession*. Thus, he stated on August 29, 1946, that "if some units wanted to part company, they might do so," prompting a Bengali supporter to defend the Congress position against Communist attack (Promode Sen, *Congress and the Right of Self-Determination*, Institute of New Democracy, Calcutta, 1946).

to the British cabinet mission in April 1946, set forth its position in unmistakably explicit terms:

The provisional government should be charged with the task of setting up a boundary commission to redraw boundaries on the basis of natural ancient homelands of every people. The people of each such unit should have the unfettered right of self-determination. . . . Delegates elected from each national unit shall decide by a majority whether they will join the all-India constituent assembly to form an Indian union, or remain out and form a separate sovereign state by themselves, or join another Indian union.[65]

The memorandum envisaged four units now in Pakistan (Western Punjab, Sind, Baluchistan, and Pathanland), a sprawling, Hindi-speaking Hindustan, and twelve other regions now in the Indian union—Tamilnad, Andhra, Kerala, Karnataka, Maharashtra, Gujarat, Rajasthan, Punjab, Bihar, Assam, Bengal, and Orissa.

Once the terms of freedom were settled, Pakistan had to be dropped from the Indian Communist vocabulary, but the regional components of the new Indian Union were still there to be championed. Only minor changes were necessary to bring the party line up to date, and the party central committee accordingly demanded in June 1947 that the constitution of the projected Nehru regime grant "national self-determination on the basis of linguistically demarcated provinces."[66] At the Calcutta Second Party Congress in February 1948, the ascendant anti-Joshi faction led by the victorious new secretary, B. T. Ranadive, gave vent to retroactive dismay at the alliance with the Muslim League but called the broader slogan of self-determination "fundamentally sound."[67] The March post-convention manifesto of the new party central committee called for "self-de-

[65] *Memorandum* of the Communist Party of India to the British cabinet mission, April 15, 1946 (mimeographed). See also "Declaration of Independence—Communist Resolution for the Constituent Assembly," Resolution of the Central Committee of the Communist Party of India, published in *People's Age*, December 15, 1946, p. 1. See also *People's Age*, December 29, 1946, p. 1; *People's Age*, July 7, 1946, p. 1; *People's Age*, September 1, 1946, p. 5.

[66] *People's Age*, June 29, 1947, p. 7.

[67] *Fighting front of the toiling millions*, Review of the second Congress of the Communist Party of India, CPI Publication, Bombay, March 1948, p. 21.

termination to nationalities, including the right of secession."[68]

The Indian Communist Party thus openly avowed its separatist intentions at the very outset of India's independent national existence. In so doing the party paralleled the Soviet Union's own line which, if anything, showed even less respect for Indian sensitivities than the Indian Communists themselves. In 1946 the Soviet specialist on India, A. M. Diakov, dismissed Indian unity with the abrupt declaration that "one cannot consider the whole population of India a single nation."[69] Reading between the lines, in fact, one notices a distinct Soviet suspicion that Indian unity might not survive at all—and that therefore, so far as Indian Communist separatism was concerned, the more the better. Gene D. Overstreet's study of Soviet writings in this period led him to conclude that

Soviet and Indian Communist leaders believed that India would indeed be in a drastically weak and disorganized condition following its assumption of independence, that its government would be unpopular and ineffectual to cope with the situation, and that the time was therefore ripe for . . . the immediate displacement of that government . . . Soviet writings showed fairly clearly an expectation that the country would be fragmented in the process of achieving independence.[70]

On his Indian tour Khrushchev asked West Bengal Chief Minister B. C. Roy how the new Nehru regime had managed to liquidate the princely states. "I was expecting to see civil war," said Khrushchev. "We had Gandhi," replied Roy.[71]

[68] *Toward the democratic front to win real independence and peoples democracy*, Statement of policy of the Central Committee of the Communist Party of India, Bombay, March 1948, p. 11. See also *People's Age*, August 8, 1948, p. 3; September 5, 1948, p. 16; December 26, 1948, p. 2.

[69] "K Voprosu O Natsional 'nom Sostave Naseleniia Indii," *Uchenye Zapiski Tikhookeanskogo Instituta*, Tom 1, p. 231, and *New Times*, March 1, 1946, pp. 25-31, cited in Gene D. Overstreet, *The Soviet View of India, 1945-48* (M.A. dissertation, Columbia University, Russian Studies Institute, February 1953, p. 45).

[70] Overstreet, *op.cit.*, p. 81. See also Overstreet, Ph.D. dissertation, Columbia University, 1955, and Romesh Chandra, *Princistan: Imperialism's Nest for Tomorrow*, People's Publishing House, Bombay, April 1947. Ruth Fischer, "Minutes of seminar meeting," Russian Research Center, Harvard University, July 11, 1952, observes that "under a curious double influence of the most conservative British ideas in India, and the recent strength of Mao, the Communists considered the new republic so unstable as to preclude the possibility of uniting the entire subcontinent."

[71] Interview with B. C. Roy, April 1956.

When Indian Independence was proclaimed in 1947, the Communists promptly went out in search of a territorial base of operations for guerrilla warfare against New Delhi and decided upon Telengana. Communist success in this Telugu-speaking southeast corner of Hyderabad is discussed at length in the chapter which follows. Insurgent Communists organized parallel village governments policed by their own terrorist night riders. Not until 1951 did Nehru crush separatism in Telengana—the sorest point in early Indo-Soviet relations.

Until 1953, when the party line changed, the governing Soviet interpretation of Indian nationality was A. M. Diakov's 1948 political tract, *The National Question and British Imperialism in India*,[72] published by the State Publishing House of Political Literature and aimed, therefore, less at scholars than at operating bureaucrats and diplomats in Moscow and in the field. Praising Stalin's prescience for having seen India's "many-sided facets, behind the outward national unity," Diakov declares his intention at the outset to show the peculiarities of India's "separate nationalities," employing, incidentally, the Russian adjective "Otdel 'nykh," which connotes separateness (rather than difference) more sharply than other suitable Russian words. Then he states:

By virtue of the fact that India has for two hundred years been a colony of England in the eyes of the outside world, India appears as something unified and its entire population as one people. . . . The presence in India of a powerful national liberating movement in which all the peoples living in India participate in this or that degree still further strengthens this illusion of a national unity of the entire Indian people. It is more or less broadly known that in India there are different religions . . . that there are a great number of castes, but few know that in India there is a number of large peoples, each of which is no less numerous than the English, the French, or the Italians; that these people are distinguished by their individual culture, language, literature, have their own mores and customs, their national character, have passed a long road of historical development. The colonial position of India which made its peoples slaves of English imperialism has depersonalized it in the eyes of the outside world.[73]

[72] *Natsional 'nyi Vopros I Angliiskii Imperialism V. Indii* (translated for the author).　　　　[73] *Ibid.*, Introduction, esp. p. 35.

He concludes that with "neither a common language nor a common national character," India cannot be considered as one nation, and adds the gratuitous comparison that the common cultural fund that has developed in India "is no greater than the common cultural fund of the different peoples of Europe, of the Far East, and of the Middle East."[74]

In a region-by-region analysis, which he develops in detail in supplementary works, Diakov divides India into fully formed nations, those in the process of formation, and those which might develop into nations barring their absorption by other nations with a head start. As fully formed nations he lists "the three peoples of East India, namely: Bengali, Oriya, and Assamese; the two peoples of Western India, the Marathi and Gujarati . . . and the four Dravidian peoples of the South, Tamil, Telugu, Kannada, and Malayalam." Still in the process of national formation are the Hindustani- and Punjabi-speaking peoples, while altogether uncertain in their national character remain the tribal hill peoples sandwiched between regions.[75]

Speculating on the disparity between the South with its compact territorial units and the indeterminate regional development in the North, Diakov echoes standard Western scholarship in explaining that the South escaped the brunt of India's foreign invasions. Only Bengal and Gujarat offer hope for "strong national movements" in the North. Bengal holds a special fascination for Diakov, who looks to eventual reunion between Pakistani East Bengal and adjacent Indian West Bengal. "There is no doubt that India and Pakistan have to face the Bengal problem," he maintains.[76] In 1952 he charged that the Indian and Pakistan governments were fomenting periodic Hindu-Muslim riots because, "following the example of their British teachers, they seek to drown the national movement of Bengal in blood." Bengal's Chief Minister, B. C. Roy, plays hand in glove with the central government because he is a "stooge of the Marwaris."[77]

[74] Ibid., p. 47.
[75] Diakov, Indiia Vo Vremia I Posle Vtoroi Mirovoi Voiny, 1939-49 (India during and after the second world war, 1939-1949), Moscow, 1952, pp. 215-217 (translated for the author). A Communist writer in New Age, July 1, 1957, p. 63, demands regional tribal autonomy.
[76] Diakov, 1952, p. 162.   [77] Ibid., p. 220.

Marwari Whipping Boy

The Marwaris, in fact, invariably turn up as the final culprits in Diakov's discussion of every region. They provide the recurring central theme of his analysis, just as Indian Communist separatist propaganda during this period points with equal certainty to the Marwaris as the major villain in India, the evil monopolist power behind the Nehru Government. In league with Anglo-American finance to create a centralized Indian economic empire, the Marwaris are the Indian counterparts of Kuomintang China's "Four Families."[78] From the start of the Independence movement, writes Diakov, the Indian answer to the British concept of India as "a formless conglomeration of heterogeneous races, tribes, castes, and religions" was not based upon correct Leninist-Stalinist "national" analysis. Instead, because the Congress has been "captured" by Gujarati and Marwari influence,[79] the Indian rejoinder was the incorrect

one-nation concept . . . the expression of the centralistic tendencies of the summit of the Indian bourgeoisie, primarily the big capitalists of the province of Gujarata and Marwara. . . . This capitalist group aspires to a monopoly to dominate the Indian market and in this sense it struggles not only against British capital but also against the bourgeoisie of other nationalities of India . . . which strives to tear its own markets from the hands of Gujarati-Marwari capital.[80]

Diakov cites Lenin's law that for capitalism anywhere to triumph over feudalism "there must be a state-like cohesion between territory and language . . . one of the most important conditions of a truly free and broad movement of goods, of close ties between the seller and purchaser."[81] Thus the bourgeoisie of each region seeks linguistic reorganization of states to secure its own basic market preserve, and conversely the Marwaris seek to promote all-India linguistic unity through Hindi, "to some degree already the all-India language in spheres of trade and industry." Brandishing Hindi as their cultural instrument to

[78] *Ibid.*, p. 211.
[79] *Ibid.*, pp. 32, 146.
[80] Diakov, 1948, pp. 45, 154.
[81] V. I. Lenin, *Collected Works*, Vol. 17, 3rd edition, p. 428, cited in Diakov, 1948, p. 138.

weaken regional solidarity, the Marwaris, in this account, next proceed to strike with the political weapon of centralism against the movement for linguistic provinces.[82]

Diakov's attack on the new Indian Constitution's "extraordinary presidential powers . . . nullifying state autonomy"[83] is surprisingly moderate next to the scornful Indian Communist charge, similarly directed at the Marwaris, that "the 'powers' given to the provinces are those enjoyed by municipalities in other countries." With exclusive central control of banking, insurance, stock exchanges, petroleum, mining, and airways, most initiative in industry and finance would be, said the Indian Communists, "in the hands of the center, to be utilized in the interests of the Birlas and Dalmias."[84] In the new Constitution,

the wide powers given to the central government in the name of the security of the state, constitute nothing but a device for unbridled domination by the Marwari-Gujarati capitalists of the economic and political life of all nationalities. . . . The constitution denies equality of all languages and imposes English and Hindi as the state languages. This monstrous attack is a weapon of perpetuating backwardness and denying culture and education to the people of these regions; it is a weapon of creating a solid basis for Marwari-Gujarati domination because such domination stands endangered if people develop their own languages and culture.[85]

Rejecting outright the very notion of a federal language in India, Communist writer Ram Bilas Sharma echoed Diakov, charging that "the demand for a *Rashtrabhasha* (national language) in the mouth of Indian big business reveals its own imperialist and colonial ambitions." Is Marwari ambition comparable to past Great Russian oppression of other nationalities in Czarist Russia? Sharma answers his own question:

The political thesis of the Communist Party of India clearly speaks of a dominating Bourgeoisie which is denying the right of secession

82 Diakov, 1952, p. 211; 1948, p. 163. See also *People's Age*, September 5, 1948, p. 16.

83 Diakov, 1948, p. 310. See also 1952, p. 210; and T. Yershov, *New Times*, March 15, 1950, pp. 5-6.

84 "Review of the Draft Constitution of India," *Marxist Miscellany*, May 1949, Bombay, p. 12.

85 *Manifesto of the Central Committee of the Communist Party on the New Constitution*, People's Publishing House, Bombay, 1949, p. 4.

to other nations. . . . Such a dominating Bourgeoisie cannot but have a national basis. . . . The dominating Bourgeoisie of India is drawn mainly from the Marwari nation. From this nation come the Birlas, the Dalmias who have spread their tentacles far and wide in the country. There are also others who form part of this gang but whose nationality is not Marwari. This would happen in any multi-national country. In Czarist Russia, big capital was controlled not by Russians alone. For example, in the Ukraine the monopolists of France, Belgium, Germany, and Britain owned eighty percent of the blast furnaces, ninety percent of the coke, and the byproduct plants, but this did not alter the fact that the Czarist Russian policy was to Russify the Ukraine. So in India it matters not a jot if the dominating Bourgeoisie has non-Marwari elements also in it.[86]

Communist student fronts during this period emphasized the twin demons of the Marwaris and Hindi, protesting that the University Education Commission recommendations would pave the way for Hindi as the medium in the universities.[87]

For Diakov the Marwaris served as convenient whipping boys because, as "typical cosmopolites, in foreign as well as internal affairs,"[88] they could readily be charged with links to Wall Street and Whitehall and thus fit into Soviet propaganda that the Nehru Government connived secretly with imperialism. But the importance of the Marwari in his analysis was even more fundamental. The notion of a Marwari oppressor ranged against the oppressed bourgeoisie of the non-Hindi regions was his grudging application to the Indian scene of the so-called "Maoist" line, which had prevailed in Moscow by 1949.

The victorious Mao Tse-tung's "New Democracy" had enshrined a multi-class Communist Party that became the representative not only of the proletariat but of the "patriotic, national" bourgeoisie and of all the peasantry as well. At the June 1947 session of the Soviet Academy of Sciences, both Diakov and another leading Soviet South Asian specialist, V. V. Balabushevich, were still opposing E. M. Zhukov's Maoist proposition that Communist-led united fronts in other Asian countries

[86] "On the language question in India—an article for discussion," *The Communist*, September-October 1949, p. 47.

[87] "Review of the twelfth conference of the All-India Students Federation," *The Communist*, September-October 1949, p. 18. See also *Young Guard*, March 1950, p. 32.

[88] Diakov, 1952, p. 212.

should include, on occasion, a section of the national bourgeoisie.[89] By 1949, however, Balabushevich had conceded at the Academy's Pacific Institute that "individual groupings" in the national bourgeoisie were admissible, including

the rising Bourgeoisie of those national regions of India which are more backward in their development. This Bourgeoisie is dissatisfied with the predominance of the already constituted monopolist group. . . . The process of the formation and growth in the Bourgeoisie of the different nationalities of India is intimately bound up with the process of capitalist development and the formation of nationalities. At present in India there exist not merely large enterprises owned by native capital but national monopolist combinations have also been formed. The Gujarati and Marwari groupings of the Bourgeoisie occupy a dominant position in these monopolist combinations and it is, in the first instance, these monopolist combinations that the right wing leadership of the national Congress and the Indian dominion government represent.[90]

To save face, Balabushevich warned that "these oppositional strata . . . ought not to be regarded as reliable or stable members of the anti-imperialist camp," just as Diakov, also by then in step with the new line, characterized any bourgeois allies as "unreliable." But no matter how much they minimize their conversion, both Soviet Indologists had by 1949 made an inglorious retreat before the advancing Maoist line. The repentant Diakov, whose 1948 treatise on India is replete with excoriations of Marwari oppression, nonetheless felt compelled to apologize in 1952 for presenting the Indian bourgeoisie in some of his writings as "an undifferentiated whole . . . for failing to clearly separate out the contradictions between the monopolistic apex and the larger part of the national bourgeoisie." As his final capitulation, he argued that alliances with local business interests, while "perhaps not too reliable, nevertheless must be taken into consideration . . . overlooking their weakness and unreliability."[91]

[89] John Kautsky, *Moscow and the Communist Party of India*, Technology Press and John Wiley and Sons, 1956, p. 300.
[90] V. V. Balabushevich, "New stage in the national liberation struggle of the people of India," *Colonial Peoples Struggle for Liberation*, People's Publishing House, Bombay, 1950, pp. 53, 58.
[91] Diakov, 1952, pp. 1, 216-217.

Diakov's emphasis on the Marwaris signalled an historic ideological turning-point in international Communism, but the Indian Communists, or at least important non-Hindi Communist groups, made the Marwari their whipping boy for simpler tactical reasons that had little to do with grand strategy. Communist parties in the non-Hindi regions wanted a doctrinal pretext for local alliances with aggrieved regional caste groups whose interests conflicted with those of the Marwaris, or who could, in any event, be plausibly depicted as victims of Marwari oppression. To ally with any capitalist or landowner was intolerable, of course, for the doctrinaire B. T. Ranadive, then secretary of the Indian Party. He screamed heresy at the Andhra Communists for even proposing such a thing. But Ranadive's proved to be a small voice, swallowed up in the ideological din emanating from the centers of international Communist power.

With their leadership in the wealthy Kamma landowning caste, the Andhra Communists, as we shall see in the following two chapters, had good reason to espouse the Maoist line in India. The Andhra Communist leaders established ground rules at the start of the Telengana insurrection in 1948 which assured that most of their Kamma brethren went unscathed. So long as the middling-rich farmers who make up the bulk of the caste stayed above the battle, they were classified in Communist strategy as "neutralized."[92] This was outright deviation, not only from the Ranadive line, which saw all landowners as equally villainous, but also from Moscow's early postwar Zdhanov line decreeing unequivocal guerrilla offensives throughout Asia. Ranadive, attacking the Andhra Secretariat, publicly charged that in Andhra Communist ranks "it is the rural intellectuals, sons of rich peasants and middle peasants, that preponderate in important positions. The party politically based itself on the vacillating politics of the middle peasants and allowed itself to be influenced even by rich peasant ideology." He contrasted Andhra's "wrong social base" with the working class base of the Tamilnad party and the "poor peasant" base in Kerala.[93]

[92] An example of this characterization is in *The Communist*, June-July 1949.
[93] *Ibid.*, p. 34.

162

The Andhra Communists had made no secret of their "rich peasant" policy within the party. They explicitly declared themselves on this point in a 1948 program report for the Indian Communist Politburo which stressed two major tactical rules of thumb:

1. In delta areas the pressure of population would be heavy, and as such slogans should be raised for the distribution of lands belonging to rich ryots among poor peasants and laborers . . .
2. Propaganda should be carried on to convince the ryots about the just demands of the workers, and we should also effect compromises with such of those ryots who would follow with us. Assurance should be given that we should not touch the lands of rich ryots.[94]

B. T. Ranadive singled out for special attack another statement of this position in a 1948 Andhra Secretariat document discussing tactics toward government rice procurement for rationing:

In the matter of procurement of paddy, the Secretariat believes that it is possible to neutralize the rich peasants as the government plan goes against the rich peasantry also. Though the rich peasantry as a class is not standing firmly in the fight, it is parting with paddy with dissatisfaction.

This, Ranadive charged, "constitutes the real practical gist of the document, a program of class collaboration in rural areas, of bowing down before the rich peasant."[95]

Ranadive and the Andhra Secretariat waged unabashed open warfare that may well have been a reverberation of the larger struggle in world communism. For then, in mid-1949, Mao Tse-tung did not yet control the Chinese mainland. Soviet writers were only beginning to see virtue in Mao's "New Democracy," with its expansive welcome to "patriotic" capitalists and rich peasants. The Andhra document specifically justified its "rich peasant" policies by pointing to Mao. But, Ranadive declared, Mao's "horrifying" departures from accepted Stalinist dogma "are such that no Communist Party can accept them;

[94] The 1948 report appears in part in *Self-Critical Report of the Andhra Communist Committee, January 1948-February 1952*, Part Two, March 1949-March 1950, a party document not intended for publication.
[95] *The Communist*, June-July 1949, p. 72.

they are in contradiction to the world understanding of the Communist Parties." Ranadive scolded the Andhra comrades, who "should have thought ten times before making such a formulation."[96] It was not until the summer of 1950, after the Cominform Journal had endorsed the "path taken by the Chinese people,"[97] that the Indian Communists replaced Ranadive with the Andhra leader C. Rajeshwar Rao, profusely apologizing to Mao and praising "New Democracy" as a model for India.[98]

But the new Rao leadership, while minimizing the reckless terrorism of Ranadive's tenure and condemning his failure to fight for linguistic provinces, was slow to catch up with the full implications of the new Maoist line. Rao's new central committee sounded faintly like the reluctant convert Diakov when it said in a party circular that

the middle Bourgeoisie may be progressive to a certain extent. The middle Bourgeoisie also includes the rising Bourgeoisie of nationalities dominated or suppressed by Gujarati-Marwari big business. But not all of them would be progressive. . . . Only those sections of the Bourgeoisie which stand up against the big Bourgeoisie on the question of linguistic provinces, as on other issues, can be considered as an ally.[99]

Three months later, Bombay Communist leader S. A. Dange attacked the Central Committee's ideological sluggishness in another major intraparty document. He cited a dictum by Stalin in 1925 that "the compromising section of the national Bourgeoisie has already managed *in the main* to come to an agreement with imperialism. Dreading revolution more than imperialism, this *wealthiest and most influential section* is completely going over to the camp of irreconcilable enemies of the revolution [Dange's italics]." Dange asked:

What made us forget that the Bourgeoisie is itself divided into competing sections? Why did we fail to notice the significance of the words 'in the main' and 'wealthiest sections'? The explanation of the

[96] *Ibid.*, p. 60.
[97] Editorial in *For a Lasting Peace, For a People's Democracy*, January 27, 1950.
[98] *The Communist*, July-August 1950, pp. 6-35.
[99] *Letter of the new Central Committee*, to all party members and sympathizers, Mimeographed, June 1, 1950, p. 7.

politbureau in its resolution is that because we were fighting 'all shades' of Bourgeois nationalism, therefore it attacked and denounced all sections of the Bourgeoisie as having gone over to the counter-revolution and in order to unite all workers, attacked all Bourgeoisie, including the Bourgeoisie of various nationalities, though it should have distinguished between the big Bourgeoisie and the Bourgeoisie of the nationalities who are not yet in power.[100]

Former party secretary P. C. Joshi joined the attack, charging that the Ranadive and Rao leaderships had failed equally dismally to exploit differences in business ranks. The Rao leadership, charged Joshi, is "as touch-me-not Brahman in practical politics as it is ignorantly doctrinaire in its understanding of principles." The demand for linguistic provinces

is being voiced by local Bourgeoisie leaders and even the feudal elements, both from inside and outside the Congress. It is a hot popular issue, and for the party of the proletariat to take initiative and lead in this campaign would have been to build up a powerful mass opposition against the big Bourgeoisie Nehru-Patel Government. . . . Comrade Ranadive's idea was that all this—the demand for separate linguistic provinces—was Bourgeois nationalist reformism and the party had only to expose it all, concentrate upon leading popular struggles to a higher and higher pitch and realize peoples democracy in all the national units of India—when alone self determination could be really enjoyed.[101]

Joshi's regional lieutenants in Maharashtra echoed his attack in a pamphlet which declared that Indian business was "not a monolithic capitalist bloc" but that "regional capitalist sections have ranged themselves in opposition to the monopolists, for example over the tussle for inclusion of Bombay in Maharashtra."[102]

When their intraparty debate was finally resolved in favor of the new flexible line, the Communists in Maharashtra, as in other linguistic regions, could now proceed without ideological hindrance to join local business interests in the demand for linguistic provinces and to point accusing fingers at the Mar-

[100] *Some notes on the roots of our mistakes after Calcutta*, Mimeographed, August 19, 1950, pp. 20-21.

[101] "Letters to Foreign Comrades," *Views*, 1, January 18, 1950, p. 9.

[102] *Struggle against sectarian legacy and for a new perspective*, signed by Bhayyaji Kalkarni, G. D. Sane, K. N. Phadke, D. K. Bedekar, Meenakshi Karadkar, Poona, September 15, 1950, p. 14.

waris. Indeed, in the case of Maharashtra, the villain responsible for the denial of Bombay to Maharashtra has been consistently labeled. What the Communist press said in 1948, deploring proposals to constitute Bombay as a separate city state "to placate a few capitalists,"[103] recurred in 1956 when the party weekly shed tears for Maharashtra, "a serf nation in the service of the commerce of Bombay City."[104]

For the Bengal Communists, the conspicuous Marwari presence in Calcutta could now be trotted out on almost any propaganda occasion. The headquarters of the eastern India railway had been shifted to Calcutta in 1952, said a Bengal Communist writer, "so that Marwari big business . . . could have the best of the bargain."[105] The Bengal Communists took their cue so readily from Diakov's revised thesis in 1949 that their Revolutionary Socialist foe, Tridip K. Chaudhuri, taunted them for the

sudden anxiety displayed by the Bengal provincial committee, criticizing the Polit-bureau about the ruin of Bengali banks and Bengali trade and industries in the 'unequal competition' with the Birlas. In other words, attempts will be made from now onward to bring the dissatisfied and disgruntled Bengali bankers and industrialists (and their counter parts in other provinces) into the 'broad nation-wide united front.' . . . The stalwarts of the Bengal national chamber of commerce ranged in revolutionary array with the workers and peasants against the Gujarati-Marwari collaborators of imperialism![106]

In Karnataka the Communists pamphleteered against alien moneylenders, Marathi Brahmans as well as Marwaris and Gujaratis, for foreclosing mortgages and reducing peasant owners to tenant farmers.[107] The Kerala Communists who bid for election support in 1951 from local owners of coir mat factories,[108] were still flailing in 1956 at "profiteering by Indian

103 *People's Age*, September 10, 1948, p. 1.

104 *New Age*, January 8, 1956, p. 2.

105 Bhowani Sen, *Nutan Bangla* (*New Bengal*), Bengal Communist Committee, Calcutta, 1946, p. 10. See also pp. 17-19, and *India Today*, July 1952, p. 21.

106 Tridip K. Chaudhuri, "In Search of Capitalist Fellow-Travelers," *The Swing Back*, Revolutionary Socialist Party, Calcutta, 1949, p. 125.

107 *The Goondas of Karnataka*, CPI Publication. See also G. Adhikari, *Pakistan and National Unity*, p. 24.

108 K. K. Warior, "Elections and after in Travancore-Cochin," *India Today*, February 1952, p. 18.

monopolists at the expense of Malayalees."[109] And in Andhra, where Marwaris and Gujaratis outnumber indigenous money-lenders by an unusually big ratio, Communist propaganda pressed down heavily on the charge that

The *sahukars* continue to loot: through business, trade and interest it continues. The exploitation is not confined to the villages but to the whole country. The Birlas and Dalmias are sucking the blood of the poor.[110]

"Marwari and Gujarati big business hold under their sway the entire Andhra internal trade,"[111] complained a Communist writer. Andhra Communist leader P. Sundarayya, pointing to the cotton crops of Rayalaseema, lamented that:

We are being forced to export our raw cotton and feed the textile mills of Bombay and Ahmedabad; our growers are not getting reasonable prices; Bombay merchants' agents are selling the stocks with excessive profits in the black market.[112]

Monopoly capital, said the national Communist weekly, opposes the formation of Andhra State out of fear "that linguistic national states, each wishing to develop its own homeland economy for its people, will obstruct the loot carried away by the all-pervading tentacles of the narrow clique of big bankers and landlords who are now in power at the Center."[113]

Of all the slogans used in the Telengana movement, reports one party leader, none carried more force than: " 'Abolish all debts of the peasantry.' No landlord or moneylender dared collect old usurious debts. Six to nine percent interest was decreed by the people's councils on debts taken during the current or past year. Previously interest varied from twenty-five to one hundred percent. For the first time in generations, people in these

[109] *New Age*, July 22, 1956, p. 4.

[110] Cited in *Communist Crimes in Hyderabad*, Government Press, Hyderabad, 1950, p. 19. See also second supplement, April 22, 1949, *Memorandum* of the Agriculturalists Association, p. 30.

[111] A. S. Rao, "Andhras struggle for their own State," *New Age*, November 1953, p. 103.

[112] *Vishalandhralu Prajarajvan* (People's Rule in Vishalandhra), Vijayawada, Vishalandhra Publishing House, 1946, Chap. 3 (translated from Telugu for the author).

[113] *Crossroads*, December 21, 1952, p. 1.

167

villages were free from the rapacious moneylenders."[114] A study of seized Telengana Communist pamphlets in the files of the Hyderabad Government shows attacks on one Hyderabad Congress leader as an "agent of the Marwari capitalists" and on another as "a big Gujarati *sahukar*."[115]

The Communist accent on linguistic provinces sharpened with Rao's replacement as party secretary on the eve of the 1951 national elections. With the admission of regional business and rich peasant groups to the united front the party was ready to accept the Nehru Government's terms—an end to terrorism—to gain credentials for participating in the elections. The Kremlin summoned party stalwarts S. A. Dange, M. Basava Punniah, and Ajoy K. Ghosh to Moscow and tapped Ghosh as the compromise "apparatus man" who could unite rival factions for the important election test. As a keystone of the new united front policy, linguistic provinces became a central party election issue.

Shortly after the elections, P. C. Joshi promptly renewed his demand for emphasis on linguistic provinces, declaring in his organ *India Today* that "if, in the post-election period, anti-Communism is being provoked from above, the national problem is rising from below and the Communists are known and respected as the party that saw first the importance of this basic problem."[116] The newly-elected leader of the Communist bloc in the lower house of Parliament, A. K. Gopalan, exultantly described the formation of linguistic provinces as "India's most important problem, the Communists' number one goal."[117] Gopalan's sweeping invitation to other opposition groups for a joint parliamentary front listed as the second plank in a proposed common platform "immediate formation of linguistic national states . . . wider provincial autonomy."[118] It was this emphasis on linguistic reorganization, in fact, which was pri-

[114] *On Telengana*, Information Document No. 7 (2) to all Party Units, October 7, 1950, by "An Andhra Provincial Member," p. 4.
[115] "Shadow of a change in the Congress-Nizam Government, a cunning drama to mislead the people," p. 2.
[116] Notes of the month, *India Today*, June 1952, pp. 5-6.
[117] *Times of India*, May 26, 1952, p. 1.
[118] "Minimum Program for United Democratic Front," Mimeographed, Issued by "The Communist MP's and MC's," 1 Windsor Place, New Delhi, April 25, 1952.

marily responsible for the decision of Acharya J. B. Kripalani's Kisan Mazdoor Praja (Peasants Workers Peoples) Party to decline membership in the front. The main difference between the Communists and the K.M.P., as *The Statesman* reported at the time, came in "the approach to the problem of 'linguistic autonomy,' which was emphasized in the draft program circulated by the Communist Party. Most K.M.P. members appear to consider this move as a danger to national unity."[119] Despite this rebuff the Communists promptly proceeded to cast themselves as the only true friends of linguistic provinces. Communist deputies stalked out of Parliament on one occasion to protest delivery of speeches in Hindi and then rallied seventy-seven votes for a resolution demanding linguistic reorganization.[120] In December 1952, Communist-led rioting made the fast unto death of an Andhra leader the frantic occasion for the central government's surrender not only to Andhra demands but to demands for a broad reorganization of states.

A Respite for Nehru

It was a bitter irony that, at the very moment when the clamor of contending regions reached its highest pitch since Independence, the exigencies of Indo-Soviet relations compelled the Indian Communists to accent Indian unity. By late 1953, when Stalin's successors decided to reckon with the Indian Union as an established fact, the avowed separatist policies of the Indian Communists clearly required modification. In this case the doctrinal flexibility built into the nationality weapon made it less cumbersome than usual to reverse the party line. But it must have tested the aplomb even of "apparatus-man" Ghosh to stand before the Third Indian Party Congress at Madura in December 1953, and feign shame that "in the past, many a

---

[119] Vedette, "The Political Scene—a still-born parliamentary opposition," May 17, 1952, p. 6. The resignation of Dr. N. D. Jaisoorya, a son of the late Independence leader Sarojini Naidu, from the Communist-led People's Democratic Front in Hyderabad, was couched in part in terms of nationalist objections to the CP's self-determination line. See P. Ramamurthy's defense against "disruptionist" charges, *Indian Communist Party Documents, 1930-56*, Democratic Research Service, Bombay, and Institute of Pacific Relations, New York, 1957, p. 193.

[120] *The Hindu*, July 13, 1952.

time we scoffed at the concept of Indian unity and glorified separatism." In campaigning for linguistic provinces, said Ghosh, "bourgeois-nationalist deviations have been allowed to penetrate our own ranks. . . . The unity of the toiling masses is the most precious thing." While the 1951 Party Program correctly stated that the use of Hindi "will not be obligatory," he explained, introducing the sole amendment to the party program,

at the same time, we have to realize that the Communist Party stands for the unity of India. . . . Hindi is to be encouraged as the language for communication between governments and peoples in different provinces. . . . Where Hindi is not spoken, the party while upholding the rights of the national languages must also encourage and popularize Hindi.[121]

Ghosh spelled out the new line in the party's monthly organ in May 1954, repudiating the "myth of a Marwari oppressor nation" that had been the cornerstone of the party's policy for seven years. A Soviet attack on the managing agency system at about the same time referred only to "intra-caste crediting . . . by large merchant moneylenders,"[122] without directly mentioning the Marwaris. By 1956, an intraparty circular proposing program amendments for the Fourth Party Congress could speak of conflicts between "monopolists" and "smaller industrialists and traders" without any reference to distinctions between centralist Marwaris and regional interests.[123]

This reversal necessitated a spate of explanatory polemics that laid down a new rationale for Communist support of Hindi. What the Third Party Congress had decided, wrote the party's Bengali theoretician on nationality, S. N. Mazumdar, was actually only a reasonable response to extremists—those who, at one end of the spectrum, would impose Hindi at the expense of the regional languages, and those others who would deny any

121 Ajoy Ghosh, "On the work of the third party Congress," *New Age*, January 24, 1954, p. 13.
122 A. I. Levkovshij, "Sistema Upravljajushchikh Agen Tstv-Orudie Poraboshchenija I Ekspluatatsii Narodod Indii Anglijskim Imperializmom" (India and Burma), *Essays in History and Economics*, Vol. 10, pp. 193-194, *Uchenye Zapiski Instituta Vostokovedemia (Learned Notes)*, Vols. 1-10, 1950-1954, Moscow, 1954, Izdatel'stvo Akademii Nauk SSSR (translated for the author).
123 *Amendments to the Party Program*, Fourth Party Congress, Document No. 1, CPI Publication, September 1955, p. 4.

status to Hindi. No longer should Hindi and the regional languages be viewed as deadly rivals. Mazumdar blithely defines the new line in terms indistinguishable from the Congress orthodoxy:

In a multi-lingual country like India, there must be a medium of intercourse. . . . In reality, there is not and should not be any conflict between the federal language and the regional languages. Their spheres of action are different and each can fulfil its functions without encroaching on the sphere of the other. Given a proper and correct understanding of their respective roles, they can enrich one another.[124]

Another writer on nationality found it necessary to rewrite the existing Communist version of Indian history. In the existing version the British were blamed for disrupting the growth of separate linguistic nationalities in India. Now Ram Bilas Sharma argued that as early as the 16th century Hindi had spread throughout India. The existence of Hindi poets in Maharashtra and remote Tanjore, he declared, "brings out the wide popularity of the language. The British actually arrested and hindered the natural process of the unification of the country, a process in which the Hindustani language was playing an important part."[125]

By the eve of Republic Day, January 26, 1955, *Pravda* signalled in an historic editorial that Soviet policy had completed its full 180-degree revolution—from condemnation of Nehru as an imperialist ally to praise of his "outstanding statesmanship" and of India as "a peace-loving state upholding its national independence." Foreign Minister V. M. Molotov echoed the new line in his foreign policy review on February 8, 1955, when he noted the fact, "of great historic significance, that at present there is no colonial India, but instead the Indian republic. More and more rises the international authority of India."[126] The leader of a Soviet delegation to India praised American-assisted

---

[124] S. N. Mazumdar, "Stalin's work on linguistics," II, *New Age*, April 1954, p. 76.

[125] *The Question of an Obligatory State Language in India*, New Delhi, People's Publishing House, 1954, p. 17.

[126] *New York Times*, February 9, 1955, p. 3.

village development projects and India's Five-Year Plan.[127] *Pravda* took the new line on Hindi in its greeting to an Indian Parliament delegation:

As yet, English is the main language used in parliament, as this is the only language comprehensible to all deputies. However, the use of one of the languages of India—Hindi—is receiving more and more encouragement from the Indian Government and deputies frequently deliver speeches in Hindi.[128]

After Nehru's triumphal tour of the Soviet Union in 1955, the Indian Communist Central Committee adapted itself still further to the new turn in Indo-Soviet relations. The Committee passed a comprehensive resolution on the Indian scene in which there was not a single reference to linguistic states or even to the States Reorganization Commission then touring the country.[129]

When the Commission issued its report, the Central Committee went out of its way to emphasize its "general satisfaction," leaving it to local party units to exploit local dissatisfaction with specific recommendations. Ghosh fulsomely welcomed the proposal to abolish the institution of Rajpramukhs (princely rulers) as state governors and the decision to grant "the demands of the peoples of Tamilnad, Kerala, and Karnataka for the formation of their linguistic states," criticizing in unusually restrained terms the postponement of the formation of Vishalandhra and the rejection of the demand for a separate Maharashtra.[130] Local Communist units gave at least nominal credence to the central line in their own statements. The Kerala leader E. M. S. Nambudripad judged that the Commission had gone "a long way in accepting the concrete proposals made by the Communist Party." In place of past excoriations of Marwaris and Gujaratis,

127 " 'Those Soviet reactionaries' Indian Communists might say," *The Indian Worker*, March 5, 1955, p. 3.

128 O. Orestov, *Pravda*, May 10, 1955, p. 3, cited in *Current Digest of the Soviet Press*, June 22, 1955, p. 14.

129 *Communist Party in the struggle for peace, democracy and national advance*, Resolution of the Communist Party Central Committee, CPI Publication, New Delhi, June 1955. See also *Times of India*, August 25, 1955, p. 8, which notes that the Communist Party feels "linguistic rivalries should not be encouraged. . . . The present party line favors responsive cooperation with the government."

130 *New Age*, October 16, 1955, p. 1.

Nambudripad carefully worded his charge that the Commission had denied Bombay City to Maharashtra as a result of its "unwillingness to resist the pressure of non-Maharashtrian big business in Bombay."[131] The Fourth Party Congress in 1956, while protesting the government's stand on Maharashtra and on the abortive Bihar-Bengal merger, praised the government's reorganization program in general as "a great triumph of all patriotic and democratic forces."[132]

Despite its conciliatory phraseology, however, even the present Indian Communist line on nationality with its nominal restraint can be changed on short notice whenever the needs of Soviet foreign policy dictate. Today the Soviet Union attaches high importance to cordial relations with Nehru's India. Whether this would continue to be the case with a lesser leadership remains to be seen. Lesser leadership, moreover, means in all likelihood some decline in India's internal stability, which, in turn, could well tempt regional Communist parties beyond endurance.

In any event, the Indian Communists have never fully relinquished the nationality weapon's most potent ammunition—each "nation's" right to secede from the Indian Union. The right of secession has not been an explicit part of the Indian Communist program since its pointed omission from the 1951 election manifesto. But published policy statements indicate that it is as implicit as ever. Nambudripad, voicing official party policy in 1953, qualified the right but did not deny it in explaining why it had been omitted from the manifesto. Only three months before the party's radical change of front on nationality policy at its Third Congress, Nambudripad tipped off what was to come with references to the "overemphasis" placed on the right of secession. "The right of secession," he wrote, "should not be confused with the *expediency* of the formation of separate states." This remains in each instance "for the working class and its allies in every nation to decide." In the case of the Soviet Union, great Russian oppression of other nationalities

131 *New Age*, October 16, 1955, pp. 8-9. See also B. T. Ranadive's reference to "non-Maharashtrian capitalists" in *New Age*, September 25, 1955, p. 13.
132 *New Age*, May 13, 1956, p. 5.

made the right of secession vital to the Bolshevik cause. But with all due respect to the Marwari bogeyman of the previous seven years,

It would be wrong to mechanically apply this solution to the entirely different situation in India. For here is a state which is not militarist-feudal, dominated by the landlords and Bourgeoisie of a particular nationality in India itself, but a semi-feudal, semi-colonial social and state system in which all the nationalities in India are dominated by British finance capital. . . . Hence, though for India too, the principle of self-determination means and naturally includes the right of separation, it is inexpedient for Indian nationalities to exercise the right.[133]

In 1955, the British Communist Party's oracle on Indian Communist affairs, R. Palme Dutt, carefully left the door ajar with the statement that each "distinct nationality" in India could justly claim "the right to exist as an autonomous state if it so wishes within the free Indian federation (including the right to secede)."[134]

Opportunism, of course, is inherent in Communist nationality doctrine. But there is astonishing elasticity in a rationale that can so easily be alternated to justify, or not to justify, the right of secession. In 1944, G. Adhikari wrote that "the question of when, whether, how to separate cannot and must not be decided today. This question can only be decided in any particular case at any particular time in terms of . . . whether separation serves the interests of social and political development taken as a whole."[135] How similar this is to the open-ended logic of a member of the Indian Communist Central Committee who told the writer that conceivably an Indian region under Communist leadership, such as his own Andhra, might someday be forced to secede, but that

The right of secession is brought into the picture only when connected with imperialism—otherwise it is a question of union. We don't rule out those situations, but we doubt that any Indian gov-

---

[133] "Questions and Answers: Nationalities and the right of secession," *Crossroads*, September 6, 1953, p. 10.

[134] *India Today & Tomorrow*, revised edition, 1955, Lawrence and Wishart, London, pp. 244-245.

[135] *Pakistan and National Unity*, p. 48.

ernment any more will risk imperialist connections. Anyway, the central government is not sitting in the air. They would think very seriously before they would force us to that point. If they force a solution of their problems on the people, not by democracy but by the bayonet, then the people will decide for themselves. Why should we talk of secession now?[136]

Would the Communists invoke the right of secession if the Congress-controlled central government should ever try to starve out a Communist-controlled Andhra? Another Andhra Communist leader replied that

We could always dissolve the state assembly and get the Andhra people's verdict. If the center would not compromise, it would depend on the people how they were going to take the future into their own hands. But if such a stage is reached, the center will in its own interests compromise. Because when there would be a bursting point there, there would be a bursting point in other places. We don't want independent states, but we do want greater residuary powers in the hands of the states than in the center.[137]

To take away the threat to secede even tentatively is to handicap the party in its relations with other regional groups. The slow start of the Kerala Communists on their road to success in the 1951 elections can be attributed in part to the limitations on their united election front with the separatist Kerala Socialist Party (KSP). "What are the main differences in the united front?" asked a Communist writer. "In the first place, there is the KSP slogan of an independent Kerala . . . independent of the rest of India."[138] Since the Communists and the Revolutionary Socialist Party could not accept the KSP line as part of a joint manifesto, the three parties maintained only a nominal united front in the 1951 election campaign and the Congress remained in power. Writing at the same time, in neighboring Tamilnad, the Tamil Communist Sankara Narayan objected strenuously to the fact that the national Communist leadership had disassociated itself from the demand for a sovereign Dravidastan in its 1951 election alliance with the Dravida Kazagham:

[136] Interview with M. Basavapunniah, September 22, 1953, New Delhi.
[137] Interview with T. Nagi Reddi, Gandhi Nagar, Madras City, December 14, 1952.
[138] *Crossroads*, March 7, 1952, p. 5.

The unity of India is not an article of faith for us. The democratic movement in India is not uniform. A contingency may arise in the future when the democratic anti-imperialist and anti-feudal movement to the south may grow so strong that it may capture political power, while unfortunately the movement in the north may be unable to reach that happy consummation.

Should we on such an occasion, because of our desire to have a united India, oppose the secession of the southern region from the imperialist and monopoly finance-ridden north? . . . If people belonging to a certain nationality give their verdict in favor of a separate state, the CPI, true to its Marxian principles on the national question, cannot oppose them.[139]

As it happens, Indian Communism need be true only to principles convenient at a given time. Even at present, when it is necessary, if inconvenient, to dull the edge of separatism, the Indian Communists continue to attack "the reactionary Congress concept of India as one nation,"[140] to oppose interstate administrative zones,[141] to warn that "monopoly capital" is growing stronger,[142] and to resist central government control over strategic cities such as Bombay.[143] While official policy avoids insults to Hindi, operative Communist policy continues to emphasize "as speedy a transition as possible"[144] to the regional languages and their use as optional media of national civil service examinations.[145] Removal of English, which "constitutes the biggest obstacle in the path of India's cultural advance," is the "paramount task."[146] To contend, as Indian Communist leaders did in 1956, that "the demands of the various nationalities of

---

[139] *Crossroads*, January 18, 1952, p. 10.

[140] *New Age*, March 1956, p. 4.

[141] *New Age*, January 1, 1956, p. 4. For an excellent review of the zonal council plan, see *Regionalism Versus Provincialism: A Study of the Problems of Indian National Unity*, Joan V. Bondurant, Indian Press Digests—Monograph Series No. 4, December 1958, University of California, Berkeley.

[142] "Report to the Party Congress—1956," *Indian Communist Party Documents, 1930-1956*, pp. 284-286. See also *New Age*, July 1957, p. 34, and December 1957, p. 2.

[143] *New Age*, February 6, 1955, p. 1.

[144] The Communist Chief Minister of Kerala, E. M. S. Nambudripad, discussed language policy in a party conference on January 4, 1958, according to *The Hindu Weekly Review*, January 10, 1958.

[145] Ajoy Ghosh, "Language Policy," *New Age*, March 1958, p. 12.

[146] Ajoy Ghosh, "Report of the Official Language Commission," *New Age*, December 1957, p. 10.

India for their free development are denied,"[147] is but a short step away from provoking a constitutional crisis. The victory of the Kerala Communists in 1957 came at a time when such a crisis between the central government and its most distant outpost could not be precipitated without undercutting Soviet strategy in India. But what will Soviet strategy be five or ten years from now?

In future as in past relations with the Soviet Union and Communist China, Indian leaders will be influenced in considerable degree by the desire to forestall the full fury of Communist separatism. For their part, the Indian Communists, who would be the first to crush separatism once they were in power, cannot be expected to forsake their best weapon indefinitely. Their isolation from nationalist forces in the wake of Chinese border incursions in 1959 may very well leave them no other effective means for taking the political offensive. Given a total demoralization and collapse of non-Communist forces, of course, the Indian Communists would not need to employ this weapon and might instead aim for power via a nationalist united front. They are ready for this eventuality: Ajoy Ghosh declared in 1958 that "the unity of India can today be maintained only by strengthening the Communist Party and democratic forces."[148] But only a mercurial change in that intangible and perhaps unmeasurable quantity—national state of mind—might enable one to envisage the wholesale pro-Communist defections necessary for a successful united front strategy. Weighing the tangible and measurable facts of existing Indian Communist machinery and of the location of Indian Communist strength, one must hesitate before assuming, as so many do, that pro-Communist susceptibilities among Indian intellectuals will be translated into political power—that governmental centralization in India merely prepares an apparatus all the more convenient for the Communists to take over.

[147] *Amendments to the Party Program*, pp. 3-4.
[148] *New Age*, April 13, 1958, p. 13.

VI · INDIAN COMMUNISM: WHERE STRATEGY SUCCEEDED

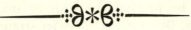

CONCEIVABLY, Indian Communism will in time yield up pan-Indian leadership so dynamic, so cohesive, that the future Indian political alignment will bear only slight resemblance to the past. But if the past is any guide, Indian Communism will not, by itself, provide a pan-Indian alternative to the Congress Party. Indian Communism is a loose federation of regional units that have succeeded, where they have in fact succeeded, only on regional ground. The uneven pattern of Communist strength corresponds to the pattern of Communist identification with regional forces. The pattern of failure, too, corresponds to regions in which rivals have monopolized regional patriotism. With its strength dispersed in scattered regional strongholds, Indian Communism seems committed by its past to a separatist future.

Painted in broad strokes, the pattern of Indian Communist strength shows a movement concentrated heavily in the non-Hindi regions. While the Congress machine is entrenched most deeply in the Hindi-speaking northern states, the strongest Communist organizations are all outside the Hindi heartland.[1] Thus Telugu delegates claimed 25 percent of the votes at the Fourth Party Congress in 1956, Malayalam 19, Bengali almost 12, and two other non-Hindi contingents, Marathi and Tamil, 7 percent each. Unlike the Soviet Communist Party, in which the dominant Soviet nationality, Great Russian, is also the dominant bloc in the party, the Hindi belt represented only 21 percent of Indian Communist strength.[2] Not surprisingly,

---

[1] "As one Communist leader despairingly pointed out," reported the *Times of India*, May 5, 1956, p. 1, from the Fourth C.P.I. Congress at Palghat, "the entire Hindi belt from Bihar to Rajasthan is overwhelmingly Congress in its loyalties." See also Amlan Datta, *The Radical Humanist*, March 23, 1952, p. 139.

[2] Party press releases at the Congress listed delegate representation. Membership figures announced in February 1958, according to *The Hindu Weekly Review*, February 17, 1958, showed that Kerala, with 25 percent, and Andhra, with 19 percent, had been juxtaposed.

in view of this pattern of organization, the Communists have won their significant electoral representation mainly in the legislatures of such non-Hindi regions as Andhra, Kerala, and Bengal. This was the case in the 1951 elections; and again in 1957, despite Communist attempts to emphasize nation-wide distribution of strength, Communist victories were overwhelmingly concentrated in established strongholds. Although placing in the field fifty-six percent more candidates in 1957 than in 1951—thus inevitably assuring victories here and there in all states—the Communists still won nearly half of their total parliamentary votes in Andhra and Kerala alone.[3] It is in Kerala that the Communists captured their only state government and in Andhra, where they polled 2,695,562 votes in 1955, that they have claimed their biggest electoral following.[4]

To some extent, notably in the cases of Andhra and Kerala, the pattern of Communist strength can be explained as the result of historical accident. During the prewar Communist-Socialist united front the Communists infiltrated and captured units of the Congress Socialist Party (CSP) which happened to be in non-Hindi regions. Communist Party members constituted a majority in six CSP regional units.[5] In the cases of Andhra and Kerala, the CSP units were well-organized adjuncts

[3] In regional literary and cultural activities, too, it is in the non-Hindi regions that the Communists have been most successful. For a revealing summary in a party organ, see Ram Bilas Sharma, "Report to the Sixth Session, All India Progressive Writers Conference," *Indian Literature*, No. 2, 1953, p. 53. For other references to this regional disparity in Communist cultural activities, see also, Niranjan Sen, *Unity*, December 1952, p. 47, and February 1953, p. 48; *Indian Literature*, No. 1, 1952, pp. 1, 44; and *Crossroads*, April 19, 1953, p. 1. The Communist press has thrived best in non-Hindi regions, according to *New Age*, October 4, 1953, p. 3. See also *Crossroads*, February 29, 1952, pp. 15-16; and *Party Letter*, June 8, 1943, Vol. III, No. 11. *Party Letter*, May 1, 1943, p. 3, shows leading circulations then were *Janayuddha*, Bengali, 12,500, and *Prajasakti*, Telugu, 7,500.

[4] The Andhra Communists in defeat polled more than the 2,156,012 registered by the victorious Kerala Communists in capturing their legislative majority.

[5] Jayaprakash Narayan, *Towards Struggle*, Padma Publications, Bombay, 1946, pp. 171, 174. Minoo Masani cites the Communist circular "Plan of Work," dated May 9, 1938, in "Communist Plot Against the C.S.P.," *Indian Communist Party Documents, 1930-1956*, Democratic Research Service, Bombay, and Institute of Pacific Relations, New York, 1957, pp. 40-44, in which the Communists claimed majorities in the Andhra, Kerala, Tamilnad, Orissa, Bengal, and Punjab party units.

to the Congress machine,[6] solid bases for regional Communist parties which gained from the beginning a head start over Communist units in other parts of India. But it is clearly not enough to explain the non-Hindi character of Indian Communism as a mere accident of history. For all the importance of the CSP legacy, the fact remains that there has been a marked disparity in Communist fortunes from one non-Hindi region to another that only partially corresponds to the CSP pattern. Why, for example, did the Andhra and Kerala parties develop such strength while another of the six Communist-majority CSP units, that in Tamilnad, failed to grow into an effective Communist organization? Why has Maharashtra yielded a relatively insignificant Communist movement?

"A Bunch of Brahman Boys"

In part the pattern of Communist strength in India has coincided with those regions, such as Andhra and Kerala, where the sense of regional subjection in a multilingual political unit became most acute and where Communist parties were able to outdo others in championing the demand for regional autonomy. The Communists themselves attributed the location of their successes in 1951 in substantial degree to the regional issue. In an intraparty circular issued two months after the elections, most of the seven reasons cited for the disparity in Communist electoral fortunes put the blame outside the party or on local organizational details. Only one important condition for victory related directly to Communist strategy and tactics:

Where provincial units of the party brought out their own manifestoes, where agitation was positive and such concrete factors as the *national* factor, the factor of the unification of the nationality into linguistic provinces, were effectively utilized. The contrast between Andhra and Kerala on the one hand and Maharashtra on the other is striking.[7]

[6] P. C. Joshi, in *Among Kisan Patriots*, a pamphlet review of the Vijayawada, Andhra, Session of the All India Kisan Sabha, People's Publishing House, Bombay, 1946, p. 4, recounts that an Andhra Communist claimed to him in 1946: "It is we who built the Congress organization in the villages, and becoming Communists did not make us any the less Congressmen in the eyes of the masses, simply because the party taught us to become organizers."

[7] "On the results of the general elections and the tasks before the party,"

Only part of the answer, however, lies in the manipulation of regional patriotism, for a region-by-region analysis shows that nowhere does this fully explain, in and of itself, the basis of Communist power. It is where the Communist leadership at the same time holds a footing in politically strategic regional castes, which are in most cases rising non-Brahman castes, that Communist activities have gained decisive leverage. Indeed, divided as power is in every region among the new caste lobbies, regional caste ground is the only solid ground on which the manipulator can stand.

The success story of the Andhra Communists is a striking case in point, so instructive, in fact, that it is set forth as a separate documented case study in the following section. Not only could the Andhra leadership exploit India's most intense regional agitation for autonomy; in addition, the Andhra leadership happened to be based in a politically strategic regional caste, the Kamma gentry of the Krishna-Godavari delta. With their base in the Kammas, who own an estimated eighty percent of the fertile delta land, the Andhra Communist leaders "belonged" in their regional social and economic power structure. Where regional Communist parties have been unsuccessful, on the other hand, it is often because predominantly Brahman Communist leaderships have competed as social strangers for the allegiance of newly-assertive non-Brahman caste lobbies.

Prior to the 1951 elections the existence of a strong Communist movement in Andhra was attributed to Andhra's high population density, especially to the unusual concentration of untouchable landless labor—thirty-seven percent of the agricultural population in the delta. But when in 1951 the Andhra Communists won not only most of the seats reserved for untouchable landless labor, but twenty-five general seats as well,

---

Party Letter, No. 5, April 1952, p. 15. For another reference to Marathi-Telugu disparity, contrasting Telengana and Marathwada, see *Crossroads*, March 21, 1952, p. 14. A. M. Diakov, in *Crisis of the Colonial System* (People's Publishing House, Bombay, 1950, p. 35), declared that "the national liberation movement bears particularly sharp forms where there already exist developed nations. This movement is distinguished by the greatest acuteness in the bounds of the national regions of Andhra, Maharashtra, Kerala, and Karnataka. It is much weaker in Tamilnad and Gujarat."

this explanation could no longer account for Andhra Communist strength. The crucial element in fourteen of these twenty-five upset victories was, as we will see, simply that the Kamma Communist leaders could compete for financial support and votes from a caste group, their own, which held the balance of political power. By winning a share of Kamma support at the same time that they were exploiting the Andhra State issue, then at its highest emotional pitch, the Andhra Communists gained the margin of strength necessary to win their 1951 victories. Neither the caste base of their leadership nor the manipulation of regional patriotism would have been sufficient alone to provide this margin of success.

If the Andhra Communist success story appeared to be momentarily darkened in 1955, when Congress election victories cut in half Communist seats in the state legislature, it was precisely because the party failed to command the bloc strength in delta constituencies that Kamma support had made possible in 1951. While the party actually polled more votes than ever, the Congress, bargaining hard to regain Kamma support, commanded the margin of victory in Kamma strongholds, which were once again the decisive battleground. In view of their economic stake as peasant proprietors, of course, Kamma patriarchs may never have intended to remain bedfellows with the Communists for long. Kamma Communist leaders were able to capitalize on their social ties at a time when the Kammas had lost factional ground inside the Congress to the Reddis, a rival non-Brahman peasant proprietor caste group. But the coincidence that the Communists could, in fact, exploit the Kamma-Reddi rivalry should not be minimized. Indeed, the social base of their leadership has been invariably decisive in the success or failure of Communist parties in most regions of India.

Tamilnad

In the case of Tamilnad, where the Dravidian movement has appropriated regional patriotism, the Communists are consigned at least temporarily to political outer darkness by the added handicap of a predominantly Brahman leadership. Only with a base in the same influential non-Brahman castes that provide the base of the Dravidian movement could the Communists compete against the whole-hog Dravidian demand for separation from the Union.

The short-lived 1951 Communist-Dravidian election alliance demonstrated how dependent the Communists were on Dravidian support for even their negligible measure of election success. The Dravida Kazagham or Dravidian Federation supported sixteen of the fifty Communist election contestants. While thirteen of these Kazagham-supported Communist candidates were successful, only two other Communist candidates, in Srirangam and Erode, were able to win election in all Tamilnad without Kazagham support (see Table I). Furthermore, the sixteen Kazagham-supported candidates polled an average 37 percent of the vote in their constituencies; the thirty-four other Communist candidates who were not supported by the Kazagham polled only 18.4 percent, while the fifty-seven Kazagham candidates who ran without the benefit of an alliance were strong enough to poll an average 45.1 percent.

Even in Tanjore, where the Communists had directed their appeal to Tamil landless laborers, it was the particularist rather than the economic appeal which seems to have been decisive. In Tanjore the Communists had attached themselves to the cause of sharecroppers who had finally won the right in 1948, after decades of agitation, to retain 25 percent of their produce. Then, when the owners of the rich Kaveri delta land would not accede to new demands for 30 percent, the Communists had incited the laborers in 1951 to harvest and carry off their crops without any payment at all. This defiance, on the eve of the 1951 elections, prompted wide-spread evictions, a state of virtual siege in the countryside, and finally promulgation of the so-called Tanjore Ordinance by Rajagopalachari's Madras Congress Ministry to restore tenancy rights and fix compromise payment scales.[8] The Communists were riding the crest of local popularity at election time, but strong as their position was in Tanjore, strong at least in contrast to other Tamil

[8] See B. Srinivasa Rao, *Crossroads*, September 1, 1952, p. 8, and *News Bulletin of the All-India Kisan Sabha*, December 1952, p. 1.

TABLE I

COMMUNIST CANDIDATES IN TAMILNAD IN 1951 STATE ASSEMBLY
ELECTION: ALLIANCE WITH DRAVIDA KAZAGHAM

District	Constituency Supported by DK	Percent of Vote	Constituency Not Supported by DK	Percent of Vote
North Arcot			Vellore General	11
			Gudiyatham	9
			Chengam	19
			Arni	6
			Tirupattur	24
South Arcot			Gingee	5
Chingleput			Kanchipuram	8
Coimbatore	Uttukuli	39*	Udamalpet	25
			Madukkarai	22
			Pollachi Gen.	22
			Pollachi Res.	20
			Erode	41*
			Bhavani	11
Madras	Washermanpet	33*	Triplicane	9
	Perambur	16		
	Choolai	10		
Madura	Madura North	37*	Cumbum	15
	Vedanchendur	51*	Palni	14
			Ottanchatram	13
			Nilakkottai Res.	7
			Melur Res.	10
			Dindigul	38
Ramnad	Ramanathapuram	23	Manamadura	19
			Paramakudi	20
Salem	Tiruchengode	27*	Krishnagiri	23
	Namakkal	38*	Salem Town	32
Tanjore	Tanjore Gen.	18*	Nannilam Gen.	12
	Nidamangalam	54*	Nannilam Res.	14
	Mannargudi Gen.	50*	Mayuram Gen.	7
	Mannargudi Res.	48*	Kumbakonam	46
	Nagapattinam Gen.	46*	Adhiramapattinam	34
	Nagapattinam Res.	47*	Sirkali	32
Tirunelveli			Tuticorin	15
			Tirunelveli Gen.	14
			Nanguneri	17
Trichinopoly	Trichy North	59*	Srirangam	53*

* Elected.
Percentages in this table were computed with the assistance of the Littauer Statistical Laboratory, Harvard University, on the basis of official election returns.

184

districts, it was still the Dravidian movement which made the most impressive showing in the alliance. Although six of the joint Communist-Dravidian victories were in Tanjore, in six other constituencies in which they contested without Dravidian support the Communists lost decisively.[9]

For such unavoidable rivals the alliance was destined to be one of mere convenience from the start, and the two protagonists relapsed, accordingly, to their fundamental mistrust soon after the elections. Periyar had justified the pact with the simple explanation that "my enemy's enemy is my friend." He likened it to a

railway travel friendship. Passengers traveling in a compartment become friends, their friendship lasts until they reach their destinations. Each passenger gets down at his particular way station and goes his own way. That is the friendship between the Communist Party and the Dravida Kazagham. We want to see the Congress Party defeated at the polls.[10]

Although Periyar gave a plethora of reasons afterward for breaking off the friendship, charging the Communists, among other treachery, with "secret attempts to convert Dravida Kazagham branches into Communist Party units," the fundamental reason lay in the Brahman preponderance in the Tamil Communist leadership and what the Kazagham would have us believe to be its logical consequence, Tamil Communist subservience to north Indian domination. In a Tanjore constituency, alleged Periyar, the Communists surreptitiously supported a Congress Brahman candidate against the Kazagham choice.

---

[9] *The Hindu*, February 3, 1952, p. 6, attributed Communist victories in Tanjore to the fact that "the ground was prepared for them" by the Dravidian movement.

[10] *Viduthalai*, November 27, 1951, p. 1. The resolution passed by the Kazagham Executive Committee at Trichinopoly, November 15, 1951, translated from Tamil for the author, is as follows:

A. This committee resolves that the primary object of the Dravida Kazagham so far as the election is concerned is to get the Congress candidate defeated in the general elections.

B. It is therefore resolved that as a party, the Communist Party candidates should be supported in the election.

C. It is resolved that, where there is no chance of success for the Communist candidate in any constituency, those candidates who stand in the name of any other party against the Congress, and those who stand as independents, should be supported by the Kazagham, if it is felt that such candidates have got a chance of success against the Congress.

"The Communists have their office at a foreign place, Bombay or Delhi," said Periyar, "and they are just as interested in exploiting our country as any of the other foreign-controlled parties. Besides, most of the Communist leaders are Brahmans. Ramamurthi is a *pucca* (grade A) Brahman. The editors of *Janashakti* (Tamil Communist weekly) are Brahmans. Wherever a Brahman goes, into the Communist Party or anywhere else, he wants to support caste distinctions."[11]

The special object of Periyar's scorn is P. Ramamurthy, member of the Indian Communist Politburo, just as the Communist apple of his eye is the party's leading non-Brahman, the Madras City labor leader Jeevanandam. Once Periyar's supporter in the old Justice Party, precursor of the Dravidian movement, Jeevanandam bolted to the Communists to protest Justice ties to non-Brahman landlords. When the new Communist line denied the right of secession from the Indian Union in 1953, it fell to Jeevanandam's lot to mount the attack on the Dravidasthan demand. The revised Communist emphasis on language and its denial of Dravidian racial claims compelled Jeevanandam to argue in a special tract, *The Unity of Tamilnad*, that all Tamils could be identified by their Tamilian birthright irrespective of their caste. The Dravidian writer Kunrathol countered quickly that Jeevanandam

is denied the right to defend Tamilnad because the Communist Party in Tamilnad is dominated by Brahmans and Mr. Jeevanandam's position is utterly unimportant. . . . Mr. Jeevanandam argues that C. P. Ramaswami Iyer and Rajagopalachari are Tamilians. In the same way Nehru and Prakasam are known as Kashmiri and Andhra instead of Aryan. This is the trick of the Brahmans.[12]

The central Communist Party exploits poor Jeevanandam through his Brahman superiors, just as the Soviets, for all their claims to national justice, exploit their hinterland out-

[11] Interview, December 14, 1952, Madras. The Trichinopoly District Kazagham, in a resolution on December 14, 1951, blamed the rupture with the Communists on Communist opposition to the demand for a separate Dravidian state, according to T. Balakrishnan Nayar, "Madras," *Indian General Elections, 1951-52*, S. V. Kogekar and R. L. Park, eds., Popular Book Depot, Bombay, 1956, p. 95.
[12] *Jeevavukku Bathil* (Answer to Jeeva), Madras, 1954, pp. 25, 31-32.

posts.[13] Thus, runs the rebuttal, Jeevanandam serves the cause of Hindi and Marwari imperialism.[14] What should all good Communist non-Brahmans do? Stay right where they are, inside Communist ranks, but begin behaving as non-Brahmans, infiltrating in reverse through a species of political squatters' rights!

For their part, the Communists justified the alliance up until the elections with all the proper protestations, pointing to Periyar's courageous departure from the Justice Party to found "a huge mass organization," one which "has its origin in the revolt against severe caste oppression."[15] Bombay Communist leader S. A. Dange, himself a Brahman, explained that agrarian revolts in the South were naturally anti-Brahman since the masses are non-Brahmans and untouchables. He called the Kazagham "more a progressive mass movement than a communal organization."[16] But it was not long until the end of the election signalled the end of the lip service that Tamil Communists had continued to pay to the right of secession for the sake of a facade of unity with the Kazagham. The end was unannounced but nonetheless definite. On February 11, with the elections barely over, Ramamurthy, in a speech delivered at Periyar's side, referred to "the right to secede from the union on the basis of language, culture, and contiguity of territory."[17] But less than two weeks after that statement, which received India-wide publicity to the discomfiture of the Tamil party leaders, Ramamurthy made it clear that even the facade could be maintained no longer. The Kazagham executive committee meeting on February 24 declared that there was no hope for Communist conversion on the separation issue. "The Communist Party had definitely decided to oppose us on this," recalled Periyar, "whatever they may have said for

13 *Ibid.*, pp. 36-37.
14 *Ibid.*, pp. 15, 19.
15 *Crossroads*, December 28, 1951, p. 7.
16 The author was present at Dange's press conference in Constitution House, New Delhi, December 23, 1952, when he discussed the Communist-Kazagham alliance.
17 *Free Press Journal*, Bombay, February 11, 1952, p. 1.

their purposes in the elections, but they, not we, will suffer for it."[18]

If the 1957 elections provide any indication, Periyar's prophecy has been vindicated, for the Communists in Tamilnad dropped from seventeen seats in 1951 to a mere four in the State assembly in 1957. "It must be admitted that many of us did not grasp the tremendous democratic significance of the national factor," wrote a party leader. With a nod to C. N. Annadurai's Dravida Munnetra Kazagham or Dravidian Progressive Federation, which had displaced Periyar's Kazagham to a great extent by 1957, he declared that "without doubt, the minimization of this factor by us helped the DMK to capitalize anti-Congress sentiment in a big way."[19]

Dravidian propagandist A. S. Venu has explicitly claimed that it is the Dravidasthan demand which gives his movement its unique position in Tamilnad, relegating other anti-Congress parties to insignificance. "Barring a few differences, there is nothing novel in the motives of other parties," argues Venu. "The Congress stands for a united India. All other parties too stand for one united India. It is proved and known that the people of the South do not like the one united India any longer. They uphold the theory of separation."[20] Whether or not Venu's estimate of his opponents is justified, the Tamil Communists indeed present a sorry spectacle next to their partisans in Andhra and Kerala. In his estimate of Communist strength in the regional literatures, Ram Bilas Sharma places Tamil very near the bottom of the list.[21] Moreover, Communist prospects in Tamilnad seem darker than ever now that Annadurai has become the major Dravidian leader. For Annadurai's appeal is frankly directed to the non-Brahman dispossessed, rather than the non-Brahman well-to-do. True, Periyar, in his long career, made periodic gestures to the goodwill

[18] Interview cited.

[19] New Age, June 1957, p. 6. See also Hindustan Times, April 8, 1957, p. 4.

[20] Dravidasthan, Kalai Manram, Madras, 1953, pp. 71, 73.

[21] "Report to the Sixth Session, All-India Progressive Writers Conference," Indian Literature, p. 64. See also discussions of Tamil Communist cultural activity by M. B. Srinivasan, Crossroads, September 6, 1953, p. 11, and New Age, September 24, 1954, p. 10.

enjoyed by the Communists in Asia, such as when he returned from a Soviet visit in 1932 to write "vague Socialist slogans" into the Justice Party's so-called Erode Program.[22] But for all his gestures, he has undeniably represented the non-Brahman elite rather than the non-Brahman masses. Annadurai, too, is no doubt on the receiving end of donations from non-Brahman mercantile and landed interests, but he goes to great pains to discount such charges and to talk in proletarian language. In 1951 the Socialists called the Dravida Kazagham "the party of the weak and timid south Indian capitalist class. . . . It is an open secret that the DK movement is financed by the mill owners of Coimbatore."[23] Annadurai, speaking for his own wing of the movement, replied that it would be convenient to accept capitalist support but

we will not fall into that trap. It is very easy to secure the support of the capitalists and industrialists to our cause by giving them a blank check. They will be only too willing to support us because of their natural desire to step into the shoes of their North Indian counterparts. But we are not here to oblige Dravidian capitalism. In the Dravida Nad which we envisage we will not countenance capitalism of any sort, be it North Indian or Dravidian. And this is the reason why the Dravidian capitalists are not with us.[24]

A Bengali Communist, writing in the national party weekly in 1958, dismissed DMK promises of nationalization of industry and land reform as "Socialist sauce to whet the intellectuals' appetite." But he could not deny that Annadurai's popularity "is something to be seen." "The DMK advances with its cult of unreason," he lamented. "Hard work lies ahead in Tamilnad for those who believe in India, her unity and her future of Socialism." And as the 1962 elections approached, the possibility arose that the Dravidian movement and the Communists would ally once again. In 1959 Communist votes helped elect DMK men as mayors of the Madras and Coimba-

[22] *Delhi Express*, August 6, 1952, p. 6.
[23] *Janata*, July 29, 1951, p. 9.
[24] Cited in S. Vedaratnam, *A Plea for Understanding*, Vanguard Publishing House, Conjeevaram, 1951, p. 34.
[25] *Link* (New Delhi newsweekly), May 31, 1959, p. 11.

tore municipalities.[25] Annadurai told a May Day rally in Madras that the Communists "are of the poor, for the poor, and so are we," and predicted that "ultimately we may agree that both of us should jointly represent Communism."[26]

Maharashtra

Anti-Brahmanism as a political cult has flourished in Maharashtra quite as much as in Tamilnad. But far from exploiting caste tensions, the Maharashtra Communists, too, have been handicapped by the predominantly Brahman base of their own leadership. Neither the dominant non-Brahman caste in Maharashtra—the Maratha peasant proprietors—nor the potentially powerful Mahar untouchables are to be found represented among the high-caste urban intellectuals who founded Maharashtra Communism. Maharashtra Communist B. T. Ranadive, a former secretary of the Indian Communist Party, belongs to a Maharashtra caste subordinate only to the Brahmans, the Kayasth Prabhus; S. A. Dange, G. S. Sardesai, S. V. Ghate, and G. Adhikari, his fellow Maharashtra Communist notables, all belong to various Brahman castes. The Communist press has conceded that "a broad-based *kisan* movement is practically non-existent in the Marathi-speaking areas,"[27] which S. S. More, former leader of the Maratha caste political vehicle, the Peasants and Workers Party, has explained in straightforward caste terms. More dismisses the Communists in his region as "mostly from the advanced classes. Look at Sardesai and Ghate. They are Brahmans all the way."[28] The late Dr. B. R. Ambedkar, who organized the Mahars as a political force, accounted similarly for Communist weakness in Maharashtra:

The Communist Party was originally in the hands of some Brahman boys—Dange and others. They have been trying to win over the Maratha community and the scheduled castes. But they have made no headway in Maharashtra. Why? Because they are mostly

[26] *Op.cit.*, May 10, 1959, p. 9.
[27] *News Bulletin of the All-India Kisan Sabha*, August 1953, Vol. 2, No. 8, p. 1. For a scholar's discussion of the Maharashtra Communists and caste tensions, see Nalini Pandit, *Maharashtraleela Rashtravadacha Vikasa* (Growth of Nationalism in Maharashtra), published by the author, Bombay, 1956, p. 215.
[28] Interview with S. S. More, New Delhi, July 1, 1953.

a bunch of Brahman boys. The Russians made a great mistake to entrust the Communist movement in India to them. Either the Russians didn't want Communism in India—they wanted only drummer boys—or they didn't understand.[29]

Although Ambedkar's Scheduled Castes Federation never became a well-organized party on a national scale, among the Mahars Ambedkar could claim enough organized support to frustrate most Communist attempts to control Mahar labor both in Bombay and in Maharashtra proper. But all Maharashtra labor is not Mahar. Many young Marathas leave their villages for part of the year to earn factory wages in such provincial industrial centers as Ahmednagar. These Maratha workers with one leg in the village responded not to the Communists but to a labor wing of the Peasants and Workers Party led by the Maratha Datta Deshmukh. Although Deshmukh went over to the Communists in 1953, together with a dissident rural faction in the Peasants and Workers Party, even this limited Maratha integration with the Communists has remained incomplete.[30] This was so, said Ambedkar, because Deshmukh "is not a Communist in that sense. He is just a poor boy who has been misled by some Brahmans."

It was the Maratha leader More, not the Communists, who capitalized on the formation of a new movement for a separate Maharashtra in 1948. While the Andhra Communists were taking over the campaign for an Andhra State, the Maharashtra Communists were complaining that the Maharashtra Conference was "initiated by some intellectuals and Congress leaders as almost a private affair of their own."[31] Not until after the 1951 elections did the Maharashtra Communists begin what was to become furiously repentant activity in behalf of a separate Maharashtra, and then only when the national high command rapped their knuckles in public:

[29] Interviews with Dr. B. R. Ambedkar, February 21, February 28, and October 9, 1953, Alipore Road, Delhi.

[30] See *New Age*, May 29, 1953, p. 3, for an account of the merger negotiations which accompanied Deshmukh's merger with the C P. For an earlier phase of C P relations with Maratha leaders, see Peasants and Workers Party, Executive Committee, *Scrutiny of the Draft Program of the Communist Party of India*, July 1951, Poona.

[31] *People's Age*, October 31, 1948, p. 5.

The Party in Maharashtra has to take up the issue of Samyukta Maharashtra in right earnest. The ignoring of this issue by the Party is a serious failing which has nothing in common with the Marxist principle that the party of the proletariat has to fight for unification of national homelands. The relative strength and stability of the Congress in Bombay and Madhya Pradesh is due, among other reasons, to the fact that the movement for linguistic provinces has remained weak.[32]

As late as 1957, Ranadive conceded, many party leaders "vacillated" when instructed to participate in the Samyukta Maharashtra Samiti, a united front of all parties formed to press the linguistic demand. Ranadive attributed this vacillation to their "failure to understand properly the depth of democratic feeling behind the demand for linguistic states."[33] But it is likely that the doctrinaire urban trade unionists who control Maharashtra Communism understood all too well. Dange, for example, pointed with alarm to the prospect of Samiti-operated trade unions, which "would not be proletarian internationalism. If you divide the workers on a national basis, it will create complications. How to deal with this situation?"[34]

Even Dange, however, does not dispute that the Maharashtra Party's long-overdue identification with regional patriotism promises to pay dividends. When the chance came to set up a new cotton textile union in collaboration with a Socialist Samiti colleague he forgot about the complications. "Labor and linguism," concluded an observer, "are in grand alliance."[35] In the 1957 elections eighteen Communists who went before the electorate as Samiti candidates won seats in the Bombay Assembly.[36] Perhaps, as Ranadive argued, the Samiti united front has even "laid the basis of healing the great split between the dem-

[32] "On the Results of the General Elections and the Tasks Before the Party," *Party Letter*, p. 24.

[33] B. T. Ranadive, "Maharashtra Election Review," *New Age*, July 1957, p. 21. For examples of Communist attempts to capture the Maharashtra issue, *Unity*, December 1952, pp. 27-30, and February 1953, p. 48, and *Indian Literature*, p. 74. "My Bombay," an adaptation of the Maharashtra *tamasha* folk art form, pleading the case for Bombay City's inclusion in Maharashtra and addressed to Mahar laborers, is published in part in *New Age*, October 4, 1953, p. 2.

[34] S. A. Dange, "Trade Union Tasks," *New Age*, December 1957, pp. 10-11.

[35] *Hindustan Times*, June 22, 1959, p. 6.

[36] *Hindu Weekly Review*, July 29, 1957, p. 7.

ocratic movement and the untouchable masses, led by the late Doctor Ambedkar."[37] But for the present the Maharashtra Communists are still cut off from the Mahars and, even more important, from most politically organized Marathas.

Kerala

The success of the Kerala Communist Party as the first regional Communist Party in India to capture control of a state government can be explained, above all, by its ability to manipulate the regional patriotism of all Kerala at the same time that it manipulated politically strategic caste lobbies within linguistic boundaries. As in the case of Andhra, the Kerala Communists have exploited unusually acute economic despair. But this is not enough to account for the fact that the Kerala Communists in their 1957 victory actually polled less votes— 36.5 percent to 38.2 percent—than the losing Congress Party. As in Andhra, the Kerala Communists mobilized mass support around regional slogans; as in Andhra, the Kerala Communists were able to transform economic despair into a legislative majority because their footing on regional caste ground, notably among the numerous Ezhavas, provided the necessary margin of bloc strength in the necessary number of constituencies.

Like the Andhra Communists, and in contrast to the belated regional patriotism of the Maharashtra Communists, the Kerala Communists can with justification claim to have been among the most vociferous early advocates of a separate Malayalam-speaking state. The Kerala Communists claim flatly that the anti-Congress sentiment leading to their victory was in effect "a real national demand," nothing less than "national" antagonism to a party, the Congress, which "was against the formation of a united Kerala state as the homeland of the Malayalees."[38] In making this claim they were only saying in exaggerated language what two of India's staunchest anti-Communists, A. D. Gorwala and Asoka Mehta, also pointed out following the 1957 elections. "The Government of India waited many years," observed Gorwala. "Meanwhile the Communists became more

[37] "Maharashtra Election Review," op.cit., p. 15.
[38] New Age, June 1957, p. 2.

and more closely identified in the public mind with the cause of a united Kerala."[39] The Communists, said Mehta, have "functioned as the regional party of Kerala."[40]

Before Independence, the Congress did not maintain branches of its own in princely states, leaving the field to the companion All-India States Peoples Conference. Thus the bulk of the Malayalam area, princely Travancore-Cochin, was anything but a Congress stronghold at the time of Independence. The Communists, on the other hand, had organized from the start on a strictly linguistic basis, so that, claims E. M. S. Nambudripad,

It was the emergence of the socialist movement and its transformation into the Communist Party that created an all-Kerala political party, an all-Kerala political leadership.[41]

As Independence loomed, the Communists specifically demanded the formation of a linguistic state of Kerala at the same time that the Tamil Dewan of Travancore, Sir C. P. Ramaswami Iyer, was proposing a sovereign independent Travancore (omitting the Malayalam-speaking Malabar District of Madras), and the Congress was struggling to assure accession of the princely domain to the new Indian Union. Although the splinter Kerala Socialist Party outdid them with its call for a sovereign linguistic Kerala, the Communists with their far superior organization could best exploit the linguistic demand. In the 1951 election the Communists made the regional appeal central in their joint six-point election manifesto with the Congress-rump Praja Party in Malabar:

1. To separate Malabar from Madras Presidency,
2. To end the rule of the king in Travancore-Cochin,
3. To form a united Kerala with definite boundaries,
4. To give half of the duty from tea, rubber, and pepper to Kerala,
5. To establish a Kerala University, a Malayalam encyclopedia, and a Malayalam Radio Station,

39 "The State of Kerala," *Encounter*, April 1957, p. 2.
40 "The Political Mind of India," *Foreign Affairs*, July 1957, p. 683.
41 *The National Question in Kerala*, People's Publishing House, Bombay, 1952, p. 163.

6. To get our local necessities, we the Malayalees must vote for Communist and Peoples Party candidates![42]

In 1954, after the Malabar Communist Party won eighteen seats on the Malabar District Board, the Communist members of the Board demanded that the district board "force" the central government as well as the government of multilingual Madras to return a fair share of taxes collected in the district.[43] Like the Andhra Communists, the Kerala Communists have recruited influential regional literary figures to identify the party with local aspirations.[44] What the Andhra Communists triumphantly —and prematurely—boasted after the 1951 election, Nambudripad echoed in 1953: The Communists are Kerala's "national party";[45] Vallathol, the late literary figure and mentor of Kathakali dancers, its "national poet."[46]

Once in power, Kerala's Communists were supremely situated to pose as the champion of "even those Congress state governments which are struggling for more power from the central government . . . for greater allotment to backward or less developed areas."[47] Nor can it be doubted that charges of neglect in New Delhi, which Kerala Congress leaders blamed for their 1957 defeat,[48] will be heard increasingly in the future to justify new Communist assaults on national unity. Indeed, Nambudripad has readied a theoretical justification unique in Indian

[42] *Voters! Please vote for Communist and Peoples Party Candidates to Form a Government That Will Take Care of the Malayalee Nation,* Marxist Book Stall, Calicut, December 2, 1951, p. 5. See also *Why You Should Vote for the Peoples Party,* signed Peoples Party, Malabar Committee, APP Press, Calicut, p. 1. Translated from Malayalam.

[43] *New Age,* November 28, 1954, p. 10.

[44] P. V. Kunnil, "The United Front of Kerala Writers," cited in Rohit Dave, *The Communist Culture Front,* Indian Congress for Cultural Freedom, March 1951, p. 20. See also *Indian Literature,* No. 2, November 1952, p. 81; *New Age,* June 7, 1953, p. 11; *Crossroads,* August 2, 1953, p. 10; *Free Press Journal,* January 16, 1953, p. 3; *Unity,* May-June, 1953, pp. 61-63; and *A Brochure on the Progress of Malayalam Literature from 1948 to 1954,* p. 3 (no identification).

[45] *New Age,* December 1, 1953, p. 1.

[46] *People's Age,* June 29, 1947, p. 16. Vallathol's school, Kerala Kalamandalam, at Cheruthuruthi, was scheduled to be managed by a state-operated arts group, according to a report in the *Times of India,* June 13, 1957, p. 7.

[47] *New Age,* June 1957, p. 7.

[48] "We could not spend enough money for development there," said T. T. Krishnamachari in a *New York Times* interview, September 14, 1957. See also *Hindustan Times,* August 8, 1957, p. 6.

Communism for any future Kerala separatist adventure: Kerala, he explained in a 1952 book, is distinctively different not only from north India but from other regions of south India. In fact, it is the only south Indian region which is the authentic southern commodity, for Tamilnad, Andhra, and Karnataka all "built up their superstructure on the same lines as, though independently of, north India." There is "something distinctive"[49] in the very territory of Kerala, making the canals and other artificial irrigation of other regions unnecessary; "something particularly Malayali"[50] about the beliefs of Hindu, Christian, and Muslim in Kerala; "a distinctive cultural sensitiveness"[51] in psychological makeup. It was only natural for Kerala to stage the "first national revolt against the British" in all India with its Kundara rebellion in 1809.[52] But for British rule,[53] which checked a final stage of national consolidation dating back to the 16th century,[54] and but for capitalist "socio-economic barriers" in the present day, Kerala would already be "an advanced industrial nation."[55]

Most significant of all, perhaps, Nambudripad goes to great lengths to seek to prove that all Kerala castes are indigenous to the soil of Kerala and that—contrary to conventional anthropological accounts—the Nambudri Brahmans at the top of the scale and the Ezhavas, near the bottom, are not interlopers from the outside. They have lived there as long as anyone else. Malayalees of all castes, therefore, constitute an integrated national whole. All evidence shows that the Nambudris and the Nayars, the wealthiest non-Brahman caste, "belong to the same racial stock" and thus to a distinct nation.[56]

For all his emphasis on the unity of Kerala castes in their relation to other regions, however, Nambudripad is even more interested in the possibilities for manipulation in inter-caste relationships. While caste separatism in peasant ranks "has to be broken, if they are to be organized as a class,"[57] "the first

---

[49] E. M. S. Nambudripad, *The National Question in Kerala*, p. 14. See also book review, *New Age*, May 1953, p. 68.
[50] Nambudripad, *op.cit.*, p. 31.   [51] *Ibid.*, p. 47.
[52] *Ibid.*, p. 95.   [53] *Ibid.*, p. 60.   [54] *Ibid.*, p. 58.
[55] *Ibid.*, p. 4.   [56] *Ibid.*, pp. 15, 56.   [57] *Ibid.*, p. 103.

form in which the peasant masses rise in struggle against feudalism . . . to progress from a defeated and leaderless mass . . . is the form of caste organizations."[58] This is a candid rationale for close ties with the Nayar Service Society and another caste group representing the Ezhavas, the Sri Narayan Dharma Paripalana (S.N.D.P.), named after the late Ezhava religious leader Narayan Guru. The prosperous Nayars and the Ezhavas have provided the lion's share of the Kerala Communist leadership: a majority of the 61 Communist legislators elected in 1957 were either Nayars (23) or Ezhavas (21). Kerala Communist Secretary Govindan Nair was at one time a director of the Nayar Service Society, and N.S.S. support in the central and north Travancore section of Kerala was a crucial factor underlying Communist success in 1957 in at least five specific constituencies.[59] It was this firm footing on Nayar and Ezhava ground that made it possible for the Kerala Communists to bring about a polarization in 1957 between a Congress identified with Kerala's two-million-strong Syrian Christians and a Hindu-oriented Communist Party.[60] By the same token it was the outraged response of the Nayar Service Society to the Communists' Education Act and in particular Clause 11 that was primarily responsible for the bizarre Nayar-Christian political alliance in 1959 and the downfall of the Communist Ministry.

The Syrian Christians—so called because of their historic association with the Church in Syria and the use of Syriac as their language of liturgy—are about half Roman Catholic and for the rest loyal in most cases to the Patriarch of Antioch.[61] Because many claim their ancestors were personally converted by Thomas the Apostle in 52 A.D., the Syrian Christians are also known as St. Thomas Christians. As an influential community with great power in Kerala's commercial life the Syrian Chris-

[58] *Ibid.*, p. 106.

[59] *New Socialist*, New Delhi, October 1958, p. 17, cites the Perumpavoor, Changanacherry, Thiruvella, and Kottarakkara assembly constituencies and the Thiruvella parliamentary constituency.

[60] For analyses of this polarization, see M. N. Srinivas, "Caste in Modern India," p. 543; *Times of India*, January 25, 1952, p. 6; *The People*, New Delhi, March 15, 1952, p. 4; and *Jayakeralam*, Madras weekly, December 1, 1951.

[61] See Samuel Mathai, "St. Thomas Christians of India," *March of India*, June 1955, pp. 17-22.

tians are powerful in political life as well. Yet while the Congress has become more and more a political focus for Christian influence, the Communists have been consistently Hindu-oriented. Just as there were less than half a dozen Christians in the legislative ranks of the Communist-led "United Front of Leftists" in 1951,[62] so there were in 1957 only six Christians among the Communist legislators.

The Communist Ministry took a remarkable step in promulgating the controversial Clause 11 because the requirement that teachers in privately-owned schools be recruited from lists prepared by the Communist-controlled civil service commission was certain to alienate the Nayars with their estimated 3,000 educational institutions. Since civil service recruitment to all public posts in Kerala is governed by rules setting aside specified numbers of jobs for certain designated "backward" social groups, notably the Ezhavas, this new rule meant in effect that the Nayars and Christians would have to choose their teachers from restricted lists sure to include a goodly number of Ezhava names. At bottom the furor was thus inspired not over ideological indoctrination, as the Western press speculated, but rather over communal job competition in a state with one of the highest rates of educated unemployment in India. What the Communists "had in view," as the *Hindustan Times* speculated at the height of the crisis leading to central intervention, was "a communal split based on Ezhava defection from the Congress." Their strategy represented, among other things, a bold bid to consolidate Communist power among the three-million-strong Ezhavas. In losing their Ministry, the Communists clearly appear to have enhanced their future prospects for the support of this rising, politically militant, social force. Numerically, most of the Ezhavas are, according to their traditional occupational niche, toddy-tappers.[63] But there are now young Ezhava civil servants, the sons of village clerks who got their white-collar start during British rule,[64] and Ezhava landholders too,

[62] *National Herald*, January 10, 1952, p. 6.

[63] The exploitation of toddy-tappers', which is to say Ezhavas', cooperatives for party ends is discussed in *Hindustan Times*, June 16, 1959, p. 6.

[64] *Report of the Backward Classes Commission*, Vol. I, Government of India Press, 1956, p. 131.

such as pepper farmers, who made quick money during the war.[65] That the Communists in Kerala have made a prominent place for this rising caste would seem, on the record at least, less an accident than the deliberate plan of a shrewd leadership. Nambudripad, although a Brahman, is a lone Brahman in a non-Brahman ruling group. Moreover, Nambudripad's own 1952 study, published a year after a wholesale Ezhava defection from the Congress,[66] shows clearly that he long ago perceived the crucial importance of the Ezhavas for the Communist cause:

The Ezhavas are a community which is numerically the strongest, and socially and culturally the most advanced, among the non-caste Hindus. . . . Being socially and culturally more advanced than the Scheduled Castes, they could, more easily than the latter, create those forms of agitation and organization which would prove useful in the struggle for social equality. They, therefore, became the main source of inspiration to, and the virtual leaders of, all the oppressed and untouchable castes.[67]

It was an Ezhava leader who was "the pioneer of modern lyrical poetry in Malayalam," and it was the first stirrings of Ezhava caste consciousness which were, in fact, "the beginnings . . . of the national upsurge which swept Kerala in the Twenties and Thirties."[68] The land reform law, which was one of the first enactments of the new Communist regime in Kerala, frankly favored "the tenant," observed the *Hindustan Times*, "in most cases the Ezhava."[69] At the same time, the Communists were careful to direct their legislative damage primarily at big plantation owners—mostly British—rather than at middling Hindu landlords—Nayars and the wealthy Ezhava upper crust.[70]

The Pattern of Success

To account for the success or failure of Communist Parties in each and every region is, of course, a task far beyond the

[65] *Ibid.*, pp. 96, 132. One Ezhava notable, the diplomat V. Raghavan, represented India in Communist China in 1953-1954.

[66] *Times of India*, January 25, 1952, p. 6.

[67] Nambudripad, *op.cit.*, p. 101.   [68] *Ibid.*, pp. 112-113.

[69] July 18, 1957, p. 8. See also *Times of India*, August 3, 1957, p. 1.

[70] See Nambudripad, "Agrarian Problems of Kerala," *New Age*, August 1957, p. 32.

reach of any one study. In each instance local factors, which can only be discovered through detailed case histories, may be crucial to conclusive analysis. Moreover, the success or failure of a particular Communist Party may be explained by the mere fact of dynamic leadership or of effective exploitation of isolated local grievances. With a study in depth of the Andhra experience as a basis for comparison, however, the evidence available for other regions does support in general a consistent explanation of the pattern of Communist strength in India.

It appears, for example, that the Karnataka and Gujarat Communist Parties have been unsuccessful for virtually the same reasons which explain the unsuccessful records of the Tamil and Maharashtra Communist Parties. If there is any single pre-eminent Karnataka Communist leader it is the Brahman K. L. Upadhyaya, this in a region where anti-Brahmanism has acquired the dignity of a reformist religious sect in Lingayatism. The party lacks leaders drawn from both strategic regional non-Brahman peasant proprietor castes, the Lingayats and the Vakkaligas. When a lone Communist won a seat in the Mysore Assembly in 1957, he turned out to be a domiciled Telugu, Ganga Reddi.[71] Thus rival caste cliques inside the Karnataka Congress have been able to keep as their family feud a competition comparable to the Kamma-Reddi rivalry inside the Andhra Congress that was so profitably exploited by the Andhra Communists. Similarly, not a single major Gujarat Communist leader belongs to the Patidar peasant proprietor caste, which dominates the fertile Charotar heartland of central Gujarat and functions as the most cohesive caste bloc in Gujarat politics. Powerful Patidar politicians such as the late Sardar Vallabhbhai Patel have, on the other hand, built for the Congress a region-wide rural base in Gujarat.

The fact that both the Karnataka and Gujarat Communist Parties have directed appeals to regional patriotism has mattered little for the simple reason that they have failed to elbow out other parties in competing for the regional banner. This, in turn, has been so because their leaders have occupied an

[71] *Times of India*, March 11, 1957, p. 3.

insignificant position in the regional social and economic power structure. What sets apart the successful regional Communist Parties in India is that fortuitous combination of the right tactics, in the right political circumstances, with roots spread deeply in the right places in regional society.

The Bengal Party is a relatively successful regional arm of Indian Communism. So important, indeed, is it likely to be in the future that it merits the most searching study. Yet even a superficial examination reveals the obvious disparity between the strength of the party in Calcutta and its weakness throughout most of the rest of Bengal. Is this related to the possibility that, while the party has appropriated regional patriotism, the absence of marked cleavages within Bengal Hindu society denies to all parties the opportunity for social leverage available in other regions? Certainly the Bengal Party has vigorously identified itself with Bengali regional sentiment. In 1946, the Bengal Communists hinted at a sovereign Bengal and fought partition, which "provides for the extinction of Bengalis as a nationality and Bengal as a country."[72] During the 1954 Bihar-Bengal boundary dispute, not only were the Bengal Communists at the forefront of Bengal chauvinism, but the national Communist line in effect took Bengal's side.[73] In multilingual Calcutta the Bengal Communists have based their union organizing in the ranks of Bengalis—a minority of the labor force—rather than in Hindi-speaking "floating labor."[74] They have gained great influence in Bengali letters, but here, as in all their activities, the party sees its own weakness in "our urban orientation . . . our defective outlook."[75] For all of its strength in Calcutta, the party does not enjoy the region-wide base made possible by the rural orientation to a Kamma in Andhra or an Ezhava in Kerala.

[72] Bhowani Sen, *Nutan Bangla* (New Bengal), Bengal Communist Committee, Calcutta, 1946, pp. 62, 64.

[73] *New Age*, July 4, 1954, p. 3.

[74] In 1957, "the leftist parties were unable to poll more than ten percent of non-Bengali working class votes," according to *New Age*, May 1957, p. 45. See also *New Age*, July 1957, pp. 32-35.

[75] *Unity*, December 1952, pp. 14-17. Here Sachin Sengupta urges the use of "national" themes to "reach this consciousness of the mass mind of Bengal." See also *Indian Literature*, No. 1, 1952, p. 94, and *Unity*, July 1953, pp. 4-20.

In the Punjab, by contrast, the Communist movement has been oriented from the very beginning to the region's most distinct particularist force, the Sikh peasantry, and today the Communists in the Punjab are patently a Sikh Party. Even before World War I, pressure on the land at home sent large contingents of Sikh peasants from the Punjab to the United States and Canada, especially to California. The expatriate Sikhs soon organized the Ghadr Party, dedicated to Indian Independence. They looked first to Germany for support and finally, after Germany's defeat, to the new Soviet Union.[76]

The Ghadr Party was a valuable prize when its leaders gradually turned to the Soviet Union as "the only consistently anti-imperialist power."[77] Two of its founders, Santokh Singh and Gurmukh Singh, went to Russia in the early 1920's with Moscow's help and pledged aid for the Soviet cause. The trickle of Sikhs who went back and forth between the United States and India passed regularly through Shanghai, where numerous resident Sikhs, employed mostly as policemen, had fallen under the influence of the emerging Chinese Communist movement. Communist control of the Ghadr cause became complete with the capture of the Kaidi Pariwar Sahayak or National Protection Committee, which collected funds among prosperous Sikhs abroad to assist the Sikh revolutionaries jailed by the British in India. "Besides helping the families of the patriots," a former Punjab Hindu Communist writes, "the spread of the Communist movement was made a fundamental item of the committee program. This marked the real beginning of the Communist movement in the Punjab."[78]

The venerable Sikh "Babas" who served terms in British prisons, joined by the new Moscow-trained "Babas," became the controlling clique in the relief committee and its political offshoot, the Kirti Kisan Party. In at least one instance recalled from first-hand experience, a check from the United States

[76] Tilak Raj Chaddha, *A Study of the Communist Movement in the Punjab*, Jyoti Prakashan, Ghaziabad, 1954, p. 3. See also Robert Sloss, *Some Facts About India (Interviews with Lord Islington)*, London, Burrup Mathieson and Spraig, 1917.
[77] *Hindustan Times*, September 21, 1953.
[78] Tilak Raj Chaddha, *op.cit.*, p. 4.

addressed to the relief committee was cashed and converted to immediate Communist use.[79] But in Communist affairs the Baba patriarchs maintained separate identity as the so-called Kirti group, shying away from disciplined adherence to the national Communist organization. Not until after factionalism had spoiled Communist chances in the 1951 elections in the Punjab did the Kirti group—also known as the Lal (Red) Communist Party—finally make its formal entrance to the official Communist fold at a special convention in Bhatinda District, Communist stronghold in the Sikh tenant farmer belt.[80] In the merged Punjab Communist forces the importance of the Sikh leaders has been more pronounced than ever.

While the historical accident of the Soviet-oriented Ghadr Party helps to explain the Sikh base of Punjab Communism, there are other reasons why the rural Sikh masses respond to the Communist appeal. As an aggrieved community, blaming the Congress for the partition of the Punjab, the Sikhs are quick to suspect authority—especially when it is the authority of a Kashmiri Brahman leader who personifies "Pandit" rule and therefore, implies the propagandist, anti-Sikh rule.[81] The Communists in the Punjab have treated with great solicitude the main champion of Sikh grievances, Master Tara Singh's Akali Party, seeking to break away "leftist" sections to the Communist cause.[82] Moreover, the Babas have maintained a toe hold in the religious affairs of the Sikhs since 1936, when they won virtual control of the committee that operates Sikh religious shrines, and in 1954, the Communists allied with the Akalis to capture the committee presidency.[83] Communist success in Pun-

[79] *Ibid.*, p. 2.

[80] *Times of India*, July 9, 1952, p. 1. See also *Party Letter*, June 8, 1943, Vol. III, No. 11 ("Open letter to All Party Members in the Punjab: Why Factionalism?") and July 12, 1943, Vol. III, No. 13.

[81] "Pandit" rule has been frequently mentioned by Sikh members of all Punjab parties in conversations, including the Communist leader Achar Singh Chinna, interviewed May 6, 1953.

[82] See *India Today*, September 1952, p. 33; *People's Age*, March 30, 1947, p. 1; *New Age*, July 12, 1953, p. 2, August 1953 (monthly), p. 23, April 1954 (monthly), p. 25; *Times of India*, November 8, 1954, p. 7; *Hindustan Times*, January 3, 1953.

[83] *Times of India*, October 6, 1954, p. 1.

jabi literature has been limited to Punjabi Sikh writers.[84] For all their efforts to build pockets of strength outside Sikh areas, Punjab Communist strength remains "mainly confined to the districts of Bhatinda, Barnala, Sangrur, and Kapurthala"—all Sikh peasant proprietor strongholds.[85]

The pattern of Communist success in India, it is clear in virtually every regional experience, is in no sense a national pattern. In the first decade of Independence Indian Communism did not develop a national character. Nor did Indian Communist leaders make a sustained attempt to address the nation from a national platform. Since 1951 Communist leaders have made the most of their representation in the central Parliament. They have still concentrated, however, in regional strongholds that have been located, by and large, where their leadership has "belonged" within the social and economic power structure and where this leadership has appropriated particularist disaffection. What has been true for the decade past need not be true for the decades immediately ahead, but in this instance the past may well offer a mere foretaste of what the future holds in store. For the social conflict set in motion by economic development will, more than ever, invite political manipulation, and the record of the Indian Communists tells us that they will be the very first to clasp the invitation as their own.

Kulaks in Andhra: A Case Study

The primary raw material of Communist power in economically less developed countries is neither the landless peasant with outstretched rice bowl nor the intellectual in search of a cause. Even more basic than these often summoned symbols, the *realpolitik* of social tensions determines political events where economic scarcity aggravates the divisions setting off man from man. Thus in India, as we have seen, the successful regional Communist Parties have been those able to manipulate to their own advantage tensions between one region and an-

---

[84] *Unity*, November 1952, p. 11, and *Indian Literature*, No. 2, 1953, pp. 32-39.
[85] *Crossroads* (July 5, 1953, p. 1) recounts the unsuccessful attempt of the Punjab Communists to gain Hindu support in Hariana Prant.

other, between regions and the central authority, and between caste lobbies within each region.

The experience of Andhra State on the southeast coast of India, which is the subject of this case study, is in its main outline a prototype for the study of other regional Communist strongholds. A comparative analysis spanning three elections in Andhra shows that Communist success has depended primarily on exploiting the rivalry between two rising peasant proprietor caste groups and, at the same time, the struggle of all Telugu-speaking Andhra to win separate linguistic identity within the Indian Union. Communist candidates won their margins of victory most often when they were able to exploit allegiance to caste and to language region. They made the most of economic despair, decay in the governing Congress Party, and the reflected glory of international Communism, but these alone do not get to the bottom of the Communist roots in Andhra soil.

The accident of three free elections within a decade in Andhra—1946, 1951, and 1955—makes Andhra a uniquely convenient unit of study. The first of these elections came only a year before Independence. The British Indian regime conducted a limited franchise ballot to choose provincial legislatures which, in turn, named the constitution-writers of India's first Constituent Assembly. By 1951, Prime Minister Nehru's government had launched nation-wide direct elections on a basis of general adult franchise to select new members for the lower house of the Indian Parliament and for state assemblies. The 1951 balloting set a relatively stable political pattern throughout India, with the notable exceptions of Andhra, Travancore-Cochin, and the Patiala and East Punjab States Union (PEPSU).

In the case of Andhra, the legislators elected in 1951 were seated alongside deputies speaking Tamil, Malayalam, and Kannada, in the legislature of multilingual Madras State, a sprawling political Babel carved out by British map-makers with little regard to south India's cultural differences. It was only after Potti Sriramulu, a prominent Gandhian advocate of provincial autonomy, fasted unto death in 1952 that the Nehru government demarcated Andhra as a separate state. When the new unit was inaugurated in October 1953, the 160 Telugu members of the Madras legislature, including a forty-one-member Communist bloc, became the new Andhra legislature. A Congress cabinet took office, but factionalism within and Communist harassment from the outside brought its collapse on a non-confidence motion by November 1954. New elections had to be conducted in February 1955, the third in less than ten years.[86]

For all Andhra political groups, this decade of near-deadlock was a rigorous exercise. Only in Kerala has a major Asian Communist party experienced an equally intensive testing process at the polls. Moreover, checkered as the course of Andhra Communist strategy was during this decade, the primacy of caste and language manipulation in Andhra Communist success persisted throughout a wartime united front, four bloody guerrilla years, and the present parliamentary phase of Indian Communism.

By focusing on caste and language it is possible to discover why the Andhra Communists, while successively increasing their popular vote from 258,974 (on a limited franchise in 1946) to 1,208,656 (1951) to 2,695,562 (1955), were able to win a significant number of seats in the legislature only in 1951. It is possible to discover, too, why this popular vote could increase without disturbing the localized concentration of Communist power. In all three elections Andhra Communism demonstrated its greatest strength in the fertile rice delta where the Krishna and Godavari rivers empty into the Bay of Bengal. Contrary to the theme that poverty above all breeds Communism, arid Rayalaseema in west Andhra has consistently failed to produce a significant Communist response.

"Kulak Pettamdars"

To find the keys to this puzzling situation it is necessary first of all to establish the major caste contours of the Andhra political landscape. In the case of the Andhra Communists, the effective use of caste does not arise full-blown out of a bottomless tactical armory but rather out of the caste homogeneity of

---

[86] The 1955 elections obviated the need for state legislature elections in 1957, when Andhra voted only for members of Parliament.

the Andhra Communist leadership itself. Since the founding of the Andhra Communist Party in 1934, the party leadership has been the property of a single subcaste, the Kamma landlords.[87] The party's historians date the awakening of political consciousness in its emerging leadership to the slump of agricultural prices in 1929 and the subsequent no-tax campaigns of pauperized delta Kammas.[88] This base in the Kammas carries enormous importance in view of the rising influence of the Kammas in Andhra life. World War II and the postwar years were a boom period for the Kamma farmers,[89] who own an estimated eighty percent of the fertile delta land.[90] High prices for both food and cash crops made many Indian peasant-proprietor castes newly rich, but for the Kammas, presiding over land as productive as any in all India, the boom was especially potent.

Kamma funds have made the Andhra party better able to support itself than any other regional arm of Indian Communism. In fair political weather or foul, a virile, expensively produced Communist press in Andhra's Telugu language has been kept alive by a Kamma publisher, Katragadda Rajagopal Rao,[91] whose family also operates one of India's largest Virginia tobacco plantations and virtually monopolizes the fertilizer market in

[87] G. S. Bhargava discusses this in *A Study of the Communist Movement in Andhra*, Delhi, Siddhartha Publications, 1955, pp. 2, 14, 22-34; see also K. B. Choudary, *A Brief History of the Kammas* (Sangamjagarlamudi, Andhra, published by the author, 1955), pp. 98, 123; and V. Lingamurthy, "Elections in Andhra," *Indian Journal of Political Science*, Vol. XVI, No. 2, April-June 1955, p. 157. He deplores "the diabolic forces of casteism. . . . For a Brahman to succeed in a constituency dominated by non-Brahmans or for a Reddi to succeed in a constituency dominated by Kammas is more an exception than a rule."

[88] P. Sundarayya, *Vishalandhralu Prajarajvan* (People's Rule in Vishalandhra), Vijayawada, Vishalandhra Publishing House, 1946, p. 34 (translated from Telugu for the author). See also A. S. Rao, "Andhras Struggle for Their Own State," *New Age*, November 1953, p. 106, who states that "these peasant youth began to grope for a new path. . . . This way was born the Communist movement on the soil of Andhra."

[89] Choudary (*A Brief History of the Kammas*, p. 124) notes that "the Second World War and the years that have followed have once again seen rocketing of the prices of paddy, pulses, turmeric, tobacco and fruits. These have been very prosperous years for agricultural communities like Kammas."

[90] This is the private consensus of members of different Andhra castes. No official figures exist showing caste land ownership in Madras.

[91] Katragadda Rajagopal Rao's role is noted in "The Future of Andhra," *Thought*, New Delhi weekly, October 3, 1953, p. 4.

Andhra.[92] As "the people who count"[93] in the villages of the delta districts, even relatively modest Kamma landholders have been in a position to put decisive influence on the side of the Communist Party.[94] For not only are rich peasants numerous in the delta, as the Andhra Communists have themselves pointed out,

but also through exchange loans, family relations, physical labor and various other means, they have innumerable ties with the oppressed people, mainly with the middle peasants.[95]

Aruna Asaf Ali, a former member of the Indian Communist Central Committee, has said that "a distinguishing feature of the Andhra Party is its social content. The rural intelligentsia (numerically stronger and politically a great deal more mature than in the rest of India) has provided the party with a leadership that knows its mind and is unmistakably competent."[96] Andhra Communist leaders at state, district, and village levels, wrote a party leader in 1958, are all "predominantly of rich and middle peasant stock."[97] Three wealthy Kamma intellectuals have maintained for at least the past fifteen years key control of the Andhra Communist Party: party secretary Chandrasekhar Rao, former national Indian Communist Party secretary Rajeshwar Rao, and M. Basava Punniah, a member of the Indian Communist Central Committee. As a result, an Andhra Communist dissident has coined the epithet *kulak*

92 The holdings of the six Katragadda brothers are described in P. C. Joshi, *Among Kisan Patriots*, Bombay, People's Publishing House, 1946, p. 4. This pamphlet reviews the Vijayawada, Andhra, session of the All-India Kisan Sabha.
93 Kamma status in the delta is so described in "How Red is Andhra?" *The People* (pro-Congress weekly), New Delhi, March 4, 1952, p. 8.
94 For an excellent description of the manner in which a dominant caste can mold village behavior, see *All-India Rural Credit Survey*, Vol. II, Reserve Bank of India, Bombay, 1954, pp. 56-58. See also Alan Beals, "Leadership in a Mysore Village," *Leadership and Political Institutions in India*, Richard L. Park and Irene Tinker, eds., Princeton University Press, p. 428, where, speaking of the "group basis of decisions," he distinguishes between villages all of one caste, those with a dominant caste, and those with equivalent castes.
95 *Andhra Provincial Committee Letter*, Telengana Documents, I, cited in O. P. Sangal, *Telengana and the Rajeshwar Rao Leadership*, Adhunik Pustak Bhandar, Allahabad, 1951, p. 8.
96 In an interview with an editor of *New Age*, February 13, 1955, p. 7.
97 M. Basava Punniah, "Andhra Communists and Their Tasks," *New Age*, March 1958, p. 15.

pettamdar to attack the Andhra leadership, coupling the Russian word for rich peasant with the Telugu word for head of a caste or tribe.[98]

In sharp contrast to Kamma control of the Communist Party, stands the power of the rival landowning Reddi subcaste in the Congress Party.[99] This posture of political competition between the two caste groups is only a modern recurrence of an historic pattern dating back to the 14th century.[100] Kamma lore evokes the image of a once-proud warrior clan reduced by Reddi chicanery to its present peasant status. Reddi duplicity, recounted by Kamma historian K. Bhavaiah Choudary, was first apparent in 1323 A.D. at the downfall of Andhra's Kakatiya dynasty. Reciting voluminous records to prove that Kammas dominated the Kakatiya court, Choudary suggests that the Reddis, also influential militarists at the time, struck a deal at Kamma expense with the Muslim conquerors of the Kakatiya regime. The Kammas lost their noble rank and were forced into farming.

In his research Choudary frankly has an axe to grind: he seeks to establish Kamma claims to *Kshatriya* rank, second in the traditional Hindu caste hierarchy. At present Kammas and Reddis both find themselves in an anomalous hierarchical status, the result, says Panikkar, of their "imperfect integration" into Hindu society.[101] Brahmans dismiss them as *Sudras*, but the Kammas and Reddis themselves have never accepted this dis-

[98] *Kulak pettamdar* recurs throughout C. V. K. Rao, *Rashtra Communist Navakathwapu Bandaram* (Bluff of the Andhra Communist Leadership) Masulipatnam, Andhra, 1946. (Partially translated from Telugu for the author.) Rao is a member of the Devadasi caste.

[99] Reddi power in the Congress figures in D. V. Raja Rao, "Election Lessons," *Swatantra*, February 15, 1952, p. 13; Choudary, *A Brief History of the Kammas*, p. 97; and an earlier article by the author, "How Nehru Did It in Andhra," *New Republic*, March 21, 1955, p. 7.

[100] See Choudary, *A Brief History of the Kammas*, p. 55, and his earlier three-volume history, *Kammacharitra Sangraham* (Sangamjagarlamudi, Andhra, published by the author, 1939), Vol. I, p. 20. (Partially translated from Telugu for the author.)

[101] K. M. Panikkar, *Hindu Society at Cross Roads*, Asia Publishing House, Bombay, 1955, p. 9. Sat- (Good) Sudra status is accorded to Kammas, Reddis, Velamas, and other Telugu peasant proprietor subcastes to distinguish them from less prosperous Sudra subcastes, according to W. Francis, *Census of India, 1901*, Vol. 15, Part 1 (Madras), Calcutta, Superintendent of Government Printing, 1903, p. 136.

missal (or for that matter even the very hierarchy of four *varnas*) and have in fact enjoyed social power equal to *Kshatriyas* in north India. Choudary's main outline of Kamma and Reddi history, however, does not differ essentially from the consensus of more disinterested scholars.[102] Both Kammas and Reddis were probably warriors in the service of the early Andhra kings. Later they became farmers, some feudal overlords and others small peasant proprietors who to this day take part in the cultivation of their land. Between them they dominated rural Andhra, leaving Brahmans beyond the pale of economic power in the countryside.

For five centuries the Kammas have centered in the four mid-Andhra delta districts, which Choudary says were once known as "Kamma Rashtra" or "Kamma Land." The 1921 census[103] shows 600,679 Kammas congregated in the delta districts, with another 560,305 scattered in other Andhra districts and in pockets in neighboring Tamil territory.[104] The extent of Kamma dominance in the delta is exemplified in Guntur district, where all other peasant proprietor castes together totalled 149,308, less than half the Kamma figure.

The Reddis[105] gravitated to the five Rayalaseema districts of west Andhra. Here Kammas are in the minority; in Cuddapah, for example, Reddis numbered 211,558 to 20,171 Kammas in the 1921 census, and in Kurnool, Reddis were 121,032 to 14,313 Kammas. Today in popular Telugu parlance the region is called "Reddiseema."

This geographical separation of the two powerful castes had a tribal logic; in any one local area, only one or the other caste group with its patriarch could be dominant. When British tax collectors came onto the scene, they formalized the status

102 See Edgar Thurston, *Castes and Tribes of Southern India*, 14 vols., Madras, Government Press, 1909, Vol. 3, p. 94; G. MacKenzie, *Manual of Kistna District*, Madras, 1883, p. 53; *Census of India, 1901*, Vol. 15, p. 159; J. H. Hutton, *Caste in India*, London, Oxford University Press, 1946, p. 11.

103 The last in which district caste tables for Madras are available.

104 *Census of India, 1921*, Vol. 13 (Madras), Part II, by G. T. Boag, Madras, Superintendent of Government Press, 1922, Table XIII, p. 119.

105 Reddis are also referred to by anthropologists as Kapus. However, this terminology is confusing in contemporary Andhra; Kapu is loosely applied to other non-Brahman peasant castes.

quo, extending the sway of leading landholders in each caste over vast zamindari estates. Fourteen Kamma zamindars became the biggest estate owners in the delta country.

Despite their wealth, the Kammas and Reddis as a village-centered rural gentry lagged behind the traditionally education-minded Brahmans in gaining the English literacy that was the entry to political leadership in the early years of the Independence movement. For example, the 1921 census showed that out of 79,740 literate Kammas, only 2,672 were able to read English, while out of 159,730 literate Telugu Brahmans, as many as 46,498 were literate in English.[106] Choudary explains this in the following way:

Shorn of their principalities, commanding officer's posts, and choudariships, Kammas had to content themselves with the lot of peasants and husbandmen. Learning only Telugu, they looked after their ryotwari [holdings]. Only about 1900 A.D., Kammas awakened to the fact that without English education they cannot better their position. The few educated Kammas who joined government service had to struggle hard to come up due to lack of patronage and the opposition of Brahman vested interests.[107]

It was inevitable that Kamma-Reddi competition would increase with the educational advancement of the two castes, and that the Brahman politicians who controlled the Andhra Congress Party would gradually lose their actual—if not titular—party control to others exercising greater local power in Andhra. This is precisely what happened between 1934 and World War II. Both Kammas and Reddis, pushing forward with the anti-Brahman movement that swept all south India, supported the Andhra branch of the short-lived Justice Party.[108] Then Reddi power lodged itself in the Congress behind a Brahman facade at the same time that a clique of young Kamma intellectuals was founding the Andhra Communist Party. Choudary notes that Kamma youth were attracted by "the Communist Party, with its slogans of social equality," but he does not seek to

[106] *Census of India, 1921*, Vol. 13, Table IX, p. 77.
[107] Choudary, *A Brief History of the Kammas*, p. 122.
[108] A coalition of aggrieved non-Brahman castes throughout south India.

explain why the party in Andhra became "predominated by Kammas" rather than Reddis.[109]

The circumstances explaining the polarization of Kamma-Reddi warfare on a Communist-Congress basis deserve further study. Perhaps, as M. N. Srinivas has argued, it was only natural for the Kammas and Reddis to fall back into their traditional rivalry once their united front in the Justice Party had reduced Brahman power.[110] But the consensus in Andhra points as well to geographical accident: the Kammas happened to be in the delta. There political activity of every stripe had always been greater than in Rayalaseema. From the beginning of the Independence movement Gandhian Congress leaders found their liveliest Andhra response in the delta rice trading towns of Vijayawada and Guntur, centers of the region's intellectual and political ferment. Thus, just as the then Brahman-dominated Congress drew its leadership from the delta, so the challenge to this leadership emerged within the strongest non-Brahman caste group in the delta. "Guntur, Krishna, and the Godavaris were the strongholds of the Gandhian movement," explains the Rayalaseema Communist leader T. Nagi Reddi. "There has always been more political consciousness there." It may or may not be true, as Reddi goes on to claim, that "the Communist strongholds of today are in those places where the national movement was strongest. That political consciousness has been transformed into a Communist consciousness."[111] But the Congress strongholds were indeed in the delta, not in Rayalaseema, and it was natural for delta Kammas to mount the Communist challenge to the established political leadership.

Although Reddis had participated in the Justice Party, the young Reddi intelligentsia in the Rayalaseema hinterlands was politically quiescent by comparison with the Kammas. The young Reddi who did desire a political career could best seek it in the Congress, where his caste group, gravitating almost by default, had cornered the market on the bulk of the party's non-Brahman patronage. Some young Reddi leaders were a

[109] *A Brief History of the Kammas*, pp. 97-98.
[110] "Caste in Modern India," *Journal of Asian Studies*, July 1957, p. 538.
[111] Interview with the author, December 14, 1952, Gandhinagar, Madras.

part of the Communist Party from its inception, but they have always been outnumbered by Kammas. Only one has held his own in the party hierarchy, Puchalapalli Sundarayya, whose real name is Puchalapalli Sundar Rama Reddi. He is in a position comparable to that of the Kamma Congress veteran, N. G. Ranga, for most of his career a nationally prominent Congress figure and another notable exception to the rule of caste politics in Andhra. Both of these politically displaced persons enjoy wide personal popularity, but in the period under discussion both strike discordant notes within the otherwise relatively homogeneous leadership cliques of their respective parties.

The Role of Landless Labor

Against this historical backdrop it is now possible to examine the course of political events surrounding the 1946, 1951, and 1955 elections in Andhra in an effort to explain the consistent concentration of the Communist popular vote in the delta as well as its special potency in 1951.

In 1946, Andhra was the only region in India where the Communists felt strong enough to enter a bloc of candidates across one large contiguous group of constituencies against the candidates of the Congress—recognized champion of Independence at a time when India remained under foreign domination. In Bengal, Malabar, and parts of north India, where the Communist Party was also an election factor, Communist entries were pinpointed in scattered centers of industrial or farm labor, but in Andhra they were massed solidly over the delta. Of the sixty-two constituencies in Andhra, as it existed prior to the reorganization of states and the formation of Vishalandhra, or Greater Andhra, in 1956,[112] the Communists contested twenty-nine, virtually side by side. Twenty-four were located in Krishna, Guntur, and in the East and West Godavari districts, the delta belt commonly called the "Circars."[113] This concen-

---

[112] "Delimitation of Madras Constituencies," *Government of India (Provincial Legislative Assemblies) Order, 1936,* cited in Jagat Narain, *Law of Elections in India and Burma,* Calcutta, Eastern Law House, 1937, pp. 250-258.

[113] *Return Showing the Results of Elections to the Central Legislative Assembly and Provincial Legislatures, 1945-46,* New Delhi, Government of India Press, 1946.

tration in the delta was no momentary accident of tactics but a reflection of the basic character of Andhra Communism.

With Communist candidates almost exclusively centered in the delta in 1946 (see Table II), it was not surprising that most

TABLE II

LOCATION OF COMMUNIST POWER IN ANDHRA, AS SHOWN IN 1946, 1951, AND 1955 STATE ASSEMBLY ELECTIONS

Year	Votes Cast in Four Delta Districts:* Percent of Total Votes Cast	Communist Votes Cast in Four Delta Districts: Percent of Total Communist Vote	Communist Candidates Contesting in Four Delta Districts: Percent of Total Communist Candidates
1946	55.1	94.7	89.2
1951	54.3	85.5	72.2
1955	56.2	72.8	57.4

* The four Andhra districts in the Krishna-Godavari delta are Krishna, Guntur, East Godavari, and West Godavari.

Percentages in this and subsequent tables were computed with the assistance of the Littauer Statistical Laboratory, Harvard University, on the basis of official election returns.

Communist votes were recorded there. Even in 1955, however, with only 57.4 percent of the Communist candidates running in the delta districts, 72.8 percent of the Communist vote still went to these delta contestants. In 1951, thirty-one of the forty-one successful Communist candidates were in delta constituencies; in 1955, eleven of fifteen. In all three elections, the delta has provided an average of 55 percent of Andhra's total vote.

View this concentration in the delta alongside the failure of the Communists in 1955 to win more than fifteen seats in a 196-member chamber[114]—at the same time that they were increasing their share of the popular vote from 18.6 to 31.2 per-

[114] The legislature was increased from 160 to 196 members before the 1955 elections in a new delimitation of constituencies. For detailed maps and lists of 1951 and 1955 constituencies, see Joan V. Bondurant and Margaret W. Fisher, *The Indian Experiment With Democratic Elections*, Indian Press Digests, Monograph No. 3, Institute of International Studies, University of California, Berkeley, 1956, pp. 197-200. See also an account of the 1955 election, pp. 79-86.

cent. Congress quarters reasoned hopefully[115] that the increased vote resulted naturally from the greater number of Communist candidates in 1955 (169 out of a total 560) than in 1951 (61 out of 614). Yet this explanation ignores the fact that the Communists retained their high proportion of the vote in their delta heartland. While their ambitious "shotgun" strategy helps explain why the Communists won comparatively few seats in 1955, other factors must be found to explain the consistent concentration of the Communist popular vote as well as its special potency in 1951.

Certainly one feature distinguishing the delta scene from other parts of Andhra is the high population density—especially the high percentage of landless laborers. Density runs from 900 to 1200 persons per square mile in the delta, as compared with 316 in the rest of Andhra. Thirty-seven percent of the total agricultural population in the delta is landless labor, a concentration second only to Malabar District on the West Indian coast.[116]

Andhra Communist leaders have from the outset attempted to organize the Adi-Andhras, an untouchable subcaste comprising the bulk of the region's landless migrants.[117] Their success has been conceded by Communist leaders outside Andhra who granted that "the organized strength of agricultural workers in Andhra is by far the biggest in any province."[118] The likelihood that the votes of landless laborers have been a bulwark to Com-

---

[115] For example, *The Hindu*, March 10, 1955, p. 4. This issue also contains detailed election statistics.

[116] Thomas Shea, "Agrarian Unrest and Reform in South India," *Far Eastern Survey*, Vol. 23, pp. 81-88, at pp. 84-85, June 1954. See also *District Census (1951) Handbooks*, Madras, Government Press, 1953, Tables D-III: Krishna, p. 183; West Godavari, p. 168; East Godavari, p. 292; Guntur, p. 206.

[117] P. Sundarayya, *Vishalandralu Prajarajvan* (People's Rule in Vishalandhra), Ch. 6, states that "since 1932, the Communists tried to organize and integrate all agricultural labor, particularly Adi-Andhras, into agricultural unions."

[118] "The Struggle for People's Democracy and Socialism, Some Questions of Strategy and Tactics," *The Communist*, Vol. 2, pp. 21-90, at p. 35, June-July 1949. This was formerly the monthly organ of the Communist Party of India. For additional references to Communist organization of agricultural labor in Andhra, see N. Prasada Rao, "Agricultural Laborers Association," *News Bulletin of the All-India Kisan Sabha*, October-November 1952, p. 22, which terms agricultural labor "the rock-like base of the (Communist) movement in Andhra"; and "Second Andhra Agricultural Labor Conference," August 1953, p. 6, setting organized strength in the region then at 94,890.

munist strength gains further support from an analysis of the concentration of Communist votes alongside the irrigation map of the delta. The same extensively irrigated delta rice country which, as a focus of farming, has dense settlements of landless labor, such as Tenali, Gudivada, Bapatla, and Bandar taluks (subdivisions) in Krishna District, is also the site of consistently high Communist voting.[119] After the 1951 elections, the Congress publicly acknowledged that Communist "canalization" of agricultural labor votes had played an important part in the election.[120] There is no evidence to suggest that this factor was absent in 1955. On the contrary, the Communists themselves claim that "the most oppressed and exploited strata of the people in the rural areas, the agricultural workers and poorest peasants, stood firmly by the party."[121] Independent press comment has accepted this as a fact.[122]

In 1946, however, the Communists could not have derived much benefit from this source of strength. Franchise limitations excluded all but thirteen percent of the population. In addition to a literacy requirement, only registered landholders owning, in addition to their homes, immovable property valued at the rupee equivalent of $10 or more were permitted to vote.[123] Therefore, landless farm laborers were unable to take part in the election.

In any case, the support of landless labor would not explain the two subsequent elections.[124] To be sure, six of the thirty-

[119] *Imperial Gazetteer of India*, Provincial Series (Madras 1), Calcutta, Superintendent of Government Printing, 1908, p. 309. See canal locations in frontispiece maps in *District Census (1951) Handbooks*; note also S. W. Cushing, "The Geography of Godavari," *Bulletin of Geographic Society of Philadelphia*, Vol. 9, pp. 2-3, October 1911, reprinted.
[120] *The Hindu*, March 3, 1952, p. 1.
[121] Ajoy Ghosh, "The Andhra Elections and the Communist Party," *New Age*, March 4, 1955, p. 1.
[122] For example, see "Andhra Victory," editorial in *Times of India*, March 10, 1955, p. 4.
[123] *Public General Acts and Measures*, Vol. 1, Sixth Schedule (Part II: Madras), London, H.M.S.O., 1935-36, pp. 256-257.
[124] A. Chakradar, Secretary of the Andhra Socialist Party, explicitly pointed to the limits to landless labor as a source of Communist strength in *Report on Communist Activity in Andhra Districts*, 1950, mimeographed, stating that Communist strongholds were in villages where the party claimed support "not only among the agricultural laborers but also in the middle peasantry."

one seats won by the delta Communists in 1951 were reserved for scheduled castes (untouchables). These seats, by their very nature, hang on the support of landless labor. In addition, these six reserved seats were in double-member constituencies in which the Communists also won the six non-reserved seats. In these double constituencies both general and scheduled caste voters can vote twice, each influencing the outcome in both seats; landless labor thus clearly played a role in the six non-reserved seats in these double-member constituencies. In the remaining nineteen of the 1951 Communist victories, landless labor votes must also have been an important prop to Communist candidates. But if dependable landless labor support alone explains Andhra communism, why then could the Communists not win as many seats in 1955 as in 1951?

It is the contention of this study that Communist victory margins in 1951 stemmed from a timely confluence of events, favorable to the manipulation of social tensions, which did not recur in 1955. In 1951 the movement to carve a separate Andhra State out of Madras had reached a high emotional pitch. The Communists surcharged the election atmosphere with propaganda keyed to Telugu patriotism, while in 1955, with Andhra State a reality, the Congress could make Indian nationalism the issue. Furthermore, at the same time that they were exploiting Telugu solidarity in 1951, the Communists made the most of a bitterly tense moment in Andhra's caste rivalries—a crisis which the Congress was able to surmount in time for 1955.

The 1946 Elections

At the end of the war, with the polarization of Andhra politics on caste-party lines almost complete, the Kamma leader, N. G. Ranga, was on the far fringes of the Andhra Congress power structure. Inside, a personal rivalry raged between two prominent Telugu Brahman politicians: Pattabhi Sitaramayya, official historian of the Indian National Congress, and Tanguturu Prakasam, "Lion of Andhra," who won a legendary reputation in the Independence movement when he bared his chest before British police, daring them to shoot. Sitaramayya typified the Brahman facade behind which Reddi power made its appearance. In 1946 he held firmly onto the Andhra Congress machinery, though Prakasam maneuvered many of his own choices into election nominations. N. G. Ranga was, then, part independent operator, part Prakasam satellite.

Frankly building his political career on a Kamma base, Ranga had articulated a "peasant socialist" theory,[125] gingered by Western class slogans but boiling down in concrete terms to a defense of peasant proprietorship as opposed to land nationalization. In Andhra he organized a compact political striking force, bent on increasing Kamma influence in the Congress while at the same time fighting the Communists by reciting the story of Stalin and the peasant. In 1946, however, with Congress activity only beginning to regain momentum after the war, there was little time to put a striking force into action before the elections. Relatively few Kammas won Congress nomination and election, even in Kamma strongholds (see Tables III and IV).

The Kamma Communist leaders were in a more favorable position. During the war the Andhra Communists fattened handsomely on the official patronage accorded all-India communism for support of the defense effort. The Congress, demanding freedom first, protested when Britain decided that India was at war. Thus, while Congress leaders spent the war in British jails, Communist leaders not only had a clear field to organize but actually had official support. The government cooperated with the party and the Communists accordingly worked to popularize rationing, filling out rice and kerosene ration forms for illiterate peasants, to fight black marketing, to assist procurement policing, and to talk down strikes.[126] In parts of India where the Communist movement had gained a foothold before the war, this favored position presented a rare oppor-

125 For example, N. G. Ranga, *Outlines of National Revolutionary Path*, Bombay, Hind Kitabs, 1945, pp. 109-110.

126 The Communist role during the war is summarized in *The Communist Party of India*, Publication No. 2681, Research and Analysis Branch, Office of Strategic Services, August 1945, p. 21; note also P. Sundarayya, *op.cit.*, Ch. 6, where it is estimated that Andhra Communist membership rose from 1,000 in 1942 to 8,000 in 1945. See also G. N. S. Raghavan, "Reprieve in Andhra," *Encounter*, July 1955, p. 54.

TABLE III

NUMBER OF CANDIDATES BY MAJOR CASTES IN ANDHRA DELTA DISTRICTS,
IN 1946, 1951, AND 1955 STATE ASSEMBLY ELECTIONS

Year	Communist				Congress			
	Kamma	Reddi	Brahman	Other	Kamma	Reddi	Brahman	Other
1946	9	–	1	1	4	3	4	7
1951	22	2	3	15	17	7	2	20
1955	32	4	6	24	28	7	7	25

NOTE: Constituencies reserved for scheduled castes and tribes have been omitted. In the case of 1946, when certain constituencies were also reserved for urban as distinct from rural voters, and on the basis of labor union membership, religion, and sex, these figures apply only to general rural constituencies.

Caste designations on which this and subsequent tables are based have been compiled through the cooperation of members of major Telugu castes. This compilation has included a cross-check test of the designations made by each cooperating informant by other persons of different castes.

TABLE IV

NUMBER OF ELECTED LEGISLATORS BY MAJOR CASTES IN ANDHRA DELTA
DISTRICTS, IN 1946, 1951, AND 1955 STATE ASSEMBLY ELECTIONS

Year	Communist				Congress			
	Kamma	Reddi	Brahman	Other	Kamma	Reddi	Brahman	Other
1946	–	–	–	–	4	3	4	7
1951	14	2	3	6	3	3	–	4
1955	1	2	3	3	24	7	7	25

NOTE: Constituencies reserved for scheduled castes and tribes have been omitted. In the case of 1946, when certain constituencies were also reserved for urban as distinct from rural voters, and on the basis of labor union membership, religion, and sex, these figures apply only to general rural constituencies.

tunity for rapid expansion. The Andhra Communists could take full advantage of the situation. Besides the wealth and influence of their Kamma leaders, they had capitalized as much as any regional Communist Party from the prewar united front with the Congress Socialist Party, walking off with almost the entire Andhra Socialist organization in 1939.[127]

The Andhra Communists waged a vigorous campaign in the

[127] In a press statement dated September 18, 1938, now in the personal files of Jayaprakash Narayan, P. Mallikarjuna Rao resigned from the Andhra Congress Socialist Party in protest against the "rank communalism" in the dominant C P faction.

1946 elections, putting their major effort into Kamma strongholds. Because the sole successful Communist contestant won in a labor stronghold,[128] the dominantly rural nature of the Communist effort in 1946 has been overlooked. Of the twenty-four delta seats for which the Communists contested, seventeen were entirely in rural areas. Of these seventeen, six were reserved seats for scheduled castes. In each of the eleven remaining "general rural" constituencies, the percent of the vote polled by the Communists was surprisingly high—ranging from a low of 11.5 to a high of 31.9, with the median falling just above 20.[129] When the franchise property restriction in 1946 is kept in mind, this figure assumes its proper importance. These were not to any substantial degree the votes of agricultural labor. Rather they were votes drawn from the general landed caste Hindu population in the countryside and from propertied voters in small rural centers.

Here a caste analysis of candidates highlights the Kamma base of the Communist leadership. Omitting the six constituencies set apart for scheduled castes, a caste breakdown of the eleven Communist caste Hindu entrants shows nine Kammas, while of eighteen caste Hindu Congress entrants for rural seats in the four delta districts only four were Kammas (Table III).

"Telugu Motherland"

It is important to keep in mind, however, that in addition to their strong Kamma base, their organized strength among migrant farm labor, and their windfall capture of the Andhra Congress Socialist machine in 1939, the Andhra Communists were well on their way to taking leadership of the Andhra State issue away from the Congress even before the 1946 elections.

Until the war the Andhra Communists paid only nominal attention to the Andhra State demand. They could trace pronunciamentos back to 1937,[130] but the issue belonged to Congress

128 P. Venkateswarulu in West Godavari-cum Kistna-cum Guntur (Non-union) Factory Labor constituency.

129 Ellore, 19.3; Bhimavaram, 19.4; Narsapur, 21.4; Bandar, 28.4; Bezwada, 31.9; Guntur, 26.9; Narasaropet, 17; Tenali, 16.6; Ongole, 14.4; Rajahmundry, 11.5; and Amalapuram, 18.4.

130 *New Age*, January 23, 1955, p. 8. A. S. Rao, "Andhras Struggle for Their Own State," p. 107, claims that the Communists demanded Vishalandhra in 1937.

leaders, who made "Swarashtra" (literally, national state) for Andhra a battle cry inseparable from Gandhi's "Swaraj" (self-rule). Andhra Communist interest in the cause coincided with the national Communist emphasis, beginning in 1942, on each "national" region's right of self-determination to the point of secession. The Andhra Party was quick to pick up its cue, infiltrating the respected Andhra Mahasabha, Congress vehicle for Andhra State agitation, and installing a Communist as president at the group's 1944 session.[131] By the 1946 elections, the Andhra Party had placed the appeal to Andhra regional sentiment at the forefront of its propaganda. Sundarayya issued a pseudo-scholarly polemic on the eve of the elections, taunting Congress leaders to say whether they agreed with national Congress refusal to support the right of secession for Andhra:

One question to Andhra Congress leaders: we are three crores of Telugu people; living in the same or only one area; our history is very ancient; we have our own language, culture and traditions; our political and economic future will be bright if all of our Telugu people should form into one political unit or state. Do you agree that all of us, Telugu people, belong to one race? Do you agree that we, as the Andhra race, have got a right to decide freely and independently whether to join or not in the Indian federation?[132]

Sundarayya then flatly charged Andhra Congress leaders with "destroying our Andhra national movement. We won't rest content with a separate Telugu province. A united Telugu nation should exist in the independent Indian federation, as an independent Telugu kingdom."

After the elections the Andhra Party organized the Telengana movement, which not only blended Kamma power, in a strange political alchemy, with the land hunger of the migrant untouchables, but provided an ideal platform for the slogans of regional patriotism. The Telengana movement, organized along standard Communist guerrilla lines with wholesale land redistribution and parallel village governments, swept clusters of villages in the delta and nearly all of Warangal and Nalgonda districts in Hyderabad under Communist control from 1948 through 1950.

[131] *People's War*, June 11, 1944.
[132] *Op.cit.*, Ch. 6.

Andhra and Telengana Communist leaders directed a two-way offensive, north into Telengana and south into the delta, from a forty-village base of operations in Munagala Jungle in northwest Krishna District.[133] Communist squads raided villages by night, police battalions by day. When Indian Army troops conducted their 1948 "police action" against the Nizam of Hyderabad, they stayed on in Warangal and Nalgonda to drive the Communists out. It took them until 1951 to restore normal local government.

Just as the delta Communists had invaded the Andhra State movement via the respected Andhra Mahasabha, so the Telengana Communists sought to capitalize on the spade work of others. As early as 1922, the Andhra Jana Sangh had launched mass Telugu language campaigns for libraries and reading rooms, and its successor, the Andhra Conference, had gained still more influence through attention to such social evils as *begar* or forced labor. The Telengana Communists infiltrated the Conference during the war, "securing an energetic section of young workers."[134] Sundarayya claimed that the eventual merger of the Conference and the Mahasabha, with its branches in Telengana, created a combined Communist-led force in Telengana of "more than one hundred thousand members and one thousand organizers, working as the sole association for the Andhras of Nizam State."[135]

The Telengana movement is normally depicted as an agrarian uprising with land reform as its slogan or as a Hindu response to the Muslim Nizam's domination of Hyderabad. But Telengana drew important motive force from the assertion of linguistic regional solidarity which the Communists made a cardinal feature of the movement. It is no doubt also true, as a Soviet commentator wrote, that "it was the combination of the anti-

[133] The designation of Munagala as headquarters during this period is part of a colorful description of the Telengana movement as seen by delta Congress leaders in *Charges Against the Madras Ministry* (by Certain MLAs), published by A. Kaleswara Rao, Madras, Renaissance Printers Ltd., 1948, p. 28.

[134] *The Hyderabad Problem.* See also *The New Danger,* Supplement to *Memorandum of the Agriculturists Association,* Hyderabad, December 24, 1948, p. 2; and Romesh Thapar, *Storm Over Hyderabad,* Kutub Publishers, Bombay, 1948.

[135] *Op.cit.,* Ch. 4.

feudal and the national struggle which conditioned the particular acuteness of the peasant struggle in Telengana."[136]

To the delta people, the Andhra Communists could present themselves as brave soldiers venturing across the border into the Nizam's Hyderabad to annex Telugu territory rightfully belonging to Andhra; in Telengana, they were liberators, joining with Telengana Communist leaders to do battle against the Nizam's feudal oppression and to unite his Telugu subjects with Andhra. Propaganda salvoes in the delta and Telengana were invariably signed jointly, "Andhra Mahasabha—Communist Party."

During this period the Andhra Communists could communicate their regional appeal to the remotest hamlet through a network of teen-age partisans—125 separate squads, leaders claimed—organized in the Andhra Youth Federation.[137] This was the leg and lung power that carried party propaganda far and wide, propaganda custom-tailored to suit rural Andhra. The pro-Communist wing of the Andhra literary world, led by the poet Srirangam Srinivasa Rao, or Sri Sri, and his Abhyudaya Rachayithala Sanghamu or Progressive Writers Association, maintained a training school at Pedapudi in Guntur District to assure a steady output of fresh colloquial material.[138] Sri Sri emphasized

---

[136] V. V. Balabushevich, "New Stage in the National Liberation Struggle of the People of India," *Colonial Peoples Struggle for Liberation*, People's Publishing House, Bombay, 1950, p. 50. See also P. Ramamurti, *New Age*, September 27, 1953, p. 4. In *People's Age*, December 15, 1946, p. 5, P. C. Joshi states that in Hyderabad and Travancore-Cochin, "the issues are the same—peoples' right to live and to win the right of self-determination."

[137] Interview with S. V. Narasaiah, former President of the Andhra Youth Federation, Vijayawada, December 20, 1952. See also *Blitz*, October 1, 1953, p. 4.

[138] Sri Sri, *Revolutionary Songs*, Vishalandhra Publishing House, Vijayawada, 1949. See especially "Nava Kavita" or "Modern Poetry," in which Sri Sri tells party poets how to stir the people through vistas of Red Flags and marching millions, and "Pledge," in which he employs the Hindu imagery of Lord Jagganath to symbolize Red Revolution. For other descriptions of Andhra Communist cultural activities, see *Unity*, September 1952, pp. 3, 11; *Indian Express*, October 1, 1953, p. 1; *New Age*, February 2, 1955, p. 3, for an account of a popular Communist play, "The Last Sacrifice," in which the Telugu actress G. N. Varalakshmi played the mother of a Congress minister who renounces her son's party, and *New Age*, August 14, 1955, p. 7, for an account of a film polemic on land reform, "Rojulu Marayi" or "Times Have Changed," written by the pro-Communist film writer Tapi Dharma Rao, and p. 11, for a report of Andhra Communist campaigning for colloquial Telugu in school textbooks.

adaptations of Telugu folk art forms, such as the *Burrakatha*, a ballad told to the rhythm of wood noise-makers, or *Burras*, clicked together by the performers. With its simple ballad sequence, the *Burrakatha* can be staged without scenery and requires few performers, so that a large number of troupes can be in the field at the same time. Into themes of everyday life the Communist creators of the latter-day *Burrakatha* weave the party's propaganda. One popular ballad in the Andhra movement sang of eighty-year-old Sitayya, an honest tenant farmer, his three sons, Kamayya, Ramayya, and Somayya, their three wives, and the inevitable villain, Krishna the landlord. Dire poverty leads Sitayya to a despairing suicide, whereupon Krishna,

> the sole monarch of all he surveys,
> assuming different forms of power and poise—
> a typical example of Congress Raj—

sets Ramayya and Kamayya to feuding, the better to dominate them both—until, enter Somayya:

> The struggle continued and continued
> till the youngest brother arrived
> a true Communist by nature
> a man of good humor and stature
>
> Separating the fighting bulls
> Somayya spoke in reverence
> that differences among the poor
> will lead them to the rich man's door.

By the happy ending, Somayya has reunited the brothers and rallied the village tenant farmers against the landlords, all to the strident strains of Telugu patriotism:

> As our landlords in fear tremble
> let all the peasants and workers unite
> for our Telugu motherland fight.[139]

The Youth Federation combined balladeering with adult education groups, especially during the three months, beginning

[139] *Kauludaru* (The Tenant), by Lakshmikant Mohan, Adarsh Granth Mandali, Vijayawada, 1952. Translated from Telugu for the author.

in January, when Andhra farm chores slacken. The Federation selected local leaders to lead study groups year-round, furnishing loud-speakers and a set of simple Telugu primers phased into successively more complicated literacy lessons, four in all, to be studied over three-month periods. One thirty-five page primer in Telugu begins:

We must have peace. We must have a good time. We must all play happily. Every one of us must have food. We must all go around as equals. Untouchability must vanish. Are things unsatisfactory now? Can you guess the reasons? Learn to read and write well.

Lesson twenty-two ends with the sentences:

The new China is like a lamp in dark Asia. And the brightness of that lamp is tremendous.

Adi-Andhras or untouchables cannot be mistaken in this passage:

They live outside the town. They till the soil and sow the seeds and reap the crop. But they have nothing to eat. What they grow by sweat and toil is enjoyed by others.

Lesson thirty, longest in the first primer, recounts the ancient glories of Andhra and makes an unabashed plea for the Andhra cause:

A few centuries back the Andhras were rulers of a vast country. Their land extended from the ocean in the east to the ocean in the west. In the north, the Andhra sway extended to the banks of the Ganges and in the south up to Tanjore which was ruled by Andhra Nayaks. Where is that domain now? Where has that great country disappeared now?
Today we lie divided and torn and our past glory is only a memory now.
Will there be misery in our country if Andhras come together again? Will there still be famine in the country? Why should there be famine in the land of the Godavari and Krishna? We can work wonders within our borders if we the Telugus come together. Are we all not brothers, people living in distant parts but talking the same Telugu language?
Let us all get together and prepare the ground for a Telugu country. We can then conduct our business and government in our own mother-tongue. We can divert the waters of our rivers wherever they are needed. We can spread the knowledge of our ancient language to every nook and corner of our Telugu country. There will be no

hungry man. We can live happily. That is the real Telugu wealth, Telugu country and Telugu community.[140]

As a result of the regional accent in their propaganda, said the Andhra Communists in an intra-party post-mortem on the Telengana years, "our party came forward as the leader of the Andhra race. It is our party that first posed the issue that Vishalandhra should be formed. With that objective in view, 4,000 heroes in Telengana sacrificed their lives."[141]

The 1951 Elections

Whether or not Communist esteem reached such exalted heights, the party clearly was acquiring new lustre during the very period when the Congress was sinking deeper and deeper into unprecedented factional difficulties. In the years between the 1946 and 1951 elections, Andhra Congress leaders were locked in a factional war, in which the fortunes of N. G. Ranga went first upward and then to rock bottom. The three-way tussle between Ranga, Pattabhi Sitaramayya, and T. Prakasam was complicated by the multilingual nature of Madras politics during that period. To score a point at any given moment, each Andhra faction could reach across not only caste but also regional lines, striking at its rival by aligning with Tamil-speaking factions in the Madras government.

Prakasam, having helped his own lieutenants win Congress seats in the Madras Assembly, commanded powerful support in the first skirmish of this period. In the 1946 wrangle for ascendancy in the multilingual Madras Legislature Congress Party, Prakasam emerged with the prize of the Madras Chief Ministership. But his majority was perilous in that Tamil members of the Assembly had joined in electing him for factional reasons of their own. The ruling Tamil Congress bloc, predominantly non-Brahman, used Prakasam, an Andhra, to head off Tamil Brahman Chakravarti Rajagopalachari in his bid for the Chief Ministership. Once successful, they hurried to hunt

[140] *Lessons*, Andhra Youth Federation, Vijayawada, 1951. Translated from Telugu for the author.
[141] *Self-Critical Report*, Andhra Communist Committee, Part 4, May 1951–January 1952.

allies to replace Prakasam. Caste loyalties on both the Andhra and the Tamil sides thus vanished at the linguistic border. The twenty Andhra supporters of Brahman Sitaramayya lined up with the non-Brahman Tamil bloc and half of the Malayalam-speaking members of the Legislature to unseat Prakasam.

To save his political position in his home territory, Prakasam joined forces with Ranga. Together they took control of the Andhra Congress machinery from Sitaramayya. Ranga won the Andhra Congress presidency, defeating N. Sanjiva Reddi, nominee of the Sitaramayya group.

In the bitter ensuing warfare, both sides aired charges of corruption, which the Communist propaganda network carried into remote rural regions. As a result, the Congress leaders soon lost the prestige of their Independence movement days. Prakasam followers charged Sitaramayya members of the new Madras regime with trafficking improperly in commercial permits and transport franchises, black marketing, and rampant nepotism. They also contended that the Communists enjoyed an unholy alliance with the active leader of Sitaramayya forces in the Madras government, Revenue Minister Kala Venkata Rao. Prakasam cited chapter and verse to allege that Rao, later a national general secretary of the Congress, helped arrange facilities for Red Flag meetings, looked the other way when Communists staged illegal squatter movements, solicited and received Communist help to defeat Prakasam candidates in local elections, and fed anti-Prakasam propaganda to Communist leaders.[142]

With the Kamma Ranga at the head of the Congress, the opposition to Prakasam and Ranga had strong caste overtones. Reddi forces were a part of the maneuvering that brought Ranga's downfall in April 1951, when N. Sanjiva Reddi won the Andhra Congress presidency in a close 87-82 decision. Ranga and Prakasam, charging that the Reddi victory hung on "irregularities," walked out of the Congress. Fifty of their sympathizers on the Andhra Congress Committee followed them out of the party. Then came the final blow to Congress unity, a Ranga-

[142] *Charges Against the Madras Ministry*, pp. 6-7, 30-31.

Prakasam split. Prakasam announced that his candidates in the general elections would carry the symbol of the new Kisan Mazdoor Praja (Peasants Workers Peoples) Party led by Acharya J. B. Kripalani. Ranga formed a Kamma front, the Krishikar Lok (Farmers') Party. Therefore, in delta election constituencies where Kamma influence counted, the three-way Congress split meant that at least two Kammas, a Ranga candidate and a nominee of the official Congress, and in many cases other Kammas named by Prakasam, the Socialist Party, or independent local groups, all competed for the campaign support of their wealthy caste fellows.

It was into this inviting situation that the Andhra Communists strode in the fall of 1951. With many top Andhra leaders—the party's strongest election contenders—still in prison, the national Communist leadership had sent out feelers in midsummer offering to behave as a legal party in exchange for the release of Telengana *détenus*. At first, the Communist press complained that the government of Hyderabad, where the initial overtures were made, "did not even bother to reply."[143] In a Parliament speech on August 14, the then Home Minister Chakravarti Rajagopalachari declared that "the party cannot have it both ways, delivering speeches and carrying on other election activities while killing and terrorizing." As late as November 19, the official Congress Party organ said that "it would be unprecedented for any government to release men convicted by courts or reasonably detained as enemies of the state."[144] Still, in spite of these declarations, the government had an historic last-minute change of heart and released most of the Madras Communist prisoners.[145]

Communist leaders hurried from South Indian jails to their home districts with all the martyr's aura reserved in Indian

---

[143] "For Settlement in Telengana," *Crossroads*, August 3, 1951, p. 1.
[144] "Reds' Threat," *Congress Sandesh*, November 19, 1951, p. 4.
[145] The decision to release the Communist *detenus* is generally attributed to Prime Minister Nehru. A high Indian official with responsibilities in this matter told the author at the time that Nehru felt the Communists would be the gainers if permitted to increase their martyrdom behind bars. Given enough rope, reasoned Nehru, they might eventually be their own undoing.

society for those who suffer privation at the hands of authority. A notification in the *Gazette of India* dated August 11, 1951, showed 202 Communist prisoners in Madras, most of them—although district by district breakdowns are not available—from Andhra. Month by month figures in Home Ministry files show the Madras total of its *détenus* dropping to eighty-six in December and four by February 1952. These figures do not include an almost equal number placed on parole at this time and later declared free. Thus, most of the Andhra Communist high command were freed in time to map strategy for the January balloting.

They campaigned feverishly to make up for their late start, well aware that the deep factional crisis then gripping the Congress camp presented a rare opportunity. Already on good terms with their Kamma brethren because of their sweet reasonableness during guerrilla days, they warned that the Reddi-dominated Congress was out to get them. Ridiculing Ranga's KLP as a splinter group, they argued that he could not possibly emerge with a majority. The Communists presented themselves as political comers who would soon be able to protect the caste from the citadels of government power. The candidate to support is *"manavadu"*—"our man"—which is to say, "our caste man."

The Kammas could well have been impressed with the apparently rising star of their caste fellows at the helm of the Communist Party. Even the Kamma historian Choudary, outspokenly anti-Communist in his writings, recites with obvious pride a long list of Communist notables, adding that "many other young Communist legislators have turned out to be able debaters and formidable opponents."[146] The Kammas must certainly have considered how desirable it would be to crystallize friendly relations with a revolutionary leadership that had already shown it could be reasonable about whose land was confiscated.[147]

[146] Choudary, *A Brief History of the Kammas*, p. 98.

[147] Terming the Andhra Communist proposal for a 20-acre ceiling on wet delta land "conservative," Vinoba Bhave (*Bhoodan*, July 24, 1957, p. 1) complained that "our 'radical' parties . . . would hardly touch the problem of the landless."

Whatever the understanding[148] between the Communists and Kamma patriarchs, a significant section of the Kammas plainly put its funds, influence, and votes behind the Communist Kamma candidates (see Table V). This factor appears to have tipped the scales in the delta. While the Kamma vote was divided, the share of Kamma support won by the Communists provided the margin of victory in fourteen of the twenty-five delta general constituencies where Communist deputies were elected.[149] Three of the six Communist members of the lower house of Parliament elected in 1951 from the delta are Kammas.

The victorious Communist in 1951 drew on the numbers of the landless laborers and protest votes of erstwhile Congress supporters, but powerful Kamma backers gave him in a substantial number of cases even more decisive support—identification with village-level authority. In a society hardly out of feudalism, this is an intangible that should not be underestimated.

To a great extent the 1951 results in the delta can be explained simply by the multiplicity of candidates, which enabled the Communists to capitalize on a divided opposition. But it is necessary to examine the nature of this multiplicity. The telling strength of the Communists in this opportunity came from the fact that they were uniquely situated to exploit the divisions in the Kamma camp. Their leaders were Kammas on Kamma ground. Kamma influence is spread evenly enough over the delta so that even in those delta constituencies where non-Kamma Communist candidates were successful, the Kamma population must have played an important role. Furthermore, a glance at the votes polled by the winning Communist Kammas places the factor of multiplicity of candidates in proper

---

[148] C. V. K. Rao, *Rashtra Communist Navakthwapu Bandaram,* said that Dharma Rao, a brother-in-law of Basava Punniah, has enrolled hundreds of Kammas as actual party members on the promise that the caste group would benefit when the C P came to power. As an example of specific allusions to Communist Kamma support, see also "CPI May Win More Seats in Madras," *The Statesman,* January 8, 1952, p. 1.

[149] The figure of twenty-five excludes six reserved constituencies in which Communists won in the delta.

TABLE V

COMMUNIST KAMMA STRONGHOLDS IN ANDHRA[a] AS SHOWN IN 1951 AND
1955 STATE ASSEMBLY ELECTIONS

Constituency	1951 Percent of Total Vote				1955 Percent of Total Vote		
	Congress	CP	KLP	Others	Congress	CP	Others
Krishna—							
Kanchikacherla	31[b]	52[b]	13[b]	4[b]	50[b]	47[b]	3[b]
Kankipadu	30[b]	54[b]	11[b]	5[b]	51[b]	49[b]	–
Divi	20[b]	44[b]	–	36[b]	59[b]	41[b]	–
Gudivada	14[b]	48[b]	–	38	–	42[b]	58[b]
Guntur—							
Chilakaluripet[c]	19[b]	55[b]	11[b]	15	56[b]	43[b]	1
Bapatla	32	36[b]	25[b]	7	56	40[b]	4
Mangalgiri	14	51[b]	23[b]	12	57	43[b]	–
Repalle	34[b]	52[b]	9[b]	5	60	40[b]	–
Ongole	12	40[b]	20[b]	28	54	46[b]	–
Ponnur	15	37[b]	21[b]	27	65[b]	35	–
East Godavari—							
Rajahmundry	27	40[b]	–	33	59	41	–
West Godavari—							
Kovvur	23[b]	30[b]	–	47[b]	63[b]	32[b]	5
Eluru[d]	26[b]	40[b]	–	34	62[b]	37[b]	1
Chintalapudi	32[b]	46[b]	–	22[b]			

[a] Constituencies shown represent all those in which Kamma Communist candidates were elected in 1951. The outcome in the same constituencies is shown in 1955, though it should be borne in mind that new delimitation of constituencies prior to the 1955 elections makes the 1955 constituencies not exactly congruent with the originals under comparison. These constituencies do not necessarily represent the sites of greatest Kamma Communist success in 1955. The site of one 1951 Communist victory—Chintalapudi (West Godavari) —cannot be compared meaningfully with any 1955 constituency.

[b] Candidates designated in this manner are members of the Kamma subcaste.

[c] Renamed Paruchur in 1955.   [d] Renamed Denduluru in 1955.

NOTE: Percentages have been rounded to the nearest decimal. Communist-supported Kamma candidates running on other party tickets or as independents in other constituencies are not included in this analysis in view of the author's inability to gain a precise picture of the division of support in the constituencies concerned. A Communist-supported Kamma won on the KMP ticket in Narasaropet (Guntur), while a C P-supported candidate lost on the KLP ticket in Tenali (Guntur) and another lost as an independent in Nuzvid (Krishna).

perspective. The average Communist Kamma winner polled 44.6 percent of the votes. In only two constituencies, Eluru and Chintalapudi, did the combined vote of non-Communist Kamma candidates exceed that of the Communist Kamma vic-

tor. Even in defeat, Communist Kamma candidates in 1951
polled 33.1 percent of the votes (see Table VI), with their

TABLE VI

DEFEATED 1951 COMMUNIST KAMMA STATE ASSEMBLY CANDIDATES
IN ANDHRA DELTA DISTRICTS

Constituency	Percent of Total Vote			
	Congress	CP	KLP	Others
Krishna—				
Kaikalur	37[a]	36[a]	–	27
Guntur—				
Guntur	24[a]	23[a]	–	53
Duggirala	42	38[a]	13[a]	7
Prathipadu	26	25	22[a]	27
East Godavari—				
Pamarru	49[a]	46[a]	–	5[a]
West Godavari—				
Tanuku	29[a]	25[a]	–	46[a]

[a] Members of the Kamma subcaste.
NOTE: Percentages have been rounded to the nearest decimal. Communist-
supported Kamma candidates running on other party tickets or as independents
in other constituencies are not included in this analysis.

margin of defeat a matter of from one to four percentage points
in every instance where the successful candidate was also a
Kamma. In sharp contrast, other defeated Communist candidates in the delta polled only an average twenty-two percent.
Thus the multiplicity of candidates alone cannot explain the
large number of Communist victories. The fact that the Communists could compete strongly for the support of the caste
group most strategically placed in delta politics was the key
to the Communist sweep.

Outside the delta, too, in constituencies where the Kammas
were a potent minority but not dominant, the Communists
chose to rely on Kamma support. For example, in the Chittoor
parliamentary contest, the Communists unsuccessfully supported a Kamma independent against a Reddi Congress candidate. In Nellore, a coastal district adjacent to the delta where
the Kammas have only half the numerical strength of the
Reddis,[150] the Communists lost out to Congress Reddis in

[150] *Census of India, 1921*, Vol. 13, Table XIII, p. 119, shows 109,969 Kammas
and 208,018 Reddis in Nellore.

three constituencies where they nominated Kammas.[151] Where they won in Nellore it was with Reddi candidates in two solidly Reddi constituencies,[152] and with a Brahman in another.[153] The two Reddis elected on the Communist ticket in Nellore may owe much of their strength to the prestige of the sole major Communist Reddi leader, Sundarayya, in his home district. Where scattered Reddis were elected in other districts, the result appears to have hinged on local and personal factors.[154] The only other Communists elected outside the delta were four Brahmans and one Velama, a petty landlord subcaste.

It was in Nellore that Kamma-Reddi bitterness in 1951 reached its high point in the defeat of the prominent Andhra Congress leader B. Gopala Reddi, Finance Minister in the Madras government, by a KMPP Kamma candidate in Udayagiri constituency. Reddi, who once remarked lightly in the Madras Assembly that his was "a Reddi government for Reddis,"[155] told reporters that Kammas had "wreaked vengeance" on him.[156] His supporters explained that a would-be Kamma candidate in Chingleput had been refused a Congress nomination by Congress leaders there. The Kammas in Udayagiri blamed it on backstage maneuvering by B. Gopala Reddi. This was one of the rare episodes in which Kamma-Reddi enmity had ever burst into the open.

Their vantage point in the competition for Kamma support, of course, does not fully explain the Communist showing. They had the issues on their side. Not only could they promise five acres and a cow to their traditional supporters, the Adi-Andhra landless laborers; they could also inflate popular discontent with food shortages and blackmarketing that grew worse while ruling Congress politicians seemed too busy

[151] Venkatagiri, Gudur, and Rapur.
[152] Kanigiri and Darsi.
[153] Kovur.
[154] Nandikotkur in Kurnool, Kamalapuram and Rajampet in Cuddapah, and Anantapur in Anantapur District were the sites of other Communist Reddi successes.
[155] Quoted by D. V. Raja Rao, "Election Lessons," p. 13.
[156] "Congress Reverses in Madras," *Hindustan Standard*, January 14, 1952, p. 8.

feuding—or wading in the trough of corruption—to take action. Most important of all, they could put the Congress on the defensive in the Andhra State issue.

Popular sentiment for an Andhra State had grown powerful by 1951, but the Nehru Government, fearful of the inevitable chain reaction in other regions, paid as little attention as possible to the mounting uproar. This only aggravated the discomfiture of Andhra Congress leaders on the eve of the national elections. While the Communists and the Prakasam-Ranga camp could make the Andhra issue a major campaign vehicle, the Congress could point to no more than general assurances from Nehru that "eventually" there would be an Andhra province—when Andhra and Tamil leaders could agree on boundary details—assurances virtually cancelled out, for all practical purposes, by Nehru's offhand confession on his Andhra campaign tour that "personally, I am against linguistic provinces, though the case of Andhra is an exception."[157]

Nehru's near-fiasco in Andhra can be read between the lines even in the account of the Congress' own election organ:

At various places the Congress President witnessed demonstrations by protagonists of an Andhra State, with slogans, placards and posters. At some places he smiled at them, at others he was enraged at their behavior. Leaders of Andhra do not seem to have been enthused about the Congress President's far-reaching statement on an Andhra State. They demand an immediate Governmental declaration, a target date for the formation of the new state.[158]

In Guntur the crowds were more disciplined, but there was a mechanical tragedy:

Nehru's throat had gone hoarse and the mikes failed, and Guntur was the place where he was to have made the best and most important speech of his Andhra tour. He was vexed. He saw it was one of the best crowds he had met and he flew into a rage and cut his one-hour speech to twenty minutes, both in English and in Hindi. Telling local Congressmen that it was more an insult to the lakhs of people gathered there than to him, he walked away in disgust.[159]

157 *The Pilgrimage and After*, A.I.C.C., 1952, pp. 22-25.
158 *Congress Sandesh*, January 7, 1952, p. 10.
159 *The Pilgrimage and After*, p. 25.

With none of the restraints of the Congress press, a Bombay weekly explained that Nehru had tried to address the throng without a microphone but was "shouted down. . . . Mr. Nehru heard nothing but 'we want Andhra State, we want Andhra State' from everywhere."[160]

To make the most of Congress discomfiture, the Communists, Prakasam, and Ranga all stepped up their propaganda on the Andhra issue,[161] but it was the Communists, with organization superior to the election-eve improvisations of the other opposition groups, who were the main beneficiaries of the clamor. Congress equivocation, charged the Communists, was nothing short of self-interested treason. "Many of our own Andhras as Ministers and members of Assembly have been thriving and making hay at the expense of their own country and people by joining hands with Tamilians,"[162] said a circular laying down the election line. The Andhra State issue contributed significantly to the concentration of Communist votes in the delta, it was generally agreed, for it was in the delta that the issue most mattered.[163]

But after the elections, Andhra State was still to be won. In an intraparty analysis the Andhra Communist Committee said that "by electing our deputies, people have placed on us not only the problems relating to different classes, but also the problem of the Andhra race as a whole, namely the Andhra State issue. The middle class intelligentsia, who ideologically differed with us in the past, are now prepared to work along with us."[164] Proclaiming the Andhra Party to be "the national party of the Telugu people," the Communist press pointed to the forty-one Communist seats in Andhra and forty-five more in Telengana, concluding that in a united Telugu State eighty-

[160] *Current*, January 2, 1952, p. 8.

[161] *Times of India*, January 3, 1952, p. 4.

[162] Confidential circular issued by N. R. Dasary, Andhra Students Federation, to all units, October 1951. See also *Crossroads*, January 4, 1952, p. 5.

[163] For example, see a Press Trust of India dispatch from Madras, *Hindustan Times*, December 30, 1951, p. 3.

[164] *Self-Critical Report*, May 1951–January 1952. See also A. S. Rao, "Andhras Struggle for Their Own State," p. 109.

six Communist deputies would be a serious threat to Congress control.[165]

Even in the existing Madras Legislature, however, the compact Andhra Communist delegation realized it could wield decisive impact by uniting all Telugu deputies with Communists elected in other Madras regions. In February 1952, with the elections less than ten days behind, the Andhra Communist Committee met for the first time after four guerrilla years and called on all Andhra legislators to declare unequivocally for an Andhra State.[166]

All Andhra members of the Madras Assembly, they demanded, should speak in Telugu as an earnest of their determination to quit the multilingual body.[167] The newly-launched Telugu Communist daily *Vishalandhra* hailed the fight for Andhra State as the first step toward "the unity of the Andhra nation."[168] In this heady atmosphere the Communists induced Prakasam to lead an anti-Congress "united democratic front" in the Legislature. For a fleeting few weeks the Congress could find no formula for resuming control in Madras until, as Richard L. Park wrote at the time, "the problem became so critical that Chakravarti Rajagopalachari was called out of retirement to form and head the Congress Ministry."[169] Rajagopalachari had been in power only a short time when the Gandhian disciple Sriramulu began the fast that ultimately ended in a martyr's death and brought Andhra State into being. Sriramulu's fifty-eight-day ordeal was not inspired by the Communists, but the party shrewdly exploited its emotional aftermath. The Communist press frankly recorded the role of the party in the wave of mob violence that followed Sriramulu's death. Nehru's decision to grant Andhra "followed years of struggle led by the Communist Party," reported the London *Daily Worker's* New Delhi correspondent, "culminating in a united movement last week which paralyzed all government

[165] *Crossroads*, March 21, 1952, p. 5. There would have been 248 seats in the combined legislatures.
[166] *The Hindu*, February 8, 1952, p. 4.
[167] *The Hindu*, October 26, 1952, p. 4.
[168] June 22, 1952, p. 1.
[169] "Indian Election Results," *Far Eastern Survey*, May 7, 1952, p. 64.

in the area."[170] *Crossroads* exulted that "railways, postal and telegraphic communications and all transport stopped. Mass demonstrations were held, in which people died and many were injured by police firing. The people made it impossible for governmental machinery to move until an Andhra province was granted."[171]

The 1955 Elections

Once Andhra State was formed, the focus for regional patriotism became the Vishalandhra demand for annexation of Telugu-speaking portions of Hyderabad. But Vishalandhra faded away into the welter of administrative snarls and shifting political alignments in the new state. Moreover, open Kamma-Reddi warfare increased with the two rivals now pitted directly against each other. No longer was there the intervening presence of non-Andhra elements in a multilingual legislature. Even Jawaharlal Nehru could not bring N. G. Ranga under the wing of Sanjiva Reddi's party leadership.[172] The controversy over the choice of the new state's capital once again polarized Andhra politics on what was now widely conceded to be a regional-caste basis, the Reddi-dominated Congress winning the selection of Kurnool in Rayalaseema over the bitter protests of the Communists and Ranga's KLP as champions of the delta.[173]

Puchalapalli Sundarayya charged that the Congress:

. . . wanted to rouse regional feelings: it wanted to rouse communal feelings, and that is why it selected Kurnool as the capital. . . . The Congress raises the slogan of Reddi vs. Kamma. It says: if you want to change from Kurnool to any centralized place, then Kamma domination will come and Reddi domination will go. These are facts that cannot be controverted by anybody who knows anything about Andhra.[174]

[170] Quoted in *Free Press Journal*, Bombay, December 25, 1952, p. 1.
[171] *Crossroads*, January 11, 1953, pp. 8-9.
[172] "Ranga Keeps Out," *Times of India*, October 2, 1953, p. 1.
[173] For example, see "Andhra Election Scene," *Times of India*, January 10, 1955, p. 6.
[174] "We Demand Free and Fair Elections," Parliament speech by P. Sundarayya, cited in *For Victory in Andhra*, CPI publication, Delhi, 1955, p. 13.

A newspaper correspondent reported during this episode that:

In recent years the rivalry between the Reddys of Rayalaseema and rich Kammas of delta districts has grown to alarming proportions. Congressmen have tended to group themselves on communal lines, and the Sanjiva Reddy-Ranga tussle for leadership which finally resulted in Ranga's exit from the Congress is a major instance in this regard. And rightly or wrongly the choice of Kurnool is looked upon by the Kammas as another major triumph for the Reddys.[175]

Ostensibly, the Congress stand for Kurnool in the capital dispute honored a 1937 commitment by Congress leaders from the delta that the underdog Rayalaseema area could have first claim in the location of the capital or High Court of the future Andhra State—with the delta getting the one left over. But in the 1953 wrangle there was more at stake. Both the Communists and the KLP were voicing not only the local pride of the delta communities seeking the capital, but real estate and mercantile interests as well.[176]

By the time the first Andhra Congress ministry had collapsed in November 1954, a scant year after its installation, Congress leaders in New Delhi had come to realize that firm intervention from outside would be necessary to forge a united front for the new elections in February 1955. From Jawaharlal Nehru down, there was a determination that the history of the 1951 Kamma defection should not repeat itself. For N. G. Ranga this was an important political moment in which his whole future as a Kamma spokesman lay at stake. Nehru summoned the forces of Ranga, T. Prakasam, Sanjiva Reddi, and assorted other anti-Communist Andhra leaders to map a united election campaign. Working closely with such Kamma Congress powers as Kotta Raghuramaiah,[177] formerly India's dele-

---

[175] *Times of India*, June 16, 1953, p. 7.

[176] In "The Future of Andhra" (*Thought*, October 3, 1953) G. S. Bhargava reports that Kamma property owners in Vijayawada had confidently based land investments on the expectation that the capital would be there, and suffered heavy losses. Similarly, Rayalaseema Member of Parliament Seshagiri Rao charged during the debate on the Andhra State Bill (*Proceedings*, House of the People, August 17, 1953, Col. 927) that "it is so many people who have purchased lands in Bezwada who are responsible for this sort of agitation."

[177] For a sketch of Raghuramaiah, "Tobacco King," reflecting Kamma power in tobacco farming, see *Times of India*, September 13, 1955, p. 3.

gate to the UN Trusteeship Council, Ranga emerged from the
negotiations with control over nominations in thirty-eight
constituencies as part of a Congress United Front—enough to
assure a single Kamma entry by Congress forces in all Kamma
strongholds. The regular Congress organization received 136
constituencies and the People's Party, a Prakasam rump group
comprising Andhra remnants of the defunct KMP, won control
of nominations in twenty constituencies.

Although Sanjiva Reddi, leader of what by then was popularly called "The Rayalaseema Junta," sulked in protest
against the very principle of alliance with Ranga,[178] the pressure for a joint front against the Communists was too much
for him. The Congress high command assigned Bombay Congress strong man S. K. Patil to enforce factional unity. With
the Congress camp united, independents shunned battle. There
were seventy-eight straight contests between the Congress and
the Communists, sixty-five more with only three contestants.
Only in the remaining fifty-three was there the dispersion of
1951. The Communists, confidently dashing into the fray, had
announced their candidate lists in the first week of December
to place themselves squarely on the offensive. But this cut two
ways: the Congress had time to match caste with caste in se-
lecting candidates. The upshot was that in their delta stronghold the Communists won only eleven seats, two of these in
reserved constituencies, as opposed to their thirty-one delta
seats in 1951. A solitary Kamma was elected on the Communist
ticket.[179]

Ironically, in 1955 their caste may in certain cases have been
a liability to Kamma Communists. The defection of C. V. K.
Rao, a Communist leader of the Devadasi caste, was openly
trumpeted in anti-Kamma terms by Rao's election-rump "Communist Unity Centre." Handbills ridiculing Communist leaders as "Red landlords" sufficiently nettled them to elicit a
special campaign appearance by Rajeshwar Rao. Announcing
that he and his brother had donated the equivalent of $40,000
over the years to Communist coffers, Rajeshwar Rao added:

[178] "Rift in Andhra Congress," *Times of India*, January 1, 1955, p. 10.
[179] V. Visweswara Rao in Mylavaram constituency, Krishna District.

"I did not say that all our property is exhausted; there is still something left. We shall spend it, along with our lives, in the service of the people."[180]

The Communists made every bit as intensive an effort in 1955 as in 1951 to capitalize on the Kamma "social base"[181] in the delta, running Kamma candidates in twenty-nine delta constituencies. Underscoring the Kamma orientation of Communist tactics is the fact that in nine of these twenty-nine constituencies, the Communist candidate was the only Kamma in the field.

With anti-Communist Kamma forces consolidated in the Congress, however, the Communists could not make their Kamma support a decisive factor in 1955. Confronted with a single Kamma opponent (see Table V), the Communist Kamma candidate was in a defensive position. N. G. Ranga had recaptured the initiative in the contest for Kamma support by showing he could drive a hard bargain for the caste within Congress councils. The twenty-eight Kamma Communist losers did win substantial support in their caste strongholds—an average 38.7 percent of the votes. But this was a drop from an average 44.6 percent polled by the fourteen Kamma Communist winners in 1951.

Despite this 6 percent decline in their Kamma strength, the Communists increased their popular vote in most of the delta just as in the rest of Andhra.[182] This is explained by the even distribution of their 1955 vote over a wide range of constituencies, in contrast to spotty 1951 voting concentrations in constituencies where they then enjoyed strong Kamma support. Unlike 1951, when the Communist Kammas fared better than other Communist candidates, the Communist Kammas in 1955 were on a par with the thirty-four other defeated Communist candidates in the delta. Defeated non-Kamma Communist candidates in the delta in 1955 averaged 38.3 percent, while in

180 *New Age*, December 26, 1954, p. 16.

181 This phrase is attributed to the Communists in "Caste Factor," *Times of India*, February 1, 1955, p. 6.

182 While the popular vote increased in Krishna District, the Communist increase did not keep pace with the over-all increase; the Communist percentage of the total in the district dropped from 48 percent in 1951 to 44 in 1955.

1951 non-Kamma Communist losers had polled only twenty-two percent, and even defeated Kammas had polled only 33.1 percent.

The Communist share of Kamma support went a long distance with the Congress Kamma camp divided in 1951, but the Ranga-Congress alliance made Communist inroads on Kamma backing less significant in 1955. Nor did the issues fall on the Communist side in 1955 as they had in 1951. The Kammas responded to the general strength of the Congress cause, coupled with a successful appeal to the caste's economic stake in keeping the Communist Party out of power. The Congress election platform stressed agricultural price support. The Communist press bitterly complained that propertied interests had ganged up against them. In a reference to Divi, the home constituency of the Kamma Rajeshwar Rao, the Communist weekly *New Age* declared that "all quarrels of caste or community have been forgotten. They [the landlords] have united to face the common people. They are all in the Congress now."[183]

While Congress leaders such as S. K. Patil deluged all Andhra with effective anti-Communist propaganda, the body blow to the delta Communists came from the fact that the veteran anti-Communist ideologian, N. G. Ranga, now had the prestige to make an effective appeal in the Kamma constituencies, the central arena of the contest. G. S. Bhargava reported from Andhra that credit for delivering the telling punch in the delta "must go to the KLP leader, Mr. N. G. Ranga, who for the first time carried the fight against communism into villages hitherto regarded as impregnable Communist fortresses."[184] A. Kaleswara Rao, a Grand Old Man of the Andhra Congress, wrote the author at the time polling was about to take place: "The Con-

---

[183] January 17, 1955, p. 3. In a post-mortem on the 1955 elections (*Resolution of the Central Committee on the Andhra Elections*, cited in *Indian Communist Party Documents, 1930-1956*, Democratic Research Service, Bombay, and Institute of Pacific Relations, New York, 1957, pp. 220-221) the Andhra Communist decline is attributed largely to Congress tactics "swinging . . . the majority of the rich and middle peasants." The elections showed the "supreme urgency . . . of winning in particular, the middle strata, while firmly relying on our basic masses."

[184] G. S. Bhargava, "Verdict on Communism," *Ambala Tribune*, March 15, 1955, p. 4.

gress United Front formed by Pandit Jawaharlal Nehru, roping in Sri Ranga . . . is very successful in the Communist-infested districts, e.g. in central Andhra. The Kamma community, which is predominant in this area, have joined the Congress United Front with patriotism."[185]

Rao's reference to patriotism echoed Congress campaign slogans. Undoubtedly the fact that a procession of respected national Congress leaders came to Andhra to denounce the Communists in unequivocal terms of nationalism played an important election role, not only in rousing Kamma support, but throughout Andhra. Jawaharlal Nehru attacked the Communists as "professional maligners of the Indian people."[186] Congress president U. N. Dhebar warned Andhra voters that "if one Communist state in India is established, our international strength will be lost."[187] S. K. Patil's posters and pamphlets blasted the Communists as outright traitors, painting gruesome pictures of horror in China and the Soviet Union.[188] The fall of Malenkov on February 8, just as polling was getting underway, was a convenient reminder of past purges. Moreover, the Congress had dulled the ideological edge of the Communist appeal at its January national session at Avadi by announcing a "socialistic pattern of society" as its goal. What hurt even more, the Communists were denied the support of Russian policy and its propaganda machine. *Pravda* published an historic editorial on the eve of India's Republic Day, January 26, marking the end of seven years of attacks on the Nehru government and confounding the Communists' election strategy. How could the Communists parade the banner of an international big brother who praised "the outstanding statesman, Mr. Jawaharlal Nehru,"[189] at the same time they were waging an election campaign against his party?

[185] Analysis prepared for the author, dated February 19, 1955, Vijayawada. Rao has served on the All-India Congress Committee for over thirty years. He was elected a member of the Andhra legislature from the Vijayawada constituency in the 1955 election.
[186] *Times of India*, January 16, 1955, p. 4.
[187] *The Hindu*, February 8, 1955, p. 4.
[188] See "Nehru's Congress Filth," *New Age*, February 6, 1955.
[189] Cited in *Times of India*, February 1, 1955, p. 3. The editorial also stated

By successfully making Indian nationalism a live issue in a state election, the Congress, still for all its sins a symbol of Independence, was calling forth its trump card. The resultant election-time atmosphere was a complete reversal of 1951, when the Communists had been able to wrap themselves in the banner of the Andhra provincial autonomy movement and make Telugu patriotism a live ballot-box issue. In 1955, the demand for Vishalandhra, anti-climactic, perhaps, so soon after the formation of Andhra, did not evoke the same emotional response, although the Communists sought to capitalize on the omission of the issue in the Congress platform.[190]

But Andhra's formation as the first frankly linguistic state in India, while relaxing the tension between the Telugus and the central government, only heightened the political struggle among Telugu castes. As we have seen in Chapter IV, the change in the vantage of castes which accompanies the formation of new linguistic provinces is a basic fact of Indian political life. In the case of Andhra, it was immediately clear that political stability could depend to a great extent on the ability of Reddi and Kamma leaders to work together in a united government.[191] Looking to the future, subcaste divisions within both Kamma and Reddi ranks could harden into a still more complex array of political battle lines. Furthermore, the formation of a united Vishalandhra with Hyderabad as its capital in 1957, following the report of the States Reorganization Commission, has foreshadowed shifts in the power balance among Telugu castes.

The power of the delta Kammas is now diffused in the new larger unit. M. Basava Punniah, the Kamma Communist leader, attributing the 1955 Congress victory to the support of Ranga's Kamma following, seemed to be bidding for renewed all-Kamma

---

that the Indian Republic was "a peace-loving state upholding its national independence," which has "set itself to the grim task of gradually eliminating colonialism."

[190] *New Age*, December 26, 1954, p. 3; January 9, 1955, p. 3, and *New Age*, monthly, January 1955, p. 2.

[191] By August 1957, the Kamma-Reddi honeymoon in the Andhra Congress had ended. "There are thirty-one members in the Executive Committee," said the *Times of India*, August 23, 1957, p. 6, "but no room has been found in such a large body for Mr. N. G. Ranga."

solidarity when he suggested in a 1959 article that Ranga's KLP Party do some "serious re-thinking and reformulation of their program." Implying that the Kammas had more to gain from the Communist alliance pattern followed in 1951, he observed that "it is yet to be seen whether the KLP leadership, *drawing on its own lessons from the past full decade . . .* gives up some of its rightist and anti-Communist positions or . . . prepares the ground once again to be out-maneuvered by the official Congress leadership at the crucial hour" (italics added).[192] Ranga, however, had taken his followers into the new national right-wing Swatantra Party by the end of 1959 and Kamma political power seemed likely to become one of the many splintered forces in a splintered Andhra body politic.

The delta Kammas confront in the new larger unit not only the Reddis of Rayalaseema but also the politically distinct Telengana Reddis—whose rivals on their home ground have been the Telengana Brahmans. Once Vishalandhra became imminent, the Reddi-Brahman rivals in Telengana and the Kamma-Reddi antagonists in Andhra could each be seen jockeying to establish ties across intra-regional borders. To complicate matters still more, the Telengana Communist leadership has lacked homogeneity. Ravi Narayan Reddi and a Brahman, D. V. Rao, have led rival factions that must now adapt themselves to a new common relationship to the delta Communist leaders.[193]

Paradoxically, the success of the Andhra Communists in finally winning Vishalandhra could be their undoing. With their leadership uneasily balanced between intra-regional factions, they will perhaps be as frustrated by the strength of regional caste alignments in the future as they have been blessed by them in the past. But in any event, the Andhra Communist leadership, Kammas and Reddis alike, can be counted upon

---

[192] M. Basava Punniah, "Andhra Congress Conflicts," *New Age*, January 1959, p. 9.

[193] The thirteen-member Visalandhra Communist secretariat elected in July 1956, numbered six Kammas, four Reddis, two Brahmans, and one Muslim, with the Kamma Rajeshwar Rao as secretary. See *New Age* (weekly), April 22, 1956, p. 2, and July 29, 1956, p. 5.

to manipulate the regional patriotism which all Telugus will share in common. It is in time of conflict between the Telugus and New Delhi that the Andhra Communists can still come into their own.

WILL INDIA develop as a strong centrally directed political whole, or will she, under the stresses of regionalism, become a congeries of loosely federated states?

To predict the future of the Union is, in effect, to predict the shape that Indian leaders will give to their political institutions in the coming decades. But it is not clear what kind of political institutions will assure what results. Under the present Indian Constitution, each state elects its own legislature. While Nehru's Congress Party survived the first general elections with control of all states, the Communists took power in Kerala for two years, and the Ganatantra Parishad only narrowly missed control of Orissa in the second general elections of 1957. The possibility of divergence on a multiplying scale between the national party in power and an assortment of ruling state parties now looms unmistakably on the Indian political horizon. Not only did more regional political groupings, and more potent ones, emerge in 1957, but their emergence occurred at the expense of national parties. Thus the great issue before Indian leaders is whether the present Constitution, drafted at a time when a national party system seemed to be in the making, will be adequate to a new time in which the interplay of national parties makes way for the new contest between the central power and regionally based political forces.

The Indiscipline of Indian Communism

Indian Communist experience demonstrates the central dilemma of a party system in India. By and large, as we have seen, Indian Communist organizations have found success where they have embodied dominant parochial interests and have therefore been able to exploit local chauvinisms to their own advantage. Yet this disparate character is a source of weakness rather than strength when the Communist Party, or any Indian party, seeks to be national. The regional pattern of Indian Communist success merely underscores the fact that Indian Communism cannot yet claim the discipline implicit in its commitment to centralized unity. In the loose federation called the Communist Party of India—"not a single monolithic autocracy but rather a cluster of autocracies, functional and regional"[1]—strong units have been free to get stronger while the weak remain weak.

The Communist experience reveals the strains that a political party must endure in India when it has no Gandhis or Nehrus. As a movement that played a nationalist role only for a brief period in the thirties, Indian Communism naturally threw up leadership which addressed local grievances from local platforms, rather than pan-Indian leadership which voiced the common anti-British grievance from a national platform. Although the founders of Indian Communism in the twenties were the "Old Bolsheviks" of the northern industrial centers, such as S. A. Dange in Bombay, the young intellectuals in the hinterlands who founded regional units in the thirties were to become the party's most powerful leaders. "We haven't got anyone who can compete with Nehru," granted Ajoy Ghosh, "but in the provinces we do have people. Not mass leaders on the all-India level, but local mass leaders like P. Sundarayya and A. K. Gopalan."[2] When the author asked the late M. N. Roy, a founder of Indian Communism and later one of its vocal opponents, who were the party's most significant leaders, it was Gopalan again who came to Roy's mind as a characteristic figure of future importance, precisely, he explained, because the party could claim so few leaders with local mass standing.[3] Although the Brahman E. M. S. Nambudripad, as the Kerala party's prime intellectual, became Chief Minister when the Communists came to power in the state in 1957, Gopalan, as

---

[1] Gene D. Overstreet and Marshall Windmiller, *Communism in India*, University of California Press, Berkeley, 1958, p. 458.
[2] Interview with Ajoy K. Ghosh, Delhi, September 10, 1951.
[3] M. N. Roy, analysis prepared for the author, July 1952, p. 2.

a bright young light of the Nayars, is the Kerala party's popular idol and stump orator.[4] Known as "AKG," Gopalan commands worshipful young followers who come to national party congresses sporting buttons complete with smiling Gopalan images in the best Rotarian manner. In the same way the non-Brahman Sundarayya in Andhra has established a grassroots reputation in his region, especially in his own Reddi stronghold of Rayalaseema.[5] Both Gopalan and Sundarayya exemplify the bedrock reserves of regional leadership without which the party could claim little substantial mass following. In the absence of any all-India leader who is more than the "apparatus man" personified in Ghosh, it is in this regional leadership that effective party power resides. The main cause of Indian Communism's weakness at the national level, Marshall Windmiller has speculated, "seems to be that real power exists primarily at the state level and that control of a mass following either in a particular region or in a trade union organization is more important than holding national office."[6]

This power of the regional leadership is reinforced by the fact, already noted, that the numerical membership strength of the party itself is greatest in the non-Hindi regions; that at the Fourth Party Congress in 1956, for example, the Telugu belt accounted for nearly 25 percent of delegate strength, Malayalam 19, Bengal almost 12, and two other non-Hindi regions, Marathi- and Tamil-speaking, 7 percent each. The former leader of the Communist-led Peoples Democratic Front in Hyderabad, Dr. N. M. Jaisoorya, charged flatly in abandoning his post in 1954 that the (then) Andhra and Telengana party units "dominate the Communist Party setup today through numerically higher votes."[7] Unlike the Soviet Com-

[4] For sketches of Gopalan, see *Hindustan Standard*, April 17, 1952, p. 10, and *Crossroads*, December 1, 1951, p. 2.

[5] For sketches of Sundarayya, see *Amrita Bazar Patrika*, June 8, 1952, p. 3; *New Age*, January 9, 1955, pp. 1, 12; A. S. R. Chari, *The Lid Off Andhra Anti-Communism*, People's Publishing House, Bombay, 1945, p. 12; and P. C. Joshi, *Among Kisan Patriots*, Bombay, People's Publishing House, 1946, p. 4. The author interviewed Sundarayya at 3 Windsor Place, New Delhi, March 10, 1952.

[6] Marshall Windmiller, "Indian Communism and the New Soviet Line," *Pacific Affairs*, December 1956, p. 357.

[7] *Times of India*, December 10, 1954, p. 3.

munist Party, in which the dominant Soviet nationality, Great Russian, is also the dominant bloc in the party, the entire north Indian region embracing Hindi and its variants, bordered by Bengal in the east, Gujarat in the west, and Kashmir in the north, claimed only 21 percent at both the Third and Fourth Party Congresses. By contrast, the majority of members of the Soviet Party have been Great Russians from the beginning.[8] The bulk of the original members of the Soviet Party came from urban and industrial centers in the Russian component of the Soviet Union. In 1922, Great Russians accounted for 72 percent of party membership; in 1927, 65 percent, even though the Russian component of the population totalled 53 percent at that time. The delegate roster to the Sixteenth Party Congress in 1930 showed 57.4 percent Great Russians, which corresponds to current estimates placing the Great Russian percentage of the population at 58.4 percent.[9]

The Loyalties of a Communist

Perhaps, as Gene D. Overstreet maintains, Indian Communism "has by and large succeeded in reducing regional antagonisms within the Party to a level below that prevailing in the country as a whole."[10] But it is doubtful whether the level is much below. For all the discipline that their commitment presupposes, Communist leaders remain very much the human captives of their own birthright, which they may exploit, as have the Kammas in Andhra, or permit to be their undoing, as in the case of the Tamil and Marathi leaders. Certainly the Indian Communist movement, like the Congress and other parties, has produced only a few authentic cosmopolitan leaders. Just as Nehru, representing as he does the Islamicized, Western-trained "universal" aristocracy of Uttar Pradesh, had to "discover" the local cultural integrity of India's diverse regional

8 Richard Pipes, *The Formation of the Soviet Union,* Harvard University Press, Cambridge, 1954, p. 269.

9 Frederick C. Barghoorn, *Soviet Russian Nationalism,* Oxford University Press, New York, 1956, pp. 87-89.

10 Gene D. Overstreet, "Leadership in the Communist Party," *Leadership and Political Institutions in India,* R. L. Park and Irene Tinker, eds., Princeton University Press, 1959, p. 243.

life—the life of most Congress leaders—so the global perspective of that *doyen* of Indian Communism, Rajani Palme Dutt, born in Cambridge, England, the son of a Swedish mother and a Bengali father, is very different from the regional perspectives of the great majority of Communist leaders.

Thus, while regional Communist leaders such as the Marathi writer on nationality, Dr. G. Adhikari, were preparing the ground for Indian Communism's multi-national view of India, Dutt in *India Today* (1940) stressed that India was a single nationality and that the Muslim league was "reactionary."[11] The Soviet Indologist Diakov scolded Dutt,[12] and by 1949, Dutt had to insert an entire new chapter in which he recanted, declaring that "the unity of the Indian people in their struggle for freedom against imperialism . . . does not mean that the Indian people must therefore be regarded as a single homogeneous whole. On the contrary, there are strong grounds for recognizing the multi-national character of the Indian people."[13]

In contrast to Dutt, who had to be brought around to supporting the regionalist line on nationality, many another prominent Indian Communist has required periodic reminders of his party's subcontinental scope. The Maharashtrian Brahman Communist leader S. A. Dange must have ruminated on the adage 'it is dangerous for a politician to write a book' when a 1951 treatise (*India: From Primitive Communism to Slavery*) brought forth charges that he had permitted his inheritance— both in its Maharashtrian and in its Brahman aspects—to color what was presented as a work of trail-blazing Marxist investigation. A British Communist reviewer charged that Dange had glorified the early Aryan ancestors of many modern Brahman communities, including Dange's, "endowing the Aryans with a unity far removed from time and space and crediting them with all the basic inventions of human progress—the discovery

---

[11] R. P. Dutt, *India Today*, People's Publishing House, Bombay, 1940, p. 412.
[12] A. M. Diakov, "K Voprosu O Natsional'nom Sostave Naseleniia Indii," *Uchenye Zapiski Tikhookeanskogo Instituta*, Tom 1, p. 231, cited in Gene D. Overstreet, "Soviet View of India, 1945-48" (M.A. dissertation, Russian Studies Institute, Columbia University, February 1953).
[13] Dutt, *op.cit.*, 1947 edition, p. 381.

of fire, agriculture, and metallurgy."[14] In effect, charged the Marathi Marxist writer D. K. Bedekar, also a Brahman, Dange "creates a concept, namely the Aryans, and then seeks to examine it in the light of Marxism. He breaks down all barriers and, one might say, freely migrates with his Aryans!"[15] Dange takes the Aryan side against the south Indian claim that an advanced Dravidian civilization was in existence when the Aryans arrived on the Indian scene. The explanation for this "utter disregard of Marxist objectivity" is, as a subheading in bold type proclaims, that "Dange follows not Engels, but Kunte!" Bedekar shows through elaborate citations that Dange has indeed borrowed wholesale from the analysis of two Maharashtrian loyalists of the turn of the century, the historians M. M. Kunte and V. K. Rajwade. One of their concepts, that of the origin of the *Sudras* as slaves rather than as the victims of caste oppression, was to Bedekar a patent white-washing of Aryan Brahman tyranny. For a Communist to offer as an apologia for the pristine evil of caste the notion of an ideal Aryan society in which slavery was something different from caste inferiority, "is to give up scientific categories and substitute mere agitational or sentimental parallelisms."[16] The Soviet Indologist Diakov echoed this objection in a later review.[17] Dange, in addition to purveying this Brahman interpretation of early Aryan society, speaks of "the peculiar genius of the Marathas" in the course of his book, tilting at one point with historians who have in his opinion done violence to Shivaji and thereby to all Maharashtrians:

Avzal Khan was killed—it is a fact; but relate this fact in a proper setting and do not argue like the English that Shivaji was a treacherous man, that all Marathas are so and their ethics are low.

Defending the so-called saint poetry in Marathi traditional literature against "critics of the left," Dange insisted on another

[14] *Modern Quarterly*, London, Summer 1950, p. 278.
[15] "Marxism and Ancient India," *India Today*, July 1951, p. 27. Since 1951 Bedekar has drifted away from his Marxist moorings, so that today, the Indian Congress for Cultural Freedom states, it would be "perhaps unjust even to call him a neo-Marxist."
[16] *Ibid.*, pp. 28-33.
[17] Cited in *India Today*, August 1951, p. 33.

occasion that Communist attempts to put the words of anti-caste protest into the mouths of the Marathi saints is the result of a failure to

understand the law of development of the village community. Saint poetry as a whole does not demand abolition of caste. It could not. On the contrary, it demanded normal proper relations of castes and varnas. Why? Because the disturbance of these relations meant social and economic crisis. . . . Hence they wanted the proper relation of *Dharma* to be restored and thereby the crisis eliminated.[18]

The Bengali Communist leader Hiren Mukerjee, recounting the 1905 partition of Bengal, describes his region matter-of-factly as "the most advanced province in India." When Lord Curzon issued the partition edict, "driving to desperation a sensitive people . . . Bengal did not groan in agony, she roared."[19]

The Uttar Pradesh Muslim Communist writer Sardar Ali Jafri writes that the Sepoy Mutiny of 1857, which the Nehru government commemorates as a landmark of India's struggle against the British, was "particularly the national struggle of the Hindustani people." He cites Karl Marx's statement that the Sepoy Army had 40,000 Avadhi soldiers, "linked to one another through caste and national unity." Then, in a final burst of regional pride, Jafri declares that

the Hindustani people, constituting one of the biggest nations of the world numerically after the Chinese, will rise to their feet. It is they who have given such eminent writers as Tulsidas, Mir Ghalib, and Prem Chand to India, who have constructed the Taj, and led such struggles as the freedom struggle of 1857. Once they begin to stir, the face of India will change quickly.[20]

E. M. S. Nambudripad expounds at length on the distinctive excellence of Malayalis in *The National Question in Kerala*, and in the earlier Malayalam version of this work, published in 1948, *Kerala—Homeland of the Malayalees*, he displayed a Nambudri Brahman bias as well. It was necessary to rewrite

[18] "Notes on Medieval Maratha Literature," *Indian Literature*, No. 2, November 1952, p. 32.

[19] *India Struggles for Freedom*, Kutub, Bombay, 1946, p. 79.

[20] "Unification of Hindi and Urdu," *Indian Literature*, No. 3, 1953, pp. 18, 27, 29-30.

the work and to withdraw all copies from circulation because, as Nambudripad later wrote in masterful understatement,

Being the first effort to apply the general principles of historical materialism to the national democratic movement of Kerala, that book was bound to suffer from various discrepancies. Various friends offered criticisms and suggestions to me, some of which took the form of polemical articles in the press. These criticisms and suggestions helped me to see the inadequacies and fallacies of the various generalizations made by me in the previous book. I therefore decided to completely revise it.[21]

Whatever their regional ties, Communist leaders in all parts of India are subject alike to the tugs of Hindu caste loyalty. After allowing for the possible margin of error in any opinion sampling procedure, it is interesting, nonetheless, that Robert T. Bower found greater caste bias among student Communists polled in Indian universities than among Socialists and partisans of Congress and the Jan Sangh. One percent of those declaring themselves as Communists said they would accept *Bhangis,* or untouchable sweepers, as marriage partners, compared to two and three percent for students of other political faiths; five percent said they would accept a *Bhangi* for an intimate friend, compared to eight percent for Socialist students and nine percent for Jan Sangh adherents, and six percent said they would accept *Bhangi* fellow workers, compared to a response of ten percent by Socialist students.[22] Former Indian Communist secretary P. C. Joshi confessed in the course of a 1950 attack on his factional opponents that the doctrinal flip-flops expected of loyal Communists, back and forth in

blind and servile idol worship, come very naturally and easily to the Indian intellectual with our traditional outlook determined by the caste-ridden and Brahman-dominated feudal society.[23]

The Andhra Reddi leader Sundarayya wrote in a moment of gloom during the caste wars of the Andhra Congress Social-

---

[21] *The National Question in Kerala,* People's Publishing House, Bombay, 1952, p. 1.

[22] *Political Attitudes of Indian Students,* Bureau of Social Science Research, American University, Washington, December 1955, pp. 66-68.

[23] *For A Mass Policy,* Part I, *Letter to Foreign Comrades,* Allahabad, 1950, p. 15.

ist Party that his despondence "arises, perhaps, from myself coming from a petty bourgeois class and not yet completely overcoming the caste and class prejudices."[24] Twenty years later, Sundarayya was allied with his caste fellow Ravi Narayan Reddi, the Telengana Communist leader, in intra-regional party jockeying to curb the power of the Kamma leaders who dominate Communist machinery in the Telugu-speaking territory.[25] In Telengana Communist ranks, the rivalry for leadership follows strictly the lines of Telengana's Brahman versus non-Brahman rivalry, with Reddy's followers ranged against those of Brahman leader D. V. Rao. In 1953, with control of the Congress Government in multilingual Hyderabad State in the hands of a Brahman, Burgula Ramakrishna Rao, the caste conflict in the Communist Party came very near to enabling a rival Reddy Congress faction to get enough state legislature votes to overthrow the Burgula Ministry. An employee in the Hyderabad State Government, who was in a position to observe this episode, wrote the author at the time:

Brahman and non-Brahman feelings are rampant among the ranks of the Communist Party members and there are differences of opinion between Narayana Reddy and Devulapalli Venkateswara Rao. These feelings are even rampant in Congress ranks and the Reddy group in the Congress (the group of the Minister Ranga Reddy) is trying its level best to take reins from Burgula, who is a Brahman. In order to attain his cherished ambition, Ranga Reddy is having secret discussions with Narayana Reddy, and at any time the Burgula cabinet may be dissolved.[26]

Multilingual Revolutionists

Even if individual Communists were immune to caste and regional loyalties, however, the cohesion of the all-India Communist machine would be sorely tested by the mere mechanical obstacles to the conduct of national political activity in India. From the very beginning the Indian party has faced something unique in Communist organizing annals, which did

24 P. Sundarayya, letter to Jayaprakash Narayan, dated January 29, 1938, Camp Lankla Koderu, West Godavari District.
25 The *Hindustan Times* referred to the "Ravi Narayan Reddy-Sundarayya group" on December 25, 1953, p. 2.
26 Letter to the author, April 16, 1953, p. 1.

not, of course, prevent foreign advisers from dispensing advice based on dissimilar experience elsewhere.

In 1933, answering questions submitted by the Communist parties of two multilingual Asian states, India and Indo-China, the *Pan-Pacific Worker* succeeded in thoroughly muddying the waters:

QUESTION 16. How should the central committee work when it is in part composed of workers who do not know English, of comrades who speak Hindi or other native languages? Under such conditions will not the intellectuals always be the leaders? How should we help the workers in this matter?

ANSWER. Why should the central committee be obliged to use the English language? If the majority speaks Hindi, then this language should be used and translations should be made from this language into the other languages, including English. Language difficulties should not hinder common work and should not serve as a reason for the intellectuals to be the sole leaders. In the past few years there were big strikes in India. Surely, the leaders in these strikes were workers. . . . And finally, is it so difficult to learn English? It is necessary to teach English to really revolutionary workers.
What we require is really good workers who know their tasks and are willing to work. . . . There is nothing terrible if they do not know the English language. Why should it be a rule to speak English on the central committee, why not speak Hindi or some other language?[27]

Obviously, the Indian party could expect no guidance from outsiders who knew neither the strength of the regional languages in their own right nor the weakness of Hindi in relation to the regional languages. Twenty years later, the party was still confessing its inability to overcome linguistic obstacles to all-India organizing. If a region did not throw up enough of its own leadership, as happened to be the case in Karnataka, the center could be of little help to local party stalwarts. For it was not a mere matter of dispatching manpower, any manpower, irrespective of linguistic considerations:

The Karnatak peasantry in the whole area are coming to us, requesting us to go over to their villages. Our organizers do not know

[27] Orgwald, "Tactical and Organizational Questions of the Communist Parties of India and Indo-China," *The Pan-Pacific Worker*, 1933.

the language. They are feeling it difficult to fulfill the wishes of the Karnatak masses and send repeated demands on the party center to send them Karnatak-speaking organizers![28]

The fact that English provides the only means of inter-regional communication, party secretary Ajoy Ghosh wrote in 1957, has

hampered the growth of the democratic movement. Today the work of most all-India organizations, including the organizations of the working class and the peasantry, has to be conducted in English. Inevitably, only well-educated members of the middle and upper-middle classes can participate in the deliberations of these organizations at the all-India level. They alone, in practice, can function as members of the all-India executives of these organizations. Even delegates not knowing English find it hard to participate effectively in the deliberations of all-India conferences. Everyone who has any experience of the mass movement knows what difficulties this creates.[29]

At the 1954 session of the Communist-dominated All-India Trade Union Congress it was necessary to use eight languages in the proceedings.[30] The mere operation of the party Politburo as a clearinghouse and exchange-point of provincial experience has suffered seriously because, said a review report, even those state branches which submit reports "have sent them in their own languages, which for obvious reasons are thus remaining in the files."[31] The Politburo abandoned as "unrealistic" its plan for an all-India Cultural Commission to carry on centralized cultural infiltration when it was found that "burning problems of culture in one nationality (Hindustani-speaking nationality) are posed and discussed in detail while the comrades coming from other nationalities are unable even to follow the discussions, much less participate in them."[32]

[28] *On Telengana,* Information Document No. 7 (2), To all Party Units, October 7, 1950, by "An Andhra Provincial Member," p. 20.

[29] *New Age,* December 1957, p. 9.

[30] *Reports and Resolutions,* 24th Session of the All-India Trade Union Congress, May 27-29, 1954, p. 6.

[31] Cited in Windmiller, "Indian Communism and the New Soviet Line," p. 361. See also *Communist Conspiracy at Madura,* Democratic Research Service, Bombay, 1955, pp. 133-138.

[32] *Unity,* December 1952, p. 48. In *Indian Literature* (No. 2, 1953, p. 66), Ram Bilas Sharma disputed the "notion that the Progressive Writers Associa-

Because the Politburo could not get regular reports from branches or otherwise maintain effective contact with local party activity, it has become impossible, confessed the review report, "for the center to do anything more than function as a technical center."[33] The Politburo itself cannot even be sure of a quorum at meetings, said the CPI's 1956 Organizational Report, and "there were occasions when, for several days together, there was no PB member at all at the Centre." The party's provincial press in the Indian languages has "been run practically entirely on the initiative and with the resources of the provincial committee," complained a circular to party journalists, "without any appreciable political guidance from the party center."[34] Although the Indian party rules provide for greater centralization than even those of the Russian Party, in actual practice, observes Gene D. Overstreet, the CPI displays "a higher degree of indiscipline . . . than any other Communist Party of which we have detailed knowledge."[35] If Indian Communism can lay claim to "glorious achievements," in short, these must be credited to local leadership rather than to a coordinated national political program. Telengana, the Punnapra-Vayalar terrorism in Travancore, the Tebhaga peasant risings in Bengal—all these, concedes E. M. S. Nambudripad, "were solely due to the initiative and organizing capacity of the leadership locally."[36] Indian Communism, summarized a post-election intraparty analysis, is characterized by "great unevenness."[37]

---

tion is the business of different languages and that we can dispense with an all-India executive."

[33] *Communist Conspiracy at Madura*, p. 133.

[34] Circular to all P C's and Editorial Boards of Party dailies and weeklies, Communist Party of India, 38 Mount Road, Madras, August 6, 1952, p. 1. The circular was issued to call a meeting of party editors in Madras, September 6-8, 1952.

[35] Overstreet, *"Leadership in the Communist Party,"* pp. 5, 9.

[36] *On the Agrarian Question in India*, People's Publishing House, Bombay, p. 58.

[37] *Party Letter*, No. 2, January 30, 1953, Barat Vijaya Printing Press, New Delhi, p. 4.

The Hindi Controversy

What this outside observer at the Third Party Congress in 1953 sensed but could not confirm, barred as he was from convention sessions, party leaders themselves spelled out afterward in their own words. Indian Communism's most sensitive problems are organizational rather than doctrinal, and of the organizational matters discussed at Madura, stated Ghosh in his post-Congress report, "the most important point made . . . was the urgency about building a strong and effective party center."[38] The indiscipline of Indian Communism's regional components is a persistent theme in party documents. Madura brought to a climax a decade of inter-regional conflict within the party, which was much the same in microcosm as the pulling and hauling within the general Indian body politic. The Hindi question—whether the party should disengage itself from its policy of unequivocal opposition to Hindi, and if so, how far to move toward a pro-Hindi position—was the vexing operative issue for the Communist Party as it has been and remains for the Union.

British Communist leader Harry Pollitt, who attended the Madura Congress, wrote in a report for his own party's consumption that in the discussion of amendments to the party program, delegates from the non-Hindi regions "wanted to delete a reference to 'a single popular assembly' and substitute 'a house of the people and a house of nationalities,' "[39] proposals which Ghosh obviously had in mind when he explained in his report that the "wrong" idea of oppressing and oppressed nations in India

finds expression sometimes in proposals for a double chamber, for a chamber of nationalities in the future Indian State. It is forgotten that a single chamber is always preferable. . . . A mechanical parallel should not be drawn with the position obtaining in the Soviet Union. . . .

Among major topics discussed at Madura, Pollitt also observed, were "linguistic problems, with a highly critical note running

[38] Ajoy K. Ghosh, "On the Work of the Third Party Congress," *New Age*, January 24, 1954, p. 19.
[39] *Indian Diary*, Communist Party of Great Britain, 1954, London, p. 23.

through the discussions." The major "linguistic problem" was an amendment of the party program plank on Hindi—"use of Hindi as all-India state language will not be obligatory"—adding the words, "but will be encouraged for state intercourse and trade." This compromise on Hindi policy came about, according to Pollitt, only after delegates from Uttar Pradesh forced the Congress steering committee to introduce the revised language as its sole amendment to the party program. When the pro-Hindi amendment reached the convention floor, said an Indian Government intelligence report,

serious controversy was exhibited. Delegates from Tamilnad opposed this imposition of an alien language against the desire of the people, terming this undemocratic and also detrimental to the regional language.[40]

The crisis in the party over Hindi that came to the fore at Madura is not a simple matter of north versus south, but a more complicated dilemma which will be resolved, if it is resolved, by the Communists in Hindi territory. On the one hand, Communists in Uttar Pradesh do not wish to alienate their strong Muslim following, especially among the pro-Urdu literati. At the same time they wish to attune the party to nationalist sentiment in north India—above all, to the Hindi literati—which will take some doing after the party's decade of attack on "Hindi imperialism." For the party had not escaped from its separatist adventures without paying a high price. With its centers of power outside the Hindi heartland of India, Indian Communism had been driven by its own internal compulsions to weaken, rather than strengthen, its position in the one part of India where the party most needs new roots. The historical accident of the party's early growth in the non-Hindi regions even today sets in motion its own vicious circle.

The intraparty debate that had simmered for a decade prior to Madura was complicated by the prevailing inability of Communist theoreticians to decide whether the Hindi region was

[40] This report, which was made available to the author at Madura, was written by a Tamil operative whose sources included the Communist daughter of a prominent Tamil Brahman Congress leader.

to be described as an already "formed" nation or, for that matter, even as one likely to grow to unified nationhood in coming decades. Diakov, in his analysis of the national composition of India in 1948, dismissed the "Hindustani nation" as indeterminate, its future unfathomable, and he did not rule out the possibility that two separate nations would rise on the basis of dialect differences between east and west Uttar Pradesh.[41] But even if a single unified Hindustani nation was in the making, would its linguistic foundation be Urdu, a Sanskritized Hindi, or some standardized union of both with spoken dialect forms?

In 1945, a bitter party debate on this issue began when S. Sajjad Zaheer, later a leading Communist in Pakistan, called on the party to support a hybrid Hindustani language with a liberal inclusion of Urdu.[42] By 1949, the Hindi Communist writer Ram Bilas Sharma was speaking in similar terms, advocating the adoption of a modified Devanagari script to fuse Hindi and Urdu, and denouncing the proposal of the widely-read Hindi Communist scholar Rahul Sankrityayana for separate political units or republics along the historic dialect lines of Avadhi, Brajbhasha, and Bundeli, a proposal which gave scant respect to Urdu. Taking issue with Rahul's proposal and others like it, Sharma declared that a standard language had developed across all these dialect areas during Muslim overlordship in India. As an indication of the havoc wreaked by the party's anti-Hindi line during this period, Sharma publicly rebuked a party supporter for suggesting that Hindi could become an all-India language in a natural way, objecting to the very phrase "all-India language" as embodying "a loop-hole for chauvinist trends to creep in."[43]

There were many Communists in Uttar Pradesh, however,

[41] A. M. Diakov, *Indiia Vo Vremia I Posle Vtoroi Mirovoi Voiny, 1939-49* (India During and After the Second World War), Moscow, 1952, p. 89; Diakov, *Natsional 'nyi Vopros I Angliiskii Imperialism V. Indiia* (The National Question and British Imperialism in India), 1948, pp. 114, 117, 121.

[42] *Marxist Miscellany*, People's Publishing House, Bombay, October 1945, Vol. 4, pp. 91-120, at p. 120.

[43] "On the Language Question in India," *The Communist*, September-October 1949, p. 76.

who had a vested interest in preserving their credentials among the Hindi intelligentsia, and in 1952 their dissent grew vocal enough to place the defenders of the then existing line on the defensive. The party's Central Cultural Commission, which was soon to be abandoned as an "unrealistic" experiment in all-India cultural activity, appointed a subcommittee to air all viewpoints on "the formation of the Hindustani nation and the problem of its national language."[44] The draft subcommittee statement advanced by the Muslim Communist writer Sardar Ali Jafri was an unabashed defense of Urdu.[45] Jafri maintained that the "existence of a Hindustani people . . . and the consciousness of their national unity" are indisputable facts of political life. The British came on the scene in the 18th century to disrupt "a nation in the making . . . the process of the formation of the national market, of the consolidation of the national language." Since the Congress today undermines this historic unity by suppressing one of the literary forms of the Hindustani language, Urdu, "the task of the unification of the Hindustani nation and its national language has fallen on the working class and its vanguard, the Communist Party."

Bitterly attacking attempts to suppress Urdu, Jafri charged that "even some of the progressive circles have been infected. In words they oppose suppression but in practice they do it. The result is that in northern India Urdu has been practically thrown out of elementary and secondary schools and government offices." He then proceeded to strike out at Rahul, whose scholarly eminence as a Sanskritist and whose adventurous missions to the Soviet Union and Tibet, recounted in best-selling books, had elevated him to a position not easily assailed. Rahul's affiliation with the Communist Party had been in doubt ever since the party's support for the Pakistan demand, and to win him back was a cherished objective of many in the party. Jafri caused a sensation, therefore, when he charged Rahul with Hindu "communalist frenzy" and with behaving

[44] *Indian Literature*, No. 1, 1952, p. 95.
[45] "On the Formation of the Hindustani Nation and the Problem of its National Language," *Indian Literature*, No. 1, 1953, pp. 1-46.

as a "ready servant" of the Hindu extremist Congress leader P. D. Tandon.[46]

If Jafri's draft statement was intended to pacify the dissenters, it was a complete failure, for he only provoked a more furious protest than ever. One writer challenged his central thesis, arguing that "a Hindustani national consciousness has yet to emerge, and if we run ahead of popular consciousness, we are likely to do more harm than good."[47] A Bengali Communist predicted the formation of many nations within the Hindi region.[48] But it was Jafri's attack on Rahul which evoked the most emphatic reaction. Rahul himself drily observed that Urdu protagonists "should get over their fascination for the Arabic script and accept Nagari,"[49] and Amrit Rai depicted Rahul as the very symbol of the Hindi intelligentsia which had been alienated by Communist hostility to Hindi:

Our attitude on the language question has already isolated us a great deal from the mass of democratic Hindi writers, and if we allow this kind of attitude to persist any longer, then we are only digging the grave of the Hindi Progressive Writers Association as the forum of the democratic literary movement in Hindi. The attitude represented by Rahulji is in essence the outlook of the average democratic Hindi writer with all the points of strength and weakness and should be accepted by us as such. . . .[50]

That the party was isolated from Hindi writers could not be disputed, for only shortly before the publication of this rebuttal to Jafri, the prominent Hindi poet Sumitranandan Pant had called on Hindi writers to boycott the 1953 Progressive Writers Conference barring a specific avowal that the group "has nothing to do with the language policy of the Communist Party, and it accepts Hindi as the state language."[51] A meeting

[46] Rahul's anti-Pakistan statements in *Aj Ki Rajniti*, published in 1950, were singled out for special condemnation by Jafri, *op.cit.*, p. 25.

[47] Satish Chandra in "Discussion on the Central Cultural Commission's Note on the Formation of the Hindustani Nation," *Indian Literature*, No. 3, 1953, p. 14.

[48] *Ibid.*, p. 16.

[49] Rahul Sankrityayana, *op.cit.*, p. 19.

[50] Amrit Rai, *op.cit.*, p. 22.

[51] *Free Press Journal*, Bombay, June 10, 1953, p. 10. Discussions of Pant's place in Hindi poetry appeared in the *Times of India*, April 7, 1957, p. 8, and

of "progressive Hindi publishers" in early 1953, reported a Communist organ, had "noted the sad fact that there was not a single progressive monthly paper in Hindi now existing."[52] Moreover, continued Rai, the party's weakness in Hindi literary circles was only one relatively isolated example of still broader consequences of the party's Hindi policy. Rai complained that Jafri's preoccupation with the status of Urdu led him to "side-track the one main issue which is agitating the democratic mind today: the issue of Hindi as the state or union language. The people want to know from us in clear-cut terms if we can see the possibility of a language for inter-state purposes, and if we think that Hindi can be that language." The Hindi extremists should admittedly be opposed, said Rai, "but while we do that, we would be wise not to throw away the baby with the bath water." As a result of having advocated Pakistan, he warned,

the popular mind tends to regard us as poor friends indeed, if not enemies, of Indian unity! We cannot get away from the consequences of supporting separatist tendencies in the past. . . . It is in this context that the walkout of the Communist MPS on the question of the use of Hindi has to be seen. It galled every democrat that, whereas we could stomach English many a time, we could not suffer Hindi even once!

In conclusion, Rai issued an appeal to the national leadership which, dated as it was in early 1953, makes interesting reading in the context of the amendment to the party program at Madura:

Let not the language controversy further divide us and deplete our ranks, which, I am afraid, is bound to happen so long as we do not adopt a patriotic democratic line on the question. We should like to know why this is not being done even at this juncture when the CPI is being misunderstood and maligned a great deal on just this issue and when a forthright declaration on the issue would greatly help the party in its growth.

The Statesman, April 10, 1957, p. 3, on the occasion of one of his visits to New Delhi.

[52] *Indian Literature*, No. 2, 1953, back cover.

The Madura amendment did not resound with Hindi chauvinism, but it represented enough of a definite break with the past to appease the dissenters and to mitigate, at least temporarily, one of the most serious strains then weakening party unity. By February 1955, with the change in Hindi policy a settled fact, Rahul quietly returned to the fold to be welcomed with open arms by the party press.[53]

Proletarian "Internationalism"

Clearly the party made its historic change of front on nationality at Madura not merely to get in step with the new Soviet line. The party's own unity had been perilously tested both by the Hindi controversy and, as Ghosh quite frankly admitted, by a wide assortment of separatist excesses accompanying the old line. In conducting campaigns for linguistic provinces, Ghosh wrote after the Congress, "we have even allowed bourgeois-nationalist deviations to penetrate our ranks. The party Congress declared that in India today the unity of the toiling masses of all nationalities is the most important thing." When disputes arise between two provincial party units over policy in linguistic controversies, "no party unit can be allowed to come out on its own in demanding some areas from a neighboring province."[54]

In the year immediately preceding this injunction Ghosh had to take time out for a personal rescue mission to south India when the Andhra and Orissa party units became hopelessly embroiled in inter-regional border wrangling. In the heat of the Communist campaign for Andhra State, the Communist weekly *Crossroads* published a map, supplied by Andhra comrades, delimiting the greater Andhra that was the ultimate goal of Andhra Communism.[55] This map showed shaded "Andhra areas in other states," including portions of Orissa,

---

[53] *New Age*, February 13, 1955, p. 1. Rahul's early career is discussed in an appendix to *The Communist Party of India*, Research and Analysis Branch, Office of Strategic Services, No. 2681, August 1945.

[54] Ajoy K. Ghosh, "On the Work of the Third Party Congress," p. 21. *New Age*, June 1956, p. 32, recalls that the Madura Congress "nailed down bourgeois nationalism in the party."

[55] *Crossroads*, June 29, 1952, p. 1.

and led to such an uproar that Ghosh rushed to the Orissa capital of Cuttack to assure the Oriyas that central Communist policy took no sides and that "the Andhra Committee cannot on its own claim that certain territories in Orissa should be incorporated in Andhra."[56]

The old accent on separatism, Ghosh declared at the 1953 Party Congress, especially the notion of oppressing and oppressed nationalities, has very serious implications, which

would mean disruption of the common movement itself, especially of the working class movement. For, in many of the most important industrial centers—Calcutta, Jamshedpur, and Bombay—the working class is to a great extent multi-national in composition. It should be obvious therefore that the whole understanding is not merely wrong but has disastrous implications which strike at the root of the unity of the toiling masses and of the working class itself.[57]

If any contributing domestic factors were needed to justify the 1953 reversal on nationality (see Chapter V), once the dictates of Soviet policy had become clear, it was eminently reasonable for the party leadership to trot out this dilemma of the multilingual labor centers. For it is indeed true that union organization, by the Communists or anyone else, runs into perplexing complications when the labor force is divided, often within the same plant, along rigid linguistic and caste lines. The Communist reflex is to opt in a given plant for the numerically dominant group, or where there are evenly matched groups, for one strategically situated in the local social or economic setting. But this is only the lesser of evils among available tactical alternatives. While making a choice between groups can guarantee a definite measure of allegiance, rather than risk ending up with no support at all, this alternative also incurs

[56] *The Hindu*, October 14, 1952, p. 4. *New Age*, December 24, 1954, p. 2, blamed "reactionary government policies" for Andhra-Oriya border riots.

[57] Ajoy K. Ghosh, "The Movement for Linguistic States and the Struggle Against Bourgeois Nationalism," *New Age*, May 1954, p. 17. See also *New Age*, January 17, 1954, p. 15, and *New Age*, February 1954, p. 39. Ram Bilas Sharma, in *The Question of an Obligatory State Language in India* (People's Publishing House, New Delhi, 1954, p. 21), refers to the "problem" faced by the Indian working class in "developing political and cultural intercourse among the different nationalities."

heavy obligations to the chosen group. Thus S. A. Dange, secretary of the All-India Trade Union Congress, advised the Communist trade union functionary in 1952 to learn the "caste and national composition of the workers in his union and trade" so that the party could defeat divide-and-conquer tactics by employers. "The caste, nation and tribe in the worker," said Dange, "must be harnessed in the service of building the class outlook."[58] "The nationalism of the worker," he warned on another occasion,

must not be allowed to destroy his internationalism as a class. It is the task of our trade unions to see that while supporting the demand for linguistic provinces, the workers of one language and nationality do not trail behind the Bourgeoisie of their language and nationality and break with their working class brothers of another nationality or be unfriendly or hostile to them.[59]

Dange's own home ground of Bombay has long been the scene of intraparty strife arising from the city's cosmopolitan character. South Indian elements inside the Bombay Party have complained that the Bombay Communist leadership is dominated by Dange and a Maharashtrian clique, and in 1955 two of the most prominent Communist leaders in Bombay, A. S. R. Chari and the petroleum workers' G. Sundaram, both Tamil Brahmans, were denied seats in the newly-created Maharashtra Communist Committee that was formed following merger of the Bombay and Maharashtra units.

The Bombay City labor force is divided between Mahars and Marathas from Maharashtra (55 percent), Gujaratis, south Indians of all the major linguistic groups, and north Indians, predominantly Hindustani-speaking.[60] The party's Maharashtrian leadership in Bombay has consistently concentrated on the Marathi-speaking majority,[61] so much so that party leader

58 *On the Trade Union Movement*, Reports to a convention of Communist trade unionists, May 20-22, 1952, CPI Publication, Bombay, 1952, p. 41.

59 This is an extract from a report by Dange, as secretary of the AITUC, to the AITUC working committee, August 17, 1953, circulated among party trade unionists and not intended for publication.

60 R. M. Birjay, *Textile Labor in Bombay City*, cited in *Memorandum* submitted to the States Reorganization Commission, Bombay Citizens Committee, 1954, p. 67.

61 Diakov, 1952, *op.cit.*, p. 214, citing *Peoples Age*, September 5, 1948, frankly

B. T. Ranadive, reviewing the 1957 election results in Bombay City, pointed to the "alarming" polarization of votes between "Maharashtrian and non-Maharashtrian sections," Communist and non-Communist, which could become a permanent feature of Bombay politics. Could the party stand this sort of prosperity? "Unless fought, this will end in dividing the working class movement in Bombay on linguistic lines," concluded Ranadive, "and give a big blow to the common democratic movement." Nor was there much more to be gained from this polarization. As a result of the Samyukta Maharashtra movement, the party had already "reached the limit of Maharashtrian support."[62]

In multilingual Bombay the Hindustani-speaking worker or "Bhayya" has been touched least of all by Marathi-oriented Communist organizers. "Special attention must be paid to this erstwhile neglected section of the Bombay working class," warned the 1953 political report of the Bombay Communist Committee. "The dangerous attitude that the Bhayya will always remain a stranger to our movement must be banished forever from our minds." The Bhayya, added the report, unfortunately lacked the susceptibility to group manipulation of Bombay's other workers:

The understanding of our message comes naturally to nationalities like the Malayalis, the Telugus, the Kannadas who find in it a parallel to their own national aspirations. Not so the North Indian. They have no such movement in the frontiers of their own nation.[63]

As for the Southerners, the report reflected exacting attention to the possibilities in each group. The Malayalis, for example, are described as "office employees and workers in new factories which came into existence during the war. The impress of political developments in Kerala is deeply planted in them. A. K. Gopalan, our party leader, has earned the prestige of a national leader, and his name should be employed." In the

---

attributes C P support of the Maharashtra demand to the Marathi-majority population of Bombay City. See also Diakov, 1948, *op.cit.*, pp. 99, 143.

[62] "Maharashtra Election Review," *New Age*, July 1957, pp. 25-26.

[63] Bombay Committee, Communist Party of India, "Political Report," 1953 (mimeographed).

wake of Andhra State's formation, continued the report, "an extremely favorable situation has now come into existence for building up a powerful militant movement encompassing all Telugus in Bombay." Bombay Tamils, the report declared, are divided into two distinct sections. The middle classes "generally support the Congress, although progressive thought has begun influencing them." Tamil workers, located chiefly in Bombay's Dheravi section, must be weaned away from the Dravidian movement. When organizing workers on nationality lines, concluded the report, it is vital "to integrate any such movement with the wider democratic movement in Bombay right from its commencement." Otherwise, Communist leaders would function in separate enclaves. Malayalam and Telugu party leaders in the city, for example, were charged with "deviations . . . which must be combatted."

While in Calcutta, too, the working force is multilingual, there the Communists have based their organization not in a majority, such as Bombay's Marathi-speaking 55 percent, but in the indigenous Bengali work force—37 percent. This Bengali orientation leaves the larger 'floating' non-Bengali workers from U. P. and Bihar—56 percent of jute labor alone—to the pro-Congress INTUC unions, with the result that the Bengal Communists are forever blaming their shortcomings on this handicap. After a strike in 1952, *Crossroads* bewailed the fact that "the great bulk of the Hindustani workers, particularly in the jute belt, kept out of it and did not join the strike."[64] In spite of their best efforts at "patient, fraternal persuasion," said Bengal Communist leaders after the anti-merger movement of 1956, protesting a united state of Bihar-Bengal, "large sections of Hindustani-speaking people, in Calcutta and in industrial suburbs, were somewhat confused and were not very enthusiastic about the movement."[65] The polarization in Calcutta is precisely the reverse of Bombay, with the Communists in this instance on the short end of the bargain. "This is the Achilles heel of the Left," said a 1957 election review, blaming the 80

[64] *Crossroads*, May 16, 1952, p. 2. See also *India Today*, May 9, 1952.
[65] Bhupesh Gupta, "Anti-Merger Movement," *New Age*, July 1956, p. 12.

percent Congress majority in Calcutta's non-Bengali labor ranks on Congress propaganda that the Communists would evict all out-of-state workers from their jobs.[66]

Caste and Class

As if it were not enough to confront the linguistic variety of the urban melting pots, the Indian Communists face obstacles to organization quite as complex in the caste alignments which characterize equally both city and countryside. The peculiarly integral position of caste in Hindu society makes the organization of a centralized national Communist Party a task unique in international Communist experience. If Hindu caste units corresponded neatly to economic gradations, one caste per gradation, it might be argued that the Indian social structure provided exceptional opportunities for classic Marxist exploitation. But caste and class do not in fact necessarily coincide. More often than not there will be more than one subcaste unit within each economic gradation in a given region, which cannot always prove so fortuitous as it has for the Kammas in Andhra or the Ezhavas in Kerala.

"Probably Marx, even Lenin or Mao, would have wilted in the Indian climate," editorialized the Lucknow *National Herald* on the occasion of Nambudripad's statement in 1953 that the CPI would suit its Marxism to Indian conditions. "The inchoateness of the class situation, the indeterminate, undefined intermediate forces which are largely British-made, the peculiarly hard social structure defy analysis."[67]

Even more than in the multilingual cities, it is in rural organizing, above all, that caste divisions make it completely impossible for Communist organization to follow traditional Marxist class preconceptions. In the northwest U. P. district of Bijnor, for example, a case study by the author[68] found the

[66] *New Age*, April 1957, pp. 45, 51.

[67] "Marx in India," *National Herald*, January 5, 1954, p. 4. See also the review of M. R. Masani's *Communist Party of India*, in the *Times of India*, August 10, 1954, p. 8. The reviewer scolds the Indian Communists for their failure to "study caste and village factions as they affect class conflict, or to consider in what way the class relations of a U. P. village differ from those of the Godavari delta."

[68] The author visited Bijnor District in early 1953 and subsequently obtained

rural population divided into three major caste alignments: Jats, eighteen percent of the district; Chauhans, sixteen percent, both peasant proprietors, as well as various grades of outcaste or semi-outcaste communities, thirty percent. Communist organizing tactics must take into account the cleavage between the rival Jats and Chauhans, who would for the most part be classified together as middle peasants in conventional Communist terms but who are in fact entities socially and politically distinct. As for the outcaste and semi-outcaste communities, these, too, are divided between untouchables such as Chamars (leather workers) with their own local caste body, the Raidas Sabha (named after the Chamar saint Raidas) and the Shoshit Sangh ("League of the Exploited"), a coalition of low-caste groups such as gardeners and potters who rank higher than the untouchables but are not accepted fully as caste Hindus. As it happens, the Communist-led Kisan Sabha in the district is based on the Jats. The Sabha's chairman is a veteran Jat political leader who moved in 1948 from the Congress to the Socialists and decided finally that the Communists could provide better political sanctuary. He can claim an organized Jat following for the party. But the Chauhans must then be forfeited to the Congress, which has traditionally been Chauhan property in district affairs and now seems destined to stay that way under the new polarization. The Chauhans will not follow behind a dominant Jat faction, and the untouchables, too, will keep their votes intact for sale to the highest bidder rather than enter into an inevitably subordinate relationship to any caste Hindu peasant faction. Here, in the militant solidarity of the untouchables, the Communists face an almost insoluble problem.

Confronted with conflict between peasant proprietors and the untouchable "rural proletariat" the party is constantly compelled to make a choice between caste and outcaste, and invariably expediency forces Communist preference for the landed peasant. The president of the All-India Kisan Sabha, N. Prasada

detailed case study data in correspondence, translated from the Hindi, dated Bijnor, June 28 and July 26, 1953.

Rao, is an Andhra Kamma who knows well the value of a base in a strategic peasant-proprietor caste. Rao urges Kisan Sabha organizers to proceed with all haste, since "so many caste organizations have been formed or are being formed." He frankly advocates that the Communists, too, follow caste lines, forming separate agricultural labor unions alongside parallel poor peasant and rich peasant organizations. Rao propounds the Andhra line that regardless of the size of his holdings, any peasant who actually cultivates his land, "if he himself is a cultivator, should be neutralized and should not be disturbed."[69]

It would be useless to combine all the peasantry in the Kisan Sabha, a Central Committee commentary on agrarian problems explained, because

the struggles that we have been conducting all these years, mainly based as they were on the middle peasant, have not yet succeeded in battering down the caste walls even in our areas. The fact that both the middle peasant and the poor peasant has sometimes to use the services of the rural workers of other trades will make them antagonistic to rural worker wage demands made by a separate movement. . . . The danger should not be under-estimated. The touchable peasant in many places quite casually says that the untouchable is getting cheeky.[70]

Since most agricultural laborers belong to "socially backward" castes, said a Central Committee resolution on peasant activity in 1954, it would be notably "difficult to draw them and activize them in Kisan Sabhas directly along with the other caste peasants, or even if we succeed in drawing them in, it may lead to the other peasants not joining the Kisan Sabha in large numbers."[71]

As a result of the Communist decision to keep caste and outcaste apart, reported a Socialist writer who observed the national Kisan Sabha session in 1954, the Sabha now consists "mostly of middle and well-to-do peasant proprietors. Landless laborers, who are mostly untouchables, were conspicuous by

[69] "Agricultural Laborers Association," *News Bulletin of the All-India Kisan Sabha*, October-November 1952, pp. 13, 21.

[70] *The Communist*, January 1949, p. 48.

[71] *Our Tasks Among the Peasant Masses*, Resolution of the Central Committee, Communist Party of India, April 1954, New Delhi, p. 16.

their absence, and the Stalinist organizers of the show were not sorry for it."[72] The Communists, in short, recognize that the landed peasant is a source of great strength to the Congress, as well as to some of their own regional organizations, and they hope to meet the Congress on its own ground on a national scale. In pursuing this hope, however, they are neither building a "revolutionary" instrument of India's most numerous proletariat, the landless untouchables, nor are they "battering down" the walls of the Hindu social structure any more now than in the past.

India's social landscape bends all parties to its contours, and the Communists are no exception. The party and its labor and peasant fronts are riven first by India's regional divisions and then by each region's caste structure. Paradoxically, the separatist period from 1946 to 1953 aggravated the stresses and strains inherent in Indian Communism. After 1953 the nominal restraint of the softened Communist line did not conceal tensions between national and local party leaders over the use of separatist tactics in the regional controversies accompanying states reorganization. Maharashtrian outrage over the refusal of the States Reorganization Commission to award Bombay City to Maharashtra, for example, caught the Marathi Communists and their leader, Dange, at the diabolically inconvenient moment of the Soviet leaders' Indian tour. Bulganin and Khrushchev arrived in New Delhi on November 18, the same day demonstrations against the Commission report began in Bombay. As Marshall Windmiller has shown in a searching case study,[73] the central party leadership did nothing to encourage Communist violence in Bombay. But the party Politburo notwithstanding, rank-and-file pressure at the local level forced Dange's entry into the Bombay riots.

[72] *Janata*, October 10, 1954, p. 9. See also E. M. S. Nambudripad, *Peasants Meet at Moga*, CPI Publication, New Delhi, 1954, for a Communist account of the debate.

[73] "The Politics of States Reorganization in India: The Case of Bombay," *Far Eastern Survey*, September 1956, pp. 136-138. Windmiller cites *The Call*, organ of the Revolutionary Socialist Party, one of the constituents in the united leftist action in Bombay, for the MKP role in forcing the strike. See also *Free Labor Herald*, organ of the Bombay Association of Free Trade Unionists, November-December 1955, p. 3, which credits Dange with desiring "to play a lone hand to impress his Soviet bosses."

Significantly, Dange's hand had been forced by the militance of a solitary regional splinter group, the Mazdoor Kisan Party (MKP), a group restricted to Maharashtra which had no national responsibilities and could afford to press regional demands to the limit. Here we see the essential weakness of all Indian parties before the onslaught of parochial pressures. The Maharashtrian demand cried for leadership, and any party that failed to act automatically forfeited leadership to its rivals. In the showdown Dange could not afford to make this sacrifice —even though national party discipline is a more explicit article of faith with the Communists than with any other party in India.

The Congress: Strengths and Strains

Before Independence, the Congress, as the party of the freedom movement, claimed a degree of unity and loyalty impossible for the Communists. But for all the binding strength of nationalism, the Congress, too, has endured profound and persistent regional stresses. The stresses within the Congress were not always visible beneath a surface unity. Yet they were there from the start; they were, from the start, the same stresses which have risen so clearly to the surface since 1947.

In contrast to the Communist Party with its non-Hindi base, the Congress sunk its firmest roots in the northcentral Hindi heartland. Membership figures have consistently revealed a party in which outnumbered non-Hindi regions have had to fight for their place in the sun against dominant Uttar Pradesh, Bihar, and Mahakoshal. In 1929 the province-by-province roster showed 44 percent of the membership centered in these three Congress units, only to jump to 46 percent in 1946.[74] Moreover, no matter what the distribution of membership at any time, the strategic position of the Hindi heartland remains constant:

[74] These percentages are based on figures in the *Congress Handbook*, 1946, A.I.C.C., Allahabad, p. 222, and additional figures for 1946 in *The Hindu*, February 26, 1946, p. 4. For an interesting corollary, see membership figures for the pro-Congress Indian National Trade Union Congress as of October 31, 1954, in *I.N.T.U.C. Annual Report*, Nagpur, 1955, Appendix B, p. 184. See also Rawle Knox, *The Observer*, February 17, 1951, for a discussion of the northern roots of the Congress.

Hindi strength is concentrated heavily in a single state, Uttar Pradesh, and the possibility of U. P. bloc dominance is inherent in a Congress Constitution that provides for representation on Congress governing bodies strictly on the basis of regional population. Each regional or state committee sends one delegate per 100,000 of its population to general Congress conventions, and one-eighth of the number of convention delegates to the All-India Congress Committee—ruling body of the party between conventions.[75] K. M. Panikkar in his Dissent to the Report of the States Reorganization Commission gave voice to a long-smouldering sense of injustice among non-Hindi party units. Attacking "the dominance of Uttar Pradesh in all-India matters" and calling for its dissolution into smaller units, Panikkar noted, in a pointed reference to U. P. power in the Congress, that "modern governments are controlled to a greater or lesser extent by party machines, within which the voting power of a numerically strong group goes a very long way."[76] On the basis of population U. P. send seventy-nine delegates to the A.I.C.C., while Panikkar's Malayalam-speaking region sends sixteen.

The Hinterlands Win

From time to time in the pre-Independence years it was necessary for national Congress discipline to resolve the same inter-regional disputes within the party which were to be resolved once again later in the larger context of the Indian Union. After Andhra won its own separate Congress unit in 1920, for example, both Andhra and Karnataka Congress leaders were claiming jurisdiction over the bilingual border district of Bellary, and from January to May 1921, two district Congress committees maintained offices in Bellary Town. The first national Congress fund-raising drive to fall in this period provided the occasion for a showdown and the All-India Congress Committee had to appoint the Marathi Congress leader N. C.

[75] *Constitution of the Indian National Congress,* as amended at the Bombay meeting of the All-India Congress Committee, June 1956, A.I.C.C., New Delhi, 1956, p. 6. See also *Congress Handbook,* 1946, p. 228, and N. V. Rajkumar, *Development of the Congress Constitution,* A.I.C.C., New Delhi, 1949, esp. p. 106.
[76] *Report of the States Reorganization Commission,* Manager, Government of India Press, Delhi, 1955, p. 245.

Kelkar to arbitrate. The so-called Kelkar award of 1921, maintained the Karnataka Congress years later, "actually gave away to the Andhras the most contested parts which Kannadigas rightly claimed as their own . . . although Mr. Kelkar expressed admirable sentiments to assuage the Kannadigas." Bitterness grew all the greater, and when a committee of Andhra Congressmen met in Bellary in October 1943, "the Kannadigas gave such a hot reception to them that it became next to impossible for the Andhras to carry on their deliberations."[77] Karnataka feared, and time has justified this fear, that concessions to Andhra in the intraparty dispute would lead to still more Andhra gains in the inevitable linguistic reorganization of state boundaries.

In the Independence movement itself there were significant regional variations. The non-violent Gandhian credo was explicitly repudiated in Bengal, as the most notable example, where "Indian nationalism was expressed through the agency of Bengali patriotism,"[78] and in Maharashtra, where Jayakar and Kelkar organized the Responsivist Party as a deliberate regional defection from Gandhi's leadership. "Amongst the provinces that have not reconciled themselves to the cult of Gandhi these ten years," wrote the Congress historian Pattabhi Sitaramayya, "the two outstanding are Maharashtra and Banga. . . . Outstanding men from the provinces either fought the movement inaugurated by Gandhi or stood sullenly aloof from it."[79] "Swarashtra" for Andhra was a battle cry indistinguishable from "Swaraj" for India as a whole, and in the Punjab, as well, a marked regional flavor infused the nationalist struggle right from the disturbances of 1919.[80]

Congress leaders recognized, of course, that regional partici-

[77] *Replies and Memoranda to the Linguistic Provinces Commission*, by the representatives and associations of Madras Karnataka, 1948, All-Karnataka Unification Sangha, Mangalore, pp. 125-127.

[78] Richard L. Park, "The Rise of Militant Nationalism in Bengal: A Regional Study of Indian Nationalism" (Ph.D. dissertation, Harvard University, 1950, p. 3).

[79] *Janmabhumi*, English-language Andhra weekly (now defunct), January 18, 1930, p. 87. For a description of the Maharashtra defection, see Nalini Pandit, *Maharashtrateela Rashtravadacha Vikasa* (Growth of Nationalism in Maharashtra), published by the author, Professor of Political Science, Poddar College of Commerce, Bombay, 1956, esp. "The Mahatma and Maharashtra," pp. 166-170.

[80] Mark Naidis, "Punjab Disturbances of 1919: A Study in Indian Nationalism" (Ph.D. dissertation, Stanford University, 1951, p. 237).

pation in the Independence movement need not necessarily follow a uniform pattern. But this recognition, and indeed the high place of the non-Hindi regions in Congress councils, came about only with the insistent encouragement of the regional parties concerned. The vulnerability of the Congress to internal pressures today can best be appreciated in the light of this clear but frequently misstated record. Today the fact that the Congress organization was established on the basis of linguistic party units is commonly attributed to the deliberate desire of the founders to reach a mass audience and to use the slogan of linguistic provinces as a weapon against the British. There can be no disputing Nehru when he cites the demarcation of Congress provincial machinery on a linguistic basis in 1920 as the turning point which saw the Congress transformed from a middle-class assembly of leaders to a mass movement able to speak to the people in their own language.[81] Nor can we dispute the judgment of the States Reorganization Commission that "the national movement . . . was built up by harnessing the forces of regionalism,"[82] and of the Karnataka Congress Committee that the Congress "would not have acquired the strength it did if it had ignored the factor of language in framing its constitution."[83] It is one thing, however, to judge results and quite another to suggest, as is so often done, that Gandhi worked with a consciously deeper wisdom when he sided with the demand for linguistic demarcation in 1920.

It was only under pressure from the non-Hindi regions that the Congress reluctantly agreed—after five years of indifference and outright opposition—to the 1920 linguistic reorganization at Nagpur. Congress historian Pattabhi, an Andhra, has recounted his own fate at the hands of the north Indian high command during this period. At the 1915 Bombay session of the Congress he made the first attempt to get Congress endorsement for the principle of linguistic reorganization. But when he presented his resolution, "who cared for it or for me? Lin-

---

[81] Jawaharlal Nehru, *Toward Freedom*, John Day, New York, 1941, p. 66.
[82] *Report of the States Reorganization Commission*, p. 38.
[83] *Linguistic Provinces and the Karnataka Problem*, Karnataka Pradesh Congress Committee, Hubli, 1948, p. 7.

guistic provinces was only a cry in the wilderness then." The Congress leaders of the day, who hailed from Bihar and U. P., looked askance on the resolution as disruptionist. After whispered consultations on the platform, the chairman ruled it out of order "for want of time," whereupon Pattabhi proceeded to see that every subsequent resolution introduced on that morning was ruled out for the same reason. "The whole house rose in utter confusion, bitterness, and impotent rage, and collapsed," he recalls. The Andhras once again were rebuffed at the Lucknow Congress of 1916, but they won a clear promise that their demand for a separate Telugu Congress body would be aired at the Calcutta Congress a year later.[84]

At Calcutta, writes Pattabhi, the Andhras won the day only after a bitter wrangle in which the Marathi leader Tilak, spokesman of another region with a strong sense of its own identity, took the Andhra side against a recalcitrant Gandhi:

The subject was hotly contested in the Subjects Committee. Even Gandhi thought that the question might wait . . . but Lokmanya Tilak saw the point, namely that linguistic provinces were an essential prerequisite to provincial autonomy. The subject held the field for over two hours in Calcutta, and was ultimately accepted at 10:15 P.M. . . .[85]

Calcutta—and finally Nagpur—decided the linguistic foundation of the Congress organization.[86] But it was one thing to debate the structure of a party in the limited terms of mechanical convenience and of the tactical necessity to take the movement to the people; to champion linguistic boundaries as the basis for a nation was another matter. There were doubters who objected on grounds of national unity to any definite Congress commitment—useful as the linguistic demand could be to club the British. At the All-Parties Conference in 1928,

[84] Pattabhi Sitaramayya, "Congress and Linguistic States," *Times of India*, November 14, 1956, p. 18.

[85] Pattabhi Sitaramayya, *History of the Indian National Congress*, Vol. 1 (1885-1935), Padma Publications, Bombay, 1935, p. 147. See also Vol. 2, p. 93. Tilak's position is recalled in the *Memorandum* submitted by the Samyukta Maharashtra Parishad to the States Reorganization Commission, 1954, p. 111.

[86] See Article 5 of the Congress Constitution, cited in *The Indian National Congress, 1920-23*, Allahabad Law Journal Press, 1924, p. 40.

presided over by Motilal Nehru, "there was not a little difficulty." Pattabhi reported to the Andhras that whatever the north may think, "we must not exaggerate the 'success' of the Conference. On the plain question of linguistic provinces, the drafting committee had not the vision to see that the Andhra Province was a foregone conclusion." North Indians, wrote Pattabhi, "are as much strangers to the difficulties and even discussions arising from these differences of language . . . as the people in the south are apt to be ignorant of the difficulties in the north arising from differences in religion."[87]

Hindi and the South

The North-South cleavage has from the start been the central internal problem of the Congress just as it has been the fundamental challenge to would-be unifiers of India throughout history. With exceptions such as Chakravarti Rajagopalachari, the top Congress leadership, reflecting the party's regional origins and balance of organizational power, has been predominantly north Indian. When national party leaders ventured south, they were linguistic outsiders whose political effectiveness suffered accordingly. Gandhi was no exception, and the fact that his visits to Madras were normally accompanied by preachments in behalf of the propagation of Hindi only made matters worse. Gandhi's 1946 visit for the silver jubilee of the Dakshina Hindi Sabha, one of his last to the south before his assassination, was a fiasco not uncharacteristic of north Indian encounters below the Vindhyas. Telugu delegates to the Sabha sessions protested when he used a word of Tamil, Tamils objected when he used Telugu, and neither knew what he was saying when he delivered the body of his remarks in Hindustani. When Gandhi began to address his first prayer meeting in Hindustani, *The Hindu* reported that

as the Tamil translation of a few sentences Gandhiji had spoken was rendered, a member of the audience, an Andhra, asked for a Telugu translation and kept on shouting even when Gandhiji appealed to him to cool down. Gandhiji refused to submit to his dictation and declared that henceforth there would be no trans-

[87] "The All-Parties Conference," *Triveni*, July-September 1928, p. 5.

lation of his speech in Tamil or Telugu. Those who did not care to know Hindustani should afterward gather from newspaper reports or from friends what he had said.[88]

Whereupon he stalked away from the meeting, followed by the irate and unrepentant Andhra. "Gandhi rebuked him," said *The Hindu*, "saying that he . . . had only forced him to a decision that prevented his coming into contact with the people in the manner he wanted."

Gandhi pronounced it intolerable that the silver jubilee of the Hindi cause in the south should yield an audience unable, for the most part, to follow him in the simplest Hindustani. On the second day of his visit he tried to induce his Tamil and Telugu audience to join in the singing of the prayer song which was a fixture of his prayer meetings in north India. Gandhi recited the song in advance, complete with instructions on how to handclap to the rhythm, but the bulk of the crowd sat in uncomprehending silence as Gandhi and his devotees sang alone on the platform. Proceeding to scold his audience, Gandhi did not spare even Rajagopalachari:

When I spoke in Hindustani, Rajaji himself did not fully understand it. He is the defaulter number one in this respect. He addressed you in Tamil, but when he goes outside the province he talks in English. Well, if the sea water should lose its salt, wherewith shall it be flavored? All over the country, he is reputed to be one of the finest speakers in the English language, but he has not learned to speak in Hindustani. I want a pledge from you here and now— that you will all learn Hindustani. . . . I say it is your *dharma* to learn Hindustani, which will link the south with the north.

In the course of this same visit, Gandhi, addressing 1,500 Congress workers in Madras, asked how many present could understand him in Hindustani. Fifty put their hands up, but Congress leader Kamaraj Nadar was conspicuously among the missing. With a mixture of laughter and scorn, Gandhi exclaimed: "You too!" In this instance Nadar provided a more meaningful linguistic foretaste of future Indian leadership than Rajaji, for he speaks neither Hindi nor English, and even

[88] Gandhi's visit to Madras is described in detail in *The Hindu*, January 22-30, 1946.

today he seldom submits to important negotiations with Nehru, as we have seen, without the backstop of an English-trained secretary. On discovering that the jubilee's own souvenir program was printed in English, Gandhi's rebuke to Hindi Sabha workers was so sharp that the Tamil Gandhian G. Ramachandran gently reminded "his north Indian friends" later in the meeting that they, for their part, should feel obliged to learn south Indian languages.

Even the south Indian Congressman with the best of intentions labors on the short end of a difficult linguistic bargain in his national party activities. Pattabhi recounts a characteristic Congress meeting at Sabarmati in 1930 when Gandhi insisted one evening that all must speak in Hindi,

and who could dare to break the rule? We had to speak in our broken, *thuti puti* Hindi, Hindustani, Persian, Arabic and Urdu with an occasional admixture of Sanskrit and English and an unwitting lapse into Telugu and Tamil. However, we were understood. What is required now is that we should not merely earmark Hindi for ceremonies as we do our silk clothes, but that it should be an article of daily wear or use. . . . We have taken it for granted that south of the Vindhya range of mountains we are exempt from this infliction of Hindi. In the north we resent Hindi, in the south we neglect it. This is bad.[89]

Gandhi could cajole his south Indian disciples on a rare occasion to suffer such linguistic discomfiture, but it has never been seriously suggested that Hindi be made even nominally compulsory for Congress deliberations. While "desirable" that Hindi should be used for Congress circulars and as the medium of party meetings, said the working committee in 1921, it would be "premature to set down any hard and fast rules imposing Hindustani."[90] Today it is still premature so far as Congressmen from non-Hindi regions are concerned, notwithstanding a 1939 amendment to the party Constitution providing that

the proceedings of the Congress, A.I.C.C., and working committee shall ordinarily be conducted in Hindustani. The English language

[89] *Janmabhumi*, March 1, 1930, p. 183.
[90] Resolution of the Working Committee, Bombay, November 22, 1921, cited in *The Indian National Congress, 1920-23*, p. 139.

or any provincial language may be used if the speaker is unable to speak in Hindustani or whenever permitted by the president.[91]

Nehru normally addresses Congress meetings in Hindi as a concession to this stricture—and then delivers his message again in English, as he said at the 1957 session, "for the benefit of our friends from the south." When general secretary Balwantrai Mehta advised Congressmen at the 1954 Kalyani Congress session to "make themselves fully prepared to use Hindi in all meetings and in correspondence" and proposed a Hindi examination for Congress officers, Andhra Congress president Gopala Reddi objected that "even after years of training, it is difficult for south Indians to use Hindi in debates and conferences, and so the idea of enforcing the use of Hindi at this stage is not acceptable to us."[92] A Bengali delegate promptly rose to address the session in his own language over the protests of Hindi protagonists but with the support of Nehru. Only one out of forty Congressmen in Tamilnad, according to a 1949 report, would even buy the Hindi edition of the Congress Bulletin—let alone read it.[93]

Once it was no longer a patriotic necessity to subordinate internal grievances to the common anti-British struggle, south Indian Congress leaders promptly raised voices in the open that might until then have been confined to party meetings. The report of the Dar Commission on linguistic reorganization in 1948 aroused bitter protest. The Commission's postponement of linguistic reorganization inspired charges from party leaders in all southern regions that the Commission had been constituted deliberately of persons of Hindi origin. Even the sedate *Hindu* pronounced it "extreme . . . for the commission to equate the demand for linguistic autonomy with an ambition for sub-national status,"[94] and an Andhra Congressman, attacking it as the "No-Linguistic Provinces Commission," spoke

[91] *Congress Handbook*, 1946, p. 236.
[92] *Congress Bulletin*, A.I.C.C., New Delhi, January 1954, p. 31, and February-March 1954, p. 46.
[93] Cited by P. Subbaroyan during debate on the language provisions of the Constitution, *Constituent Assembly Debates*, Vol. IX, No. 33, September 13, 1949, p. 1398.
[94] *The Hindu*, December 15, 1948, p. 4, and December 16, p. 6.

threateningly of "rumblings of secession of the regions south of the Vindhyas from the Indian Union if the Dar conclusions are to be adopted by the powers-that-be."[95]

What threatened Congress unity most fundamentally in the first years after Independence, however, was the decision to designate Hindi in the Devanagari script as the federal language—a decision to which non-Hindi Congress leaders agreed only with loudly proclaimed reluctance and even dismay. For two years after Independence the issue had remained unresolved. Language provisions were pointedly omitted from the Draft Constitution of October 1947, as well as from all subsequent versions until the very last. The late Dr. B. R. Ambedkar, a non-Congressman who was admitted to Congress meetings in his capacity as Law Minister, revealed shortly before his death (and he has not been challenged) that at the Congress meeting to consider the Draft Constitution

there was no article which proved more controversial than Article 115, which deals with the (Hindi) question. No article produced more opposition. No article, more heat. After a prolonged discussion, when the question was put, the vote was 78 against 78. The tie could not be resolved. After a long time when the question was put to the meeting once more the result was 77 against 78 for Hindi. Hindi won its place as national language by one vote.[96]

When the Constitution-writers of the Constituent Assembly finally faced up to the language question on September 12, 1949, it was the signal for each non-Hindi deputy to join in prolonged filibustering for the benefit of his regional grandstand. No one seriously challenged the decision as such. But all unanimously unburdened their resentment when confronted with the insistence on Devanagari numerals by "the austere, wholehogger Hindi group"—as a Bengali deputy put it—adding insult to the injury already inflicted by the choice of Devanagari script. One by one, the non-Hindi spokesmen placed themselves on record.

[95] G. V. Subha Rao, *Linguistic Provinces and the Dar Commission Report*, Goshti Publishing House, Vijayawada, 1941, pp. 16, 28.
[96] *Thoughts on Linguistic States*, Ramkrishna Press, Bombay, 1955, p. 14.

T. A. Ramalingam Chettiar of Tamilnad warned grimly that the south was faced with

a matter of life and death. . . . If there is the feeling of having obtained liberty, freedom and all that, there is very little of it felt in the south. Sir, coming here to the capital in the northern-most part of the country, and feeling ourselves as strangers in this land, we do not feel that we are a nation to whom the whole thing belongs. It is not even the things that are said—we have given up our language in favor of Hindi—but the way in which the Hindi-speaking people treat us and the way in which they want to demand things which is more galling. . . .[97]

Even the mild-mannered and cosmopolitan Tamil Congress leader, Dr. P. Subbarayan, added his own reminder

of the Tamil proverb which says, if a man comes and asks for a little place on the verandah and if you grant it, he will next ask for entry into the house itself. That is the position of most of you gentlemen today. It is very important, sir, that you should understand the south Indian position.[98]

Orissa Congressman Biswanath Das—objecting to the fact that in a debate on the very selection of a Union language, Hindi protagonist Seth Govind Das had insisted on speaking in Hindi—warned that "we are not going to allow that sort of attitude. That way you will not make us cooperate in future or even now."[99]

Marathi Congress leader Shankarrao Deo declared bitterly that

the chief of the R.S.S. organization appeals in the name of culture. Some Congressmen also appeal in the name of culture. Nobody tells us what this word culture means. Today, as it is interpreted and understood, it only means the domination of the few over the many. . . . If you sincerely believe that this country requires one language, all the regional languages, whatever may be their past, whatever may be their present position, they must go. Those who have their regional languages will at least know where they stand and what they have gained by attaining freedom.[100]

When the late pro-Hindi chief minister of Madhya Pradesh, Ravi Shankar Shukla, advised south Indians not to fear inabil-

[97] *Constituent Assembly Debates*, September 13, 1949, Vol. IX, No. 33, p. 1370.
[98] *Ibid.*, p. 1398. [99] *Ibid.*, p. 1396. [100] *Ibid.*, p. 1430.

ity to learn Hindi because "frankly, they are very intelligent people, very industrious,"[101] Nehru responded to this patronizing lecture with a concluding preachment of his own:

Is your approach going to be a democratic approach or what might be termed an authoritarian approach? . . . In some of the speeches I have listened to here and elsewhere, there is very much a tone of authoritarianism, very much a tone of the Hindi-speaking area being the centre of things in India, the centre of gravity, and others being just the fringes of India. That is not only an incorrect approach, but it is a dangerous approach.[102]

Andhra—Pandora's Box

Once the die had been cast and Hindi's designation in the Constitution settled, Congress internal tensions momentarily subsided. Even in the first general elections local Congress grievances against the high command on regional issues did major damage to the party's electoral fortunes only in Andhra, though there were minor defections in Karnataka, where the Ekikarana or Reunification Front splintered from the party,[103] and in the eastern border areas of Bihar, where Bengali Congressmen seceded from the Bihar Congress.[104] The damage inflicted by Communist victories in Andhra, however, isolated as it was in the national Congress landslide, proved to be momentous from a psychological standpoint.

Communist exploitation of the regional demand had been generally credited with a major role in the Andhra vote, so that the Communists could plausibly seize upon the demand for linguistic states as a national rallying cry. They stepped up their agitation in Andhra and at the same time placed Congressmen on the defensive in all linguistic regions. In the newly elected Parliament, the Communist bloc staged walkouts to protest delivery of speeches in Hindi and introduced a motion for "immediate" linguistic reorganization, which most non-Hindi Congressmen would have supported but for a supreme effort by

101 *Ibid.*, p. 1411.   102 *Ibid.*, p. 1420.
103 *Memorandum for a United Karnataka State,* submitted to the States Reorganization Commission by the Karnataka Provincial Congress Committee, Hubli, 1954, p. 15.
104 This is recalled in the *Times of India,* January 29, 1955, p. 6.

the Party Whip.[105] Finally, amid a heightened propaganda barrage throughout the country, the Andhra Communists were able to organize a violent conclusion to the fast unto death for an Andhra State of the Telugu Gandhian disciple Potti Sriramulu in December 1952. The rampant hysteria in Andhra which followed Sriramulu's death forced the Congress central government to concede the Andhra demand gracelessly, under the threat of mob destruction, which could only encourage other regions to do business with New Delhi in an equally bellicose spirit. Nehru's announcement that Andhra would be formed brought immediate demands from other regions.

At the Hyderabad Congress session in mid-January 1953, inconveniently close upon the emotion-packed weeks following Sriramulu's death, the equivocation of the high command marked the end of the three years of intraparty good feeling that had prevailed since the resolution of the Hindi issue. "Never since Independence," reported *The Statesman*, "has a Congress session been marked for such lively debates as were caused over linguistic states."[106] The session passed a resolution on linguistic states that was a hocus-pocus reaffirming the linguistic commitment but evading definite pledges beyond the formation of a separate Andhra. Nehru spoke ominously of further linguistic reorganization as opening a "Pandora's Box," which only infuriated concerned Congress leaders all the more; Maulana Azad said flatly that "we are not prepared to take up the question of any other linguistic state for the next four or five years." The session settled nothing, and party leaders were threatening mass action in their regions before they left Hyderabad.[107]

What has happened since does not require elaboration. For since the Hyderabad session the Congress has not even attempted to wash its dirty linen, which is to say that of India as a nation, within the privacy of caucuses or closed-door meetings. Hyderabad could only postpone linguistic reorganization,

[105] E. M. S. Nambudripad, "Notes of the Week," *Crossroads*, July 13, 1952, p. 2.
[106] January 19, 1953, p. 1.
[107] *Hindustan Times*, January 19, 1953, p. 1. See also *Crossroads*, February 1, 1953, p. 2.

which was turned over to a hastily appointed States Reorganization Commission. In the years that followed, the growing internal tensions in what was the governing party inevitably occupied the forefront of the political scene. It would have been virtually impossible, for example, to ignore the noisy exchange between the Congress governments of Bengal and Bihar—originating in border disputes but rising to a crescendo in which each managed to suggest that the other should be gerrymandered out of existence, and in which Nehru had to plead with both to "stop behaving like two independent countries on the brink of war."[108] When the appointment of the Commission merely intensified the clamor, the Working Committee appealed in edict after edict to state committees "not to act in a manner hostile to other states and PCCs"—only to yield in the showdown with Karnataka and Maharashtra leaders who insisted that the party's survival demanded freedom to lobby publicly for local claims in conjunction with other regional parties.[109]

The Marathi-Gujarati riots over the future of Bombay City in January 1956, prompted Nehru to exclaim that "inside the Congress itself, this tribalism is stronger than the whole party."[110] Enactment into law in 1956 of the Commission's major recommendations, conceding most linguistic demands, silenced the noisier clamor inside the Congress. But Nehru was still admonishing the A.I.C.C. in the wake of the 1957 elections:

We say we are against communalism, casteism, provincialism and all that. And yet you know well enough how poisoned we are to the very core. . . . Which of us, I or you, is completely free of this?[111]

[108] *Hindu Weekly Review*, April 12, 1954, p. 3, and May 31, 1954, p. 4. Notable examples of intra-Congress bickering associated with the reorganization of states include *Times of India*. December 24, 1954, p. 7 (PEPSU); *Times of India*, September 28, 1955, p. 6 (Andhra-Tamilnad); and *National Herald*, December 21, 1955, p. 2, and *Hindustan Standard*, December 17, 1955, p. 1 (Maharashtra-Gujarat). Editorial discussion of the Congress dilemma may be found in the *Times of India*, September 5, October 27, and November 8, 1955.

[109] *Congress Bulletin*, February-March 1954, p. 91, and April 1954, p. 120.

[110] *Times of India*, February 8, 1956, p. 10.

[111] *New York Times*, June 2, 1957, p. 8.

The Tartar and the Chinese

The 1957 elections underscored the dilemma which the Congress confronts as a national party when parochial forces gain the political ascendancy in a given region. National Congress leaders had learned by 1957 to shift tactical ground with the shifting strength of regional caste lobbies; to go along with whatever regional leadership seemed to offer the strongest temporary base for the party. The rise of a non-Brahman caste lobby within the Congress took place with few national consequences when the high command acquiesced in the advent of Maratha leadership of the Maharashtra Congress at the expense of long-entrenched local Brahmans.[112] But Tamilnad exemplifies the dilemma in another, more perplexing form, for here politically assertive caste lobbies happen to espouse regional aims directly contrary to nationalist Congress aims. National party leaders looked the other way and hoped for the best when Kamraj Nadar pushed out Rajagopalachari and other Tamil Congress Brahmans in 1954. Yet for years Nadar's support within the party had come in part from Dravidian movement sympathizers. Periyar had openly claimed credit for "my followers"[113] whenever Nadar's fortunes took an upswing.

When the Indian press gave Periyar credit for the Congress sweep of the Tamilnad local elections in 1954—at the same time that the Congress in Malabar was being routed—Nadar, apologizing for his acceptance of Periyar's support, explained that "between the Communists and the communalists, the former constituted a graver threat to the state."[114] But in time the tone of apology was to disappear. By the 1957 elections a

112 Darem (*Times of India*, May 18, 1955, p. 6) recalls that "in Madras and Maharashtra, the Congress Trojan Horse was driven right into the non-Brahman camp. . . . The non-Brahman leaders were given control of the Pradesh Congress organizations." S. S. More, in the interview cited, July 1, 1953, specifically attributed the prominence of Maratha Congress leaders such as B. S. Hirey (at the expense of Brahmans such as N. V. Gadgil) to the defection of K. S. Jedhe and himself and the launching of a separate Maratha front party.

113 *The Hindu*, January 14, 1946, p. 4. For a description of the caste struggle in Tamilnad Congress affairs many years before Independence, see "President's Tamilnad Tour," *A.I.C.C. Letter*, No. 31, November 14, 1935.

114 *Times of India*, November 3, 1954, p. 6.

Brahman Congress faction, outraged at the number of Periyar's men named as Congress candidates and at what was, indeed, an alliance in all but name between Nadar and Periyar's Dravida Kazagham or Dravidian Federation, seceded to form a rump "Congress Reforms Committee."[115]

Tamilnad exemplifies at once the short-term political advantages in doing business with ascendant parochialism as well as the long-term dangers to national unity. The Congress strategist can argue that the Tartar, in this case Periyar, storms the Great Wall only to find in time that he has become Chinese. But the risk cuts both ways. For the leaders of the Dravidian movement have long looked to the day when they could capture the Congress and, hoisting the mantle of nationalism, pursue the ends of sectionalism. "Some may think," wrote the Dravidian propagandist A. S. Venu in 1951,

that I am asking them to desert Congress and join the Dravidian movement. . . . But even in free Dravidasthan, Congress can and should function as a sister organization. Today Congress is guided by the people in the north and that gives little or no scope for safeguarding the interests of the south. But in free Dravidasthan, Congress as a body can shape and scheme out plans to serve the people. I appeal to every Congressman . . . to get themselves freed from the Center so they can be of greater service to the masses.[116]

The weakness and discomfiture of the central Congress leadership once regional lieutenants have made their commitment to parochial forces was apparent in Congress president U. N. Dhebar's gingerly treatment of Kamraj Nadar when Tamil Congress ties with the Dravida Kazagham were aired in the press in 1956. Far from condemning Nadar, Dhebar avowed that he could "not imagine Kakkaji or anyone else in a position of leadership in Tamilnad working for the Kazagham."[117]

[115] *The Economist*, February 23, 1957, p. 8; *Times of India*, May 17, 1956, p. 6, and June 14, 1956, p. 6.

[116] A. S. Venu, *Dravidasthan*, Kalai Manram, Madras, 1954, p. 73. See also pp. 77, 95.

[117] *Times of India*, May 27, 1956, p. 6. Phillips Talbot, in his American Universities Field Staff Letter dated May 20, 1957, observes that the Congress is Nadar's "party and his vehicle to power, but it is locally-based power that leaves him relatively untroubled by any frowns that may come from Prime Minister Nehru and the party's high command over the way he runs his machine."

For the sake of the Congress alliance, Periyar's Dravida Kazagham has since early 1956 made relatively little mention of its demand for a sovereign Dravidasthan. However, C. N. Annadurai's militant wing of the Dravidian movement, the Dravida Munnetra Kazagham or Dravidian Progressive Federation, is more committed than ever to the separatist slogan. As a member of the Madras Legislature Annadurai has been able to draw Congress non-Brahmans into debate on the secession demand, thus compelling their disclosure that they consider this a debatable matter,[118] and he has also, on repeated occasions, publicly taunted the Congress, offering up his movement as "an instrument" that the Congress should use to get bigger development allocations from New Delhi.[119] While the two Kazaghams represent differing economic levels among the non-Brahmans, at any vital juncture these two kindred forces might well reunite. Certainly Annadurai's separatist line will constantly test the adherence of the Tamilnad Congress to central directives, and in meeting this test the regional Congress will be conditioned by regionalist forces within its own house.

So long as the figure of Nehru looms over all regions, of course, the high command can have it both ways. Regional alliances can safely be made as opportunity dictates according to shifting local balances of power. The high command will still be able to exercise sufficient control over the party machinery in most regions to obviate serious departures from national discipline. Thus in the selection of candidates for the 1957 election the high command extended its authority down to individual constituencies throughout India. Itinerant subcommittees of the Congress Central Election Committee, consisting of party leaders from outside the region concerned, spent "days and days" with each regional election committee. They moderated between factions, heard the grievances of disgruntled individuals, and when necessary, "knocked a few heads to-

[118] *Hindu Weekly Review*, June 3, 1957, p. 4.
[119] *Deccan Herald*, May 8, 1957, p. 6.

gether."[120] In the case of Bihar, Jayaprakash Narayan charged that Gujarati Congress leader Morarji Desai, as a member of the Committee, manipulated the choice of candidates to serve the direct interests of a particular Bihar party leader and, indirectly at least, to serve Desai's own interests in national party affairs.[121] But the ability of the high command to rule between factions as a moderator of power rivalries is not the same as the power to control a single dominant faction, which has for all practical purposes come to constitute the regional party unit. The Central Election Committee cannot, for example, order Kamaraj to jettison the support of the Dravidian movement. Here is a fundamental incapacity for a party with national pretensions at a time when new regional elites and caste lobbies are assuming progressively greater control of all political life in all regions. Here indeed is occasion to ask: after Nehru what?

For if the Congress high command cannot challenge a Kamraj now, given a stable political order, what high command of the future can be expected to do better? After Nehru, if not in these years of Nehru's fading influence, the central party leadership will face increasingly difficult choices. Even if we assume that a party oligarchy will be able to agree on a successor to Nehru, and stay agreed, the Central Election Committees of a post-Nehru order are not likely to reach into regional political life with the same authority exercised by the Central Election Committee in 1957. Yet such a decline in actual authority would most probably not stop high commands from reaching into regions all the same. The most frequent pattern of events would probably find high commands intervening in regional political decisions, but in a wishy-washy and ineffectual manner. Their intervention would be just assertive enough to arouse resentment but not sufficiently determined to be the last word. Instability and conflict, in short, may become congenital maladies of the Indian body politic. The situation would only be

[120] Phillips Talbot, American Universities Field Staff Letter dated February 12, 1957, pp. 10-13. Cited with permission.
[121] *Times of India*, January 25, 1957, p. 6. See also *The Statesman*, January 30, 1957, p. 2.

aggravated by those high commands which prove so insensitive to regional sentiments as to preclude any wishy-washy indecision. If the response of an insensitive oligarchy in New Delhi to recalcitrant regional units is a stiff-necked effort to handpick candidates and lay down unanswerable mandates, then the consequences, as V. K. Krishna Menon prophesies, can only be "either splinter parties or the selection of prominent local individuals who bargain with the national party on their own terms, thereby making national unity either at party or at national level very unstable."[122] Yet if, on the other extreme, the high command makes no attempt whatsoever to assert itself, local Congress units, and especially those which have even today been opened to parochial forces, would be free to behave as they please unrestrained by any national party discipline.

A National Party System?

National party discipline, in fact, is likely to count for less and less as the shift to the regional languages shifts the center of attraction in all political life to the regional level. While the high command of any party in power can exercise certain brute powers in a showdown, the Congress high command, when it no longer acts in the name of Nehru, may suffer from the same failure of nerve that even now inhibits the growth of effective national parties opposed to the Congress. If even the special Communist commitment to discipline has failed to yield a strong national party, as we have seen, it is not surprising that other opposition parties with a commitment to democratic procedure have failed still more dismally.

The first effort to form a national conservative coalition in India, Dr. Syama Prasad Mookerjee's "National Democratic Group" in Parliament, lasted for less than a year in 1952-1953. The party collapsed when the militant anti-Pakistan emphasis of such north Indian constituents as the Jan Sangh and Hindu Mahasabha convinced Southerners that Mookerjee's horizon did not extend below the Vindhyas. The leader of a southern bloc in the group, Dr. A. Krishnaswami, one of Tamilnad's wealthy

[122] V. K. Krishna Menon, "On Parliamentary Democracy in India," *National Herald*, February 14, 1957, p. 5.

Mudaliars, resigned with a specific blast at the north Indian bias reflected in single-minded attention to Pakistan.[123]

When former Congress president J. B. Kripalani seceded from the Congress on the eve of the 1951 elections, he launched a sort of small-scale Congress consisting of affiliated state groups, fresh from the parent party, which could claim with justification to be the "real" Congress in some regions. But Kripalani was not Nehru, nor was he in power, and his affiliated state groups subscribed to his leadership only with very definite reservations. These are the same reservations, in kind if not in degree, which will no doubt be held by regional Congress leaders as they face the Congress high command itself in years to come. Kripalani and his fellow north Indian leaders were cool to linguistic provinces, but his principal southern lieutenants, T. Prakasam in Andhra and K. Kelappan in Malabar, made this a rallying cry in the elections. Furthermore, opposed as he was to alliance with Communists, Kripalani could not control Prakasam and Kelappan, who saw in alignment with local Communists the only basis for a strong anti-Congress front. All that Kripalani could do to save face was to explain that local units had been given "autonomy" to decide their own relations with other parties. There was no all-India policy on this important issue, so that in the perspective of history, Kripalani's defection from the Congress may have been most significant as a source of strength for the Communists in Kerala and Andhra.

Unlike Kripalani's pre-election contrivance, which lacked dramatic leadership and advanced a vague good-government program, the Socialist Party offered in Jayaprakash Narayan the leadership of a youthful hero of the Independence movement and claimed to represent a clear ideological alternative to the Congress. As it happened, the Congress moved more and more explicitly toward nominal allegiance to socialism, stealing Socialist thunder. But initially in 1948, when Jayaprakash led his followers out of the Congress, he symbolized a distinct alternative to the conservative Congress leadership of the late Sardar

[123] *The Statesman,* April 25, 1953, p. 1.

Vallabhbhai Patel. If ever there was an opportunity in India for a democratic opposition, in short, it was the opportunity lost by the Socialists. Disaffection between leaders and the absence of a tough party organizer to be Patel to Jayaprakash's Nehru are factors often cited—together with the advantageous position of the Congress—to explain the Socialist debacle in India. But it is important to remember the pervasive fact that the Socialists, like any would-be organizers of a national party in India, must constantly combat centrifugal forces which both sap the party within and restrict its tactical freedom. Like Nehru, Socialist leaders such as Jayaprakash, the late Acharya Narendra Dev, and Asoka Mehta have balked at compromising nationalist ideals for the sake of manipulating regional grievances. This has exposed a sensitive nerve to their Communist competitors in the opposition at the same time that they were struggling against the governing Congress.

At the insistence of Asoka Mehta, the party even changed its organizational boundaries in 1949 to coincide with those of the new Indian Union, rather than with linguistic boundaries,[124] and at its 1949 convention, the party drafted as its major pronouncement a Program for National Revival which summoned all patriots to "declare war on the forces of disintegration."[125] When a party militant criticized the program for being soft on the Congress, Mehta responded in a party circular that "there are many fissiparous tendencies in the country represented by communalism, casteism and linguism. These tendencies, if unchecked, will not only defeat the forces of progress but destroy the integrity and independence of our country. The program for national revival has been put forward not to win electoral victories but to create in the country that strength and solidarity that can put an end to the fissiparous tendencies and enable the country to march forward. It is in fact a program of consolidation which must be put through before we can hope to make any spectacular advance."[126] The party expected the scorn of the Communists, who proclaimed

---

[124] *Proceedings*, Socialist Party Convention, March 1949, Patna.
[125] *Proceedings*, Socialist Party Convention, July 1950, Madras.
[126] Socialist Party Circular No. 2, 1950-51, August 9, 1950, p. 1.

that Socialist endorsement of Hindi proved "the Socialist leaders have sold their souls to the big bourgeoisie."[127] But some party leaders may well have hoped that nationalism might prove to be good politics in its own way by providing the basis for a political friendship with the Congress and perhaps even coalition government. In 1953 Mehta wrote his *Political Compulsions of a Planned Economy*, a plea for the solidarity of democratic and nationalist forces. At the party's Betul convention in that year he argued that it would be "anti-national" to ally "even in opposition" with the Communists or Hindu revivalist parties, which he labeled disruptive forces.[128] Nehru and Jayaprakash did explore prospects for a reconciliation in 1953, but their negotiations did not yield even a political non-aggression pact, let alone coalition, and the Socialists found themselves adrift on the mounting regional tides in the country.

At the very moment when Jayaprakash was withdrawing from partisan activity to enter *Bhoodan*, Vinoba Bhave's land-gift movement, and when personal rivalries were vitiating the cohesion of its remaining leadership, the party had to face its most difficult test in the inter-regional disputes associated with states reorganization. There had been skirmishes over linguistic issues before, such as the protest of the Maharashtra Committee in 1948 over northern antipathy to linguistic provinces,[129] but the 1953 debate at Betul degenerated into tense, angry bickering. Karnataka delegates objected to endorsement of the demarcation of the new Andhra boundaries.[130] Uttar Pradesh delegates inveighed against a reference in the draft resolution to bisecting U. P., inspiring the presiding officer, Acharya Kripalani, to exclaim that "we appear to be no better than the others on the question of linguistic redistribution. Let not the world say that our party suffers from the terrible disease

[127] R. Gupta, *The Real Face of 'Democratic Socialism,'* C.P.I. Publication, Bombay, October 1950, p. 15.

[128] Report of the General Secretary, *Proceedings*, Socialist Party Convention, June 1953, Betul.

[129] *Report*, submitted to the National Executive Committee of the Socialist Party by the Maharashtra Executive Committee, 1948, p. 3.

[130] *Proceedings*, Socialist Party Convention, June 1953, Betul, p. 38.

of . . . provincial neurasthenia. I am not against the formation of linguistic provinces. But let us have no language riots over them."[131]

In Bombay City the Socialists had lost the 1951 elections in good part because the party's alliance with Dr. B. R. Ambedkar had identified it with the untouchable leader's vocal pro-Marathi stand on the future of Bombay City, which was just enough to alienate the "Gujarati vote," while not enough to exploit pro-Marathi sentiment.[132] By the time of the riots over the disposition of Bombay in 1956, as well as the general and municipal elections of 1957, the party leaders were in no such equivocal position. Their firm commitment to the Marathi side of the issue, which was also the side of the working-class majority in the city, provoked an opponent of Bombay's inclusion in Maharashtra to deplore the fact that "a party like the Socialist, which is generally expected to view the problems concerning the country in a rational, objective and dispassionate manner, has not escaped the appeal of the 'irrational' represented by the forces of linguism. The views presented by the party in various states betray an utter lack of a unified approach on this vital question. The party leadership seems to have been divided in terms of linguistic allegiance, weakening and undermining the ideological unity of the party as a whole. . . . Instead of giving a bold and correct lead to the masses of the country on this important question, it is disappointing to find the party following the line of least resistance and supporting the so-called 'popular' agitation carried on by the protagonists of linguism."[133]

The prominent Socialist intellectual M. L. Dantwala, one of India's leading agricultural economists, charged that "the Socialists have thrown overboard the economic interpretation of

---

[131] *Ibid.*, p. 148.

[132] M. Venkatarangaiya, *General Elections in Bombay, 1952*, Popular Book Depot, Bombay, p. 67. In two or three constituencies, it is specifically recounted here, "some Socialist workers who belonged to a particular community suddenly deserted their party at the last moment and were lured into the Congress camp by their community leaders."

[133] C. L. Gheevala, *Linguistic States and the Communist Approach*, Bombay Citizens Committee, 1954, pp. 12-13.

history and invested language with the prestige and position of a fundamental factor in the political life of the people.

"In fact the political realignments born out of this controversy have made complete nonsense of party organization in Indian politics. Every political party has been blown into numerous splinters which are getting realigned into linguistic united fronts. For the Socialist Party the phenomenon has an exact parallel in what happened to the Second International on the outbreak of the first World War. Nationalism triumphed over Socialism and the national Socialist parties declared war against each other and forgot all about the unity of the working class. In India today the Socialist Party, at the first touch of linguistic frenzy, has broken up into linguistic groups demonstrating that their faith in class solidarity was but skin deep."[134]

The dilemma is a real one, for there is no escape when political life in a city such as Bombay turns, for years on end, upon Marathi-Gujarati enmity above all else. Asoka Mehta can complain on one occasion that "mutual jealousies and internal antagonisms . . . are destroying the fighting strength of the have-nots,"[135] and yet concede candidly on another that in Calcutta, it is regionalism, not socialism, which provides the grist of a proletarian movement. "Efforts at a joint front of all the exploited people against the exploiters," he writes, "evoke only a limited response." He is forced to confess that "these efforts get strength only when provincial feelings are brought into play. The demand for the inclusion of Manbhum and Singbhum in Bengal, their detachment from Bihar, have shown great evocative force."[136]

Once regional units of a party can dictate separate strategy and tactics on any widespread scale, the party's own internal

[134] M. L. Dantwala, letter to the *Times of India*, December 10, 1956, p. 6. It is interesting to note that Rammanohar Lohia's rump Socialist Party joined with the Dravida Kazagham to threaten civil disobedience to secure the change of the name 'Madras' to 'Tamilnad' soon after his secession from the parent Praja Socialist Party. This is described in *Bhoodan*, July 3, 1957, p. 5.

[135] Presidential Address, *Proceedings*, Socialist Party Convention, July 1950, Madras.

[136] C. N. Vakil, ed., *Group Prejudices in India*, Vora, Bombay, 1953, pp. 167-173.

strife is only multiplied. Yet it certainly seems likely that in India after Nehru the regions will be dictating to the central high commands rather than vice-versa. The high commands, so long as they remain committed to the politics of democratic consent, will be forced to bend before the regional component to hold it in line. And since one region's meat will be another's poison, only political craftsmen of the highest order will be able to maintain a semblance of a national party system.

Will the Union Survive?

The great issue now on the anvil in India is whether representative institutions founded upon one implicit assumption, a national party system, will become an intolerable luxury in a political competition conducted between the central authority and regionally-based political forces. Even in the stable political climate of the 1957 elections, regional forces won more seats in the state assemblies and the lower house of the central Parliament than any national party in opposition to the Congress. When a region wants to direct its discontent against "that universal whipping boy, the Union Government,"[137] regional rather than national leadership will be trusted most often in the decades ahead. The regional party's limited horizon, its allegiance to the region alone, is an asset inherently denied to the national party. In the agitation for the linguistic division of Bombay State the Congress proved no more able to control defections in an historic party stronghold—Gandhi's Gujarat—than in Maharashtra. The Maha Gujarat Parishad and the Samyukta Maharashtra Samiti together won 190 seats out of 360 in the Bombay Assembly. Both were constituted as

[137] Asoka Mehta, "The Political Mind of India," *Foreign Affairs*, July 1957, p. 683. For significant discussions of the potential importance of regional forces, see V. K. Krishna Menon, "On Parliamentary Democracy in India," *National Herald*, February 14, 1957, p. 5, who predicts that the development of state parties comparable to those which he believes to exist in the United States "would spell disintegration and the inevitable prospect of loss of national sovereignty"; and Raja Kulkarni, "Parliamentary Democracy in Asia," *Freedom First*, April 1957, p. 9, who believes that the formation of linguistic states and the emergence of regional parties "introduce a conflict of a permanent nature between forces of national sovereignty and regional independence, between national economic development and regional economic progress."

regional united fronts cutting across party lines: the fact that opposition groups from the Hindu right to the Communists can combine, for years in succession, as an electoral and legislative bloc shows the mercurial manner in which the clash of parties is transmuted in the Indian setting into a clash between sectional and national interests.

The Constitutional Issue

As a constitutional problem, the issue is whether the federal features of the Constitution put too much rope in the hands of regionally-based political forces—rope enough to tie the Union in political and economic knots—and should therefore be supplanted by the tighter controls of a unitary state. The issue is complicated by the fact that the Indian Constitution does not fit neatly into either conventional category, unitary or federal, and can be described accurately only in such an indefinite term as "quasi-federal."[138]

On the one hand it is clear that the central authority in India, far from being powerless in its contest with regional forces, can indeed summon potent constitutional reserves not necessarily associated with a federal system. If the central authority in India exhibits weakness, this is a weakness relative to the strength of state resistance to central incursions. It is not weakness in formal constitutional authority. Under Article 352, the President holds emergency authority to take over any unit where national security is threatened by war, external aggression or "internal disturbance." The President has final power of review over state legislation if the governor of a state, whom he appoints, withholds legislation for presidential approval. In addition to these presidential powers, the upper house of Parliament can by a two-thirds vote assume prerogatives assigned to the states in the Constitution. Parliament, by a simple majority, can form new states.[139] Under Article 368, Parliament

---

[138] Champions of regional autonomy have charged that the Constitution-drafters consciously tilted the balance to a unitary state at the eleventh hour. For example, see M. N. Roy, "Are Linguistic States Desirable?" *Illustrated Weekly of India*, June 14, 1953, p. 15.

[139] Krishna Mukerji (*Reorganization of Indian States*, Popular Book Depot,

holds power to amend much of the Constitution by a simple majority without referral to the state legislatures. Finally, the Indian Constitution specifically circumvents the separation of powers by giving to the Supreme Court unusual jurisdiction and authority. "Unique among the highest courts of the accepted federations,"[140] the Indian Court hears final appeals in all matters whether arising in respect to state or central laws.

But commanding as the position of the central authority would therefore seem to be, the Constitution does at the same time carry certain built-in concessions to the federal principle which in practice invite the states to resist central direction. The Seventh Schedule of the Constitution spells out explicitly the division of powers between the central government and the states, placing such crucial categories as education and agriculture among the sixty-six powers on the State List.[141] By allocating powers between the central government and the states "so precisely," objects Paul H. Appleby, India is strait-jacketed to a degree found in no other important federal nation[142] and the Constitution is virtually incapable of evolution according to changing circumstances. While Parliament can arrogate to the central government powers on the State List, such action is limited in time and can be taken only by the upper chamber, where the states hold greater proportionate voting power than in the lower chamber. The State List and the representation of states in Parliament are set apart for special treatment in the amending clause; no amendment affecting these provisions of the Constitution can be enacted by

---

Bombay, 1955, p. 27) observes that "if this is not the very definition of a unitary government, we do not know what else is."

[140] M. C. Setalvad, address before the International Legal Conference, New Delhi, June 1953.

[141] The Seventh Schedule's allocation of exclusive or concurrent jurisdiction over certain commodities encourages "local protectionism," exclusive of out-of-state buyers and sellers, according to Lawrence Ebb, "Interstate Preferences and Discriminations," *Public Law Problems in India*, Lawrence Ebb, ed., Stanford University Law School, 1957, esp. pp. 138, 148, 153, 155.

[142] Paul H. Appleby, *Report on a Survey of Public Administration in India*, Cabinet Secretariat, New Delhi, 1954, p. 7. G. N. Joshi ("Operations and Effect of the Amending Provision of the Constitution of India," *Public Law Problems in India*, p. 109) refers to the Indian Constitution as "the longest and most detailed constitution operative today."

Parliament without ratification by the legislatures of half the states. The states, moreover, can by speaking in the name of the State List make it almost impossible as a practical political matter for the President to exercise his power of review to the detriment of state legislation. When the controversial Education Bill introduced in 1957 by the new Communist Ministry in Kerala reached President Rajendra Prasad, the Kerala Communists all but challenged his Constitutional right to do more than ratify their action. Because their bill concerned education, which falls within the State List, they argued, the President should have consulted no central officials in making his decision.[143] As for the President's emergency authority to intervene in any state, the Constitution itself circumscribes this power; Presidential rule is always to "come to an end with the termination of the emergency, when the state as a whole is reconverted to its previous federal shape."[144]

Even in the sphere of financial controls, where the central government undeniably holds the upper hand, the states can exercise unusual leverage as a result of tax powers allocated to them in the Seventh Schedule. The central government's financial whip hand over the states is exercised through grants, subsidies, and in a showdown, by withholding funds due a particular state as its share of central tax revenues. Under Article 360, the President can proclaim a state to be financially unstable and assume control of its fiscal policy, reserving money and tax bills for his own disposition. Moreover, the so-called elastic revenues nominally assured to the states, albeit collected

143 *New Age*, April 27, 1958, p. 1.
144 C. H. Alexandrowicz, "Is India a Federation?" *International and Comparative Law Quarterly*, July 1954, p. 400. In *Constitutional Developments in India* (Oxford University Press, London, 1957, pp. 165-169), Alexandrowicz maintains that India is "undoubtedly a federation . . . a federation with a vertically-divided sovereignty." He argues that "disparity between the political structure of the center and of local states may tend to disturb the homogeneity of government throughout the country. . . . The impact of developments on the federal balance is such that it tends to strengthen the position of local states vis-à-vis the centre." Article 368 of the Constitution, he points out, requires that amendments affecting the State List and the representation of states in the Union must be ratified by the legislatures of not less than half of the states in the First Schedule. G. N. Joshi (*op.cit.*, pp. 41-42) describes the federal clauses as the "entrenched" clauses in the Constitution.

by the Union, include many taxes that are to be allocated "in a prescribed manner" by authorities that the Union itself designates. Here the central government gets its Constitutional support for using the distribution of the "elastic" revenues to keep the states in line.[145] But at the same time, the division of tax powers under the Seventh Schedule gives to the states control over what is potentially a source of great revenue of their own—agricultural taxation in all of its forms. Land revenue, taxes on agricultural income, and even succession and estate duties on agricultural land, are all specifically assigned to the states.

The exemption of agricultural income from the central government's general income tax power is indeed, as Matthew J. Kust has observed, "a most unique feature" of the Indian tax system.[146] Because peasant proprietor caste lobbies are in most regions of India strategically placed, if not dominant, in state politics, this is also a feature that has tended to minimize the agricultural tax yield. Not more than one percent of gross agricultural output gets back to the government through taxation in India, compared to twenty-five percent in China. Land revenues yield a negligible sum—only eight percent of all state and central revenues combined in 1950-1951. Yet the owner and renter of land in the Indian countryside is beneficiary number one of increases in agricultural productivity. State governments simply do not make the most of this potential source of income for the obvious political reason that they are, more or less, creatures of the very interests concerned. Thus the yield from agricultural taxation has gone steadily down.

[145] N. Das, "Federalism and Regional Autonomy," *The Statesman*, January 26, 1957, Republic Day Supplement. P. Kodanda Rao ("Is India a Federation?" *Parliamentary Studies*, February 1957, pp. 32-33) points out, too, that "it is the center which determines the shares, not the units" in the assignment of revenues. He adds that the units must get central permission to raise loans in the open market. For an interesting general discussion of the respective powers of the center and the states, see *Times of India*, January 8, 1952, p. 6.

[146] Matthew J. Kust, *Taxation for Economic Development—A Discussion Within the Institutional and Constitutional Framework of India*, International Legal Studies Program, Harvard Law School, Cambridge, June 1, 1955, p. 25. See also Myron Weiner, "Changing Patterns of Political Leadership in West Bengal," *Pacific Affairs*, Fall 1959, for a discussion of the growth of rural political power and its impact on center-state relations.

But the fact that Congress governments have not to date exploited this source of revenue does not guarantee that other parties, perhaps willing and able to antagonize powerful peasant proprietor interests, will not take full advantage of the Constitutional leverage available to them. The Communists in Kerala, for example, flirted ostentatiously with proposals for tightening up the collection of agricultural income taxes.

More crucial to the states' leverage than admittedly circumscribed tax powers, however, is the dependence of the central government on the states for the programming and administration of national development programs. Most governmental functions of a development nature, such as those relating to agriculture, forests, public health and education, fall within the State List. Appleby blames the "restrictive" constitutional allocation of exclusive powers to the states in many key spheres for the fact that the center is "dependent on its capacity for influencing and coordinating administration which is actually within the states' systems, and not on directing or controlling the states or holding them strictly and specifically accountable."[147] To some extent, as Appleby himself suggests, administrative reforms within the existing constitutional framework could go far to expand the central role in development. For example, while New Delhi operates field offices for national "service" functions such as customs, railways, and postal facilities, the central government does not carry on development activities through its own administrative structure. Nothing in the Constitution stops the central government from establishing its own "action" agencies in certain development spheres, agencies which would have field offices of their own, which could attempt to work around state administrative machinery rather than through it, as at present, and which could attempt to oversee the use of central funds turned over to the states. But while there is nothing in the Constitution to stop the center, political resistance on the part of the states themselves is in actual practice sufficient, reinforced as it is by the powers on the State List, to limit sharply the center's conduct of national develop-

[147] Paul H. Appleby, *op.cit.*, p. 11.

ment programs of its own and its control over state-administered programs conceived and paid for by New Delhi.

In practice, major responsibilities for development activities are assumed by civil servants who, while they may be hired and fired through central channels such as the Indian Administrative Service, remain nonetheless, under all but conditions of grave emergency, subject to the direction of the state governments to whom they are immediately responsible.[148] Thus the District Collector, who has in most states become the chief economic development officer on top of his duties as revenue collector and law-and-order officer, is more likely to receive guidance on development issues from state ministries or perhaps non-governmental sources than from New Delhi.[149]

The Imbalance of the Union

The constitutional scheme which has so deliberately balanced the strength of the states against the central authority may prove to be a work of political genius. It may prove to be, as its defenders maintain, elastic enough to permit increasing centralization while, at the same time, protecting the Union against a man on horseback. Precisely because of its diversity the Indian Union may, indeed, demand for its survival constitutional restraints on the central authority which leave great scope for local cultural and political integrity. But paradoxically, the same delicate balance between the components of the Union which makes restraints so necessary is also a fundamental source of frustrated impatience with the existing Constitution.

In India, stresses and strains between the central government and the regions, and between the regions themselves, are of a magnitude unknown to other multilingual states because of the peculiar constellation of power relationships among regions. In the inter-regional balance of power in India, the Hindi region does not enjoy a position of dominance as an

[148] Merrill Goodall, "Organization of Administrative Leadership in the Five-Year Plans," *Leadership and Political Institutions in India*, p. 324.

[149] Richard L. Park, "District Administration and Local Self-Government," *Leadership and Political Institutions in India*, pp. 341-342.

overpowering "majority" region surrounded by supine "minorities." Even at the friendly statistical hands of the Indian Government, which listed 149 million Hindi speakers in its 1951 Census by lumping Hindi together with Urdu, Punjabi, Bihari, and Rajasthani, this total Hindi bloc constitutes at the most 46 percent of the total speakers of the ten major Indian languages. Opponents of Hindi dominance, charging that the government juggled its figures in favor of Hindi, stress the differences between Hindi and its variants, especially the existence of separate scripts in the cases of Urdu and Punjabi (Gurmukhi). If one takes the anti-Hindi argument into account only partially—that is, deducting the number of Muslim and Sikh users of Urdu and Gurmukhi but not deducting Hindu users of Urdu and Punjabi, and ignoring the existence of Bihari and Rajasthani—the Hindi total dwindles to slightly over 100 million or 31 percent of the total population. Nehru has set the Hindi bloc at 120 million or 37 percent. By contrast, in multilingual Switzerland German overwhelms the other languages—totalling 72 percent.[150] Great Russian accounts for 58.4 percent in the Soviet Union. In Yugoslavia, Serbo-Croatian with fourteen million speakers claims 83 percent of the population and can afford to grant concessions to Macedonian and Slovenian minorities of little more than one million each. China's sixty national minorities confront a Han majority of more than 90 percent which, while it is divided by regional dialects, is generally considered an homogeneous whole. Indonesia's 35 million Javanese constitute 58 percent of the national population; the Sundanese, half their number, together with the lesser Madurese and Balinese, do not equal, when combined, the strength of the Javanese. However, the dispersion of the Indonesian island federation in physically separated parts confounds any comparison of this case with others.

[150] Hans Kohn, in Selig S. Harrison, *The Most Dangerous Decades* (Language and Communication Research Center, Columbia University, 1957, Appendix B, "Language as a Political Issue," p. 74), attributes Switzerland's multi-lingual stability in part "to the fact that Switzerland did not attempt to force one of the languages as the official language upon the whole nation, though German holds a much greater proportionate position in Switzerland than Hindi does in India."

The peculiar balance of power in India pits nine significant territorial language components against a tenth which is sufficiently larger than any of them to assert a dominant position but not quite large enough to achieve it. Unlike the Yugoslav minorities or the numerous non-Russian regions of the Soviet Union, which with the notable exception of the Ukraine are individually small next to Great Russia, the non-Hindi regions of India embody significant populations. If we take Nehru's estimate of 37 percent to be the Hindi share of the total speakers of the ten major Indian languages, for example, we find ranged against it Telugu, 10 percent; Marathi and Tamil, each 8, and Bengali, 7, to mention the most powerful non-Hindi components of the Union. The position of Hindi can be compared to the place of the German component in the Hapsburg Monarchy, which totalled 23 percent, largest single bloc in the Empire, but faced powerful Magyar, Slav, and Rumanian rivals.

The Hindi region's position as the political and geographical heartland of India engenders profound resentment precisely because its rivals are sufficiently strong to have a sense of their own importance and destiny. Moreover, since Hindi cannot compare in literary development to at least three of its rivals, Bengali, Tamil, and Marathi, the choice of Hindi as the official language of the Union came as a new affront on top of the psychological injury implicit in the numerical dominance of the Hindi belt. To the non-Hindi regions, the Hindi belt "sprawls across the continent of India like a leviathan,"[151] as Malabar leader K. Kelappan expressed it. In the eyes of south Indian linguistic regions it is less the north as a general geographic area than the Hindi belt as a specific and compact power center that looms oppressively large. Thus the Karnataka-eye view of India as expressed by a variety of writers lumps not only the neighboring Deccan regions of Maharashtra and Orissa but even Gujarat as components of "South India."[152]

Fears of Hindi dominance as the embodiment of northern

[151] House of the People, *Proceedings*, July 12, 1952, col. 3706.
[152] C. H. Rao, *Mysore Gazetteer*, Vol. 1, Government Press, Bangalore, 1927, p. 213. See also K. R. Karanth, *Report*, Akhand Karnataka Rajya Nirman Parishad, 1953, Mangalore, p. 16.

domination come to a still more specific focus upon the political unit of Uttar Pradesh. As the largest Hindi state, with a population of 63,200,000 in 1957, U. P. is virtually as large as the combined Telugu, Malayalam, and Kannada regions. British constitutional authority Sir Ivor Jennings has stated flatly that the Indian Constitution "vests control in the Hindus of the north"[153] through its failure to safeguard against the dominance of this one unit of the Union over others. It is certainly striking that the Indian Constitution contains none of the safeguards present in many other federal constitutions, such as the equality accorded to states large and small in a powerful upper chamber in the United States Congress. Out of 499 members of the lower house of the Indian Parliament, Uttar Pradesh claims 86, and of 216 in the upper house, 31. It was this "major and basic weakness of the Indian Constitution—the extraordinary disparity between one unit and the rest," which prompted K. M. Panikkar to file his formal dissent from the States Reorganization Commission decision to maintain U. P. in its present form. Panikkar advocated splitting U. P. into two large Hindi-speaking states as the only means of assuring a proper federal balance in India. He ruled out the alternative of changes in the weightage of representation in the upper house on the ground that the lower house, in any event, would hold the "dominant position" under the Constitution and that it was the power of the U. P. in the lower house that had to be diffused, especially the power of the Uttar Pradesh bloc within the governing Congress Party.[154]

Representatives of Uttar Pradesh betrayed their own case, said Panikkar, when they appeared before the States Reorganization Commission to plead for the retention of the present Uttar Pradesh boundaries. The U. P. leaders invariably argued "that the existence of a large, powerful and well-organized state in the Gangetic Valley was a guarantee for India's unity; that

[153] Sir Ivor Jennings, *Some Characteristics of the Indian Constitution*, Oxford University Press, 1953, p. 58.

[154] *Report of the States Reorganization Commission*, Manager, Government of India Press, Delhi, 1955, p. 245.

such a State would be able to correct the disruptive tendencies of other states and to ensure the ordered progress of India. The same idea has been put to us in many other forms, such as that Uttar Pradesh is 'the backbone of India,' the center from which all other states derive their ideas and their culture. It is not necessary to examine these claims seriously, for nothing is more certain to undermine our growing sense of unity than this claim of suzerainty or paramountcy by one state over others."[155] Panikkar objected on another occasion to U. P.'s pretensions as the "homeland" of such Hindu mythological heroes as Rama and Krishna, figures who belonged to all India.[156] The *Times of India* singled out in a similar vein the chauvinistic bad example set by certain U. P. Congress leaders at a meeting of the U. P. Congress Committee to discuss states reorganization. The meeting had been called to proclaim U. P.'s right to expand even beyond its present boundaries through annexation of adjacent Baghelkhand, a right justified variously in the name of "the land of Rama and Krishna . . . whose sons are guiding the country's destiny" and the land which is "the main source of the country's cultural and religious life."[157] Perhaps, as Panikkar's critics maintain, political motivations prompted him to make the most of his Commission assignment as a champion of the non-Hindi regions. At least one member of Parliament from Uttar Pradesh observed drily that Panikkar had registered no dissent during the Constitution-drafting period and that only later, at a time when the reorganization of state boundaries brought inter-regional tensions to political life, did he see "the beatitude of the concept of federalism."[158] But the fact remains that the sons of U. P. do, in fact, guide the country's destiny; seventy-one percent of the Council of Ministers, according to a 1956 study,[159] were native to the Gangetic watershed and the Bombay region. U. P.'s claim to paramountcy is continually asserted in Indian affairs to the

[155] *Ibid.*, p. 246.

[156] *Times of India,* December 4, 1955, p. 3.

[157] *Times of India,* May 2, 1956, p. 6.

[158] *Hindustan Times,* October 10, 1955, p. 8.

[159] Robert C. North, "The Indian Council of Ministers," *Leadership and Political Institutions in India,* pp. 108-109.

profound dismay and resentment of nationalists in non-Hindi regions. It is this claim which prompted Nehru to warn during the Constituent Assembly debates on the Union language that the Hindi-speaking deputies must cease to see themselves as "the center of things," the heartland, with the rest of India grouped around the fringes.

It would be one thing for the Hindi belt to assert its claim to paramountcy if the non-Hindi regions were in fact "minorities" in their power relationship to an overwhelming "majority." But arithmetic makes the balance of power in the Indian Union quite another matter. Not only do the non-Hindi regions, when combined, outnumber the single largest component of the Union; they are separately powerful enough to compete with each other as well as with their common rival. It is because the balance of power in India is so uniquely unstable that regional tensions can truly be said to be built into the Union.

Totalitarian Equilibrium?

This unique imbalance imposes a strain on the Union which is intensified when it is imposed within representative institutions. When the clash between regions, and between regional and national interests, becomes the basis of party politics, the political process serves only to drive on rather than to relieve centrifugal forces. Here is the crux of the political dilemma in India. On the one hand the nationalist urge is for a strong and united India which can confront other world powers on equal terms. On the other hand centrifugal stresses constantly impart to the Union a pervasive inner strife and frustration. To the impatient nationalist the only way out seems to be a strong central authority, strong enough to subdue centrifugal forces and lead the nation along a path of planned and directed development. The nationalist in a hurry more and more comes to believe that he cannot tolerate the political luxury of centrifugal stress and strain. He comes to brush aside more and more impatiently warnings that the deeper political wisdom does lie with giving scope to local integrity.

Indeed, as we have seen, the attractive power of the Soviet

image in Asia is derived in large part from the totalitarian opportunity that the Soviet path seems to offer to telescope at one stroke the processes of national consolidation and economic development. It is commonly said that the example of the undeveloped Soviet Union mobilizing its resources in the short space of forty years is compelling to Asians. But it is little recognized that the record of economic achievement is seen together with the fact that the Soviet Union, too, confronted the challenge of national consolidation that now faces the new multilingual states. The Marxist-Leninist-Stalinist scriptures on the "national question" seem to be addressed unmistakably to the special difficulties of economically less developed multilingual states. That the Soviet model is a totalitarian one takes on peculiar relevance in Indian eyes.

The totalitarian short-cut became newly fashionable as a theme for public discussion soon after the rioting that followed the report of the States Reorganization Commission in 1955. The debate on the report in Parliament and the press evoked attacks on the "fissiparous extravagances"[160] of parliamentary democracy and appeals for an early choice between a stronger central authority or chaos,[161] prompting the *Times of India* to note with alarm that "the average Indian," disgusted with fanaticism, "has tended to swing to the extreme of advocating a unitary state."[162]

Despite all the residuary powers legally available to the central government under the present Constitution, in practice, it is argued increasingly, governments seldom confess their political bankruptcy by resorting to a final test of strength. Inexorably, Indian leaders of all persuasions appear to be coming to the common conviction that the exercise of supreme central power can no longer be the exception in time of emer-

[160] S. F. B. Tyabji, "One Party Rule is Not Denial of Democracy," *Times of India*, September 25, 1955, p. 6.

[161] For example, see the comments by C. Rajagopalachari in *Times of India*, November 28, 1955, p. 4. M. C. Mahajan, former Chief Justice of India, urged abolition of state legislatures and the establishment of a unitary state empowered to deal directly with district officers in *The Hindu Weekly Review*, February 20, 1956, p. 7. See also *The Statesman*, December 13, 1955, p. 6, and *The Radical Humanist*, December 25, 1955, p. 617.

[162] *Times of India*, February 12, 1956, p. 6.

gency, but must become the everyday rule. This conviction, though arrived at from differing premises and expressed in a variety of significantly different terms, is nonetheless a serious challenge to the premises of the present Constitution.

The pressure for a stronger central government gets its most insistent propulsion from the economic argument that the state must gain more and more total control of the national economy, supported by whatever accompanying political controls may be necessary to generate an active process of economic growth. Not only is this an article of faith for many Indian intellectuals, most notably the younger members of the government bureaucracy, but it is an argument strengthened by the independent analysis of Western economists. Alexander Eckstein argues, for example, that "a massive application of state power in the minimum spheres is one of the preconditions for averting total government operation of an underdeveloped economy in many countries such as India."[163] Wilfred Malenbaum has maintained in a similar vein that what is needed to break India's economic bottleneck is "a strengthening of the scope and intensity of government action."[164] For the Western observer, it is natural to emphasize that "a massive application of state power" in certain economic spheres in the short run is but a means for avoiding a whole-hog totalitarian pattern in the long run; or to say, as Malenbaum does, that "the government role in economic life has a far way to go before it attains in India the importance it has in the United States, to say nothing of Britain and China." But the distinction between limited political intervention for certain economic purposes, and total political intervention for total purposes, becomes a vaguely discernible nuance when viewed from the perspective of the nationalist in a hurry. To break the economic bottleneck, he, too, looks hopefully to massive state intervention. But he is less concerned with distinguishing between economic and political intervention than he is with getting some process, any process of unimpeded intervention underway. Moreover, unfettered by

[163] "Industrializing in a Hurry," *The New Republic*, May 13, 1957, p. 29.
[164] "Some Political Aspects of Economic Development in India," paper read before the Association for Asian Studies, Boston, 1956.

the Westerner's democratic commitment, he can easily justify political indiscretions with the same optimistic rationale for massive intervention today—as a safeguard against a totalitarian tomorrow—that the Westerner invokes in the economic sphere.

But the young bureaucratic intellectual is significant only because he articulates in his own terms what others more powerfully situated in Indian society express with a more forthright authoritarian logic. When civil servants and intellectuals in Pakistan insist unashamed that military dictatorship is really "directed democracy," they speak in a language heard in private, with few variations, from some of their opposite numbers in India. So long as the unifying presence of Nehru provides political stability, few voices in India will be raised for structural constitutional change. But a new political environment would quickly bring to the surface a profound conflict between regional spokesmen and advocates of a stronger central authority.

Few regional politicians would accept the suggestion of the civil service veteran M. N. Kaul, secretary of the Indian Parliament, that state legislatures are really only branches of the central Parliament.[165] Nor is there common ground between the stern prescription of central direction laid down by such Congress leaders as Food Minister S. K. Patil, on the one hand, and the insistence of regional leaders on the other hand for still more autonomy than they even now claim. The position of Patil and like-minded Congress leaders, such as the sixty members of the "National Unity Platform," which lobbied against linguistic reorganization of states in 1954,[166] is a consistent position that dates back even before Independence. Patil himself urged the Congress in 1945 to abandon the linguistic basis of its party organizational structure. Calling for a "total approach" to the nation, Patil argued that "the Congress must

[165] Kaul's speech at the conference of legislative secretaries in Gwalior in 1953 is cited in K. K. Sinha, *Towards Pluralist Society*, Writers House, Calcutta, 1957, p. 13.

[166] For an account of the National Unity Platform, see *Times of India*, November 10, 1953, p. 3, and Memorandum to the States Reorganization Commission, submitted by the Platform, New Delhi, 1954.

contact the nation in its entirety" rather than through its separate regional parts.[167] In 1954, he warned that "if India is still showing some measure of national unity it is entirely due to the unique personality of our Prime Minister"; linguistic states were a step in the wrong direction, the right direction leading to "a more powerful center with enlarged powers."[168] Educational policy above all should be shifted from the State List to the Union List.[169] When Patil declares that the only way to deal with "the linguistic mania . . . is to stamp it down ruthlessly,"[170] he betrays the same impatience with internal faction that leads another conservative Congress leader, Chief Minister Sampurnanand of Uttar Pradesh, to call on young Indians to "mercilessly root out indiscipline . . . all that divides."[171] It is an impatience that is shared to a greater or lesser extent among industrial and mercantile leaders as much as by the civil service and the military. In a crude form it is shared by those landlord and princely elements in India that can accurately be described as feudal remnants, elements epitomized by the Raja of Ramgarh in Bihar or the Ganatantra Parishad in Orissa. The Raja, whose Janata Party won twenty-three seats in the Bihar Assembly in 1957, attacks the very principle of representative democracies, encouraging as they do "the emergence of a career politician ruling class." India was not ready for universal suffrage, which should be reserved for the village level to avoid "the chances of citizens, collected in large crowds, being utilized by demigods and career politicians for strengthening their class rule. . . . The ruling class today is an upstart body and has not built up the traditions of authority and command through time with a corresponding attitude of obedience among the masses."[172]

[167] S. K. Patil, *The Indian National Congress—A Case for its Reorganization*, Aundh Publishing Trust, 1945, pp. 12, 71.

[168] *Times of India*, January 26, 1954, p. 12.

[169] *Memorandum* to the States Reorganization Commission, submitted by Patil's Bombay Congress Committee, Bombay, 1954, p. 25.

[170] *Ibid.*, p. 31.

[171] *National Herald*, December 14, 1955, p. 2. See also *Indian Worker*, June 25, 1956, p. 4.

[172] Raja Sahib Ramgarh, *Our Robot Democracy*, "A Draft Memorandum for Private Circulation Among the Promoters," Patna, 1954, entirety (22 pp.). The

Although they operate to some extent apart both from the Westernized elements in the military, bureaucratic, and industrial leadership, and from the landlord and princely elements, the Hindu revivalists reinforce in their own way the pressure for a unitary government. Indeed, theirs is the most explicit argument of all for a new Constitution. The most sophisticated ideologian of Hindu revivalism, K. M. Munshi, former Food Minister and Governor of Uttar Pradesh, was arguing as far back as 1942 in his pre-partition movement, "Akhand Hindustan," that India's historic struggle for "its truth, its culture" was one and the same as its struggle "to overcome centrifugal forces."[173] On the very eve of the adoption of the Indian Constitution, a Hindu Mahasabha pamphleteer was charging that the states were being given too much power and that "the British want us to have a federal constitution so that as more political parties grow and consequently friction increases, every Indian province may become separate and this ancient land of Bharat Varsha may break up into so many small states, usually termed Balkanization, and this country may never rise as a first rate power in the world as a rival to Europe."[174] M. S. Golwalkar, leader of the Rashtriya Swayamsevak Sangh or R.S.S., bitterly attacked the recommendations of the States Reorganization Commission in 1954 as "paving the way for ultimate disintegration of the nation"[175] and urged, in place of linguistic reorganization, "a unitary government—prime need of the hour."[176] The Bharatiya Jana Sangh, chief political arm of the R.S.S., pledged in its 1957 election manifesto that if voted into power it would amend the Constitution and declare a unitary state, since the present Constitution "inasmuch as it has established a federal structure and named the provinces as 'States' and Bharat as their 'Union,' has distributed powers

---

National Welfare Union, a political front for Tamilnad landlords, advocated in 1957 a "strong, centralist, welfare state."

[173] "Truth Which is Unity," *Akhand Hindustan*, Bombay, New Book Company, 1942, p. 242.

[174] Horilal Saxena, *Scrap This Constitution*, Nationalist Office, New Delhi, 1949, p. 1.

[175] *National Herald*, December 5, 1955, p. 1.

[176] *Times of India*, January 26, 1956, p. 3.

between them in a way as to create a feeling among provinces of rivalry with the Center and is an obstacle in the way of national solidarity."[177]

The most categorical and unabashed program for dictatorship in India's political heritage, finally, was laid down by the late Subhas Chandra Bose. He argued that India "must have a political system—a State—of an authoritarian character,"[178] "a strong central government with dictatorial powers for some years to come,"[179] "a government by a strong party bound together by military discipline . . . as the only means of holding India together."[180] The next phase in world history, Bose predicted, would produce "a synthesis between Communism and Fascism, and will it be a surprise if that synthesis is produced in India?"[181]

"God Speaks in Five"

Bose's strident nationalism may or may not find its triumphant political expression, but there can be little doubt as to the triumph, at some point, of the forces pushing India toward greater centralization, achieved one way or another. The great issue is what way. For too much power, erupting too suddenly, could aggravate inter-regional tensions beyond the point of endurance and prove the undoing rather than the making of national unity. There are some in India who point to danger signs even now, such as the 1956 copyright bill and the establishment of government book trusts and literary academies;[182] Prime Minister Nehru's suggestion that he would prefer indirect elections to Parliament;[183] and former Labor Minister V. V. Giri's com-

[177] *Election Manifesto*, Bharatiya Jana Sangh, Bharatiya Mudranalaya, New Delhi, 1957, p. 7. See also the Jan Sangh's 1951 *Manifesto*, New Delhi, October 21, 1951, p. 2; *Times of India*, January 19, 1956, p. 1, and *R.S.S.—Its Cult*, Kull-Samaj Publications, Delhi, 1949, p. 15.
[178] *The Indian Struggle*, Wishart and Co., London, 1935, p. 344.
[179] *Ibid.*, p. 345. [180] *Ibid.*, p. 346.
[181] Jagat S. Bright, ed., *Important Speeches and Writings of Subhas Chandra Bose*, Indian Printing Works, Lahore, 1946, p. 378.
[182] See *The Radical Humanist*, August 19, 1956, p. 1; *Freedom First*, May 1956, pp. 6-7; and "Where is India Heading?" editorial in *Times of India*, February 14, 1956, p. 6.
[183] The Congress weekly *A.I.C.C. Economic Review*, July 1, 1957, reproduced on its back page Nehru's oft-repeated suggestion, as originally advanced in

ment that he sees in the five new zonal councils a stepping stone to a future unitary state.[184] Political scientist K. V. Rao has charged that the central government, especially the Planning Commission, is in practice usurping powers which it does not formally possess even under the present Constitution.[185] This process of usurpation has been described by Myron Weiner as "a kind of 'unprincipled' authoritarianism, where the ideals of a democratic, pluralistic society operate but where in reality government is centralized, leadership tends to be authoritarian, decisions are made by a relative few, and responsibility . . . is weak and remote."[186]

There is, undoubtedly, a great danger that 'unprincipled' practices embraced as temporary expedients could in fact become the institutionalized beginnings of a fundamental change in the nature of the state. If many Indian leaders fail to share a sense of danger it is because there is a widespread conviction, even among the staunchest adherents to democratic values, that the forms of Western party democracy are not suited to India at this stage of development. This conviction is implicit in the proposals of Jayaprakash Narayan and Asoka Mehta for a coalition or national front government of democratic centrist elements; and it is set forth explicitly by Vinoba Bhave, who advocates an end to parties as a prelude to a "no-party" regime uniting all men of good will. Vinoba points to the Hindu political principle inherent in the institution of the village *panchayat*, or five-man council. Here there is no place for a majority victory over a minority. As in the Indonesian *mukafat* tradition of compromise among village elders,[187] all must deliberate together until unanimity is possible. "God Speaks in

---

Discovery of India, for indirect elections based on the village *panchayat*. The *panchayat* would choose electors who would then represent the village in the election of all leadership at higher levels.

[184] *Times of India*, February 22, 1956, p. 4.

[185] "Center-State Relations in Theory and Practice," *Indian Journal of Political Science*, October-December 1953, pp. 247-355.

[186] "Some Hypotheses on the Politics of Westernization in India," *Leadership and Political Institutions in India*, p. 24. See also Weiner, *Party Politics in India*, Princeton University Press, 1957, p. 21.

[187] J. D. N. Versluys, "Social Factors in Asian Rural Development," *Pacific Affairs*, June 1957, p. 170.

Five," according to Bhave's interpretation of Vedic tradition. At the time of the 1957 elections, when many Indians were congratulating themselves on their orderly performance, Vinoba dissented: "We are copying this from the West. It is a common saying in India that if Five speak with one voice, it should be understood as the word of God; that is, our ancients believed in working with the consent of all. Today a proposition is carried by a majority of votes; it creates a conflict between the majority and the minority." In a country with India's diversity, the scramble for votes "has given casteism a new lease on life."[188]

Finance Minister Morarji Desai, a nominal Gandhian and ascetic if not Vinoba's active votary, has argued in much the same terms:

Democracy has been defined by the political thinkers of the West as government of the people, by the people and for the people. That definition is good in a way. But in actual practice the people means a majority. Thus, according to the Western conception of democracy, if a majority of 51 percent goes on flouting the wishes of 49 percent, and even goes on oppressing them, still it is called a good government. But our conception of democracy is entirely different. We have been taught democracy by Gandhiji, who has called it *sarvodaya*, which means the good of everybody.[189]

"True discipline," Morarji then concludes, "constitutes the very essence of democracy." To Western ears the notion of democracy without parties, especially when coupled with references to "true discipline," carries a totalitarian ring. But the Gandhian would say, as does Jayaprakash, that it is only by beginning from a political starting point entirely alien to Western conceptions that India can in fact reverse the present trend to a centralization which is, by its very nature, bound to become totalitarian. This starting point is decentralization with self-governing village councils as the basic units of government. These units would be responsible directly to the central government in New Delhi and only to intervening agencies, such as provincial governments, whose powers have been carefully circumscribed.[190]

[188] *Bhoodan*, February 13, 1957, pp. 44-45, and August 7, 1957, pp. 1-2.
[189] Chandrakant Mehta, ed., *Selected Speeches of Morarji Desai*, Hind Kitabs, Bombay, 1956, p. 5.
[190] *Bhoodan*, March 27, 1957, p. 1.

In his letter to Nehru at the time of the 1953 Congress-Socialist coalition talks, Jayaprakash declared that "we should make up our mind as to what kind of political system we want. Centralization of political power and authority would be disastrous. We must deliberately work for devolution of powers and decentralization of authority."[191] Freedom in India is endangered more by an all-powerful central authority which hides behind a parliamentary façade, Jayaprakash warns, than by a Gandhian system in which the price of authentic local self-government might be a less strictly "representative"—but more restricted—government in distant New Delhi. In the India of Vinoba's and Jayaprakash's conception, basic human rights would be inviolate: freedom from arbitrary arrest, freedom to criticize authority, freedom to assemble, and freedom of movement. To be sure, a conception which presumes to guarantee these personal freedoms but seems to deny their corollary— the right to organize a political opposition—is not "democracy" as the West knows it. But neither is it totalitarianism as the West knows it.[192]

The Gandhian ideal of decentralization cannot be expected to triumph in the space age. Yet the voice of Vinoba and Jayaprakash is important for two reasons. It is, on the one hand, a tragic last protest against the trend to a dominant central authority. At the same time it is the protest of traditional India against a transplanted Western politics of party and parliament, and as such, it is a voice which may in the end pronounce a most un-Gandhian central authority to be the legitimate inheritor of the Gandhian tradition. Perhaps the best that votaries of democratic values can hope for is that the dominant central authority that must at some point arise in India will rest with

[191] Interview with Jayaprakash, November 22, 1953. See also Jayaprakash's Letter to Nehru, March 4, 1953, Statesman, March 5, 1953.

[192] For a persuasive and perhaps classic statement of the argument that a unitary state should not be equated with repression, and a federal state with liberty, see Franz Neumann, "On the Theory of the Federal State," The Democratic and Authoritarian State, Macmillan, 1956, esp. pp. 224-229. See also John J. McCloy, Commentary on a paper by Patrick Gordon Walker, "Policy Choices Before the Western World," in Philip Thayer, ed., Nationalism and Progress in Free Asia, Johns Hopkins University Press, 1956, pp. 369, 373-376, for a discussion of the relevance of "democracy" in evolving U.S. policies in Asia.

men in the tradition of Gandhi and Nehru rather than that of Bose. Given India's internal power relationships, the process of centralization is not likely to occur with the smooth, gradual, almost imperceptible balance that has marked the growth of the federal system in the United States. Instead the process will be fitful, a succession of convulsions in a volcanic political landscape. The frustration to nationalist ambitions in a Union locked in a disequilibrium of competing regions and regional lobbies will generate and regenerate these convulsions. Yet to escape from frustration through the surrender of total power to a man on horseback could be in the light of history the sure way to destroy the Union.

——————:·ϑ✳ϱ:·——————

After the "Tall Leaders"

ONCE, recalls Nehru, when a crowd of villagers shouted the inevitable *Bharat Mata Ki Jai*!—Victory to Mother India!—he conducted an unpremeditated experiment in the semantics of nationalism. "Who," he asked, "is this Mata you salute?" *Dharti*—the earth—responded the villagers. "Whose earth? Your village earth? Your province? India? The world?"[1] The villagers were, of course, struck dumb, a fact of little consequence in itself but all too symbolic of the larger inability of India as a whole to discover a coherent nationalism. The Indian who shouted anti-British slogans during the movement for Independence and who now shouts to the victory of "Bharat Mata" senses that change is in the air, that change for the better is possible, and that to shout for it, to claim it, is a prerequisite for getting it. But who is this Mata in whose name he joins the revolution of rising expectations?

"Bharat Mata" is the standard of a nationalism that is subcontinental in its horizons. The horizons of those summoned to the standard, however, are in most cases still the limited ones of a caste unit or a linguistic region. Thus Mata is in practice the name for whatever horizon the manipulator chooses to fix upon in a particular political circumstance. It is the responsiveness of the new nationalism to contradictory political invitations which above all guarantees that the decades ahead will be turbulent ones for India. Political invitations will multiply with each year that change penetrates more deeply into Indian society, churning up new desires and claims at a rate that will outdistance the capacity of any central government to deliver. The bravest attempts to keep pace with rising demands will

[1] Frank Moraes, *Jawaharlal Nehru*, Macmillan, New York, 1956, p. 262.

319

require a political foundation of national unity. Yet the central authority in India is caught in a vicious circle: unity depends on rapid development as much as development presupposes unity.

Although, on the one hand, development demands central direction, the economic upheaval set in motion by planning on a subcontinental scale carries its own endemic challenge to national unity. The central authority in making planned economic expansion possible gives rise to new and perhaps self-defeating forces. It is a commonplace that nationalism is a response to the spread of industrialization and the shift from subsistence agriculture to an exchange economy, a turn to a new form of community to replace old communities that are in the process of atomization.[2] As the social unity of village life is destroyed by the new competition between castes, as more and more villagers leave their folk culture for towns and cities, men grope accordingly for new allegiances. Millions disengaged from their native ground wander through uncharted social realms. The man who once talked only to a bullock in a field now communicates with a progressively broadening circle. Language circumscribes the outer limits of this new, wider world, and so it is his regional caste and language groups which are the natural focii of his new allegiances, which provide social alliances equal in breadth and power to the new competitive challenge surrounding him. In winning the loyalty of the new groupings rising out of the dissolution of the old social order the political manipulator need only point to scapegoats and antagonists beyond the linguistic horizon. Thus the psychological underpinnings of the subcontinental state are eroded as rapidly as the state succeeds in economic development.

The period now beginning in India presents striking similarities to the rise of nationalism in nineteenth century Europe, especially the nationalist upsurge in the Balkans which culminated in the collapse of the Austro-Hungarian Empire. "Will

[2] See suggestive discussions of this process in Karl W. Deutsch, "The Growth of Nations," *World Politics*, January 1953, pp. 173, 183-184, 194-195; Rupert Emerson, "Paradoxes of Asian Nationalism," *Far Eastern Quarterly* (now *Journal of Asian Studies*), February 1954, p. 139; and J. Obrebski, "The Sociology of Rising Nations," *International Social Science Bulletin*, Summer 1951, p. 238.

India succeed in carrying out this experiment," pondered Toynbee at the time of the reorganization of states, "without bringing on herself eastern Europe's tragic fate?"[3] The Balkanization of eastern Europe along linguistic lines occurred, to be sure, in a particular historical context. Imperialism has provided a rallying-cry to the nationalist leader in multilingual India or Indonesia which distinguishes the new Asian experiments from previous European experience. But the east European outcome did come as the climax of the same historic processes now occurring in India: more and more education and literacy, more and more popular participation in political life, more and more economic opportunity, and at the same time, more and more identity of linguistic and political boundaries.[4] The rise of mass participation in politics in Austria-Hungary brought to the fore in all groups chauvinist leaders who were able to convert utopian expectations—the new popular awareness of "self-hood"[5]—into the ambitions of uncompromising nationalism. It is true, of course, that economic development in the West has to a great extent depended for its motive force on precisely such chauvinistic ambitions. Industrialization came to the Balkans, by no means accidentally, at the same time that nationalist tension reached its peak. Like regional logrollers who seek to corner India's Five-Year Plan expenditures for their own territory, "each national group tried to divert the main stream toward its own mill." David Mitrany writes in his account of the Austro-Hungarian collapse that "economic prospects and national claims became, so to speak, interchangeable; increase in one raised the level of the other."[6] Today assertive regional caste lobbies challenge Marwari power in a striking

[3] Arnold J. Toynbee, *East and West,* Oxford University Press, New York, 1958, p. 101.

[4] See E. H. Carr, *Nationalism and After,* Macmillan, New York, 1945, pp. 10-20; and Karl W. Deutsch, "Large and Small States in the Integration of Large Political Communities," a paper delivered at the Stockholm Congress of the International Political Science Association, August 21-27, 1955.

[5] Hans Kohn, "A New Look at Nationalism," *Virginia Quarterly Review,* Summer 1956, p. 329.

[6] David Mitrany, *The Effect of the War in Southeastern Europe,* Yale University Press, New Haven, 1936 (for the Carnegie Endowment for International Peace), pp. 27-28, 31. See also Robert A. Kann, *The Multinational Empire,* Vol. I, Columbia University Press, 1950, p. 340.

321

parallel to the contest between the Balkan nationalist middle classes and the Viennese financiers. But in the age of space travel and the multilingual state, Balkanization is out of date. Today a repetition of Balkan economic rivalries can only lead to an impasse in economic development and, as a consequence, to increasing social and political tension.

Economic stagnation does not rally men together, as logic might dictate, for shared sacrifices and shared progress. In practice quite the reverse happens. "While few men have the patience and skill to ponder over increasing the size of the cake," writes Asoka Mehta, "attention easily turns to its slicing up."[7] The scramble to see who gets the biggest slice of the economic cake in India is an unregulated scramble of regions and regional caste lobbies with none of the common overriding loyalty to a national feudal hierarchy and an emperor—and hence to a national state—which gave Japan the social control for its rapid modernization.[8] This undisciplined character of India's competition need not of itself choke off all economic development; indeed, according to one line of analysis, the pursuit of equality on the part of subordinated social groups can provide the greatest dynamism for economic effort in the less developed countries.[9] But an unregulated scramble in multilingual India —where the competition between regions is reinforced by the competition between caste units delimited along regional lines —propels centrifugal forces and therefore cancels out whatever economic progress it generates. There is an economic law, moreover, which dictates that inequalities between regions increase in direct proportion to the persistence of economic stagnation. What Gunnar Myrdal calls "the principle of circular causation"[10]

[7] "Politics of a Planned Economy," *Janata*, August 2, 1953.

[8] Marion J. Levy's analysis of the Japanese experience can be found in "Some Social Obstacles to Capital Formation in Underdeveloped Areas," *Capital Formation and Economic Growth*, Princeton University Press, 1955, esp. p. 466, and "Contrasting Factors in the Modernization of China and Japan," *Economic Growth: Brazil, India, Japan*, edited by S. Kuznets, W. E. Moore, and J. J. Spengler, Duke University Press, Durham, N.C., 1955, pp. 496-536.

[9] Everett J. Hagen, *An Analytical Model of the Transition to Economic Growth*, Center for International Studies, Massachusetts Institute of Technology, 1957, esp. pp. 60, 65, 87-88.

[10] *Rich Lands and Poor*, Harper and Brothers, New York, 1957, esp. pp. 32,

is known by the Biblical truth that "unto everyone that hath shall be given, but from him that hath not shall be taken away even that which he hath," and by the simple Yankee logic that "them that has, gits." Thus, since widening inequalities prompt aggrieved regions to press their claims with progressively greater vigor, the vicious circle becomes more and more inescapable.

The intensity of the inter-regional competition in India gains with each year that the unity achieved in opposition to the British ruler slips away. When opportunities for development were denied equally to all of India, all regions blamed the outside oppressor for their plight. But now that India is independent, as the States Reorganization Commission has observed, "consciousness of the lack of a community of interests between different language groups tends to become deeper and deeper with the progressive realization of their divergent economic and other needs."[11] If Nehru can to some extent hold down the claims of regional self-interest it is because he embodies a link with the Independence movement and its spirit of a common cause. Even Nehru's lieutenants in Assam protested for months on end when the central government sought for economic reasons to locate an oil refinery drawing on Assam oil outside the state. But this was restrained protest, warned one of them, compared to what could be expected in years hence. "Now, so long as our tall leaders, our all-India leaders, are there," he said, "perhaps people will be submitting to their advice. But this cannot be stretched too long."[12]

To the extent that all regions can look to New Delhi for the wherewithal of progress, the financing and know-how that build dams, irrigation canals, and industries, the Indian Union gains in strength. Conversely, the exercise of economic development power demands statesmanlike care. For to the extent that regions believe the central authority discriminates in the allocation of capital, the Union is weakened.

34, 40-45. See also Amlan Datta, *Essays on Economic Development,* Bookland Private, Ltd., Calcutta, 1957, p. 7.

[11] *Report of the States Reorganization Commission,* Government of India Press, New Delhi, 1955, p. 37.

[12] *Debates on the Report of the States Reorganization Commission,* December 14-23, 1955, Vol. 1, Lok Sabha Secretariat, New Delhi, 1956, col. 575.

The central government calls on the regions to trust in an ephemeral national unity, but the regions demand down payments before they will trust to an uncertain future. On the one hand they demand their down payments in development expenditure. At the same time they watch to see that they are not surrendering more tax money than they can see returning to their own home ground. "You want us to make a fetish of Indian unity," exclaims the propagandist for a sovereign Mithila republic in northern Bihar. "But the unity of India is a mere means to an end, which is our social well-being, a higher standard of living. If this unity, this Leviathan of an Indian State, is a bar to our progress, a weapon in the hands of our opponents, we should frankly go against it."[13] And are we not forging the weapons of our own suppression, he asks, by paying the taxes that give power to New Delhi and to the state capital?

To all regions it can easily appear or be made to appear that New Delhi, as the real or imagined agent of other regions, invariably manages to take away more treasure than it returns in development expenditure. Thus the Communist Party in Andhra emphasizes demands that the excise and export duties on Andhra minerals, peanuts, and tobacco go for use in local river valley projects.[14] In Kerala Communist Chief Minister E. M. S. Nambudripad took his oath of office and then promptly complained that the central government returned to West Bengal a portion of revenues on jute production but denied Kerala development income commensurate with revenues gained from the state's coconut, pepper and rubber production.[15] The use of this issue is not confined to the Communists, however, and long before the Communists came to power in Kerala the proceedings of the Travancore-Cochin Legislature revealed constant preoccupation with the distribution of tax revenues between the state and central governments. Rather than take subsidies from New Delhi which "will curtail our freedom,"

[13] Lakshman Jha, *Mithila—A Sovereign Republic*, Mithila Mandal, Darbhanga, 1954, p. 14.
[14] For example, see *New Age*, December 26, 1954, p. 14.
[15] *The Statesman*, April 6, 1957, p. 7.

one deputy went so far as to say, the state should tax more funds for its own use in development and refuse to surrender so much of its revenue to the central government.[16] The Dravidian movement in Tamilnad claims that a sovereign Dravidasthan would command at least 1,000,000,000 rupees ($210,-500,000) in annual revenue and charges that New Delhi "is really robbing Peter to pay Paul"[17]—an accusation paralleled indirectly by the movement's arch-rival in Tamilnad, the *Hindu*, in its demand for a greater share of central excise duties.[18]

The tax grievance is a convenient handle against the central government, but it is only as powerful as a region's sense of discrimination in development expenditure or in its general treatment by the central authority. At a time of food scarcity in Tamilnad the Dravidian movement made such effective use of alleged "heartless complacency" on the part of New Delhi in rice allocations to Madras that the issue was credited with the defeat of the Congress Chief Minister in the 1951 elections.[19] In Parliament the movement's sympathizers persistently complain that new community projects,[20] scientific laboratories,[21] and for that matter, "the bulk of our social overhead capital"[22] are concentrated by discriminatory design in north India. "I have tried to understand what this so-called all-India outlook means," said Dr. A. Krishnaswami in the House of the People, "but I invariably find that it leads to the concentration of particular industries in those regions where there has already

16 *Proceedings*, Travancore-Cochin Legislative Assembly, Assembly Secretariat, Trivandrum, March 14, 1953, p. 1126. For other examples of tax grievances, see *Proceedings*, March 13, 1953, p. 1036; Dr. P. J. Thomas, "The Second Five Year Plan and Kerala," *A.I.C.C. Economic Review*, December 1, 1955, p. 16; Lakshman Jha, *Mithila Will Rise*, Mithila Mandal, Darbhanga, 1955, p. 5; and Jha, *Mithila—A Sovereign Republic*, p. 14.

17 A. S. Venu, *Dravidasthan*, Kalai Manram, Madras, 1954, p. 92.

18 For example, *The Hindu*, December 24, 1956, p. 6.

19 *The Statesman*, January 15, 1952, p. 1, and *The Hindustan Standard*, January 21, 1952, p. 8. See also S. Vedaratnam, *A Plea for Understanding; A Reply to the Critics of the Dravidian Progressive Federation*, Vanguard Publishing House, Conjeevaram, 1951, p. 37.

20 *Proceedings*, House of the People, Lok Sabha Secretariat, New Delhi, March 11, 1953, col. 1781.

21 A. S. Venu, *op.cit.*, p. 51.

22 *Proceedings*, House of the People, Lok Sabha Secretariat, New Delhi, December 16, 1952, col. 2496.

been greater prosperity."[23] Moreover, he no doubt said to himself, where the government does not step in to initiate industrial development, the Marwaris do; in Madras, as well as Bombay, Calcutta,[24] or Poona, the enthusiasm for getting a just share of central government industrial investment is accompanied by an enthusiastic invitation to oncoming Marwari investors to stay out, or if they are already there, to get out. Wealthy Tamil communities such as Krishnaswami's Mudaliars, rivals of the Marwaris, thus feel doubly aggrieved at the north for what it does as well as for what it fails to do. Tamilnad's sense of discrimination differs only in degree, however, from that of other regions. In kind it is identical. In Orissa, the Ganatantra Parishad points to the Oriyas as the poor relations of the Union.[25] In all parts of India the Communists, with none of the responsibilities of all-India leadership, can argue that "any deficit in any single state has to be met by the center"[26] and that it is, in fact, the "duty"[27] of the center to help the less developed states. Yet the Communists only heighten grievances which even local Congress Party organizations are quick to exploit. When the central government decided against Assam as the location for the new oil refinery it was a Congress member who uttered the bitter complaint that "every drop of oil in Assam is as sacred as a drop of blood of every Assamese. We cannot allow it to be sucked by others."[28]

[23] *Ibid.*

[24] *Hands Off Bombay,* memorandum submitted by the Bombay Pradesh Congress Committee to the States Reorganization Commission, Bombay, 1954, pp. 27-28, states that non-Bengali businessmen in Calcutta "fear that they would not be welcome in that state in time to come."

[25] *Times of India,* May 27, 1956, p. 4.

[26] *New Age,* April 25, 1954, p. 11.   [27] *New Age,* May 2, 1954, pp. 8-9.

[28] *Bhoodan,* July 3, 1957, p. 4. The *Report of the States Reorganization Commission,* p. 225, pointed to regional Congress leaders in its observation that most of the demands for constituting new states were based primarily on alleged unfair and unequal distribution of development expenditure in existing multilingual states. See the *Memorandum* submitted to the Commission by the Bihar Association, Patna, 1954, pp. 98-103, for detailed charges of industrial maldistribution in India, and p. 168 for the specific charge that Bihar's border claims against Bengal can be justified solely on the ground that the state is "insignificantly developed, far behind Bengal." See also *Proceedings,* House of the People, Lok Sabha Secretariat, New Delhi, August 19, 1953, cols. 1103-1112, for a discussion of regional economic grievances within states, such as Rayalaseema's charges of neglect in Andhra and those of the Hariana Prant in the Punjab.

With all parties equally ready to use New Delhi as a whipping boy, the central government is placed on the defensive and must constantly justify every planning decision, not only in economic terms but in political terms as well. The Second Five Year Plan pledged that "in the location of new enterprises, whether public or private . . . every effort should be made to provide for balanced development in different parts of the country."[29] Nehru has on repeated occasions reassured India's own underdeveloped areas that they would be helped to catch up with the rest of the country.[30] Indian leaders must steer a narrow passage between "this Scylla and Charibdis"[31]—too much care, on the one hand, and not enough, on the other, that each region gets its fair share of development expenditure. As Maurice Zinkin points out, the planner cannot decide where he will build new railway lines simply on the basis of traffic offering—or where he will put new dams simply on the basis of the acres irrigated per million spent—if that means some states will get a great many railway lines or dams and others none at all. Yet at the same time, if he goes too far in appeasing regional leaders, "though there may be more equality, or greater regional fairness, or possibly, fewer revolutions, there is also less development."[32]

Already the dragging effect of inter-regional rivalries has materially held down India's economic progress. This is especially so in far-reaching ventures, such as river valley projects, which by their very nature cut across state lines. At the time of Independence existing statutes gave to state governments primary legislative and administrative responsibility for the planning and development of water resources. Within a year the Ramapadasagar project was hopelessly tangled in the political crossfire of Andhras and Tamils in multilingual Madras.[33] The

[29] *Second Five Year Plan—A Draft Outline*, Planning Commission, Government of India, February 1956, pp. 19-20.
[30] For example, see *Amrita Bazar Patrika*, March 6, p. 1, and April 12, p. 3, 1957.
[31] Maurice Zinkin, *Development for Free Asia*, Essential Books, Fairlawn, N.J., 1956, p. 193.
[32] *Ibid.*, pp. 237, 250.
[33] This controversy is reviewed in *The Free Press Journal*, Bombay, August 15, 1952, pp. 4, 6.

Malayalees in Madras, too, prior to the linguistic division of the state, remained constantly vigilant against the designs of both on rivers crossing their territory en route to the Arabian Ocean—lest "an Andhra Rau and a Tamil Subramanian" (references to P. S. Rau, then Presidential adviser in the state, and Madras Finance Minister C. Subramanian) divert Malayalee waters through engineering ruses.[34] Andhras and Kannadas, meanwhile, bickered over the Tungabhadra project, which provides 55 percent of its water and 80 percent of its planned electricity to Andhra but, for political reasons, has half of its headworks in Mysore. The dependence of Andhra farmers and power customers on a headworks in another state was certain, as Henry C. Hart writes, to invite "the controversy, the lost motion, and the second-best solutions which plague a project divided by a border."[35]

In contrast to the stalemate that has prevailed wherever river valley development has rested administratively in state hands, the Damodar Valley Corporation, an autonomous central agency in which Bihar and Bengal have representation, demonstrates how a sensitive national leadership can overcome the obstacles presented when linguistic lines divide river valley systems. Even in this instance, however, the interstate representation on such bodies as D.V.C. has greatly impeded rapid progress. Since the states hold the power of inspection, they are able to assert their claims at every stage of the way, when workers are hired, contracts are let, or funds are allocated for irrigation and power facilities.[36]

[34] *Times of India*, May 29, 1956, p. 6.
[35] *New India's Rivers*, Orient Longmans, Calcutta, 1956, pp. 56-58. See also *Proceedings*, House of the People, Lok Sabha Secretariat, New Delhi, August 19, 1953, cols. 1122-1123, and August 24, 1953, cols. 1431-1434, for debates on Tungabhadra between Andhra and Kannada deputies.
[36] K. K. Sinha, editor of the *Indian Journal of Power and River Valley Development*, discusses the problem of inter-state representation in an informal analysis prepared for the author, January 1956, p. 2. In its *Memorandum* to the D.V.C. Inquiry Committee, Calcutta, January 1953, p. 8, the *Indian Journal of Power and River Valley Development* pleaded for autonomous central agencies to carry out all future river valley projects. Henry C. Hart, *New India's Rivers*, *op.cit.*, pp. 74-75, 166, and 268, stresses the role of the central government in river valley development. M. S. Thirumal Iyengar, then president of the Central Board of Irrigation and Power, appealed in a significant address before the

It is the recruitment of labor which perhaps best illustrates India's vicious circle. The migration of laborers across regional lines to a new factory or river valley project is commonly assumed to exercise a unifying influence.[37] As industrialization proceeds and more and more people migrate between regions, this assumption runs, regional consciousness will give way to new cosmopolitan loyalties. But in fact the political consequences of inter-regional migration are quite different. The recruitment of labor for skilled and unskilled jobs alike becomes the grist of political controversy between regions. Nor is this phenomenon inconsistent with the entire history of nationalism, which is in essence, Deutsch writes, "the attempt at improving the position of one's 'own' group without any sharing with outsiders."[38] When nationalism spread through the new industrial masses in the nineteenth century one of the first imperatives confronting the new nationalist regimes was the defense of the wages and jobs of their workers through the exclusion of immigrant labor.[39] Today state governments in India find their political compulsions not too different. The Orissa government has been able to preserve the numerous "Grade IV" posts in the central government's Rourkela steel mill for Oriyas only, prompting a Bihar journalist to exclaim: "The Biharis are nowhere in the picture, not even in the so-called national projects."[40] To the extent that it does not militantly champion Oriya jobs, the Congress government in the state exposes itself to the onslaughts of the Ganatantra Parishad with its slogan of "Orissa for the Oriyas."[41] The Parishad's election promise to reserve all unskilled jobs on the Hirakud Dam Project held great appeal for Oriyas who see thousands of Punjabis, South Indians, Bengalis, and Biharis employed

Silver Jubilee session of the Board, November 17, 1952, for river valley zonal redistribution of Indian political boundaries.

[37] For example, see *Report of the States Reorganization Commission, op.cit.,* p. 236 and *Bhoodan,* November 7, 1956, p. 5.

[38] Karl W. Deutsch, "The Growth of Nations," *op.cit.,* p. 181.

[39] E. H. Carr, *Nationalism and After,* p. 23.

[40] *Times of India,* January 21, 1956, p. 6.

[41] See discussions of Parishad propaganda in Phillips Talbot, *The Second General Elections,* American Universities Field Staff, 1957, p. 51, and *The Hindustan Times,* March 9, 1957, p. 8.

there at wages which can easily be blamed for the high local cost of living.[42]

When recruitment controversies are over, and the chosen workers settle down in the new multilingual melting pots, the effects of close contact are not necessarily favorable to the growth of national unity. The man who leaves his native region to find greater economic opportunity seldom does so without misgivings. To stay loo long away from home, away from the group observance of marriage and eating restrictions, of religious and social strictures, is to endanger his position should he ever return. Therefore, since he normally migrates as a member of a group of his kinsmen or caste-fellows, he tends to settle with them in his new environment. As a result, observes a UNESCO report, Indian cities are little more than "an agglomeration of what are in effect villages within the urban framework. Not only do primary groups of kinsmen and caste-fellows fail to dissolve into an urban mass. Instead, they formalize their organization and accentuate their distinctiveness."[43] It is a commonplace in Indian cities to find enclaves within which linguistic minorities, far from becoming assimilated into new patterns of life, maintain their own schools and cultural institutions.[44] Unlike the immigrant in New York or Chicago, who pulls away from group discipline in the second or third generation, the Tamil in Calcutta or the Gujarati in Trivandrum holds tenaciously to his mother tongue and social ties. The industrial suburbs of Calcutta are in reality a chain of small cities in which linguistic minorities dispersed during working hours return after-hours to their own separate social

[42] The cost of living factor is discussed in *National Herald*, March 24, 1957, p. 5. See also *Hands Off Bombay*, pp. 27-28, for references to the impediments to industrial progress in state restrictions on the recruitment of labor.

[43] *Report of a Seminar on Urbanization in Asia*, UNESCO Research Center on the Social Implications of Industrialization in Southern Asia, cited in *Bhoodan*, June 19, 1957, p. 6. See also McKim Marriott, "Some Comments on India's Urbanization," *Economic Development and Cultural Change*, October 1954, pp. 50, 52.

[44] James Marshall ("Asia's Challenge to Education," *New York Times Magazine*, November 28, 1954, p. 40) discusses the obstacles to education resulting from linguistic multiplicity of schools. Congress secretary Sriman Narayan specifically deplored chauvinistic regional songs used in the schools of linguistic minorities in *Proceedings*, House of the People, Lok Sabha Secretariat, New Delhi, August 27, 1953, col. 1712.

and political unity.[45] Near Madura in Tamilnad, 225,000 "Kathiawadies," handloom weavers who migrated from Saurashtra 800 years ago, continue to use a distinctive version of Gujarati which dates back to the time of their migration.[46] The Tambats, a coppersmith community in Marathi-speaking Nasik, use Gujarati in their homes 500 years after their migration.[47] The more tempestuous social climate of the multilingual industrial centers now emerging in India could conceivably unsettle group solidarity to a degree unknown in the past. But the example of new multilingual industrial centers already in existence, such as Jamshedpur[48] in Bihar and Bhadravati in Mysore, points instead to more and more centers of multilingual instability that will infect national political life in the short run without promoting unity in the long run.

Urbanization in Asia now runs ahead of industrialization. Migration to the cities is more often impelled by the "push" of underemployment and overpopulation in the countryside than by the "pull" of assured employment in the city.[49] Even the present urban populations in India cannot be kept employed under the Second Five Year Plan. Yet urban centers continue to grow. Mere density of population by itself increases the risk of irresponsible political action,[50] and in the case of Indian cities, density aggravates tension between easily manipu-

[45] *The Bharati Jayanti Souvenir*, December 1953, published by the Bharati Tamil Sangham, Calcutta, on the occasion of the birthday of the Tamil poet Bharati, describes the group life of Tamils in Calcutta. See also "Profile of West Bengal," *Economic Weekly*, September 15, 1956, pp. 1095-1097.

[46] I. R. Dave, *Dakshina Bharatna Saurashtrio (Saurashtris of South India)*, Saurashtra Sanshodhan Mandal, Rajkot, 1957.

[47] H. Acharya, "Caste and Joint Family in an Immigrant Community," *Sociological Bulletin (Bombay)*, September 1955, pp. 129-138.

[48] The fragmentation of the work force in multilingual centers is noted in Morris David Morris, "Commitment of the Industrial Labor Force in India," a paper prepared for the annual meeting of the Association for Asian Studies, 1958, p. 12. Specific references to the multilingual character of Jamshedpur are found on pp. 8-11. Mr. Morris, however, is concerned with the economic consequences of a multilingual labor force.

[49] Bert F. Hoselitz, *Urbanization and Economic Growth in Asia*, a paper delivered at the Tokyo Conference on "Problems of Economic Growth," April 1957, p. 7.

[50] Wilfred Malenbaum, "Some Political Aspects of Economic Development in India," a paper delivered at the annual meeting of the Association for Asian Studies, 1957.

lated social groups. The fact that these groups are often away from home explains to some extent the militant tenor of discontent in the new multilingual centers. Absence has indeed been found to make the heart grow fonder: students of nationalism cite numerous cases to show that native allegiances are accentuated in alien surroundings.[51] But this reawakened sense of identity only serves to channel a more fundamental Indian psychological urge to find a group commitment, any group commitment, for its own sake. The dissolution of the individual into an endless unknown in both Hinduism and Buddhism—the indifference to the "brute particular"[52] in favor of the universal type in Indian philosophical systems—is the parallel of a political authoritarian personality.[53] The militance of the search for new group allegiances does not necessarily correspond in intensity to economic misery; Henry Hart found at D.V.C. and Hirakud that the greatest discontent prevails not among the petty contractor's workers, living in hovels and paid at the caprice of a foreman, but among the drivers of the earth moving machines—"lords materially, but lonely psychically."[54] The drivers were the men most fully disengaged from their old allegiances. They provided the leadership of discontent. At the same time their laborers—transplanted as a body in their "villages within the urban framework"—provided easily manipulated blocs of political manpower whenever there was a strike or a demonstration to be called. For both the drivers and the laborers it is the "changing of worlds" which guarantees a surcharged political atmosphere.

In this changing of worlds, this readiness to cross regional frontiers for new opportunity, India understandably looks for a ray of hope. In a society with a settled level of population, the

[51] Karl W. Deutsch, "The Growth of Nations," p. 185, discusses *fremdheitserlebnis*, "the experience of strangeness," as it is called in German literature on nationalism.

[52] Humayun Kabir, *The Indian Heritage*, Harper and Bros., New York, 1957, p. 134.

[53] See Edmond Taylor, *Richer by Asia*, Houghton Mifflin and Co., Boston, 1947, esp. p. 127; Amlan Datta, *Essays in Economic Development*, p. 135; Beni Prasad, *India's Hindu-Moslem Questions*, George Allen and Unwin, London, 1946, p. 46; and K. K. Sinha, "The Curse of Cultural Nationalism," *Radical Humanist*, December 25, 1955, p. 618.

[54] Henry C. Hart, *New India's Rivers*, pp. 186-187.

promise of progress would gradually become a reality as increasing mobility coupled with increasing national wealth relieved the social tensions dividing men from each other. But the social upheaval that accompanies economic change in India becomes an increasing irritant to social tensions, rather than a source of relief, in a society which has yet to achieve a settled level of population. As population mounts, densely populated regions cry *lebensraum* at their neighbors. Bihari laborers flock to jobs in the mining and industrial towns bordering Bengal, and overcrowded Bengal protests in return that the towns should be the preserve of its own jobless. The tea plantations of Assam become a battleground between rival groups of Assamese and Bengali unemployed.[55] Tamilnad demands the border plantation land of Malayalam-speaking Travancore-Cochin to protect Tamil coolies from Malayalee competition.[56] With each year that more and more people—made more and more group-conscious by scarcity—compete ever more feverishly for limited economic spoils, the hope for ultimate escape from India's vicious circle grows more remote.

India, China and the West

On the assumption that the birth rate will not significantly decline, India's population will almost certainly reach 500 million by 1971. Demographers may estimate slightly more[57] or slightly less, but all agree that this is no alarmist exaggeration.[58] By 1986, according to the projections of Ansley C. Coale

[55] For the Bengali case, see *Memorandum* of the Indian Association to the States Reorganization Commission, Calcutta, 1954, p. 28; for the Bihari case, *Memorandum* of the Bihar Association, Patna, 1955, p. 25, and for a Parliamentary debate, *Proceedings,* House of the People, Lok Sabha Secretariat, New Delhi, July 12, 1952, cols. 3711-3712.

[56] See *Times of India,* January 25, 1956, p. 6, and *Amrita Bazar Patrika,* December 11, 1955, p. 3.

[57] Ansley C. Coale and Edgar M. Hoover in *Population Growth and Economic Development in Low-Income Countries: A Case Study of India's Prospects,* Princeton University Press, 1958, assume 532 million in their highest projection by 1971 and 775 million by 1986. The official Indian Government projection for use in the preparation of the Third Five Year Plan pointed to 430,800,000 by 1961 and 527,800,000 by 1971, according to *The Hindu Weekly Review.* September 28, 1959, p. 11.

[58] Ajit K. Biswas and Max G. Mueller, "Population Growth and Economic

and Edgar M. Hoover, the population may climb to 775,000,000. Even assuming a downward trend in the birth rate, initiated after 1966 and progressing to a fifty percent drop by 1981, the minimum would be 634 million.[59]

The strain that population growth will impose upon food resources is a grim preoccupation of responsible Indians. Former Census Registrar R. A. Gopalaswami has placed foodgrains requirements for a population of 520,000,000 at a minimum of 108,000,000 tons per year[60]—a disquieting figure in the light of recent (1957-1958) production figures of 62,000,000 tons and estimates that annual domestic output in the early 1960's cannot be expected to exceed 77,500,000 tons.[61] Even allowing for a population of 480 million by the end of the Third Five Year Plan (1966), a Ford Foundation Agricultural Production Team, reporting in 1959, fixed a 100 to 110 million ton annual foodgrains requirement and warned that, on the basis of the 3.2 percent yearly rate of increase recorded between 1952 and 1959, the annual gap between supply and demand as of 1966 would be 28 million tons. "No conceivable program of imports or rationing could meet a crisis of this magnitude," declared the Team, urging "an all-out emergency food production program."[62] A proliferating population, moreover, means a proliferating legion of job-seekers[63] in an industrial economy expected at the very most to double in capacity every decade.[64] As the distance between economic necessity and

---

Development in India," *Indian Economic Journal*, January 1955. See also Warren S. Thompson, "The Population Problem of India," *Antioch Review*, Winter 1957, pp. 25, 27; and Kingsley Davis, *The Population of India and Pakistan*, Princeton University Press, 1952.

[59] Coale and Hoover, *op.cit.*, p. 39.

[60] *Census of India*, 1951, Vol. I, Part 1-A-Report, Government of India Press, New Delhi, 1953, p. 194.

[61] *Report of the Foodgrains Enquiry Commission*, Manager, Government of India Press, New Delhi, 1958, pp. 56-62.

[62] *Report on India's Food Crisis and Steps to Meet It*, The Agricultural Production Team, Government of India. Ministry of Food and Agriculture, April 1959, pp. 11-13.

[63] Ansley C. Coale and Edgar M. Hoover, *op.cit.*, p. 232.

[64] Harrison Brown, et al., *The Next Hundred Years*, Viking Press, 1957, pp. 40-41. The possibility of a doubling of industrial capacity is not generally accepted; for example, see George Rosen's differences with the Brown projections, *Far Eastern Survey*, July 1958, p. 10.

economic possibility widens, the political crisis of unfulfilled expectations deepens. The Coale-Hoover projections point to the conclusion that even a downward trend in the birth rate beginning as soon as 1966 may well be too late to permit increased living standards. With no check in the birth rate at all the rate of increase in income per consumer now taking place will in this analysis begin an immediate decline.[65]

Population control is, to be sure, a nominal objective even now of public policy in India. But can population be controlled on a sufficiently grand scale to change the course of events? Can action be taken in time, before India passes what may be her demographic point of no return in 1966? Only, more and more Indians are answering, if the conditions and incentives for low fertility can be brought within practical control of a highly centralized authoritarian regime.[66] A Union which gives to each state a legislature empowered to set policy in such important fields as education and agriculture will seem more and more intolerable as the population dilemma looms larger and larger. Population pressures will magnify and drive forward all the other pressures pushing India into authoritarian political adventures. Consider the sheer weight of numbers involved in the clashes of regional economic self-interest, in the competition for vantage between caste lobbies and regional elites. The nationalist in a hurry will be a prisoner of vast impersonal forces that will become stronger rather than weaker as population growth intensifies the conflict inherent in a Union of unevenly matched regional rivals.

In not too many years the nationalist ambition to confront the West as an equal must be reconciled with the fact that the political and economic order in India is in crucial respects dependent on outside capital and, as matters stand, will be progressively more so in the future. If there are indigenous resources adequate for development, these are the untaxed

[65] Ansley C. Coale and Edgar M. Hoover, *op.cit.*, p. 273.

[66] For discussions of the possible impact of population growth on Indian political institutions, see Kingsley Davis, "Social and Demographic Aspects of Economic Development in India," in *Economic Growth: Brazil, India, Japan*, p. 291, and "The Political Impact of New Population Trends," *Foreign Affairs*, January 1958.

hoards of the upper ten percent of the peasantry. Yet the power to tax agriculture rests, as we have seen, predominantly in state hands. The dominant farmers, wholesalers and moneylenders who can most afford to pay for development[67]—and who are so often one and the same person in the Indian village—are also the powers behind state machines not only of the Congress Party but of most existing Indian parties. This is why state governments are failing to raise the revenues demanded of them, while still demanding, on their part, that New Delhi find funds for their development. This is why the peasant proprietors who form the strongest of the new caste lobbies are so often on the side of regional autonomy. As sectionalists they can best keep their margin of prosperity beyond the reach of national power. The bureaucrat in New Delhi is uniquely situated to see through to the crux of the stalemate, but he acts on his insight, all too often, by systematically putting his own wealth and the wealth of his friends into the colossal tax haven that is the Indian countryside.

The nationalist in a hurry knows well that there are unexploited resources in India. Even if massive enough Western assistance were forthcoming—which it is not—to support the whole existing order indefinitely, nationalism, by its very nature, rules out prolonged acquiescence in any such state of affairs. In the long run, nationalism dictates the attempt to minimize reliance on support from abroad no matter what the cost in institutions at home. Who is to make this or that attempt and at what cost depends less on the politics of Right versus Left than on the politics of national survival. Residual political power in India in the decades ahead will rest in the regional capitals: the makers of any regime in New Delhi, Right- or Left-inclined, will face first and foremost the necessity for coming to terms with widely dispersed centers of power. The great imponderable in India's future is the possible rise of

67 Hoarding and speculating in foodgrains are discussed in *Report of the Foodgrains Enquiry Commission*, pp. 39-44, 61-62. The National Development Council acted on one of the Commission's recommendations in its still-to-be-implemented decision to establish state-level control of wholesale trade in foodgrains (*Hindustan Times*, November 10, 1958. p. 1).

some charismatic national leader equal to this necessity; all that seems certain, in his absence, is that no one political force and no one elite group at the national level can hold a commanding position for long against the onslaught of so many divergent interests. No "final" outcome is in prospect, neither the enduring triumph of a strong central state nor irrevocable Balkanization. Instead India is likely to experience a succession of political shocks as centripetal and centrifugal forces alternately gain dominant strength. The shock might at some point be great enough to detach certain regional entities from the central power, but probably not for long.

Nationalism implies shifting coalitions in which the national political personality is impelled to share power with the strategically entrenched bureaucrat, and both align at one moment or another with the military. The Indian Army may not yet be in the strictest sense a "truly national Army."[68] But it is, relatively speaking, insulated from regional pressures. The discipline of a military establishment properly permits a degree of linguistic indoctrination inappropriate to a university campus. Varying degrees of linguistic homogeneity of the enlisted ranks in Hindustani[69] and of the officer corps in English rein-

[68] "For the first time in our history we have a truly national army," maintains K. M. Panikkar (*Geographical Factors in Indian History*, Bharatiya Vidya Bhavan, Bombay, 1955, p. 91). However, Defense Minister V. K. Krishna Menon put the case somewhat more hesitantly ("Public Administration—Federalism and National Unity," *National Herald*, February 15, 1957). "We have to some extent reversed the processes of provincial bias which obtained in the Army," he wrote, "especially in provincial units, state armies. etc., but other factors have to be guarded against." One of the "processes of provincial bias" which has no doubt been removed is the automatic allocation of a disproportionate number of officers' commissions to Sikhs. The officers corps is now drawn from all parts of India and the enlisted ranks are open to applicants of all castes and regions. But in practice the majority of the infantry forces are drawn from the same "martial classes" employed by the British, the Sikhs, Jats, Dogras, Gurkhas, and Marathas.

[69] See *Report of the Official Language Commission*, Manager, Government of India Press, Delhi, 1957, pp. 107, 227. A test of the Army's ability to serve as a linguistic crucible will come when the north Indian "martial classes" (such as Sikhs, Jats, Dogras, and Gurkhas) whose mother tongues are akin to Hindustani are not so predominant. Even now, the enlisted men's paper *Sainik Samachar* is published in nine languages, indicating that the use of Hindustani as the media of instruction and examination does not alter the basic linguistic loyalties of those whose mother tongues are not akin to Hindustani. The "Hindi" controversy in the larger Indian body politic has intruded into the Army in

337

force all the other factors giving the Army its obvious magnetism as an instrument of national control.

An outside chance does exist for orderly progress through representative civil institutions, and this is the chance that scientific breakthroughs will come sooner than now seems probable. However, most of the technological short-cuts, such as solar and nuclear energy,[70] that would give India her greatest opportunity—Nehru sees no other opportunity[71]—to maintain a program of self-sustaining development, seem to imply, necessarily, the management of a very highly centralized state. The politics of national survival will clearly not conform to Western conceptions of "democracy" and will almost certainly, at one time or another, appear "totalitarian" according to the experience and definitions of the West.

What can the West do?

Not much, or not as much as is often supposed, limited as the West is by political realities within India. What the West does cannot, first of all, control the dynamic forces within India that seem so certain to overwhelm free institutions. Enough Western economic assistance, soon enough, can improve the chances that India will escape the uglier forms of totalitarianism. But a realistic Western approach to India must rest on a clear recognition that the odds are almost wholly against the survival of freedom and that in "the most dangerous decades" the issue is, in fact, whether any Indian state can survive at all.

Persistence in an approach to India that seems to condition friendship and assistance on the democratic commitment of a particular generation of political leaders progressively forecloses the possibility of Western friendship with a new genera-

---

the attempt to evolve words of command in the Union Language. See *Times of India*, October 28, 1954, p. 14; August 14, 1955, p. 13; and November 3, 1955, p. 11; and *The Hindu Weekly Review*, December 31, 1956, p. 3.

[70] For a discussion of the cost problem in nuclear energy, see Norman L. Gold, *Regional Economic Development and Nuclear Power in India*, National Planning Association, 1957.

[71] "I do not see any way out of our vicious circle of poverty," said Nehru in 1958, "except by utilizing the new sources of power which science has placed at our disposal." ("The Tragic Paradox of Our Age," *New York Times Magazine*, September 7, 1958, p. 111.)

tion embracing a new commitment. This, in a world alive with mounting racial xenophobia, is a most dangerous and short-sighted gamble. The passing of the present generation of Indian leadership makes it more, not less, necessary for the West to remain on cooperative terms with New Delhi and to assist India in her struggle for national survival. The collapse of the Indian state into regional components would in the first instance mean partial Communist control of the Indian sub-continent and in time give the Communists their chance for power in New Delhi. At the same time a defeat for freedom in a united India need not mean India's passage into the Soviet power system. By no means is it certain, as we have seen, that Communist or even pro-Soviet forces would preside over author-itarian institutions in India. And by no means is it certain that freedom would not in the end reassert itself.

What the West does in India should have validity within the Indian context, as a contribution to the survival of the Indian state, and should not rest on the commonly accepted premise of a free India in competition with a Communist China. For the premise will lose its validity as Indian political institutions undergo change and as the contrast clearly emerges between China, on the one hand, with its relatively homogeneous pop-ulation and two-thousand-year-old tradition of political unity, and India, a most unequal competitor, striving for a new nationalism against the backdrop of historic political disarray. The centrifugal stresses certain to ravage even the most mono-lithic totalitarianism in New Delhi will not in equal measure handicap the Peking regime. At the same time that the West confronts the unmistakable fact of a dominant central author-ity in China, it is possible that in an unstable India no out-sider will be able to say with assurance where political legiti-macy resides. At times it will not be clear whether assistance to a particular central regime in India will necessarily promote long-run stability. A regime which uses authoritarian power to put down the claims of aggrieved regions in the name of stability might, depending on circumstances, merely aggravate the strains in the Union. Extraordinary restraint must be ex-ercised when Western support is invited, as it was in Indonesia in 1958, by one or another territory in a civil clash. No surer way could be devised to destroy the long-range Western interest than to exploit internal differences for temporary advantage at the expense of Indian nationalism. The West can have a constructive role in the long struggle to establish a stable Indian Union if it recognizes that outsiders can temper and mold events but cannot determine them; if it acts always on an awareness that international quite as much as domestic politics is the art of the possible.

INDEX